W9-BCU-798

THE YALE EDITIONS OF

The Private Papers of James Boswell

Boswell's London Journal, 1762–1763

Boswell in Holland, 1763–1764

Portraits, BY SIR JOSHUA REYNOLDS

Boswell on the Grand Tour: Germany and Switzerland, 1764

Boswell on the Grand Tour: Italy, Corsica, and France, 1765–1766

Boswell in Search of a Wife, 1766–1769

Boswell for the Defence, 1769–1774

Boswell's Journal of a Tour to the Hebrides

with Samuel Johnson, LL.D., *1773*

Boswell: The Ominous Years, 1774–1776

Boswell in Extremes, 1776–1778

Boswell, Laird of Auchinleck, 1778–1782

Boswell: The Applause of the Jury, 1782–1785

Boswell: The English Experiment, 1785–1789

Boswell: The Great Biographer, 1789–1795

JAMES BOSWELL (1740–1795). Pencil sketch of 1791 by Sir Thomas
Lawrence.

Boswell:

THE GREAT BIOGRAPHER

1789–1795

EDITED BY MARLIES K. DANZIGER

PROFESSOR OF ENGLISH

HUNTER COLLEGE OF THE CITY UNIVERSITY OF NEW YORK

AND FRANK BRADY

LATE DISTINGUISHED PROFESSOR OF ENGLISH

THE GRADUATE CENTER OF THE CITY UNIVERSITY OF NEW YORK

McGRAW-HILL PUBLISHING COMPANY

NEW YORK   TORONTO   LONDON

1 2 3 4 5 6 7 8 9 DOC DOC 8 9 2 1 0 9

ISBN 0-07-015374-4

LIBRARY OF CONGRESS CATALOGING-IN-PUBLICATION DATA

Boswell, James, 1740–1795.
    Boswell, the great biographer, 1789–1795 / [edited by] Marlies
K. Danziger.
        p. cm.—(the Yale editions of the private papers of James
Boswell)
    Includes index.
    ISBN 0-07-015374-4
    1. Boswell, James, 1740–1795—Diaries. 2. Authors, Scottish—
18th century—Diaries. 3. Biographers—Great Britain—Diaries.
I. Danziger, Marlies K. II. Title. III. Series: Boswell, James,
1740–1795. Selections. 1950. McGraw–Hill.
PR3325.A814 1988
828'.603—dc19
    [B]   88-27447
                                                              CIP

Book design by Sheree Goodman

In memory of

FREDERICK A. POTTLE

Boswellianissimus

1897–1987

The preparation of *Boswell: The Great Biographer, 1789–1795*
was generously supported by
the National Endowment for the Humanities.

We are also deeply grateful for
timely donations of matching funds from

The Chrysler Corporation
The James J. Colt Foundation, Inc.
The Andrew W. Mellon Foundation
The North American Watch Corporation
The L. J. Skaggs and Mary C. Skaggs Foundation
The PSC-CUNY Research Award
Barry Diller
Richard Goodyear
John R. Mapel
Arthur G. Rippey
An anonymous donor
and
A gift in memory of
Norman Floyd McGowin, Sr.

The Yale Editions of the Private Papers of James Boswell consist of two independent but parallel series. One, the "research" series, gives complete texts of Boswell's journals, diaries, and memoranda, his correspondence, and the *Life of Johnson*. It preserves the spelling and capitalization of the original documents and is provided with extensive scholarly annotation. A large group of editors is engaged in this comprehensive undertaking. The first four volumes of what will be at least thirty appeared in 1966, 1969, 1976, and 1986, respectively. The other series, the reading or "trade" edition, selects from the total mass of papers those portions that appear likely to be of general interest and presents them in modern spelling and with appropriate annotation. The publishers have also issued limited de luxe printings of some of the trade volumes, with extra illustrations and special editorial matter, but neither the trade volumes nor the de luxe printings include matter from Boswell's archives that will not appear in the research edition.

The present volume is the thirteenth in the trade edition of the journals, the fourteenth in the entire trade series.

CONTENTS

ILLUSTRATIONS

frontispiece

James Boswell, pencil sketch by Sir Thomas Lawrence, reproduced from the Denham Album by permission of the Beinecke Rare Book and Manuscript Library, Yale University.

following p. 160

"The Northern Colossus or Earl of Toadstool armed with a Poll-axe," caricature of James Lowther, 1st Earl of Lonsdale, and the Carlisle elections, published in 1786. Reproduced by permission of the Trustees of the British Museum.

Edmond Malone, painting by Sir William Beechey. Present location unknown: photograph courtesy of the Witt Library, Courtauld Institute of Art.

Boswell's *Life of Johnson,* proof of the title-page. Reproduced by permission of the Hyde Collection, Somerville, New Jersey.

"Warren Hastings and his wife with an ayah," painting by John Zoffany, now in Victoria Memorial Hall, Calcutta. Photograph reproduced by permission of The Paul Mellon Centre for Studies in British Art, London.

Mary Palmer O'Brien, Countess of Inchiquin, portrait by Sir Thomas Lawrence. Reproduced by permission of the owner.

The Double Cube Room, Wilton House. Photograph reproduced by courtesy of the Earl of Pembroke, Wilton House, nr. Salisbury.

Sir Joshua Reynolds, last known self-portrait. Reproduced by permission of the owner.

INTRODUCTION

The title we have chosen for this volume, which covers Boswell's last years, is both fitting and ironic. Between 1789 and 1795 Boswell was indeed completing his *Life of Johnson,* seeing it through the press, and having the satisfaction of being acclaimed by at least some of his contemporaries as a great biographer. But far from being a time of triumph for him, these years were marked by illusory hopes, continued disappointments, and nagging self-doubts. Ironically, Boswell was still searching for a way to make a name for himself in the world of affairs at the very time when, had he but known it, his literary achievement would assure his being remembered long after most of his contemporaries were forgotten.

Despondency, anxiety, even anguish are the dominant moods in the last journals as Boswell chronicles his winter of discontent. Yet these journals are not unremittingly gloomy, for they also record periods when he was clearly enjoying the variety of stimulating experiences that his restless nature craved. We find him, now well-known in London, maintaining his social contacts with many notable figures in politics, the law, and the arts, and at one point touring Cornwall with considerable zest. The last journals in fact offer a wide range of experiences and moods.

The immediately preceding volume of this series ended with the death of Margaret Boswell at Auchinleck in June 1789. This volume begins with Boswell, now close to fifty, both grief-stricken and contrite for not having valued his wife sufficiently, and weighed down by the burden of sole responsibility for his five children. Although he kept no journal for a period of five months after Margaret's death, we know of his feelings from his letters and other documents. When he once more began to record his doings in November, first in brief notes and then in a fully written journal, he had just returned to London and his gloom was, for the moment, lifting.

London, the great magnet that had always drawn Boswell and the place where he was now trying to establish a legal practice, again had much to offer. Although he felt numb and depressed at first, he soon enjoyed the dinner-parties given by his closest friends, Sir Joshua Reynolds, long President of the Royal Academy of Arts, and Edmond Malone, the great Shakespeare scholar. Boswell met so frequently with these two and the politician John Courtenay that the group was dubbed "the Gang." With them and other prominent intellectuals he took part in a project dear to his heart, plans to erect a monument to Dr. Johnson in Westminster Abbey (it was eventually placed in St. Paul's Cathedral). He also spent time with his old friends Charles Dilly, the publisher, and Pasquale Paoli, the Corsican general who had been living in comfortable exile in London since 1769 but who was about to return to his native island. Dinners with political associates and with actors occupied other evenings. So did a whole range of clubs. The Club with its distinguished membership was still meeting, as was the Essex Head Club founded by Johnson in his later years. The Eumelian Club organized by Dr. John Ash brought Boswell into the company of physicians and other professional men; the Friends round the Globe chaired by the keeper of Newgate put him into touch with prison officials. When nothing else was planned, Boswell met acquaintances at coffee-houses or taverns. He was drinking too liberally—on one occasion, staggering, he had to be retrieved from the streets by his eleven-year-old son James—and he got into scrapes such as disturbing the peace by correcting the way a night-watchman called the hours. Although he felt dreary at times, he was, on the whole, in fine spirits. "Full of enjoyment of London," he comments after an especially good day of dining with Reynolds and seeing his favourite play, *The Beggar's Opera.* In mid-May his friend William Johnson Temple arrived in London with his daughter for a reunion after a seven-year separation.

Then, quite unexpectedly, Boswell found himself involved in one of the most humiliating experiences of his life. James Lowther, first Earl of Lonsdale, the political patron who had made him Recorder of Carlisle, peremptorily summoned him to fulfil his duties as chief legal officer of that municipality. An immensely wealthy landowner who controlled nine seats in Parliament, Lonsdale appeared to be Boswell's best hope for achieving the seat in the House of Commons that he had long yearned for. On first acquaintance Boswell had been dazzled by Lonsdale, seeing him as "an aggregate of greatness: ancient family, immense estates, a created peerage, force of intellect, fierceness, Parliamentary interest" (Journal, 2 December 1786). He had also soon become aware of Lonsdale's cruelty and pettiness, which ranged from maltreating his subordinates to refusing to share his wine with his travelling companions. Although Boswell resented Lonsdale's caprices, he remained at his patron's beck and call. Now, torn between feeling obliged to obey the summons to Carlisle and wishing to remain in London with Temple and continue his work on the *Life of Johnson,* Boswell reluctantly joined "the Potentate" in his carriage for the trip north. On the journey the full measure of Lonsdale's brutality became clear. The description of his taunts, their quarrel culminating in a narrowly averted duel, and Boswell's pained realization that his Parliamentary hopes were dashed provide some of the most compelling reading of this volume.

The heading Boswell chose for the journal he kept while at Carlisle from 17 June to 15 July 1790, "The diary of my wretched life till my return to London," well describes the raw pain recorded in many of its pages. Before he could resign from the Recordership, as he was determined to do at the earliest opportunity, he had to dance attendance on Lonsdale, enduring his contradictory orders and malicious insults. He was burdened by an additional worry—symptoms of gonorrhoea, which he must have caught during a recent London adventure. Fortunately, the return to London brought relief and, for a time, renewed enjoyment of life.

Both before and after the Carlisle fiasco, Boswell was completing the *Life of Johnson,* an experience about which we can learn a good deal even though Boswell's comments are brief. In pursuit of any morsel of information about Johnson, he interviewed high and low—Warren Hastings, the former Governor-General of India now on trial for malfeasance in office; Mrs. Siddons, the greatest tragic actress of her day; Miss Cave, the grandniece of Johnson's printer; George Strahan, the clergyman who attended Johnson during his final days. To verify information, Boswell consulted public records as well as people who had known Johnson. Before dealing with touchy questions—for instance, the King's refusal to increase Johnson's pension at a time when Johnson had hoped to go to Italy to restore his health—he sought the advice of his friend Sir William Scott, the prominent jurist who had also been a close friend of Johnson's. Determined to cite his sources so as to authenticate his anecdotes, Boswell faced difficult situations with informants who did not wish their names to appear in print. Although he chafed at the scruples of Bishop Percy and the politician William Gerard Hamilton, "that nervous mortal," Boswell yielded when necessary and insisted when he could.

Going in search of "little Johnson particulars" was easier than working on the text. "Laboured at *Life*" is a phrase Boswell repeatedly uses to record his writing sessions. Fortunately, Malone made himself available again, as he had when Boswell was preparing the *Tour to the Hebrides* for the press. Malone, an Irishman trained as a barrister who was now devoting himself to literary and historical pursuits, notably the first scholarly edition of Shakespeare, recognized the value of Boswell's work and sat with him night after night, helping him to revise his rough draft. Many journal entries refer to their joint working sessions—sixteen in November–December 1789 and twenty-three in 1790 (fewer entries mention Boswell at work by himself, but he may well not have noted all such labours in his journal). At any rate, Boswell enjoyed seeing his *magnum opus* take shape at the press. Having brought his manuscript to the printer Henry Baldwin on 1 January 1790 so that he could say it was *at* even if it was not yet *in* the press at the beginning of the new year, he took an active part in consultations about typography, volume size, table of contents, and the like.

Perhaps the most interesting revelations about the completion of the *Life of Johnson,* however, concern Boswell's moods. Although he was occasionally optimistic about the value of his work—"I have high expectations as to fame and profit," he declared to Temple in a letter of 13 February 1790—he was more often given to uncertainty and self-questioning. "Awaked in very bad spirits, and doubting if I *could* get *Life* finished," he wrote on 2 December 1789, although he then added: "With Malone in the evening; revised and grew better." The misery of the weeks in Carlisle was intensified by worries about not completing his work and not profiting from the time Malone had available before visiting his relations in Ireland. Later, beset by financial problems, Boswell worried about the sales: were readers still interested in Johnson? Should he have accepted the offer of the bookseller Robinson and sold his copyright for a generous lump sum? Altogether, how would the public judge his work, and had he antagonized some of the people whom he had described? It is against this backdrop of self-doubt that we can imagine what is not recorded in the journal, Boswell's relief and pleasure when the *Life of Johnson* was finally published on 16 May 1791—the anniversary of his first meeting with Johnson—and was an immediate, resounding success.

We get glimpses of the effect of this success in newspaper paragraphs about Boswell's increased popularity as a dinner guest, in the letters of congratulation he received, and in his request to Edmund Burke that he put the King's praise into writing so that it could be given a permanent place in the archives of Auchinleck. On his trip to Cornwall Boswell was greeted as "the great biographer," and he and

Temple agreed that he was better off as "the distinguished biographer" than as a Lord of Session, a judge on the highest civil court of Scotland. And he was pleased with the proceeds of the sales—a sum "very flattering to me as an author"—which enabled him to pay off his debts and still retain more than £600. A second edition was soon being printed by Baldwin. We know that Boswell, dilatory at first, added extensive new material and notes to this edition while it was already in the press; indeed he even published a separate pamphlet of *Principal Corrections and Additions* for owners of the first edition. But the journal plays down these efforts: "The printing of my second edition of Dr. Johnson's *Life* was the only thing I had to do. That was little, and was now nearly ended" (21 December 1792). It was published in July 1793 and sold quite well at first, but we sense Boswell's disappointment when in late January 1794 he found that the sales "had stagnated for some time."

Finishing the *Life of Johnson* and then enjoying the crowning of his reputation as a literary figure were, in any case, not enough. We observe Boswell looking for other occupations with disappointing results. The legal practice he had hoped to establish in London never materialized. Neither the chambers in the Temple that he took for two years nor his occasional attendance at the law courts of Westminster Hall or the Old Bailey brought him clients. The Home Circuit, which he travelled several times, though made pleasant by the companionship of fellow counsel, usually cost more than the slender fees he earned. His visits to Newgate seem to have been motivated not by the search for business but rather by his lifelong morbid interest in observing executions. Yet even though he could not make a living by the law, Boswell put his professional knowledge to good use when he had the opportunity. His handling of a divorce case started by a woman—a rare event at the time—appears to have been sensitive, and his pleading of an Appeal from the Scottish Court of Session to the House of Lords earned him the praise of the former Lord Chancellor, Edward Thurlow. As in earlier years, he was eager to help the unfortunate—a young apprentice treated badly by his master, or impoverished French *émigrés* threatened with imprisonment for not paying their bills. Stirred by the pathetic story of five convicts who had managed to escape from the hellish penal colony of Botany Bay in Australia, he took up their cause, wrote pleas for their release, and even arranged for an annuity to be paid to the only woman in the group. But these few uses of his legal talents, though they attest to his humanitarian impulses, brought in neither fees nor further clients.

Getting nowhere with the law, Boswell cast about for other career possibilities, preferably in public life. Perhaps he could go to America as Secretary to his friend Richard Penn, the former lieutenant-governor of Pennsylvania and grandson of its founder, if Penn were appointed first Minister to the new United States (he was not). Perhaps he could accompany Lord Macartney to Peking in 1792 when he became the first British Ambassador to China (Macartney did not ask him). Surely he could be appointed official emissary to Corsica, the country he had made famous in England by his writings, when that little island became a British protectorate in 1794 (his request to the powerful Henry Dundas, his former schoolmate and now Home Secretary, was turned down). The hope for a seat in Parliament remained even after the Carlisle débâcle, but no suitable one became available, nor did periodic appeals to Dundas for preferment bring other opportunities.

With little regular occupation to fill his time, Boswell was constantly in search of company. As intensely sociable as ever, he dined out whenever possible. His social life in 1790—91 was dominated by Reynolds, who gave interesting dinner-parties and frequently played whist with Boswell and Malone—Mary Palmer, Reynolds's niece and companion, making up the foursome. Now blind in one eye, Reynolds, the foremost painter of his time, was no longer able to work and became increasingly depressed. Boswell, who dedicated the *Life of Johnson* to him, kept him company and encouraged him to talk about his youth so as to provide materials for a possible biography. Returning Boswell's affection, Reynolds arranged for his election as Secretary for Foreign Correspondence to the Royal Academy in July 1791. After Reynolds's death the following February Boswell continued to take an active interest in the affairs of the Royal Academy. He also joined the Royal Academy Club, a group of Academicians who dined together every other week during the winter. The architect Sir William Chambers and the painters Ozias Humphry and Joseph Farington became his good friends.

That Boswell could be a genial, high-spirited companion is attested to by his many invitations. But his behaviour was erratic. He was often raucous when drunk, subdued when he periodically stopped drinking, and alternatingly restless and listless when, for months at a time, he was in the throes of his "hypochondria" or depression. As we read of all his social engagements, we are aware of his frenetic search for distraction, his fear of being alone. The images that stay in one's mind are of Boswell wandering about in the streets in hopes of a dinner invitation from any passing friend or acquaintance, or hurrying from one coffee-house to another—six on one evening—in search of companionship.

His need for society was no doubt intensified by the fact that his home life was so unsatisfactory. He disliked the house in Great Portland Street into which he moved in January 1791. He found his two older daughters, both in their late teens, irritating and unmanageable. And he missed the company of his other children. Sandy, the older boy, was at Eton College; Jamie, Boswell's favourite, was attending Westminster School; and Betsy, the youngest child, was at a girls' boarding-school near London, for Boswell considered an English education superior to a Scottish one. Although he records some bright spots in his relations with his children—his visits to Eton, for instance, and his growing bond with Jamie that is first seen in his concern for the boy's health and well-being and later in Jamie's equally intense concern for his father's mental state—he fretted at his mounting expenses and felt guilty about not maintaining a stable family life.

Relations with women brought little solace. He often thought of re-marrying but was half-hearted in most of his addresses and unrealistic in his choices. Contemplating Frances Bagnall, Sir William Scott's sister-in-law, or Harriet Milles, a rich young woman from Newcastle, or Maria Lemon, the daughter of a Cornish Member of Parliament who flattered him by declaring she had not dared address him, the great Boswell, at a London masquerade, or even "the fair Palmeria," Reynolds's heiress, he seems to have been oblivious to the fact that they were far from accepting him as a suitor. In addition, the journal reveals his interest in a whole parade of other women, wealthy and youthful, whose interest in him existed only in his mind. He fantasized about Jane Upton, whom he saw in church but never managed to meet and who inspired him to write a charming amorous poem that he apparently never sent. He also wrote flirtatious verses to Lady Mary Lindsay, the daughter of his old family friend Lady Crawford, far away in Ayrshire, and to Selena Eardley, the daughter of a wealthy London nobleman, whom he had met only once or twice. And he kept a record on separate sheets of his periodic meetings with Wilhelmina Alexander (Burns's "Bonny Lass of Ballochmyle"), the sister of an Auchinleck neighbour, whom he clearly hoped to attract. Meanwhile, as the cryptic phrases and symbols in the journal suggest, he indulged in quick encounters with prostitutes and in at least three illicit affairs, one of which, with "C." in 1790, left him with the bout of gonorrhoea that plagued him in Carlisle. Even before he recognized the symptoms of his illness, he did not seem to understand that she preferred a titled gentleman who came to her in the evenings. And although he won the favours of "a little French mademoiselle," he soon discovered that she was mercenary. We may smile at his self-deceptions and well-deserved disappointments, but we can also recognize the loneliness of the middle-aged widower.

Nor could Boswell find much comfort or peace in religion, which
left him with unresolved contradictions. The journals show him faithfully attending divine service on Sundays, seeking out the best possible
sermons in different churches, including Catholic chapels, and feeling
uncomfortable when he was prevented from such worship. Furthermore his dream of 1 March 1791 in which Margaret assured him of
"the propitiation of our Saviour" and which immediately relieved a spell
of deep despondency attests to his religious faith. Yet he was tormented
by doubts about an afterlife. Significantly, too, he could not accept the
asceticism preached in William Law's *Serious Call to a Devout and Holy
Life*, one of Johnson's favourite texts. The journal suggests that Boswell
wanted it both ways—an assurance of heaven to come and permission
to enjoy the here and now—and that he never managed to reconcile
the conflicting claims of a life of piety and a life of pleasure.

The contradictory or at least ambivalent feelings evoked by Scotland
are also a recurring theme in the last journals. His strong attachment
to Auchinleck led him to acquire Knockroon, a property that had once
been part of the family estate, even though this purchase greatly increased his debts. Certainly he still took himself seriously as Laird, writing detailed letters of instruction to his young overseer and making
great efforts to find the best possible new minister for the parish following the death of the old one. On the other hand, his two visits to
Auchinleck were unhappy on the whole, and he resisted the suggestions of well-meaning friends and relations that he return and settle
permanently in Ayrshire. In addition, the journals show his invincible
dislike of the Scots in London, who invariably aroused feelings of disgust not only by their speech and manners but also by the memories of
Scotland they brought back to him.

Moreover, Boswell found the political events of the times profoundly
troubling. As much a monarchist and Tory as ever, he bristled at the
republican ideas being formulated in France. He deeply regretted the
return of General Paoli to Corsica under the auspices of the new French
National Assembly; he felt impelled to write, or at least begin, a heroic
play about the recently executed French royalist Favras; and he became so indignant about the ignominious death and unceremonious
burial of Louis XVI in January 1793 that he launched a proposal to
have a monument to him erected in Westminster Abbey. Forthright
in expressing his position, Boswell argued with his friend Courtenay,
an ardent republican, and attempted to dissuade his acquaintance Andrew Kippis from joining a celebration of the fall of the Bastille. Naturally Boswell opposed the attempts to introduce French radicalism
and political change into England. He joined such like-minded friends

as Malone, Sir William Scott, Edmund Burke and his son Richard, and the politician William Windham in toasting "Old England against New France" and in affirming their loyalty to the British monarch and the British Constitution.

Setting down the varied and tangled skeins of his experiences in his journals was a habit Boswell seems to have retained almost to the end of his life. Although no journal has been found for his final year, the jottings of 9 March 1795—a list of engagements and notes on snatches of conversation—suggest that he had not ceased to record his activities and impressions. Taken as a whole, the last journals are not as full and vivid as those Boswell wrote at the height of his powers, and yet they still have the immediacy and frankness of his earlier journals.

Certainly the curiosity that Forbes recognized as one of Boswell's distinctive gifts, in the lines we quote as one of our epigraphs, inspired the graphic descriptions of the banquets, festivals, and rites of the City—the venison feast at the Worshipful Company of Stationers, the ceremonies at which the Lord Mayor and aldermen called on the keeper of Newgate on the way to opening Bartholomew Fair, and the rituals observed when the new sheriffs took charge of the prisons at Michaelmas. The great dinner prepared for a select company by the host of the London Tavern is likewise presented with loving attention to detail.

The same highly developed curiosity led Boswell to write his lively account of Cornwall, where he spent a pleasant six weeks in 1792 in the company of Temple, now vicar of St. Gluvias. This journal is full of fresh impressions as he observes the pleasant or rugged landscapes, the houses and possessions of prominent residents, the tin- and copper-mines and ancient burial mounds. Boswell writes with gusto about broiled pilchards, a speciality of Penzance, and with distaste about the local Cornish butter made from hand-stirred milk. He gives brief but vivid sketches of representatives of the old aristocracy and the newer wealth, pleased to be welcomed by both groups. And he takes special pleasure in analysing the expression on Reynolds's face in his last and in Boswell's opinion best self-portrait, a gift to Reynolds's niece Offie Gwatkin and her husband, who lived in Cornwall—a portrait that we are fortunate to be able to include among our illustrations.

Moreover, he could still present dramatic moments such as those he had tried to capture in his *Life of Johnson*, which he had planned as early as 1780 to write "in scenes" (Journal, 12 October 1780). We find Boswell standing up against rioting political opponents during the Carlisle elections; Boswell relishing the sight of his daughters Veronica

and Euphemia seated under the great Van Dyck painting in Lord Pembroke's drawing-room at Wilton House; and Boswell trembling as
Veronica steps too close to the edge of the cliffs at Land's End.

The journals also show Boswell's perennial interest in recording conversation. Encouraged by Malone and Courtenay—"We talked of the
great advantage of keeping a journal so as to preserve conversations in
which knowledge and wit and anecdote occur" (13 August 1790)—he
writes out snatches of literary discussions as well as of arguments about
politics and religion. He jots down his repartee with Burke on the subject of the French Revolution, on which they agreed, and Warren Hastings's guilt, on which they held opposing views. And he cannot resist
recording other people's puns and his own witticisms, whether good,
bad, or indifferent. Sadly, we find fewer of these conversations later,
and Boswell notes that he has become less interested in them, but that
does not prevent him from devoting five pages to his conversation with
the former Lord Chancellor Thurlow.

It is, however, as a frank and detailed chronicle of Boswell's shifting moods that these journals are particularly fascinating. He makes a
point of noting when he is happy and excited, as when, at an elaborate
dinner given by a nobleman, he finds the dreams of his youth coming
true. He describes his feelings when, neither happy nor unhappy, he
is contented to be "carried along the stream of life"—a phrase he adopts
from the end of Johnson's *Rasselas*. But most frequently in these last
journals he records his states of extreme depression, caused either by
a sudden return of his hereditary melancholia or by external pressures
such as Lonsdale's insults, financial worries, the death of a favourite
young family friend in the war against the French, or the shocking suicide of a close friend of his youth. "I slunk into bed with a pitiful, low-
spirited sluggishness," he reports on 14 November 1792, and indeed
we find him retreating to his bed on several occasions. During a particularly bad period he begins a journal entry by summing up his emotional state: "It is unnecessary to repeat my listless, fretful, and
desponding feelings, which, when I do not mention something different, must be understood to continue" (18 October 1793). And he shows
himself painfully aware that he has been frittering his time away: "What
an insignificant life is this which I am now leading!...My mind was very
sickly" (25 October 1793). Yet he can also recognize when he is overstating his gloom, as in his Carlisle journal: "What a wretched register
is this! 'A lazar-house it seemed.' It is the journal of a diseased mind"
(5 July 1790). Then, when his black mood suddenly leaves him, he joyfully records his relief. Recovering from a long period of depression
and cheered by a note from the elusive Miss Upton and her mother,

he exclaims: "How many *adventures* do I meet with or contrive! But to be *capable* of any at all, after my late wretchedness, is a wonderful change" (2 March 1791).

The journals not only record Boswell's moods, however, but are also his means of taking stock of what he has and has not accomplished. As in his earlier journals, he compares himself with others—sometimes with bitterness, as when he sees London barristers with many briefs whereas he has none, and at other times with satisfaction, as when, having met his old friend Sandy Gordon, now a Lord of Session, he finds him provincial and declares his own superiority. More frequently in these pages his self-analysis is pessimistic and self-critical: "My life at present, though for some time my health and spirits have been wonderfully good, is surely as idly spent as can almost be imagined. I merely attend to the progress of my *Life of Johnson,* and that by no means with great assiduity, such as that which Malone employs on Shakespeare. I am losing for myself and children all the enjoyment of a fine Place in the country. I am following no profession. I fear I am gradually losing any claim to preferment in the law in Scotland." In this instance, however, the insight is short-lived. Having acknowledged that he may be losing precious opportunities, he proceeds to rationalize: "But with the *consciousness* which I have of the nature of my own mind, I am sure that I am escaping innumerable hours of uneasiness which I should have were I in Scotland. I am in that great scene which I have ever contemplated with admiration, and in which there are continual openings for advantage" (10 September 1790). And so he ends by justifying his decision to remain in London in hopes of some undefined opportunities.

A few other passages of self-analysis show Boswell more genuinely confronting painful truths about himself and his situation. While miserably unhappy in Carlisle, for instance, he focuses on the fact that his early ambitions to mould his character, to model himself on the great men with whom he had become intimate, have come to nought: "What sunk me very low was the sensation that I was precisely as when in wretched low spirits thirty years ago, without any addition to my character from my having had the friendship of Dr. Johnson and many eminent men, made the tour of Europe, and Corsica in particular, and written two very successful books." A stark image completes the insight: "I was as a board on which fine figures had been painted, but which some corrosive application had reduced to its original nakedness" (7 July 1790).

Later he focuses on other shortcomings and recognizes, finally, that his professional prospects in the law are nil. He had always thought that he could, if necessary, retire to a judgeship in Scotland, but the moment comes when he realizes that, having made no bones about his aversion to things Scottish, he can no longer hope to be named a Lord of Session. At the same time he acknowledges that he has no further hopes of success at the English bar either, and that he has only himself to blame: "I was conscious that I had never applied seriously to English law, and could not bear the confinement and formal course of life which practice at the bar required" (24–26 September 1793). He comes to see, then, that not just external circumstances but his own inadequacy—a lack of capacity for sustained effort—has stood in his way. Ironically, he nowhere gives himself credit for his perseverance in another field, his writing, which enabled him to complete the monumental *Life of Johnson*.

Eventually, he also comes to acknowledge that at this late stage in his life his hopes of marrying an attractive and wealthy young woman are illusory. Aware of the fact that his own "uncertain spirits and temper" as well as his strong feelings for his late wife and his children block new emotional attachments, he concludes: "I could not reasonably expect to have comfort in a second marriage, except with a very excellent woman indeed who should also bring a considerable fortune; and how vain would it be for me to think of obtaining such a match!" (9 February 1794). Whereas Boswell's earlier journals were a means of urging himself on, of reviewing his behaviour in order to improve and to succeed, the passages just quoted are sadder and wiser. They show him grappling with his flaws and limitations—attaining a degree of self-knowledge that is surely to his credit.

We are likely to wish that Boswell's final years had been more serene and contented, and it is some comfort to learn from his letters and the reports of others that he spent his last few months enjoying the bustle and variety of London life in the company of interesting friends, apparently unaware that his health was deteriorating dangerously. Nor does he seem to have realized that his sudden collapse at The Club on 14 April and his subsequent illness were serious enough to threaten his life. One is left with the impression that on 19 May 1795 death caught him unawares.

Readers of the earlier journals may be pained—though not, perhaps, surprised—to find that the narrative of the young man who set out with such high hopes to be the romantic hero of his own drama, a dashing Macheath, should end so unheroically. If this irony is distressing, another irony is more pleasant to contemplate: that the journals which Boswell kept for over thirty years and used as quarry for his published writings, but which he did not think of publishing unrevised, have finally won recognition in their own right. Through them the great biographer also reveals himself as a great autobiographer.

STATEMENT OF EDITORIAL PRACTICES

Spelling and capitalization of the text and notes (including quotations in the notes from all sources) have been brought close to modern norms. Boswell's punctuation has been retained except where it would seriously interfere with a modern reader's comprehension. The standard of spelling for all but proper names is *The Concise Oxford Dictionary,* 7th ed., 1985. For place names, F. H. Groome's *Ordnance Gazetteer of Scotland,* J. G. Bartholomew's *Survey Gazetteer of the British Isles,* and *London Past and Present* by Peter Cunningham and H. B. Wheatley have been followed. Family names conform to the usage of the *Dictionary of National Biography,* Mrs. Margaret Stuart's *Scottish Family History,* George F. Black's *Surnames of Scotland,* G. E. Cokayne's *Complete Baronetage* and *Complete Peerage,* Sir James Balfour Paul's *Scots Peerage,* and various other special books of reference.

Abbreviations and contractions have been silently expanded. Names of speakers in conversations that Boswell has cast dramatically are set in small capitals. Names of speakers that Boswell failed to provide in conversations cast dramatically are supplied silently when there is no doubt as to who is speaking. A few clear inadvertencies of various sorts have been put right without notice; otherwise, all words added by the editors are enclosed in square brackets. Omissions are indicated by ellipses. Passages inked over or scored out in the manuscripts have been restored wherever possible and are indicated by a footnote reference at the beginning of each passage. Deletions which we have attributed to Boswell are so designated; the others may be assumed to be by later owners of the journals. References to the *Life of Johnson* are made by date so that the reader can use any edition at hand; in the few instances where such references are unhelpful, the standard edition by G. B. Hill revised by L. F. Powell is cited (see Documentation, section C).

ACKNOWLEDGEMENTS

The preparation of the text and annotations for this volume of the trade edition owes much to earlier studies of Boswell and Johnson, most of which are described in the Bibliography. A great deal of unpublished research material is available in the Boswell Office, which was established at Yale University in 1931. Marion S. Pottle's forthcoming *Catalogue of the Papers of James Boswell at Yale University,* a multi-volume work incorporating bibliographical descriptions and abstracts of the many papers of the collection, has served us for many years in typescript and recently in galley proof. Charles H. Bennett's thorough and accurate annotations of the text were a valuable resource for all the journal in the present volume except for the sections reported as previously unpublished in Documentation, sections A and B. Between 1937 and 1945 Professor Pottle drew on Bennett's collection of notes and his own researches for a trade or reading edition of all the fully written journal, to be published as a set in several volumes. Lt.-Colonel Isham's acquisition in 1948, by judicial award and by purchase, of the Fettercairn and further Malahide papers, and the sale of his collection to Yale University the next year led to a radical reorganization and change of editorial policy. In 1950 the Yale Editions of the Private Papers of James Boswell and the McGraw-Hill Book Company began serial publication of a trade edition of the journal. *Boswell: The Great Biographer*, like the twelve volumes which have preceded it, was raised on a foundation of Pottle's unpublished manuscript and Bennett's findings, revised extensively to incorporate the "newer" Boswell papers, and more fully annotated, not merely to take recent scholarship into account but also to make each volume a separate, self-contained work.

The preparation of a book in the trade series of the Yale Boswell Editions is in many ways a collective enterprise. The office staff as well as Herman W. Liebert, Irma S. Lustig, Thomas H. Quinn, Patricia M. Spacks, and Marshall Waingrow of the Editorial Committee read proof. Of the Advisory Committee, Ronald D. Ireland, Sheila Lambert, Roger Lonsdale, and Nicholas T. Phillipson also kindly read the book in proof, as did Marcia W. Levinson and Maura Shaw Tantillo, former members of the office staff. Viscountess Eccles graciously provided access to, and permission to quote from, documents in the Hyde Collection. For permission to quote from other documents I am grateful to the Berg Collection of the New York Public Library, the British Library, the Earl of Crawford and Balcarres, W. F. E. Forbes, the Houghton Library of Harvard University, the Pierpont Morgan Library, the National Library of Scotland, Rear Adm. P. F. Powlett, R.N., and the Scottish Record Office.

I welcome the opportunity to acknowledge publicly the versatile staff, past and present, of the Boswell Editions, and the extraordinary range and quality of its assistance. My sincere thanks to Irene Adams, senior administrative assistant, for her unfailing helpfulness, and to Susan Bianconi, copy editor, for fulfilling a multitude of tasks with intelligence and care. Even greater thanks are due to Rachel McClellan, former research editor and now managing editor, who gave not only of her editorial skills but also of her knowledge of British history in general and Boswell in particular with extraordinary generosity. Deborah J. Knuth and Katerine Snyder made useful preliminary indexes, David Kaufmann checked the notes for accuracy, and James Caudle, Judith Dorn Depuydt, Andrew Elfenbein, and Eve Sterne helped in many ways. The final index was compiled by Susan Bianconi and revised by Rachel McClellan.

I am obliged to the staffs of Sterling Memorial Library, Beinecke Rare Book and Manuscript Library, Yale Center for British Art as well as to the staff of the Royal Academy of Arts, London, for their courteous cooperation.

I should like also to acknowledge various kinds of expert assistance from D. T. Barriskill, Jean Crawford, Thomas Crawford, John Edgcumbe, Frank Ellis, Lewis Falb, Meryl R. Foster, Kenneth Garlick, Catherine Gordon, Ronald D. Ireland, Sheila Lambert, Kurt Mitchells, Betty Muirden, Jean Munro, Robin Myers, Evelyn Newby, and Francis Sheppard. My friend and colleague G. M. Pinciss offered encouragement and helpful advice after repeatedly reading sections of the manuscript.

For his kindness, patience, and constant support, I should like to thank Thomas H. Quinn, representative of McGraw-Hill on the Editorial Committee .

Above all, I wish to express my profound debt to my former colleague Frank Brady, who guided this edition in its early stages and brought to it the knowledge of a lifetime devoted to Boswell scholarship. His sudden death in September 1986 is an immeasurable loss to the Boswell Project. I am grateful indeed to Marshall Waingrow, now General Editor, who has overseen this edition in its later stages, providing incisive comments and valuable suggestions.

M.K.D.

Boswell:

THE GREAT
BIOGRAPHER

1789–1795

[ROBERT BOSWELL:] *"To Auchinleck you must at last come."*
[BOSWELL:] *"So I must, alive or dead; but if I come alive, I will bring some addition to what I now have."*

[2 JULY 1790]

I was as far as Mr. Sewell's in Cornhill to get some little information for Johnson's Life. *Hundreds of such pieces of trouble have I been obliged to take in the course of the printing.*

[8 JUNE 1790]

His journals are, indeed, exceedingly curious, for it was a faculty he possessed and had cultivated far beyond any man I ever knew.

[SIR WILLIAM FORBES TO EDMOND MALONE, 30 JUNE 1796]

Boswell: The Great Biographer

1789-1795

SKETCH OF BOSWELL'S LIFE TO NOVEMBER 1789. James Boswell, born in Edinburgh on 29 October 1740, was proud to belong to an ancient and distinguished Scottish family. His father, the formidable Alexander Boswell of Auchinleck, was a judge on the Courts of Session and of Justiciary, the highest civil and criminal courts of Scotland, who took the style Lord Auchinleck (a judicial, not a hereditary, title) from his Ayrshire estate. Both he and Boswell's mother, Euphemia Erskine, were related to some of the noble families of Scotland and even to the royal House of Stuart.

Boswell was educated at Mundell's School, by private tutors, and from his thirteenth year at the University of Edinburgh. There he took the regular Arts course, which consisted of Latin, Greek, logic, and metaphysics, and then began the study of law. He formed lifelong friendships with John Johnston of Grange, who later became a "writer" (solicitor) in Edinburgh, and William Johnson Temple, who became an Anglican clergyman in south-west England. By the age of sixteen Boswell was experiencing bouts of the hereditary depression that was to dog him all his life. Briefly he became interested in Methodism, an even stricter form of piety than his father's Presbyterianism. A little later, to the displeasure of Lord Auchinleck, he also became unduly interested in the theatre and a married actress, whereupon he was promptly sent off, in 1759, to continue his studies away from the temptations of Edinburgh.

In the spring of 1760, after a few unhappy months of studying Civil Law at the University of Glasgow, Boswell escaped to London, where he became a convert to Roman Catholicism. He was rescued from this dangerous step, which would have stood in the way of his advancement in any profession, by the worldly Earl of Eglinton, a great Ayrshire landowner and friend of Lord Auchinleck's, who used the unorthodox method of reconverting him by introducing him into high and low society—in Boswell's own words, "into the circles of the great, the gay, and the ingenious."

Persuaded to come back to Edinburgh after only three months in London, Boswell continued his study of Civil Law. He also continued his loose living by embarking on affairs with two actresses; with the married daughter of a distinguished Scotsman, Lord Kames; and with a pretty young woman, presumably a servant, who bore his child. But he was unwilling to settle in Scotland and finally struck a bargain with his father. He could return to London with an allowance of £200 a year if he passed the examination in Civil Law. He did so in late July 1762. Before his departure he took a trip through southern Scotland during which he tried his hand at recording his impressions in his first extended diary, the lively "Journal of My Jaunt, Harvest 1762."

In London Boswell hoped to lead a pleasant life as an officer in the Foot Guards. His father would not, however, purchase a commission for him, and his own efforts to obtain a place in the Guards through influence were fruitless—not surprisingly, since regiments were being disbanded now that the Seven Years' War was coming to an end. Meanwhile Boswell tasted the varied pleasures of the town, which ranged from pursuing a young but by no means innocent actress identified in his journal only as Louisa to becoming acquainted with Samuel Johnson, the literary giant who professed to dislike Scotsmen but who at once took a great liking to the eager young Boswell. Throughout his stay in London, Boswell found pleasure in writing a journal that not only recorded his experiences but also permitted him to reflect on his behaviour and progress in life. He was to continue this record-keeping and self-observation almost to the end of his life.

Forced to give up his military ambitions, Boswell again made a bargain with Lord Auchinleck. He could travel on the Continent for a year if he would first study law in Utrecht (in Holland one could learn Roman law, the basis for the Scottish legal system, and Boswell's father and grandfather had studied in Leiden). He was lonely in Utrecht until, towards the end of his stay, he became interested in the clever, witty Belle de Zuylen (better known by her pen name, Zélide), whom he came to regard, though with ambivalent feelings, as a possible wife. Having complied with his father's wishes in studying law, he then embarked on a period of travel that extended considerably beyond the year permitted by Lord Auchinleck. He happily observed life at a series of German courts—Prussia, Brunswick, Dessau, Gotha, Mannheim, and Karlsruhe—where he was welcomed warmly by the local rulers with the exception of Frederick of Prussia, who refused to meet him. He enjoyed extended visits with Voltaire at Ferney and Rousseau at Môtiers. Proceeding to Italy, he renewed his acquaintance with the political exile John Wilkes and travelled with Lord Mount-stuart, the eldest son of Lord Bute, the Prime Minister. He also became entangled with various women, most seriously with Girolama Picco-lomini, the wife of the mayor of Siena. Then, inspired by Rousseau, who had been asked to write a constitution for the Corsicans who were trying to gain their independence from Genoa, he journeyed to the little-known island of Corsica and interviewed its leader, General Pasquale Paoli. The meeting, which marked the beginning of another lifelong friendship, made Boswell an eloquent champion of Corsican independence on his return to England and led to his first major publication, *An Account of Corsica*, in 1768.

In Paris on his return journey from Corsica Boswell learned of the death of his mother and, abandoning the idea of seeing Zélide again in Utrecht, came back to Edinburgh. There, in July 1766, he was admitted advocate after passing the required examinations in Scots Law and pub-lishing his Latin thesis. During the next twenty years he developed a sub-stantial legal practice, consisting mainly of civil suits. He also took criminal cases, and so ably defended his first client, John Reid, who was on trial for stealing more than a hundred sheep, that the jury declared the charges against Reid not proven (Boswell was not, however, able to save Reid from the gallows when he was found guilty of similar charges eight years later). Throughout his career Boswell took an interest in and was willing to de-fend lowly criminals. The most notable of his other legal activities were his volunteer efforts on behalf of Archibald Douglas, who was attempt-ing to prove that he was the long-lost son of Lady Jane Douglas and, as such, heir to the huge estates of the Douglases, one of the foremost fam-ilies of Scotland. In support of young Douglas, Boswell wrote poems, news-paper articles, and an allegorical tale entitled *Dorando*, but in July 1767 the Court of Session decided against Douglas's claim. Undaunted, Boswell published a succinct summary of the arguments on Douglas's side, *The Essence of the Douglas Cause*, in November 1767 and a few days later an edition of Lady Jane Douglas's *Letters*. In 1769 he had the sat-isfaction of seeing the House of Lords reverse the Court of Session's decision on appeal—possibly as a result of his campaign.

Meanwhile Boswell's personal life became increasingly complicated. He carried on an intense affair with Mrs. Dodds, who gave birth to a daughter in December 1767. At the same time he courted Catherine Blair, an Ayrshire heiress, and after she rejected him, turned his at-tention to a sixteen-year-old Irish heiress, Mary Ann Boyd, whom he met at the Ayrshire home of his cousin, Margaret Montgomerie. In pursuit of Miss Boyd, he went to Dublin in the spring of 1769 with Margaret Montgomerie as his companion. When his courtship of the Irish heiress ran into difficulties, he finally took notice of Margaret, a handsome young woman of spirit and good sense who clearly loved him, and they became engaged. But she was not wealthy, and his father disapproved of the match. On the day of their wedding, 25 November 1769, Lord Auchinleck married Elizabeth Boswell of Balmuto, his own cousin, in Edinburgh.

James and Margaret lived pleasantly in Edinburgh during the first few years of their marriage. A son was born in 1770 but died almost immediately. Margaret suffered several miscarriages, but five children survived: Veronica, born in 1773; Euphemia, born in 1774; Alexander ("Sandy"), born in 1775; James ("Jamie"), born in 1778; and Elizabeth ("Betsy"), born in 1780. Boswell was not, however, to be tied down by domesticity. Almost every year he spent several weeks in London, where he kept up with his friends and acquaintances, especially Dr. Johnson. In April 1773, thanks to Johnson, Boswell was elected to The Club, a highly selective group founded by Johnson and Sir Joshua Reynolds whose members were chosen to represent a variety of intellectual interests and who dined together frequently in the winter. Always glad to be in Johnson's company, Boswell eagerly observed his reactions and pithy pronouncements, recording them faithfully in his journals. Boswell's greatest *coup* was to lead Johnson on an extended tour of Scotland, including the Highlands and the Hebrides, from August to November 1773. Later he accompanied Johnson to Oxford, Lichfield, and Ashbourne.

Boswell's visits to London also offered opportunities for amorous interludes—many one-night encounters, some longer flirtations, and a more serious affair with the notorious, fascinating Mrs. Rudd, an adventuress who narrowly escaped the hanging which was the fate of her two male companions (convicted of forging promissory notes). Margaret knew of some of these diversions, suspected more, but remained patient, loyal, and supportive.

On his father's death in 1782 Boswell became Laird of Auchinleck and took his duties as Ayrshire landowner very seriously. He became interested in local politics and wrote pamphlets on Scottish problems, including two rousing *Letters to the People of Scotland* in 1783 and 1785.

Johnson's death in December 1784 made Boswell feel that he had lost the fatherly mentor he had never had in Lord Auchinleck. Soon he was under pressure to write the biography of Johnson for which he had been gathering materials for many years. He decided first to publish the journal he had kept during his Scottish travels with Johnson, but preparing it proved difficult until he obtained the help of Edmond Malone, a dedicated scholar who set aside his own work on an ambitious edition of Shakespeare to advise Boswell. The *Journal of a Tour to the Hebrides*, published in 1785, was an immediate success, even though some readers were offended on finding their conversations recorded or pungent descriptions of themselves by Johnson. For Boswell, working on the *Tour* was a useful trial run for the new kind of biography—one full of anecdotes and conversations—that he planned to present in his *Life of Johnson*.

Increasingly restless in Scotland, Boswell longed to settle in London. Having eaten the requisite number of meals at the Inner Temple, he took the crucial step, in 1786, of seeking admission to the English bar. He attended the law courts at Westminster Hall and went on the circuits in search of clients. In September 1786 he established his family in London even though Margaret, who was not in good health, would have preferred to remain at Auchinleck.

All along Boswell had had political ambitions—to win a seat in Parliament—but he lacked the necessary backing from a powerful politician or patron until, in July 1786, he met James Lowther, first Earl of Lonsdale, an immensely wealthy landowner with interests in northern England. At Lonsdale's behest Boswell was engaged as counsel to the mayor of Carlisle, whom he helped in an unsavoury election in which unqualified voters were added to the rolls by Lonsdale. Thereupon, as Boswell had hoped, Lonsdale had him appointed Recorder—that is, chief legal officer—of Carlisle, and from then on Boswell lived in hopes of being returned for one of the nine seats in Parliament that Lonsdale controlled. For his part, Boswell was expected to accompany Lonsdale, an egocentric and sadistic tyrant, in London or to the provinces at a moment's notice. Yet the seat in Commons proved elusive.

Meanwhile there were other worries. Legal clients failed to appear, leaving Boswell to live largely on the rents from his estate and borrowed money. Moreover, work on the *Life of Johnson* was progressing slowly, for although Boswell had nearly completed a draft by January 1789, he still wished to interview many people who had known Johnson, collect further letters to and from Johnson, and verify information. Besides, the draft had to be revised. It was easier to spend time with his friends: Sir Joshua Reynolds, endlessly sociable, who assembled interesting company at his dinner-table; or Paoli, exiled from Corsica, whose house had long been Boswell's home from home; or Charles Dilly, the publisher, always hospitable in his house in the Poultry. Fortunately for Boswell's work on the *Life of Johnson*, Malone was still there to prod, advise, and even help with some of the writing.

But Margaret was unhappy in London and felt increasingly unwell. She had experienced episodes of consumption since 1776, had a severe bout in 1782, and was now developing alarming symptoms. Although their stay at Auchinleck in the late summer of 1787 revived her, she suffered a relapse on her return to London. When Boswell saw her again after spending Christmas and early January with Lonsdale in the north, he found that she had been deathly ill in his absence. Finally forced to recognize that her consumption was by now incurable and that she yearned to be at home, he brought her back to Auchinleck in May 1788. Euphemia and Betsy stayed with her. But Boswell returned to London to work on the *Life of Johnson* and attend on Lonsdale. Veronica went back to her London boarding-school and the boys to their academy in Soho Square. While separated, Boswell and Margaret wrote long, affectionate letters to each other.

Boswell did not see his wife again until April 1789, when he returned in response to a warning letter from her physician, Dr. John Campbell, bringing Veronica with him. He found Margaret shockingly weak and emaciated. Informed by Dr. Campbell that although she would not recover, she might continue in her present state for some time, Boswell could not bear to be with her and sought distraction in visiting, drinking, and politicking in the neighbourhood. When he received an urgent message from Lonsdale that he was needed in London for a trial concerning Carlisle voting rights, Margaret encouraged him to go, and he left. He had been in London only a few days when the news reached him that Margaret was dying. He set out for Auchinleck immediately, taking his sons with him, but on his arrival he found that his wife had died on 4 June, the very day he had left London. He remained at Auchinleck in a state of great grief and contrition.

Even before his wife's funeral, which was held on 11 June, Boswell wrote to his demanding political patron.

[Boswell to Lord Lonsdale]

8 June 1789

My Lord,—From the anxiety in which your Lordship saw me at the sad accounts in the letter which your Lordship saw,[1] I hastened down with my two sons, without going to bed. At every inn after Borough-bridge where I was known, I was frightened that worse accounts might meet me, but I was kept in a fever of suspense till I arrived at my door yesterday, when I received the dismal intelligence from my second daughter in a burst of tears. My wife died on Thursday the 4th at three in the morning. She was my first cousin, had been from our earliest years my confidential friend and correspondent. Love and esteem for her were ever united. She proved wife and mother such as I believe are seldom found.

Your Lordship, then, of whose tenderness I am fully satisfied, will feel my distress. The resolution and generosity with which she pressed

---

[1]Boswell had received alarming letters from Dr. Campbell and Euphemia.

me to leave her when very ill, that I might attend upon your Lordship's business in London, trusting that I should return to her, must impress a high notion of her character. Alas, my Lord! I fear I gave too strong a proof of my zeal for anything in which your Lordship is concerned. I parted from her in agony of apprehension—and the fatal moment came when I was far from her. But I could not foresee this. She had often recovered from attacks of her direful disease, a consumption; I flattered myself that she might again have relief and that at any rate there would be no rapid change. I thus endeavour to free my mind from a charge of barbarous neglect which now upbraids me and may attend me to my grave.

I have fixed on Thursday the 11th for her funeral, and I hope I shall be able myself to assist in the melancholy office of doing all honour to her remains.[2] She died at last without any struggle and in serene, pious hope. I can have no doubt of her happiness in a better world. May GOD grant me His divine aid to be patient and submissive under severe affliction and to take a kind care of the poor children. Your Lordship's goodness to me has so attached me that I venture to intrude on your Lordship with my distress. I have the honour to be, my dear Lord, your Lordship's much obliged and faithful, humble servant.

Boswell's other letters of this time show a similar mingling of grief and guilt. To Lady Crawford, a close friend of Margaret Boswell's, he wrote on 13 June: "It has at last come upon me unexpectedly, for I was deluded by the various turns of her deceitful but too certain disease. O Lady Crawford! could I but have a few of those years that are past to live over with her again, I think I could be more worthy of her. But I will not intrude upon your Ladyship with what I ought to endure within my own breast, with a just sense of what I deserve." And on 27 June, as if unable to refer directly to his loss, he wrote to his old friend and advisor Sir William Forbes: "You have been informed that at length 'that which I greatly fear has come upon me.'...To have foreseen it long is no alleviation, nor can I as yet imagine that time will make me less sensible to it. On the contrary, I dread that the wound will grow deeper and deeper. Piety is my source of consolation, and that will never fail."

Boswell could bring himself to give a detailed account of the funeral and a full expression of his sorrow only later, in a letter of 3 July

---

[2] As Boswell explained in another letter, "It is not customary in Scotland for a husband to attend his wife's funeral. But I resolved if I possibly could to do her the last honours myself" (Boswell to Temple, 3 July 1789).

to William Johnson Temple, his closest friend (printed in the preceding volume of this series, *Boswell: The English Experiment*, pp. 285–87). But on 15 July, in replying to condolences from General Paoli, he again turned to indirection: "The constant kindness which I have experienced from your Excellency is peculiarly consoling to me upon this melancholy occasion when it has pleased God to deprive me of '*Her of whom I was not worthy.*'" The last phrase, as Boswell acknowledged, was one that Paoli had repeatedly used and that Boswell considered entirely deserved.

By the end of June Boswell faced the practical problem of how to care for his five children. The two older girls—Veronica, aged sixteen, and Euphemia, aged fifteen—were a special worry, for as Boswell explained to Forbes in his letter of 27 June, "From the experience which I have had how very little notice is taken in London of girls who, though well-born, have not the splendour of wealth, it appears to me that it would be very wrong for me to carry them up with me and keep them in an obscure, unprotected state." Veronica wished to become a boarder in the London home of her good friend Miss Buchanan. Boswell made the necessary arrangements with Mrs. Buchanan, a respectable widow, assuring her in a diplomatic letter of 13 July that he would defray Veronica's expenses and adding: "The truth is, I think that she is just in the state in which I would not wish her to go to Edinburgh. Were she more confirmed in English manners, I should be less unwilling to have her there." On the other hand, he hoped that Euphemia could stay in Edinburgh for the time being, perhaps with Lady Auchinleck. But his step-mother declined to take Euphemia into her own house, pleading frequent headaches, and instead suggested a nearby boarding-school where, as she put it in her letter of 16 July, Euphemia would "learn habits of submission and application which are so necessary to make her an useful and agreeable woman." As for Betsy, who was barely nine years old, Boswell played with the scheme of sending her to a boarding-school not far from Temple, and of making the trip to place her there an excuse to visit his old friend at his St. Gluvias vicarage, in Cornwall. But then Boswell could not make up his mind to send Betsy so far away.

Meanwhile Boswell made anxious inquiries about how to enrol Sandy at Eton, and whether this would be a suitable school for a fourteen-year-old boy who had been kept at home because of a hernia. Writing to Malone on 8 July, Boswell revealed his ambitions for his older son: "I wish much to send him for a year or two to one of the great schools in England to open his mind as to social life and get him some genteel companions. He is a very determined Scotch laird. But I will try to give him a tolerable share of learning and polished manners." That Sandy was proving difficult to manage is suggested by Boswell's brief further comment: "I *must* send him from me somewhere." Jamie was less of a problem. "My second son is to be continued for some time at Soho Academy. He is to be a barrister-at-law. I can manage him as I choose."

During the summer months Boswell was by no means alone at Auchinleck. The Book of Company shows daily visitors—relations, friends, and neighbours. Most came for a meal, but a few stayed for several days. John Slee, the boys' London tutor, was at Auchinleck for a month. Capt. Francis Grose visited the estate in late July during his tour of Scotland, making a sketch of the Old House, the ruined ancient seat of the Boswell family, that appears in his *Antiquities of Scotland*. Boswell also spent several days with Lady Crawford at her estate, Rozelle.

Two dreams reveal Boswell's state of mind in mid-August. They are recorded on the front and back of the same wrapper, now slightly torn.

[Dreams, summer 1789]

In the night between 13 and 14 August 1789 thought I was in a room into which Dr. Johnson entered suddenly with a very angry look at me. I said to him, "My dear Sir, you certainly have nothing to say against me." He answered sternly: "Have I nothing to say against you, Sir?" I awoke uneasy and thought this applicable to my connection with E.M.

[Reverse:] and knew she had died. That I fell on my knees, and prayed for a considerable time very fervently that GOD would be graciously pleased to make me submissive to His divine will. I recollect perfectly using this expression: "Grant me *quietness*." During all this time she appeared sitting with a placid look.

The first dream indicates strong feelings of guilt although the cause is unclear. It may suggest Boswell's uneasiness about neglecting *The Life of Johnson* and relying too much on the help of Edmond Malone, or it may point to a sexual lapse with a woman designated only by initials.[3] The second dream with its poignant memory of Margaret Boswell suggests a continuing inner turmoil as cause of the intense longing for peace.

Political interests as well as personal concerns were keeping Boswell at Auchinleck. The election of an interim M.P. for Ayrshire to replace his old friend Col. Hugh Montgomerie, who had just been appointed Inspec-

[3] Boswell uses the term "connection" more frequently for sexual than for other relationships.

tor of Military Roads in Scotland, was set for 3 August. Boswell and two others opposed William McDowall of Garthland, formerly M.P. for Renfrewshire. McDowall was backed by Boswell's former fellow under-graduate Henry Dundas, who now held several high Government posi-tions in London and was the unofficial political manager of Scotland. Although Boswell had no illusions about the possibilities of success, ei-ther in the by-election or in the forthcoming General Election, he hoped to improve his political prospects by making a good showing. In a letter to Temple he explained: "Tomorrow is the election day. I fear we shall lose it. But we shall make an admirable figure. To own the truth, I have very little chance for success at the General Election. But I may perhaps negotiate for a *part* of the Parliament." His prediction that he would lose proved accurate, and Dundas showed his power not merely by bringing in his own candidate but also by selecting someone from an-other county.

All this time no word had come from Lonsdale. Boswell sent a cau-tious note to Richard Penn, whom he knew to be his friend as well as Lonsdale's close companion, to ask whether his letter had arrived. Six weeks after Margaret's death, he finally received the following cool but not unfriendly reply from Lonsdale himself:

[Lonsdale to Boswell]

London, 20 July 1789

SIR,—The situation you would be in with your children about you after the loss of so good a woman, and the many things necessary to be done at that time relative to them and perhaps the determination of the mode of life for them to enter into in the world for their future happiness and welfare, and all this resting upon you, was a sufficient reason for me not to trouble you with a letter of ceremony. By this time I hope you have recollected yourself. I shall set out for Lowther the latter end of next week where I shall be glad to see you when it is to your convenience, and it may be some satisfaction to open your mind upon family affairs to your friend,

LONSDALE

Boswell was in any case planning to attend the Northern Circuit[4] at Carlisle for professional reasons. He left Auchinleck on 10 August, but following Lonsdale's suggestion, he went first to one of his patron's seats at Lowther in Westmorland. Still depressed by his recent loss, he decided to stay there and not attend the circuit at all.

At Lowther, Lonsdale allowed some of his followers to play a shabby

---

[4]Circuit courts held sessions in various districts twice a year; the Northern Circuit cov-ered the counties bordering on Scotland.

practical joke on his miserable guest. Boswell described this humiliating experience, as well as his continued despondency and self-questioning, in a letter to Temple written from Rose Castle—the seat of his friend John Douglas, Bishop of Carlisle—where he had sought refuge for three days.

[Boswell to Temple, 23 August 1789]

A strange accident happened. The house at Lowther was so crowded that I and two other gentlemen were laid in one room. On Thursday morning my wig was amissing. A strict search was made, all in vain. I was obliged to go all day in my nightcap and absent myself from a party of ladies and gentlemen who went and dined with the Earl on the banks of a lake, a piece of *amusement* which I was glad to shun, as well as a *dance* which they had at night. But I was in a ludicrous situation. I suspected a wanton trick, which some people think witty, but I thought it very ill-timed to one in my situation. Next morning the Earl and a colonel, who I thought might have concealed my wig, declared to me upon honour they did not know where it was.... I could not long remain an object of laughter. So I went twenty-five miles to Carlisle on Friday and luckily got a wig there fitted for me in a few hours.

Yesterday I came to this seat of the Bishop, where I find myself somewhat easier, there being more quietness. His Lordship's chaplain read prayers and preached to us in his chapel today. The scene is fine externally, and hospitable and quiet within. But alas! my grief preys upon me night and day. I am amazed when I look back. Though I often and often dreaded this loss, I had no conception how distressing it would be. May GOD have mercy upon me. I am quite restless and feeble and desponding. I return to Lowther tomorrow for two days, to show that I am not at all in pᴿt, and then I am to return to Auchinleck for a little while.

Such is my melancholy frame at present that I waver as to all my plans. I have an *avidity* for death. I *eagerly* wish to be laid by my dear, dear wife. Years of life seem insupportable. I dread that Eton may make my son expensive and vicious, and it seems hard to send my little daughter two hundred miles beyond London. Every prospect that I turn my mind's eye upon is dreary. *Why* should I struggle? I certainly am *constitutionally* unfit for any employment. The law life in Scotland amidst vulgar familiarity would now quite destroy me. I am not able to acquire the law of England. To be in Parliament unless as an independent Member would gall my spirit. To live in the country would either harass me by forced exertions or sink me into a gloomy stupor. Let me not *think* at present, far less *resolve*. The *Life of Johnson* still keeps me up.[5] I *must* bring that forth, and then I think I may bury myself in London in total obscure indifference.

Boswell returned from Lowther on 28 August, and except for a few days in Carlisle to discharge his legal responsibilities as Recorder, he stayed at Auchinleck until, on 1 October, he set out for London with Veronica, Jamie, and Betsy. Sandy joined the party at Carlisle and spent the night with his father at Lowther. There Boswell found his wig but could not discover how it had been lost. Temple, however, had no doubts about what had occurred and wondered if Boswell had brought the trick upon himself. "As to the wig," Temple wrote on 7 November, "I am sorry it was found, being a proof that they meant to divert themselves with you. There must be some levities and inconsistencies that would encourage them to take such liberties. I hope you do not one while grieve and lament, and then endeavour to forget your anxieties in wine: I fear you seem to make some confession of this sort."

Once in London Boswell felt alternately numb and agitated. "I thank GOD my mind has attained more composure than when I wrote to you from the Bishop of Carlisle's," he confessed to Temple on 13 October. "But the truth is that I am in a kind of dissipated stupor, and am afraid to think." In the same letter he complained of sleeping badly: "I am not at all well today; I have had a restless night and many painful thoughts of my irreparable loss." And to Sandy he wrote later, on 28 October: "I have had bad nights, which I did not use to have."

Still, beginning in mid-October Boswell returned to his work on the biography of Johnson, which he had left off in March, and tried to use as much of the scholarly Malone's time as possible in revising the text before Malone left for Ireland. The first session was productive but far from satisfying. As Boswell reported to Temple on 13 October, "Yesterday afternoon Malone and I revised and made ready for the press the first thirty pages of Johnson's *Life*. He is much pleased with it. But I feel a sad indifference, and he says I have not the use of my faculties. They have been torpid for some time except in conversation. I hope to recover them." He also acknowledged, "I have drunk too much wine for some time past. I fly to every mode of agitation." Once started, the meetings with Malone continued frequently, but Boswell found the task of revising his monumental work almost overwhelming.

Moreover, during this first stay in London after his wife's death, Boswell continued to be troubled by his family responsibilities. He was feeling hard pressed financially, for he realized that he would need £100

[5]Boswell means "sustains me."

to maintain each child and would have only £350 per annum left for his own use. In fact, he had to postpone repayment of a small debt to Temple.

Sandy's going to Eton was a source of pride but soon an additional cause of anxiety. Boswell had enjoyed his first visit to Eton to prepare for Sandy's arrival. Invited to dine at the fellows' table, Boswell had felt he "made a creditable figure." He had been agreeably surprised to be treated with respect, he explained to Temple in his letter of 13 October, for he had had momentary qualms about his own background. "How should one who has had only a Scotch education be quite at home at Eton? I had my classical quotations very ready." But Sandy was desperately unhappy during his first weeks at school.

[Alexander Boswell to Boswell, end of October 1789]

MY DEAR PAPA,—I received your letter today which gave me inexpressible pleasure to hear from you. You may well say to exercise my patience and resolution, but all my patience and resolution avail me nothing, for I am almost driven to despair. None of the boys suffered half so much as I do. Yes, the time of uneasiness is longer with some than others, and the uneasiness is greater, too. I now and never till now knew what it is to want both father and mother. You desire me to apply diligently to my books, but alas, how can one apply whose mind is so much disturbed as mine is? However, I do my best....O my dear Papa, have pity on poor little Jamie and do not make him to suffer what I do!...The very thought of his being as miserable makes me burst into tears. Write me soon since that and your presence are the only comforts I have.

May all-seeing Providence protect and preserve you to us all is the prayer of your very affectionate son,

ALEXANDER BOSWELL

Boswell tried to be firm. "Compose yourself and apply to your studies and think and act like a gentleman, and not like a spoiled child," he urged on 5 November. Yet he was not unsympathetic. In one of his frequent letters to Sandy he recalled his own unhappiness as a twenty-two-year-old student in Utrecht, when he wrote home as if he had been condemned to the galleys.

The children were more or less settled by mid-November. Euphemia was at a boarding-school in Edinburgh near Lady Auchinleck's house. Veronica was staying with Mrs. Buchanan and her daughter in London. Little Betsy was placed in Mrs. Hockley's boarding-school at Blacklands House, Chelsea. Jamie was continuing at Soho Academy, but Boswell was seeking advice about a boarding-school for him. All of them, however, were feeling miserable.

[Veronica to Sandy, 21 November 1789]

Phemie is very unhappy at her school and wishes to stay only six months, but my father won't hear of such a thing. Betsy is gone to Chelsea and is quite well, but she complains, too, and scolded Papa because he told her she was not to come home in the holidays. So that you see, we are all equally ill off for I declare I was better off at Mrs. Stevenson's[6] than here, for Mrs. Buchanan is tired of me and uses me very ill. When I came first she made a great fuss about me and told me I must order a dinner one day and she would do that the next. But I did not want to do that. Well, she told the maids that I eat nothing [but what I like]....She told them the other day [when] we had roast mutton and batter pudding for dinner that she was obliged to ring the bell for George to take away the pudding, otherwise I would have eat all, which was a notorious lie, as I said, "Shall I ring the bell for George?" but she said she would ring the little bell as the other was broke, and she said when I chose no more mutton, "You are saving yourself for the pudding." She is just come in squealing like a pig. She is the most deceitful, artful, cunning, greedy creature you ever saw.

By this time Boswell was once more caught up in the social life he had always enjoyed in London. In particular, he was seeing a great deal of Sir Joshua Reynolds, who had recently lost the sight of one eye but was as sociable as ever. "There is nothing deformed, nothing sad, in short no change at all in his appearance," Boswell wrote to Forbes on 7 November. "He wears a pair of spectacles with a thick black patch in one of the circles as a defence to the dark eye. The other circle has no glass in it, but only serves the purpose of uniformity. His health is quite good, and he has now perfectly recovered his spirits." Boswell reported that he had just dined with Reynolds on five consecutive days—on one of these with no other company. "I dined and sat the evening with him and had him all to myself." Boswell had not yet, however, put his grief and mourning behind him. As he explained to Forbes: "Now, my dear Sir William, this has the *appearance* of happiness. But alas! the deprivation which I have suffered is still at my heart. I may have *gratifications* enough, but the *comfort* of life is at an end....I rest very ill in the night."

---

[6]The boarding-school in Queen Square, London, which Veronica had attended from May 1788 to April 1789.

Journal in England
12 November 1789 to 9 March 1795

[EDITORIAL NOTE. Boswell resumed his journal on 1 November in the form of elliptical notes written on separate leaves. We print those beginning some days later, which record his busy social life and show him already involved in a little adventure with "C."]

THURSDAY 12 NOVEMBER. Veronica with me. Went and settled Betsy at Chelsea.

FRIDAY 13 NOVEMBER. In morning found C. at home. Appointed night. Lord Lonsdale's with Penn and Saul.[7] Studiously sober. *Mount;* Farnaby,[8] etc. Then! C. self; Miss W.A., Lady Mary L.[9] Delicious night.

SATURDAY 14 NOVEMBER. Breakfasted C.; quite easy. Afterwards more breakfast Penn, in charming spirits. He told me that a day or two ago, Lord L. and he having talked of me *not to my disadvantage,* his Lordship said, "B., I think, would like to be in Parliament," and P. said, "Undoubtedly. You may see from the *man* he would much." Sat awhile with Malone. By chance met C. Walked in Oxford Road. Spoke with Kemble.[1] Went to Smyth's[2] and got C. lavender. C. asked to [make a] call before going City. Followed to Conduit Street. Walked above an hour waiting. At last [she] came and took hackney-coach in Bond Street. I followed and was a little while at [her] lodgings. Sir Joshua's with Malone,

[7] Richard Penn, a grandson of the founder of Pennsylvania and lieutenant-governor of Pennsylvania from 1771 to 1773, was one of the M.P.s controlled by Lonsdale. George Saul was a Lancaster merchant who had attached himself to Lonsdale.

[8] Boswell had met Sir Charles Farnaby-Radcliffe, Bt., M.P., at the Mount Coffee-house in Grosvenor Street.

[9] "C. self" is ambiguous, meaning either "C., myself" or, more probably in view of Boswell's jubilant mood, "C. herself." The subsequent initials very likely mean that C. reminded Boswell of Miss Wilhelmina Alexander and the Countess of Crawford's daughter, Lady Mary Lindsay, both of whom he admired.

[1] John Philip Kemble, the great Shakespearean actor, playwright, and manager of Drury Lane Theatre.

[2] James Smyth and Nephew, Perfumers to the Queen, in New Bond Street.

Kemble, etc. Cards, and I supped. Kemble sly wink. I asked how he knew C. to be——? HE : "From extreme beauty; as fine a woman as I ever saw."

SUNDAY 15 NOVEMBER. At Oxford Chapel,[3] calm and well. Called at C.'s to *inquire*. To surprise found [her] at home. Much n*a*nsense (as C. said).[4] Dined at Lord Lonsdale's with only Saul. Drank a great deal. Came to Mount; sadly *cut*.[5] Penn took care and brought me home in a coach. Had it in head to go to C. Ran out to Wimpole Street and staggered. Little Jamie followed and brought [me] back. Wretched scene.

MONDAY 16 NOVEMBER. Penn's morning. Ill and sunk. He a worthy, mild consoler. Walked to Chelsea and saw Betsy. At four with C. and engaged evening at eleven. Dined Lord Lonsdale's with Penn, etc.; drank slowly, so was pretty well.[6] At eleven at C.'s; was told *friend* there. Walked about awhile. Returned. C. not so inviting, and I, "with wine and love oppressed,"[7] weakly deficient. Only once; ineffectual wishes. Wakeful night in feverish vexation. To crown all, the *friend* was to come in the morning, so off early.

TUESDAY 17 NOVEMBER. Angry at self. Breakfasted Chapter.[8] Read Scotch newspapers, which brought back most unpleasing sensations. Dined quiet with Malone and revised so much[9] of Johnson. Afraid of mischief from C.

WEDNESDAY 18 NOVEMBER. Dined Lord L.'s with Penn, etc. Slow again[1] and not intoxicated.

THURSDAY 19 NOVEMBER.[2] Thought myself *well* from C. Had appointed to call morning. C.: "I shall lie abed a-purpose." Went up directly. C. held door as I was going into dining-room. So I went off. Returned by and by (though I had resolved *not*). Protested would not come night again till proof I was myself again. But C. evaded and asked night. BOSWELL: "I won't." C.: "Then you shall not come again." BOSWELL: "Well, I'll try to forget." Walked off without looking back.

---

[3] An Anglican church, considered especially beautiful, that was close to Boswell's house.
[4] Boswell seems to be recording C.'s attempts to soothe his suspicion that although she had told him she would be out, she was actually at her lodgings with another man—a suspicion she calls *nansense*, dialectal for *nonsense*.
[5] Drunk.
[6] The rest of this entry has been scored out in the manuscript (see Statement of Editorial Practices).
[7] Dryden, *Alexander's Feast*, ll. 114–15: "At length, with love and wine at once oppressed/ The vanquished victor sunk upon her breast."
[8] A coffee-house in Paternoster Row that stocked newspapers from many parts of the country.
[9] An expression frequently used by Boswell, here meaning a considerable amount.
[1] That is, drank slowly, as on 16 November.
[2] The passage from "Thought myself" to "looking back" has been scored out in the manuscript.

Had at dinner with me: Wilkes, Courtenay, Malone, Penn, Sir Joshua Reynolds, Mr. Flood, and my brother T.D.[3] Such a group of eminent men! Wilkes chiefly talked. Repeated a poor *bon mot said* to be Selwyn's. "Pro rege *saepe,* pro republica *sleepy.*"[4]

FRIDAY 20 NOVEMBER. Found that I was decidedly ill; sadly vexed. Dined Lord L.'s with Saul only. Drank desperately a good deal of wine and, to crown all, half a pint of Barbados waters.[5] Carried Saul to the Mount about eleven. Much intoxicated. Had lobsters, negus,[6] and cold port. Sad work.

SATURDAY 21 NOVEMBER. Ill and cast down. Veronica dined with me, and Miss Miller, her drawing-mistress at Edinburgh, drank tea. I was wretchedly sunk.

SUNDAY 22 NOVEMBER. Very bad day. Made Jamie say sacred lessons, also Veronica, who came and dined very meritoriously because she would not go to a house where cards were played on Sunday. I dined at Mr. Flood's with Malone, Courtenay, Mr. Parsons, Member for Dublin College, and his brother, Lady Frances Flood, and a Miss Cockburn, a pretty Irish woman.[7] All splendid. I was quite sober, but felt it dull, such is the effect of bad habits. Home about half past nine.

MONDAY 23 NOVEMBER. At home in the day, I believe, and at Malone's evening revising *magnum opus.*

TUESDAY 24 NOVEMBER. Dined Governor Penn's with Lord Lonsdale, Sir Michael Le Fleming, Colonel and Mrs. Lowther,[8] and Saul.

---

[3]John Wilkes, until lately a radical M.P., was an old friend of Boswell's; John Courtenay, an Irish-born M.P., minor poet and essayist, and recently elected member of The Club, had become an increasingly close friend during the past four years. Henry Flood, a schoolmate of Malone's and former Member of the Irish Parliament, was now in the British House of Commons. Thomas David Boswell, also called David or T.D., Boswell's youngest brother, formerly a merchant in Spain, was now a free-lance business agent in London and helped manage Boswell's affairs. "We had an admirable pie with three Auchinleck moor-fowl and three Auchinleck partridges in it" (Boswell to Sandy, 23 November 1789).

[4]A rephrasing of the Duke of Buckingham's epitaph, "Pro rege saepe, pro republica semper : for the King often, for the State always." The witticism attributed to George Augustus Selwyn with its pun on *saepe* and the dialectal *slaepe* ("sleepy"), reflects his avowed loyalty to the King and lack of interest in the House of Commons, where he was silent throughout his forty-four years as M.P. and frequently asleep.

[5]A cordial flavoured with orange and lemon peel.

[6]Wine mixed with hot water and flavoured with lemon and spice.

[7]A predominantly Irish company, including Lawrence Parsons, representative of Trinity College, Dublin, in the Irish House of Commons; his brother, John Clere Parsons, a young lawyer; and Lady Frances Flood, Henry Flood's wife.

[8]Sir Michael Le Fleming, Lonsdale's ward and M.P. for Westmorland, described by Boswell as "a very fashionable baronet in the brilliant world" (*Life of Johnson,* 30 July 1763); James Lowther, colonel in the army and commander of the Cumberland Militia, equerry to the Duke of Gloucester, also M.P. for Westmorland and a faithful follower of Lonsdale's; and Mary Lowther. Both Le Fleming and Lowther were Lonsdale's kinsmen.

Was very sober. Lord L. got to talking. We had tea in drawing-room at ten; sat till near one.

WEDNESDAY 25 NOVEMBER. I have no recollection of this day.

THURSDAY 26 NOVEMBER. Dined at Sir Michael Le Fleming's with Penn and the exact company who dined at his house (except his ladies), with the addition of Mr. Carleton, who has the gothic house above Brough,[9] and Lieutenant Richardson of the navy, from Penrith. My situation was evident. I told it to Lord L. I was a good deal rallied.[1] Sir Michael cried, "'Alas, how changed from him,'"[2] etc. I kept myself quite sober. Lord L. asked us all to dinner next day.

FRIDAY 27 NOVEMBER. At Malone's in morning. Courtenay came and asked me to dine with him next day, and left me at liberty to come or not. I walked with him to Jack Devaynes's,[3] it being a very fine day. We visited Mrs. Devaynes. Courtenay advised me to consult Devaynes. I went to the lottery office, Whitehall, and *proved* two old tickets, both blanks.[4] The man who attended was a fine-talking fellow, and gave me a number of curious anecdotes of adventurers. I returned by Devaynes's and *did* consult him. I dined at Lord Lonsdale's with yesterday's company, all but Colonel Lowther, who sent an excuse. As Malone had promised me the whole evening for Johnsonian revision, I wished to send an excuse also, but Penn told me it was not to be risked, as I had said the day before I would come. I must, he said, guard beforehand to escape, but must never break an engagement. He was indulgent to me today as to drinking.

SATURDAY 28 NOVEMBER. Dined at Courtenay's with Mr. Beresford, Sir John Blaquiere, General Dalrymple, Mr. Windham,[5] Sir Joshua Reynolds, and Jack Devaynes; a very agreeable day. Blaquiere (who

---

[9]John Carleton, owner of Hillbeck Hall near Brough, Westmorland, was a Justice of the Peace in that county.

[1]Lightly ridiculed.

[2]Satan's first words to his companion Beelzebub in hell (*Paradise Lost* i. 84–85), describing the change in his appearance since he was expelled from heaven. Boswell's illness seems to have become noticeable.

[3]John Devaynes, Apothecary (general medical practitioner) to the King, was among those who had attended Johnson in his last illness. In 1788 Boswell had consulted him about Margaret's and also about Veronica's health, and they had dined together frequently.

[4]That is, submitted them to see if they were winning tickets. Boswell had bought one ticket in February.

[5]John Beresford and Sir John Blaquiere were both influential M.P.s in the Irish House of Commons; Maj.-Gen. William Dalrymple had served in the army in America and was an M.P. in the British House of Commons; William Windham, member of The Club since 1778 and M.P., was a talented classical scholar and mathematician.

revived old ideas somewhat)[6] and I were warm against Courtenay, who defended the French insurrection.[7] It was now frosty weather.

SUNDAY 29 NOVEMBER. Took Jamie to Oxford Chapel in the forenoon; was calm and recovered some degree of regular piety.[8] As it might be *possible* that C. had not done me harm, paid her a visit. She protested she was well. I was all mildness and admired her still. Told her where I lived, that she might call. *Could* not believe her, but no matter. Dined at Malone's with Sir J. Banks, Reynolds, Courtenay, Windham, Metcalfe, and young Burke, and concerted effectual measures for Dr. Johnson's monument.[9] Windham and I stayed and had negus.

MONDAY 30 NOVEMBER. Dined quietly with Malone and had a long revise of *Life*.

[EDITORIAL NOTE. On this day Boswell described both his progress and his frustrations in revising the *Life of Johnson* in a letter to Temple: "I reckon that a third of the work is *settled*, so that I shall get to press very soon. You cannot imagine what labour, what perplexity, what vexation I have endured in arranging a prodigious multiplicity of materials, in supplying omissions, in searching for papers buried in different masses—and all this besides the exertion of composing and polishing. Many a time have I thought of giving it up. However, though I shall be uneasily sensible of its many deficiencies, it will certainly be to the world a very valuable and peculiar[1] volume of biography, full of literary and characteristical anecdotes...told with authenticity and in a lively manner. Would that it were in the booksellers' shops. Methinks if I

[6]Perhaps recalling Boswell's own visit to Ireland in search of a wife in 1769.

[7]The Bastille had been stormed on 14 July, and Louis XVI and his family had been taken from Versailles to virtual imprisonment in Paris on 5 October of this year. Courtenay was one of Boswell's few friends who sympathized with the French revolutionaries.

[8]The following passage, from "As it might" to "no matter," has been scored out in the manuscript.

[9]As early as May 1785 the Dean and Chapter of Westminster Abbey had given permission for a Johnson monument to be erected there. Boswell took part in several informal planning meetings with other Johnson admirers and had a subscription for the monument announced in Scottish newspapers in June 1789. A full-length statue by John Bacon was planned. The participants at this day's meeting included Sir Joseph Banks, the botanist who had accompanied Captain Cook on his South Seas voyages and who was now President of the Royal Society; Philip Metcalfe, partner in a distillery and M.P., a close friend of Reynolds's as well as of Johnson's in his last years; and Richard Burke, a lawyer and son of Edmund Burke. All those present were members of The Club except Metcalfe, who had been blackballed—possibly by Boswell, as Mary Palmer, Reynolds's niece, believed.

[1]Special, unique.

had this *magnum opus* launched, the public has no farther claim upon me."]

TUESDAY 1 DECEMBER. At home all day. Malone, who had appointed me to come at six, went to Sir Joshua's, imagining I was to be there also.

WEDNESDAY 2 DECEMBER. Awaked in very bad spirits, and doubting if I *could* get *Life* finished. Dined at home. With Malone in the evening; revised and grew better.

THURSDAY 3 DECEMBER. Dined at Lord Lonsdale's with Governor Penn, etc. Was allowed to be moderate in wine. Went home with Penn and had negus and a pipe cordially. In our way to his house, going up Bond Street in a hackney-coach, he talked of going Ambassador to America. I said, "If you do, you must find a situation for me." "That I will," said he; "you shall be my Secretary." "Are you in earnest?" said I. "Upon my honour, I am," said he. "Then," said I, "give me your hand," which he did in a cordial manner. When at his house, I resumed this matter, and he told me that it would be a great advantage to *him,* that he would make the business very easy to me, and I should find myself very happy at Philadelphia.[2] *This was an opening for me into the New World.* He told me that Lord Lonsdale had once asked of Mr. Pitt to appoint him[3] to this embassy, and that it would be a grand circumstance for his Lordship to send out the first Ambassador and the first Secretary from Britain to America.

FRIDAY 4 DECEMBER. I was rather the worse for the wine I had taken the day before, and resolved to stay at home quietly. But Penn called and told me that Sir Richard Symons, who did not know where I lived, had bid him ask me to dine at his house at Brompton with Lord Lonsdale today. I agreed. There were just his Lordship, Sir Michael, Colonel Lowther, and Penn. A most elegant dinner from a genteel Herefordshire Baronet. I tasted his fine wines freely.

SATURDAY 5 DECEMBER. Walked to Baldwin's to get a loan of £100 which he had kindly promised.[4] I had today a letter from James

---

[2]The peace treaty between England and the new American republic had been signed in 1783, but only now was the appointment of a British Ambassador being considered. Philadelphia was the capital of the new nation until 1800.

[3]That is, Penn. But nothing came of his hopes of returning as first British Ambassador.

[4]The printer Henry Baldwin had been co-owner of the *London Magazine,* in which Boswell had bought a share in 1769, had printed the *Tour to the Hebrides,* and knew he would also print the *Life of Johnson.* He had already helped Boswell financially two years earlier.

Cuninghame that I should receive £300 soon.[5] This raised my spirits. Baldwin was to be ready for me on the 12. I went upon 'Change; took soup at Birch's;[6] dined tête-à-tête with Dilly and drank a bottle of frontignac.[7] Evening Malone's and revised more *Life*.

SUNDAY 6 DECEMBER. Took Jamie to a chapel somewhere beyond Welbeck Street. He said sacred lessons to me. Dined at Metcalfe's with Sir Joshua Reynolds, Sir Joseph Banks, Messrs. Townley, Peachey, Malone, Courtenay, and Sir W. Scott.[8] Could not resist Metcalfe's fine dishes and wines. Sir Joshua began to be a water-drinker. Evening went to the Mount and had a little negus. Sat with Penn, Sir C. Farnaby, etc.

MONDAY 7 DECEMBER. This day came on in the Court of King's Bench the important trial as to the right of the Corporation of Carlisle to make freemen without the check of their being first admitted of one of the guilds. It lasted about seven hours. Erskine and Mingay exerted themselves on different sides, and Lord Kenyon made an admirable speech to the jury. I had my brief to sit by for the Corporation in case it should be necessary to say anything for them.[9] I *felt* myself quite at home in the King's Bench, and should have had no difficulty to speak. I was resolved to ply the law close after Johnson's *Life* was done, no

---

[5] Boswell had borrowed money to lend to the orphaned Cuninghames, his second cousins as well as nephews of Margaret Boswell, to start them on their careers, and had also paid some of their debts. Lt. James Cuninghame, whose army career in India Boswell had made possible by a substantial loan, was the most appreciative and responsible of them.

[6] The Royal Exchange, the trading place of merchants, was in the angle formed by Threadneedle Street and Cornhill; Birch and Son's pastryshop was in Cornhill nearby.

[7] Charles Dilly, publisher, bookseller, and another co-owner of the *London Magazine,* had published Boswell's *Account of Corsica* as well as the *Tour to the Hebrides*. He had become so good a friend that Boswell had stayed at his house in the Poultry for extended periods. Frontignac is a French muscatel.

[8] Sir William Scott was an eminent barrister specializing in maritime and ecclesiastical law.

[9] Another round in the controversy about voting rights in Carlisle that had begun five years earlier when Lonsdale, to ensure the election of his candidates to Parliament, created almost 1,450 honorary freemen—voters without the necessary qualifications of property-ownership or guild membership—known as Lonsdale's "toadstools" or "mushrooms." This trial, which had been in the offing since Boswell was called from his wife's bedside in May, was to determine the voting rights of Robert Bennett, who was being challenged for not being a member of a guild. Appearing before the Lord Chief Justice, Lord Kenyon, were Thomas Erskine representing the guilds, James Mingay representing Bennett, and Boswell as one of two counsel for the Carlisle Corporation. The decision in favour of Bennett was a victory, though only a temporary one, for Lonsdale.

matter though late. I had now resolved *Life* into my own feelings.[1] I was the first who announced our victory to Lord Lonsdale; I dined with him with Sir Michael, Colonel Lowther, etc., etc. He was highly pleased.

TUESDAY 8 DECEMBER. Sat awhile with Penn. Jamie had not been well for some days and had not been at the Academy.[2] Took him with me to dine at General Paoli's, where I was informed of the National Assembly of France having granted an equal share of liberty to the Corsicans being announced to him in a letter from their Secretary.[3] He was quite full of this. I felt a dull indifference. Went to Malone's and revised.

WEDNESDAY 9 DECEMBER. Sandy came home from Eton for the holidays. He came in good health and much improved. Veronica and my brother T. D. dined with us. Evening at Malone's and revised.

THURSDAY 10 DECEMBER. Was at a grand dinner at the London Tavern[4] given by Lord Lonsdale on the Carlisle victory. Did not get home till between three and four.

FRIDAY 11 DECEMBER. As a brag, went to Penn's and had some breakfast with the ladies[5] before he was up. Dined quietly at home in order to be at Malone's to revise, having refused invitations from Lord Lonsdale, Penn, and General Paoli. Had a long revise, and got into spirits with respect to my work, and resolved to put it to press immediately after Christmas.

SATURDAY 12 DECEMBER. My complaint was by no means well, and gave me much uneasiness. I went to Baldwin's and got £100. I had once taken good chambers in the Inner Temple (Tanfield Court, no. 2) and given up my house. But finding the butler from whom I took them had not power to let them, I retook my house for another half-year. I thought this might do well to keep near Malone.[6] He and I dined today with Metcalfe at Sir Joshua's; played whist and supped.

SUNDAY 13 DECEMBER. Went with my son James to Oxford Chapel in the evening. Sandy was not very well. I dined and drank tea

---

[1] An obscure statement, perhaps meaning that he was now determined to finish the *Life of Johnson,* in contrast to his feelings of doubt on 2 December.

[2] Soho Academy, Jamie's school.

[3] Paoli had led the native Corsicans in their struggle against the occupying forces first of Genoa and then of France until he was driven into exile in 1769. This vote of the National Assembly, which was reorganizing the French government with the reluctant consent of Louis XVI, made Corsica part of France; it also permitted exiles to return.

[4] A large tavern in Bishopsgate Street Within, famous for its excellent meals and wines.

[5] Penn's wife Mary and their two young daughters.

[6] Malone was living in Queen Anne Street East, Boswell in Queen Anne Street West.

with them. In the morning had visited with them Mrs. Buchanan and
Veronica. At night was with Malone and had a very little revise, for he
had a Dulcinea[7] with him.

MONDAY 14 DECEMBER. At home till five, when I dined with
Malone tête-à-tête and had a good revise. Penn had paid me a visit in
the morning.

TUESDAY 15 DECEMBER. Sir Michael Le Fleming and Mr. Saul
sat some time with me. I dined at Lord Lonsdale's with Penn, Colonel
Lowther, and Saul. His Lordship was uncommonly loud and contradictory, and made us drink too much wine.

WEDNESDAY 16 DECEMBER. Awaked not well, but at present
had a kind of callous indifference, so as not to feel anything exquisitely, and was serenely satisfied to think that I might either rise into
wealth and eminence, or merely get my years passed over in my present
state, which I could not well define, but which, being in London, I *felt*
to be much better than any life at Edinburgh. I breakfasted with Penn,
who was violent against L.'s shocking ferocity and undignified manner
of living. I wrote to Lady Crawford of my children and my own state
of mind, and to Lady Mary Lindsay a knight-errant epistle, but absolutely sincere.[8] At home all the rest of the day filling up blanks in my
Life of Johnson.

THURSDAY 17 DECEMBER. Dined at Sir Joshua Reynolds's with
Lord Carysfort, Sir Charles Bunbury, Sir John Blaquiere, Dr. Laurence,[9]
Malone, Metcalfe. Sir Joshua seemed much the worse for water-drinking.
He talked scarcely at all. Malone, Metcalfe, and I played whist and supped.
I had walked to Westminster in the morning and had met C. on horse-
back, looking beautiful.

FRIDAY 18 DECEMBER. Breakfasted with Courtenay, whom I
had not seen since Sunday the 6th. Sat awhile with Malone, and got a
quotation from Bacon for my Johnsonian Introduction.[1] Visited Miss

[7]Boswell's polite term for a prostitute.
[8]On his visit to Lady Crawford at Rozelle the previous summer and in a subsequent
letter, Boswell had flirted with Lady Mary by adopting a chivalric pose.
[9]John Joshua Proby, created Earl of Carysfort only a few months earlier, was a prominent speaker in the Irish House of Lords. Sir Thomas Charles Bunbury, M.P., known
chiefly for his keen interest in horse-racing (he was a co-founder and first winner of
the Derby), was a member of The Club; French Laurence, a lawyer, was Edmund
Burke's protégé and later his literary executor. Reynolds's dinners were known for
the miscellaneous character of the guests.
[1]To justify including so many of Johnson's sayings in the *Life,* Boswell quotes Bacon's
praise of Julius Caesar, who "in his book of apophthegms...esteemed it more honour
...to take the wise and pithy words of others than to have every word of his own to be
made an apophthegm or an oracle" (*Advancement of Learning,* I. vii. 25).

Cave, grandniece of old Edward Cave, and saw his original letters from Johnson.[2] She was a stately, agreeable woman, and with blood and money would have been an excellent match for a worthy gentleman. Visited Mrs. Buchanan and my dear Veronica; also Mr. Goodall, Sandy's tutor at Eton, whom I found with Mrs. Goodall at Bates's Hotel. Dined at Courtenay's with W. G. Hamilton.[3] Talked of politics, elections, and Johnson. Had just wine enough to animate me. Went to L.'s after nine. Penn gone. Colonel Lowther a short time. Then only Saul. L. in pleasant spirits so as to be absolutely easy and agreeable.

SATURDAY 19 DECEMBER. Home all the morning except a little while at Penn's. Dined at Sir William Scott's with Sir Joshua Reynolds, Sir Joseph Banks, Malone, Metcalfe, and Dr. Laurence. Agreed that there should be a public meeting advertised of friends to the memory of Dr. Johnson on the 5 of January, to sanction a subscription. This was Sir W. Scott's circuitous delicacy.[4] I was in a flow of spirits, and contrasted with the hardship of a lawyer's life that of a fox-hunter and that of the President of the Royal Society receiving foreigners, both of which, though supposed lives of pleasure and not of profit, I thought worse. I told Sir Joshua that Dr. Warren said he would die if he drank no wine.[5] This had a good effect, for he drank a glass or two for the first time since Sunday sennight. Malone, Metcalfe, and I went home with him, played whist, and had a little supper.

SUNDAY 20 DECEMBER. Called on L. in the morning. He was busy. Also on Malone, and met there Courtenay and Kemble. Time passed away till it was too late to go to church. Was uneasy at this. Found L. at Penn's, and promised to dine with him. A thick[6] day. Veronica had come to dine with us. I felt a warmth of affection for her, and was

[2]This meeting provided Boswell with a number of letters from Johnson to Cave, the founder of the *Gentleman's Magazine,* for which Johnson did his early hack writing.

[3]William Gerard Hamilton was known as "Single-Speech" Hamilton for his brilliant maiden effort in the House of Commons, after which he seldom spoke. Although he was Boswell's second cousin and had been a friend of Johnson's, he had invited Boswell to his house for the first time only three years earlier, upon hearing of Boswell's work on the *Life of Johnson*. During this visit, Boswell was impressed by "the elegance of Hamilton's house, table, and manners, and particularly [by] his beautiful language and pronunciation" (Journal, 15 June 1786). Hamilton supplied a few Johnson letters and anecdotes.

[4]Perhaps a reference to Scott's tactful way of encouraging the admirers of Johnson to contribute funds for the monument.

[5]Richard Warren, M.D., member of The Club, who was soon to become Boswell's family physician, believed that abstention from wine by those accustomed to it could be harmful.

[6]Foggy, disagreeable.

sorry to go out. A roaring day at L.'s with Penn, etc., by no means like Friday evening. Penn and I had our negus at the Mount.

MONDAY 21 DECEMBER. Awaked in tears from a dream of M.M.[7] Was not well. Breakfasted with Penn. At home after visiting Captain Grose, as also Nichols, the printer, and Lockyer Davis for little Johnsonian particulars.[8] Made insertions in the *Life* in the evening. Was rather dull.

TUESDAY 22 DECEMBER. Penn's son breakfasted with me and my sons. He was a boy of extraordinary reading and talents at thirteen, but my sons saw something ridiculous in him. Penn himself called on me. I did something to *Life*. Dined at home. In the evening at Malone's revising.

WEDNESDAY 23 DECEMBER. Dr. Barrow[9] visited me; so did Penn, and informed me that L. had gone north the day before. Dined at home. Was now studying prosody with Sandy, who was quite reconciled to Eton and visibly *imbutus*[1] with its spirit already. In the evening at Malone's. Courtenay was with him at dinner. After Courtenay went we revised.

THURSDAY 24 DECEMBER. My brother T.D. breakfasted with me, and then I went with him to the Army Pay Office to get my brother John's half-pay, which I did after making affidavit for him as a lunatic before Justice Abington, St. Margaret's Churchyard, Westminster.[2] It was a very wet day. Called on *Marshall*, Prince's Street ⊢─┤,[3] and on Dr.Douglas and Major Maxwell. Home and dressed. Dined at Kemble's with Malone, Courtenay and son, Murphy, and Sir Joshua Reynolds. Mrs. Kemble was very pleasing.[4] At coffee and tea were Miss Farren and her mother and Lord Derby. I was quite delighted with the English accent of Mrs. Kemble and Miss Farren. I did not drink much wine.

---

[7]Boswell's habitual abbreviation for his wife, whose maiden name was Margaret Montgomerie.

[8]John Nichols, a good friend of Johnson's, provided letters and anecdotes that had first appeared in the *Gentleman's Magazine,* of which he was the editor. He had also been the printer of the *Lives of the Poets;* Davis was one of the booksellers who had published them.

[9]The Rev. William Barrow, D.D., Headmaster of Soho Academy.

[1]Imbued.

[2]The phrase "as a lunatic before Justice Abington" has been inked out in the manuscript. Boswell's younger brother John, a retired lieutenant, had to be confined intermittently and was now at St. Luke's Hospital, Newcastle; Boswell consistently treated him with care and affection.

[3]A private symbol; Marshall has not been identified.

[4]Arthur Murphy was a prolific dramatist. Kemble's wife Priscilla, daughter of the Drury Lane prompter William Hopkins and widow of the actor William Brereton, was a minor actress.

All but Sir Joshua and Courtenay stayed to supper. I felt myself not quite *expert* in easy chat, but exulted in the difference between this society and any in Scotland. Lord Derby was very pleasant. The attachment between him and Miss Farren was, I really thought, as fine a thing as I had ever seen: truly virtuous admiration on his part, respect on hers.[5]

FRIDAY 25 DECEMBER. Was too late for the full service, but heard a part both of Dr. Courtenay's sermon and of prayers at St. George's, Hanover Square. Consulted with Mr. Lambertson, an apothecary in Oxford Street, as to my illness, having found him, when buying medicines in his shop, to be a sensible, clever man. Little Betsy came home from Chelsea. Mrs. and Miss Buchanan and Veronica, my brother T. D., his wife, and Mrs. Green[6] dined and drank tea, and we had a rubber at whist.

SATURDAY 26 DECEMBER. Major Maxwell breakfasted with me. Betsy wished to stay till Monday, but I perceived her being the worse for home, and went out with her resolutely. Evening at Malone's revising.

SUNDAY 27 DECEMBER. Went into several churches, but did not get a seat. Dined with Malone tête-à-tête and revised *Life.*

MONDAY 28 DECEMBER. [No entry for this day.]

TUESDAY 29 DECEMBER. Dined at General Paoli's with Jamie. Sandy was ill.

WEDNESDAY 30 DECEMBER. [No entry for this day.]

THURSDAY 31 DECEMBER. Dined at Mr. Dilly's with Dr. Mayo, Dr. Thomson of Kensington, Dr. Gillies. After dinner Mr. Sharp joined us.[7] Walked in St. James's Park, a clear evening, to revive old ideas.[8] At Malone's and revised some *Life.*

[EDITORIAL NOTE. At this point the journal, which has been written on loose leaves since 25 March 1785, continues in a new bound quarto notebook.]

[5] Elizabeth Farren was a highly popular comic actress. She was seen frequently with her admirer, Edward Smith-Stanley, twelfth Earl of Derby, but because he was married, they behaved with great discretion; he married her in 1797 after his first wife's death.

[6] T.D. had married Anne Catherine Green; Mrs. Britannia Green was his mother-in-law.

[7] Henry Mayo, D.D., was a Nonconformist minister known as the "literary anvil" for his unflinching endurance of Dr. Johnson's verbal blows; John Gillies, LL.D., a classical historian; and Richard Sharp—called variously "Hatter," "Furrier," and "Conversation" Sharp—a hat manufacturer known for his lively talk.

[8] During his stay in London in 1762–63, Boswell had lodgings near St. James's Park and had found much of his amusement there.

1790

FRIDAY 1 JANUARY. My brother T.D. breakfasted with me. I then visited Malone and had some cheering talk. Called at Lockyer Davis's and copied a passage from Plutarch for Johnson's *Life*.[9] Then delivered the Introduction of it to Baldwin, that I might say my book was *at* if not *in* the press on New Year's Day. The honest, friendly printer was a little gruff about my mode of carrying on the work, but I made allowance for him. Dined at Mr. Ottley's in Margaret Street; his lady and daughter very pleasing. There were at dinner Mrs. and Miss Buchanan and my daughter and two Mr. Napiers from St. Christopher's,[1] where Mr. Ottley's estate is. One of them had been there twenty years without being in Britain. We had good entertainment and reasonable sociality. In the evening we had additional company to tea, cards, and music by Miss Buchanan and my daughter and Mr. Florio, who played the German flute wonderfully well. A little before ten I went to Malone's and revised a few pages of *Life*.

SATURDAY 2 JANUARY. The Rev. Dr. Coombe, an American who had been chaplain to Lord Carlisle when Lord Lieutenant of Ireland, waited on me with Dr. Johnson's letter on his Lordship's tragedy,[2]

[9]Boswell quoted Plutarch, "the prince of ancient biographers," to justify the inclusion of Johnson's conversations in the *Life of Johnson* (i. 31–32): "Nor is it always in the most distinguished achievements that men's virtues or vices may be best discerned; but very often an action of small note, a short saying, or a jest, shall distinguish a person's real character more than the greatest sieges, or the most important battles" (*Life of Alexander,* ch. i, trans. John and William Langhorne).
[1]St. Kitts, in the West Indies.
[2]A few days earlier Boswell had written to the Earl of Carlisle, asking to see Johnson's letter concerning Carlisle's tragedy *The Father's Revenge*. Carlisle was sending the letter through the Rev. Thomas Coombe, D.D., a native of Philadelphia who had settled in England in 1779.

and drank tea with me. I found him to be a pleasing, well-informed man, and very Johnsonian. Then at Malone's, where I found Courtenay, and after he left us, revised *Life*.

SUNDAY 3 JANUARY. Took Jamie with me to different churches, but found no seat; did not like this wandering. Veronica came and passed the evening with us, and we had sacred lessons. Sandy was now much better.

MONDAY 4 JANUARY. Breakfasted with Sir Joshua, which produced a dinner of the *Gang*, as Metcalfe calls him and Courtenay and Malone and me. Metcalfe came in the evening, and we had whist. I drank too much moselle, imagining it a mere diuretic.

TUESDAY 5 JANUARY. Was uneasy from the moselle. Visited Mr. Humphry, the painter.[3] Then attended at Thomas's Tavern in Dover Street a meeting called by public advertisement to take effectual measures for erecting a monument to Dr. Johnson. To the disgrace of the London booksellers, only one was there, Mr. George Nicol, a *Scotchman*, who contributed five guineas. Mr. George Chalmers, the writer on finance, etc., handsomely came and contributed the same sum.[4] There was only one unknown gentleman there, a Mr. John Sumner, who contributed two guineas and seemed very zealous for the good work, which I had now no doubt would speedily be done. Sir William Scott opened the business remarkably well. Mr. Malone, though in a strange agitation, spoke pertinently and genteelly. I said a few words briskly, but felt the difficulty of speaking calmly and distinctly. Sir William Scott, Malone, Dr. Burney,[5] Dr. Laurence, and I dined at Metcalfe's. Scott and Burney went, and then was whist, and afterwards a cold supper. I was too tumultous,[6] and I believe exceeded in wine. I drank some rum punch at night, which always hurts me.

WEDNESDAY 6 JANUARY. Awaked not well. Passed a part of the morning at Malone's, and had the pleasure of consulting with him and

[3]Ozias Humphry, a friend of Johnson's, who had done "a beautiful miniature in enamel" of him after Reynolds's 1769 portrait (*Life of Johnson* iv. 421 n.2). Boswell had met Humphry three years earlier on his return from India, where he had tried in vain to make his fortune.

[4]Nicol, Bookseller to the King, had been an acquaintance of Johnson's; Chalmers, chief clerk at the Office of Trade, wrote on historical as well as commercial subjects. Chalmers, too, was a Scotsman. ·

[5]Charles Burney, Mus.Doc., was an organist, composer, author of a respected four-volume *History of Music*, old friend of Johnson's as well as of Boswell's, member of The Club, and father of Fanny Burney.

[6]Boswell's usual spelling of words ending in "uous," presumably indicative of his pronunciation.

Mr. Selfe, the corrector of Baldwin's press, as to a specimen of my *magnum opus*. Malone and I dined at Courtenay's and had good, quiet, literary conversation.

THURSDAY 7 JANUARY. Dined with Malone tête-à-tête and revised *Life*.

FRIDAY 8 JANUARY. It was a cold, thick, misty day. I was irresistibly depressed by the weather, and had dispiriting views of my own situation. I went and dined with General Paoli; only a Count Mischi there. It was somewhat melancholy to think of the General as having now acceded to the dominion of France over Corsica (however made palatable by its natives being admitted to a participation of French privileges), and that he was preparing to quit this country. I regretted his having interfered at all,[7] as I hoped the French monarchy would be re-established. I went by invitation to Sir Joshua Reynolds's, drank tea and played whist. Metcalfe and Malone were there, and we stayed to cold meat.

SATURDAY 9 JANUARY. Dined at Mr. Dilly's with Mr. Horne Tooke (formerly the noted Parson Horne) and a pretty numerous company: Dr. Mayo, Dr. Gillies, Rev. Mr. Fell, Rev. Mr. Knox, Furrier Sharp, Mr. Braithwaite.[8] I had not met with a man so very disagreeable for a long time as Horne Tooke. He seemed to be accustomed to have an audience who looked up to him as a man of superior talents. He harangued with a smooth arrogance, and with an irony which is the most provoking mode of treating those with whom a man converses. He threw out the vulgar reflections against the clergy which showed him to be a man not in the habits of genteel company, where such abuse is now exploded, both as worn threadbare and as impolite. I stood up for the respectability of the Bench of Bishops and the worth of many parish priests, even within my limited acquaintance with the clergy. The renegado had the assurance to quote himself as one who, having been

---

[7] A Corsican commission had come to London to invite Paoli to return to lead his people. A few months earlier, Paoli had sent two separate emissaries to Paris for discussions with the leaders of the National Assembly. Unlike those Corsicans who still hoped for their island's independence, Paoli willingly agreed to having Corsica declared a French province, with the same privileges as other provinces in France.

[8] John Horne Tooke (the last name added at the request of a friend who promised an inheritance) was a clergyman turned radical politician; a philologist, he was also, according to Hazlitt, a fine gentleman and a brilliant but overbearing conversationalist. Vicesimus Knox, D.D., author of the highly popular *Essays Moral and Literary*, was Headmaster of Tunbridge School. Daniel Braithwaite, a Post Office official, was described by Boswell as an "amiable and friendly man, who, with modest and unassuming manners, has associated with many of the wits of the age" (*Life of Johnson*, 17 May 1784).

a parish priest, could best tell what they were. He talked with an insolent levity of the Articles of Religion, and was in short as offensive in his topics as Wilkes, without his wit. I was upon the verge of saying something as strong as I could to him, for indignation boiled in my breast. But I considered that I had no call to get into a quarrel with such a fellow, to whom three clergymen of different denominations quietly listened.[1] I therefore rose and left the company at an early hour. My good friend Dilly followed me, and I told him fairly that I could not bear Horne Tooke, and gave him my reasons. He said, "He is reckoned very clever," but I satisfied him that I did better to go away.

I had been at Baldwin's before dinner in consequence of a letter from him which showed me that, by using a *pica* instead of an *English* letter in printing my book, I might comprise it within such a number of sheets as a guinea-volume should contain, which I could not do in English letter unless upon a *medium* instead of a *demy* paper, so as to have a larger page.[2] I consulted with Dilly, and carried specimens of both kinds of paper to Baldwin's, where it was settled that I should on Monday have a specimen in each way. I then went to Sir Joshua Reynolds's by invitation, and found a pretty numerous company at cards, and played whist. I had not been in a company of ladies for a considerable time. I felt myself strange. And recollecting her whom I had lost, who could accommodate herself to all my wayward fancies, it seemed to me impossible that I could ever again love a woman except merely as gratifying my senses. I was repelled by disgust whenever I attempted to fancy a perfect union. I might indeed establish a civil contract of *consortium vitae*[3] with a sensible, good-tempered woman of fortune. Thus I meditated. Malone and I stayed to cold meat. Sandy had been more uneasy today, and pettishly said he would not follow Mr. Devaynes the apothecary's directions.[4] He made me angry. I was convinced how unhappy it is both for parents and children when there has been too much indulgence. I could not yet decide where to send Jamie. He implored to stay in my house till summer in so piteous a tone that I inwardly yielded.

[1] They were three clergymen of two different denominations: Knox was an Anglican; Mayo and Fell, Congregational ministers.

[2] *Pica* is one size of type smaller than *English*. According to *The New Paper Makers and Stationers Assistant* (1794), *medium* paper was either 17½″ × 22½″ or 18″ × 23″ and one size larger than *demy*, which was 17½″ × 22″.

[3] Although not a technical legal term, this phrase was used to describe the most basic obligation of marriage, cohabitation. Boswell is suggesting that he would settle for a simple marital union—a sharing of bed and board—as distinct from a more perfect or ideal union.

[4] Sandy was suffering from a severe case of scarlet fever, an extremely serious illness at the time.

SUNDAY 10 JANUARY. [No entry for this day.]

MONDAY 11 JANUARY. Was at Baldwin's and Dilly's consulting as to my *Life of Johnson*. From the computation of my manuscript, or *copy* as it is called, there were 416,000 words, which we averaged would make too many pages in quarto even upon *pica*, and therefore it was thought by Baldwin that I should make two quarto volumes on *English* and sell them at thirty shillings. I dined at my brother T.D.'s, where Veronica and Jamie should have been, but they were both ill, Veronica of a cold, Jamie of the rash fever.[5] I was comfortable and made calculations as to my book; then went to Malone's and revised *Life*.

TUESDAY 12 JANUARY. Dined at Sir Joshua Reynolds's with the two Wartons,[6] Sir William Scott, Malone, Courtenay, Metcalfe, Mr. John Palmer (Sir Joshua's nephew),[7] and Counsellor Erskine, whom I had not met for some years. I was in admirable spirits and felt myself quite a match for Erskine. He told us he was the great-grandson of Sir Thomas Browne.[8] He praised Lord Kenyon highly and said he was a better Chief Justice than Lord Mansfield. "Ay," said I, "*praesens divus habebitur Augustus*.[9] No doubt he is a much better Chief Justice. But how came you, Sir, the grandson of Sir Thomas Browne" (this was thrown in merely to swell the sentence, it having no connection whatever with the subject), "how came you to frame and lead your brethren to subscribe with you a complimentary address to that old fellow who you know did all he could to destroy the law of England?"[1] Erskine

---

[5] Jamie was also coming down with scarlet fever.

[6] Joseph Warton, D.D., Headmaster of Winchester College, and the Rev. Thomas Warton, Camden Professor of History at Oxford and Poet Laureate. Both were literary historians, critics, poets, and members of The Club.

[7] Canon of Lincoln and holder of livings in Devon and Essex.

[8] Thomas Erskine, an impecunious Scotsman who had become a brilliant and successful member of the English bar, had been a model for Boswell's attempts to practise law in England. He was the great-great-grandson of Sir Thomas Browne, the seventeenth-century physician and writer. Boswell had seen Erskine at the Carlisle Corporation trial on 7 December 1789 but may not have spoken to him.

[9] Horace, *Odes*, III. v. 2–3: "Augustus shall be thought a *present* god." In the first three lines of the ode, Horace declares that just as Jupiter the Thunderer is known to reign in heaven, so Augustus will be known as a god present on earth when he conquers the Britons and the formidable Persians. Boswell is likening Kenyon, the Lord Chief Justice of the King's Bench, to Augustus—with a pun on *praesens* to stress that Kenyon is the present holder of this office—and is also implying a comparison between the former Lord Chief Justice Mansfield, a powerful judge for many years, and Jupiter.

[1] When Mansfield retired from the King's Bench in 1788 at the age of eighty-three, Erskine had presented him with a complimentary letter from the counsel of the Court. Earlier Mansfield had been severely criticized by some of his opponents for weakening the principles of *habeas corpus* and trial by jury.

seemed a little abashed, for, to be sure, what he did was from ostentation, contrary to his opinion; but he answered quickly, "I did it as the grandson of Sir Thomas Browne, on the principle of *Religio Medici*.[2] It was *pious* to give a *cordial* to an old man." I said Wedderburn had a hard voice, an *iron* voice.[3] "Why," said Erskine, "you talk *iron*ically of him." Somebody observed that his manner was *cold*. "Yes," said I, "*cold iron*."

We talked of the Revolution, against which I always declaim. Erskine said, "This new establishment should be well watched, the Constitution should be well beat and brushed, when so many rights were sacrificed to it."[4] (Dr. Warton mentioned the famous Lords' Protest: "Under *this* family we *will* be free.")[5] "For my part," said I, "such is my Toryism that I would rather not beat and brush it, but let it grow dusty, so as at least to have the *appearance* of being old. I am for 'tauk your auld cloak about ye.'"[6] Erskine repeated Johnson's eloquent passage against war in his pamphlet on Falkland's Islands.[7] Such is my scanty *report* of this day, which was a very pleasant one. I stayed the evening and played whist. In the evening was carried to Marylebone watchhouse for calling the hour in the streets.[8]

WEDNESDAY 13 JANUARY. I had talked of printing my *Life of Johnson* in folio, rather than in two volumes. Malone said I might as

[2]Part II of Browne's *Religio Medici* extols the virtue of charity.

[3]Alexander Wedderburn, first Baron Loughborough, was another Scottish advocate who had achieved success at the English bar. Known throughout his career for his ambition, he had been Solicitor-General and Attorney-General, and was currently Lord Chief Justice of the Court of Common Pleas.

[4]Boswell, like Johnson, had always taken the conventional Tory view that the Glorious Revolution of 1688 and the deposition of James II had been unfortunate but justified to preserve the Church of England. By the "new establishment" Erskine presumably means the provisions for the Regency made during George III's first period of insanity in 1788–89; by the "Constitution" he means the Revolution Settlement of 1689 that limited the powers of the British Monarch.

[5]A group in the House of Lords protested in 1736 against George II's ungenerously limiting the funds made available to his son, the Prince of Wales, and, alluding to the tyranny of such Stuart rulers as James II, declared that "under this royal family [the Hanoverians] we are fully determined we will live free" (*A Complete Collection of Protests of the Lords*, 1767, i. 149).

[6]The title and refrain of a Scots song. "Tauk" is dialectal for "take."

[7]In his *Thoughts on Falkland's Islands* (1771), which urged restraint in a quarrel over sovereignty between England and Spain, Johnson pointed out that "War has means of destruction more formidable than the cannon and the sword. Of the thousands and ten thousands that perished in our late contests with France and Spain, a very small part ever felt the stroke of an enemy; the rest languished in tents and ships, amidst damps and putrefaction; pale, torpid, spiritless, and helpless; gasping and groaning, unpitied among men made obdurate by long continuance of hopeless misery" (*The Yale Edition of the Works of Samuel Johnson*, x. 370–71).

[8]See below, 13 January 1790.

well throw it into the Thames, for a folio would not now be read. His scheme was to print 1,000 on pica in quarto, in one volume however thick, and at the same time by *overrunning* the types, as it is called, to print 1,000 in octavo, which would be kept *in petto* and be in readiness for sale whenever the quarto was sold.[9] This scheme pleased me much, and both Dilly and Baldwin approved of it, so I had resolved on it and got a specimen of each; but having talked with Mr. John Nichols the printer, he satisfied me it was a bad plan. In the first place, by *over-running* I saved only £25 upon a hundred sheets, nothing being saved but the half of the compositor's payment, which call 10/-. In the second place, my octavo edition would have all the errors of the quarto; and thirdly, it would hurt the sale of my quarto, as its being ready would be known. He advised me rather to print 1,500 in quarto, and assured me that I would run no risk of not disposing of that number. This advice was given me *after* this day, but I put the whole history of my publication together.[1] I was much obliged to this worthy, liberal-minded man.

I this morning attended at the office in Lichfield Street, Seven Dials, to answer for the offence on account of which I had been committed to the watch-house the night before,[2] but had been allowed by the constable to go home upon my *parole*. Justice Bradshaw was the sitting magistrate. He saw no criminality in me upon the statement of the sergeant of the patrol, an old Scotchman, who charged me with being riotous because I would not desist from calling the hour. My defence was that I did it to put the watchmen right, as they never laid the emphasis on the *hour* but on *past* and *o'clock*. The Justice was of opinion that there was ground for committing me, because noise is the beginning of disturbance, and no man has a right to make any noise in the street after twelve but the watch, to whom authority is given. I took today a share of Baldwin's good family dinner and a bottle of his mountain.[3] I was somewhat intoxicated, and not finding Malone at home, went to the Oxford Arms in Bond Street, supped and had punch.

[9] For a *folio*, the largest size of book, the sheet of paper is folded only once, creating two leaves (four pages) per sheet; for a *quarto*, the sheet is folded twice, creating four leaves; and for an *octavo*, the sheet is folded three times, creating eight leaves. *Over-running* here refers to using the type again for additional printing. *In petto* means "in reserve."

[1] Boswell rewrote this entry later—probably on or after 26 January, to judge by a note in the manuscript.

[2] The Lichfield Street office was one of several public or municipal offices where complaints were heard by magistrates serving in rotation (it was therefore also known as a rotation office). Seven Dials owes its name to an earlier column that was topped by dials, each of which faced one of the seven streets that meet at this point.

[3] Malaga wine made from mountain-grown grapes.

THURSDAY 14 JANUARY. Dined at Metcalfe's with the two Wartons, Malone, Sir Joshua Reynolds, Mr. John Palmer his nephew, and some more whom I do not remember, but it was a pleasant day; played whist and supped.

FRIDAY 15 JANUARY. Dined, I think, at home, and in the evening revised at Malone's.

SATURDAY 16 JANUARY. Dined at Thomas's[4] in Dover Street with Sir Joshua Reynolds, Sir William Scott, Sir Joseph Banks, Malone, and Metcalfe, we being six out of eight, the committee for Johnson's monument.[5] We had more good living than business. Sir Joshua, Malone, and I went home with Metcalfe and had whist. Miss Palmer came and took Malone's place, who went away.

SUNDAY 17 JANUARY. Went by accident (to try a new chapel) to St. Mary's, Park Street, and heard an excellent discourse by a Dr. Steevens on the truth of Christianity: *I bear record of myself, and my record is true.*[6] His mode of arguing was clear and strong and his pronunciation very much that of Garrick.[7] I dined at Malone's with the two Wartons, Sir Joshua Reynolds and his nephew Mr. J. Palmer, Metcalfe, Courtenay, and the Hon. Thomas Erskine, who gave us several stories of second sight, and repeated exquisitely well a great part of one of Burke's speeches against taxing America.[8] Dr. Warton called him the Garrick of Burke. It was an admirable day, though I have preserved so little of it. I liked to observe Malone as an acute reasoner pin Erskine down when he declaimed, as he always does.

MONDAY 18 JANUARY. Dined at Malone's on *scraps,* as he said; that is, on some of the choice dishes of the day before, and had a long revise of my *Life of Johnson.*[9]

TUESDAY 19 JANUARY. Dined at the Literary Club (I in the chair) with Lord Lucan, Lord Macartney,[1] Sir Joshua Reynolds, the two Wartons, Dr. Burney, Malone, and Courtenay. I cannot distinctly

[4] Thomas's Tavern.
[5] Edmund Burke and William Windham were absent.
[6] John 8: 14.
[7] Presumably an allusion to David Garrick's vivid, natural way of speaking.
[8] Burke made a famous speech on the subject in Parliament in April 1774; it was published as a pamphlet, *Speech on American Taxation,* in 1775.
[9] This day Boswell wrote to Lord Hailes: "My *Life of Johnson* is in the press" (Register of Letters). On 1 January, it had been only *at* the press.
[1] Charles Bingham, first Baron Lucan of Castlebar, had been an M.P. in the Irish Parliament and then in the British House of Commons. Macartney was a distinguished diplomat, who had served as envoy to St. Petersburg, as Governor of Grenada, and as Governor of Madras.

describe my present state of mind. There was a ground of sad indifference from the consciousness of the loss of my excellent wife, which
prevented all anxiety or uneasy reflections with regard to my situation
in life, whether a good account could be given of my method of living,
or whether I should ever succeed in any scheme of future advancement. I felt as if I were done with life, that is to say, with any care
about it, so that all the considerations and fretfulness which I used to
have were no more, and I experienced quite a new state of existence.
For aught I could see then, I might at an after period experience another state as new, having still the consciousness of identity, which was
continually stirring in my mind. I at the same time had a keen relish of
every pleasure, whether sensual or intellectual. We had a great deal of
good conversation today at our Club, which was called before Parliament met on purpose for the Wartons.[2]

[EDITORIAL NOTE. The full journal breaks off at this point in the
middle of a page. However, a loose paper headed "Club, Tuesday 19
January" records some of the "good conversation" just mentioned—
chiefly literary banter and irrepressible punning. In the most compre-
hensible passage, Boswell recalls Johnson's remark that the diction in
John Gay's ballad "Sweet William's Farewell to Black-eyed Susan" is
too elegant for a simple sailor and his wench. Boswell continues: "Courtenay had found fault with the lark, but I observed it was [the] poet's
simile, not [the] sailor's. I. 'Why not [make them] Duke of Clarence
and Poll Finch, and then the finch would suggest the lark.' LORD
MACARTNEY. 'Now he is on wings, he'll soar' (or 'fly' or some such
[word])." Here Boswell, after quite properly attributing Gay's elaborate lark simile to the poet as speaker, alludes to George III's son, the
Duke of Clarence (later William IV), who had served in the navy from
an early age and who was parading about with his current prostitute-
mistress, Poll Finch. Subsequently, Gay's poem *Trivia* is declared out
of date, a line of Pope's translation of the *Iliad* is found wanting, and
then the puns deteriorate to comments about the dinner: "You [are] a
drummer, [for you have] two drumsticks."

Notes of varying length reveal Boswell's busy life during the next
few weeks. They show that Jamie was still suffering from scarlet fever
and that Dr. Warren was called in several times. Boswell was pained
and anxious—"Poor little man! I was in sad apprehension"
(26 January)—then cheered: "Jamie much better. Oh, what relief!"
(28 January). Boswell's own health remained a problem: "Earle's;

---

[2]Ordinarily The Club met only when Parliament was in session, but special meetings
were held when the Wartons could attend.

sounded;[3] almost fainted" (31 January). The treatment must have helped; he felt better two days later.

Work on the *Life of Johnson* continued. "Worked *Life*" (27 January). "Up late at *Life*" (28 January). Eager to ensure accuracy, Boswell checked birth records and accounts of divorce proceedings to verify Johnson's conclusions, in his *Life of Savage*, about Richard Savage's family background and supposed illegitimacy.

A more extensive note gives a glimpse of a heated political discussion between Boswell and Edmund Burke during a meeting of the committee on Johnson's monument. Boswell had known and admired Burke for years but had irritated him by quoting Johnson's belittling comments about his wit in the *Tour to the Hebrides* and then by other unintentionally tactless remarks. Moreover, although Burke, like Boswell, was a staunch monarchist, they had genuine differences of opinion. Ever since entering the House of Commons twenty-five years earlier, Burke had been a member of the Whig group led by the Marquess of Rockingham, whereas Boswell had long been a Tory. They also disagreed on the subject of Warren Hastings, who had been impeached for plundering India and maltreating local rulers while serving as Governor-General of that country. Burke had been the chief instigator of his trial, which had begun in February 1788; Boswell steadily sympathized with Hastings. The conversation of 23 January is recorded in elliptical phrases.]

[BURKE.] "France a disgrace to human nature; cannot call it democracy." I. "Diablacy." [BURKE.] "Imprudent in Ministry to allow motion of thanks [to the throne and] Lord Valletort to attack [the French]." I pleased him by playing: "Il a tort."[4] [BURKE.] "*I* should have said ten times as much, had it been proper, but [the attack was] imprudent. We may be negotiating with them." (Prudence taught by Burke!) [BURKE.] "Maxim 'King can do no wrong' never so true as now. Poor man, [I] believe him totally innocent. 'Cineri dolosa'"[5] ([turning] towards me). "This in France would almost make me adopt your Tory principles." I. "Nay, you are one of us. We will not part with you." BURKE. "You have the

---

[3] James Earle, surgeon at St. Bartholomew's Hospital, probed his bladder to ease a urethral stricture.

[4] At the opening of Parliament two days earlier, Lord Valletort had thanked the King for his speech, which contrasted the peaceful state of England with the political turmoil elsewhere, and had attacked the French revolutionaries for creating a state of anarchy while virtually imprisoning their monarch in his palace. Boswell puns on Valletort's name: "il a tort: he is wrong."

[5] Horace, *Odes*, II. i. 7–8, trans. C. E. Bennett, Loeb ed.: "Incedis per ignes/suppositos cineri doloso: [thou]...art walking, as it were, over fires hidden beneath treacherous ashes"—a reference to Louis XVI's difficult position now that he was being forced to give up many of his powers to the National Assembly while remaining the titular monarch.

art of reconciling contradictions beyond any man." I. "[Yes,] a Tory
and an American." BURKE. "You were not always an American." (This
an unjust suspicion of time-serving.)[6] [BURKE.] "And then asking Sir
James Lowther to come into Scotland to defend liberty.[7] You are the
greatest Encyclopédiste in politics."[8] He indelicately, I thought, mentioned Mr. Hastings. I could not but say "I am on the other side there."

[EDITORIAL NOTE. Another political discussion, this one at a meeting
of The Club, took place on 2 February. Anti-French feeling was intensi-
fying, but the Prime Minister was avoiding the drastic step of declaring
war. Boswell's note for this day shows Burke less concerned about being
prudent: "Very warm against French revolutionists. But would not be tied
down to any principles; [would act] only as circumstances [dictated]: 'ex
facto jus oritur.'[9] Talked of no spirit in this country, Pitt's tyranny.
Courtenay candidly said he could not agree. Pitt had done no more than
any Minister would do. He[1] was really unpleasant."

We continue with the notes for the following days, which show
Boswell moving in quite different circles.]

WEDNESDAY 3 FEBRUARY. Laboured *Life*. Dined at Turk's Head
Coffee-house with Const, Captain Topham, Reynolds (author of *The
Dramatist*), Holman the player,[2] etc., etc. A deal of noise. Heated my-
self somewhat. Went to Essex Head Club: Barrington, Brocklesby,
Cooke,[3] T.D. Was too keen for Hastings and against Burke, partly in

---

[6]During the American Revolution, when the Tories led by Lord North had opposed
the demands of the colonists, Boswell, although otherwise a Tory, had sympathized
with the Americans. The reason for Burke's accusation is unclear.
[7]In his 1785 *Letter to the People of Scotland* protesting against a Government attempt to
decrease the number of Lords of Session, the highest civil tribunal of Scotland, Boswell
had with total irrelevance called on Lonsdale for help: "Let not the Scottish spirit be
bowed. Let Lowther come forth and support us! We are his neighbours" (p. 28).
[8]Perhaps Burke meant that Boswell, like the *Encyclopédie*, held a great many disparate
and inconsistent views.
[9]"Right is determined by the facts."
[1]Burke. At about this time he began the first draft of his *Reflections on the Revolution in
France*, vehemently opposing the ideas of the French republicans.
[2]A group associated with the theatre. Francis Const, a barrister, was the author of pro-
logues and epilogues. Edward Topham, a captain in the Horse Guards, was a playwright as well as the proprietor of the scandalmongering newspaper the *World*, which
he was reputed to have bought to puff his actress-mistress. Frederic Reynolds was also
a playwright and Joseph George Holman, an actor.
[3]This club was founded by Johnson in 1783 to dine three times a week at the Essex Head
Tavern in Essex Street. Daines Barrington, a lawyer and antiquarian, Richard Brocklesby,
a physician who treated Johnson in his last illness, and William Cooke, a legal writer, were
original members. Cooke, later known as "Conversation" Cooke for his poem of that title,
had published a biography of Johnson two weeks after his death.

opposition to Brocklesby. But it was wrong to give him an opportunity to say I talked against Burke. Cooke and I sat after the rest, till twelve, talking of Murphy, literature, etc.

THURSDAY 4 FEBRUARY. Dined at Malone's quiet (only young Jephson[4]) and revised *Life*.

FRIDAY 5 FEBRUARY. In the morning Dilly came. Visits. Dined at Sir J. Reynolds's with Malone and evening [there] (with Metcalfe, etc.). Whist.

SATURDAY 6 FEBRUARY. Charming day. Dined at Dilly's with T.D., Cavallo, two Belshams, one a dissenting minister, violent for repeal of the Test, Mr. G. Chalmers, very intelligent and sensible, and Mr. Syms, wine-merchant.[5] I was too keen against dissenters. Syms and I stayed and eat[6] oysters. As I passed by Globe Tavern a quarter before twelve, found that Akerman was there and in the chair. Went in; a numerous and decent circle. Took my pipe and two large glasses of port negus. Many good songs. Enjoyed it much. Got at last next to Akerman and heard all about Lord George Gordon.[7] Stayed till twenty minutes past two. Dreary walk home. Oxford Chapel struck three.

SUNDAY 7 FEBRUARY. Breakfasted with General Paoli; had from him a full state of his motives in his conduct as to France, and was satisfied that unless he had been active, his great object, the delivering

---

[4]Richard Mounteney Jephson, a member of the Inner Temple, was the son of an Irish friend of Malone's; Boswell met him frequently in Malone's company.

[5]Among the guests were Tiberius Cavallo, an Italian-born physicist who had recently published treatises on electricity and magnetism; Thomas Belsham, a Unitarian minister and Professor of Theology at Hackney College; and his brother William Belsham, a political writer and historian. The Test Act, which excluded all but Anglicans from public office, was a highly controversial topic since a Bill for its repeal had just been introduced in Parliament. As a dissenter (one who refused to accept Anglican doctrines and forms of worship), Thomas Belsham naturally favoured repeal; James Renat Syms, a member of the London Common Council, opposed it when it was debated by that body.

[6]An eighteenth-century alternative for the past tense of "eat," habitually used by Boswell.

[7]Boswell had known Richard Akerman, keeper of Newgate prison, for several years and had been introduced by him to a club, "Friends round the Globe," that met nightly at the Globe Tavern, Fleet Street. Lord George Gordon was Newgate's most distinguished inmate—a fanatical political agitator, who had been acquitted of high treason for encouraging the anti-Catholic riots of 1780 but who was currently imprisoned for libel (not only had he published an attack on the British criminal justice system but he had also repeated in the *Public Advertiser* the scandalous story about the sumptuous necklace supposedly ordered but not paid for by Marie Antoinette). Gordon was now conspicuous for his recent conversion to Judaism and for his elaborate entertainments of guests at Newgate.

Corsica from oppression, could not have been accomplished.[8] Good chocolade and important conversation distended[9] and raised my mind. Walked in St. James's Park; attended evening prayer and sermon in Whitehall Chapel very agreeably. Floated upon life with really pleasing sensations. Was decidedly happy that I was not at Edinburgh. Veronica and T. D. dined and drank tea. I felt myself sink a little. Walked to Mrs. Buchanan's with Veronica and sat awhile.

[EDITORIAL NOTE. Boswell's notes for the next few days merely record dinner engagements with various friends. Only a week later is there a more informative entry; it is the last for some time.]

MONDAY 15 FEBRUARY. Dined Lord Lonsdale's. Lord Galloway there. I attacked the Union and said the nation was gone. Individuals came up to England like Jews. Lord G. opposed me. "Ay," said I. "You're a pretty gentleman. You're an instance: a lord of the bedchamber, etc."[1] Lord Lonsdale maintained ably the advantage of Scotland from the Union: that we should not have been allowed East India trade, etc. Penn and I went to the Mount.

[EDITORIAL NOTE. Boswell's mood at this point can be seen in a letter he wrote to Temple on 13 February: "As by GOD's mercy I am at present wonderfully well, I shall endeavour to write to you often and to supply you with spirits from my store. I cannot account for my 'healthful mind'[2] at this time. There is no change to the better in my circumstances. I have no better prospect of gratifying my ambition or of increasing my fortune. The irreparable loss of my valuable wife, the helpless state of my daughters—in short, all that ever hung heavy upon me—is still as it was. But my spirits are vigorous and elastic. I dine in a different company almost every day, at least scarcely ever twice running in the same company, so that I have fresh accessions of ideas. I

---

[8]Paoli was explaining his reasons for resuming the leadership of Corsica under the new French rule. He welcomed the change in Corsica's status from occupied territory to a French province because he thought that this status would free it from oppressive measures, and he basically approved of the constitution being worked out by the National Assembly.

[9]Expanded.

[1]The Act of 1707 had united the parliaments of England and Scotland. Boswell is criticizing Scotsmen for giving up their national identity in order to get ahead as individuals. John Stewart, seventh Earl of Galloway, was a prominent Scots nobleman (Knight of the Thistle and for many years a Representative Peer for Scotland), who had made a place for himself at the English court; as Lord of the Bedchamber, he was paid £1,000 a year.

[2]Johnson, *The Vanity of Human Wishes*, 1. 359.

drink with Lord Lonsdale one day; the next I am quiet in Malone's elegant study, revising my *Life of Johnson,* of which I have high expectations both as to fame and profit. I surely have the art of writing agreeably. The Lord Chancellor told me, 'He had read *every word* of my Hebridean journal; he could not help it.'"[3]

No doubt his progress on the *Life,* now finally in the press, contributed to Boswell's good spirits. By the middle of March he was able to write to his friend Thomas Percy, Bishop of Dromore, that a hundred pages had already been printed. At the same time, he kept public interest alive in the newspapers. In early February, for instance, a brief note in the *Public Advertiser,* actually written by Boswell, reported that he had attended services in Westminster Abbey "in a scratch wig and watchman's great coat, as like as he could be to old Sam Johnson."

The most amusing of the newspaper articles contrasts Boswell's work with Mrs. Piozzi's two books, *Anecdotes of the Late Samuel Johnson, LL.D.* (1786) and the two-volume *Letters to and from the Late Samuel Johnson, LL.D.* (1788), which had made her a rival on the subject of Johnson just as she had earlier been Boswell's rival for Johnson's friendship. She had irritated Boswell by minimizing his importance to Johnson and by showing that Johnson had preferred her first husband, Henry Thrale, to him. He also thought her *Anecdotes* suffered from inaccuracies and pictured Johnson as excessively demanding, gloomy, and rude. Two newspaper articles in particular dwell on Mrs. Piozzi's supposed terror at the approaching publication of Boswell's biography and pointedly emphasize his accuracy as well as his respect for Johnson. The one in the *Morning Post* of 22 February adds: "Mrs. Piozzi has, however, nothing to dread, for Boswell will be employed in pursuing an eagle, and it is not likely that he will turn from so noble a flight to pluck a feather from a tomtit." The paragraph in the *Star* of 3 March is equally complimentary to Boswell but attacks Mrs. Piozzi more crudely, stressing "his integrity, his inflexible love of the truth, and his veneration for the memory of a friend, by her made to stink in the public nose." Although neither of these pieces bears the asterisk with which Boswell marked his own contributions to the newspapers,[4] both were almost surely written by him.

In a still sharper attack on Mrs. Piozzi that appeared in the *Morning Post* of 23 February, Boswell expressed his annoyance over what he considered her niggardly contribution to the monument for Dr. Johnson as well as over the profit she had made from her two books.

---

[3]Edward Thurlow, first Baron Thurlow, had been a valued acquaintance of Johnson's and was greatly respected by Boswell.
[4]Boswell maintained a file of clippings, which has survived.

Feigning a defence of Mrs. Piozzi, Boswell claimed that "she has been vilified beyond measure for giving only five guineas to Johnson's monument out of the £737. 14s. 6d. which she pocketed by selling his anecdotes and letters." He then announced that she would, however, show her generosity to the poor by "a grand entertainment at Mr. Thrale's brewhouse in Southwark to the friends and connections of her late husband, by whose bounty she is now in affluence."

This barbed reminder of the source of Mrs. Piozzi's current fortune was followed a week later in the same newspaper by a burlesque sketch of the fictitious Brewhouse Entertainment. It celebrates Mrs. Piozzi's return to her first husband's brewery with her new husband, Gabriel Piozzi, the Italian music-master whom she had married to the dismay of her friends. Making the most of his material, Boswell cast the entertainment with appropriate figures from Mrs. Piozzi's acquaintance: "A grand procession is to take place, in which Mr. John Kemble is to walk in the character of Hamlet, holding two miniature pictures and repeating the well-known comparative passage: 'This WAS your husband,' etc." In 1788 Kemble had appeared in Bertie Greatheed's *The Regent*, for which Mrs. Piozzi had contributed an Epilogue inviting the audience's applause with the unfortunate lines, "Our bard…with antiquated art/…drives his battering-ram full at your heart." Focusing on this image, Boswell concluded his sketch, which was already full of sexual innuendo, with gleeful malice: "But what has excited the most eager impatience in the ladies of Southwark is a report that the Signora is to give, after dinner, an improvisation founded on the much-famed line in her Prologue [in fact, her Epilogue] to the tragedy *The Regent:* 'And drives his battering-ram FULL at your heart.'"

Meanwhile, Boswell's search for material for the *Life of Johnson* even at this late date led him to ask for a meeting with Warren Hastings, whose acquaintance he had made three years earlier. Hastings called without delay.

[Note on the Visit of Warren Hastings, 1 March 1790]

I think I was happy in my mode of addressing him, which was: "Sir, I would not deny myself the very great honour of a visit from you, and therefore have availed myself of your most obliging offer. Any temporary difference in your situation I assure you makes no difference in my mind. I was taught by Dr. Johnson that 'whatever makes the past, the distant, or the future predominate over the present advances us in the dignity of thinking beings.'[5] I view you, Sir, with the eye of Lord Thurlow as an Alexander; and though I am not surly and proud,

[5]From the section on Iona in Johnson's *Journey to the Western Islands of Scotland.*

I flatter myself I am in some degree a philosopher. Your visit, there-fore, to me may be compared to that of Alexander to Diogenes, for indeed my small hut is not much bigger than a tub. Let me add, Sir, that you have saved me the trouble of going into the street with a torch at noonday to look for a man."[6]

The meeting was productive; Hastings promised to send the letters he had received from Johnson.

But soon Boswell was faced with an unexpected problem. The re-spected Bishop Percy, compiler of the *Reliques of Ancient English Poetry* (1765) and a long-standing member of The Club, suddenly asked not to be named in the *Life of Johnson*. Cautious by temperament, he feared that trivial details in the Johnson anecdotes he had provided would make him look ridiculous. Boswell, replying to him on 9 April, was firm and a trifle sarcastic: "As to suppressing your Lordship's name when relating the very few anecdotes of Johnson with which you have favoured me, I will do anything to oblige your Lordship but that very thing. I owe to the authenticity of my work, to its respectability and to the credit of my illustrious friend, to introduce as many names of em-inent persons as I can. It is comparatively a very small portion which is sanctioned by that of your Lordship, and there is nothing even bor-dering on impropriety. Believe me, my Lord, you are not the only Bishop in the number of great men with which my pages are graced. I am quite resolute as to this matter."

The *Life of Johnson* did not, however, absorb all of Boswell's energy. His violent opposition to the French Revolution led him to contem-plate writing a play about Thomas de Mahy, Marquis de Favras, an ardent royalist who was executed in February 1790 for supposedly or-ganizing counter-revolutionary plots that included planning the escape of Louis XVI and his family. As reported in mid-March by the *World*, "It seems that the 'Tory soul' of Boswell is employed upon a tragedy, of which the subject is...deeply interesting. It is the death of Favras, one of the *ultimi Romanorum,*[7] the faithful and heroic martyr for the monarchy of France." The few surviving fragments of this tragedy viv-idly demonstrate the prevailing conservative reaction to the events in France, which were sending shock waves through England and the rest of the world. As his synopsis reveals, Boswell planned to pit the "highly monarchical" Favras against his boyhood friend Dumont, who "has

---

[6]Alexander visited the philosopher Diogenes, who was so eager for the simple life that he lived in a tub and so disillusioned with his society that he took a lantern by daylight to look for an honest man. Thurlow was one of the few prominent politicians who supported Hastings.

[7]Tacitus, *Annals,* iv. 34: "the last of the Romans." Ironically, the reference is not to an imperial Roman but to Cassius, one of the last republicans.

served in America with Lafayette and is full of democratical sentiments"—indeed, who "has his head full of fiery modern writings about
the rights of men" and "raves like Rousseau." Dumont urges caution,
but Favras rejects all prudence, considering it "a sneaking quality when
great duties require bold exertions." That Boswell considered the Revolution a temporary aberration is suggested by his projected poetic image of the *fleur de lis*, symbol of France: "In decay for a season, to revive
with fresh lustre in all its glory like the lily of the field." In his pro-
spectus he declared that he wished to appeal to the "generous Britons
who adore their monarch and are sensible of the blessings of our happy
Constitution." In another announcement of his play, this one in the
Public Advertiser, Boswell again made much of his loyalist theme and
was already casting Kemble in the part of Favras. But these exciting
preliminaries seem not to have been followed by any further exertions.

Boswell was also looking for other occupations, chiefly because he
was becoming increasingly conscious of his financial problems. The
scheme of accompanying Richard Penn to America having come to
nothing, he sent a letter on 26 February to his old friend Sir John Dick,
formerly British consul in Leghorn, asking for his help in finding "a
situation of affluent independence" and adding, "I am resolved to go
to any corner of the globe rather than continue any longer in embarrassed circumstances." Moreover, a draft of a letter addressed some
time in March to the Duke of Leeds, Secretary of State for Foreign
Affairs, shows Boswell playing with the idea—perhaps only half in jest—
of offering £1,000 "for any post, place, or pension."

At the same time, Boswell continued to lead a full social life, not dining at home once in the middle of March. In particular, he kept Sir Joshua
Reynolds company during a difficult period when he needed support. As
President of the Royal Academy, Reynolds had backed the Italian architect Joseph Bonomi for a professorship in the Academy but was outvoted
by supporters of the Swiss painter Henry Fuseli. In protest, Reynolds had
resigned from the Academy. "Sir Joshua has been shamefully used by a
junto of the Academicians," Boswell reported to Percy on 12 March. "I
live a great deal with him." Boswell did not, however, approve of
Reynolds's stand, and much to the relief of all concerned, Reynolds was
soon persuaded to resume his position as President.

Later in March Boswell gave a farewell dinner for General Paoli just
before his return to Corsica. In spite of his mixed feelings about Paoli's
aligning himself with the French republicans, Boswell invited a number
of distinguished guests, including the Sardinian and Portuguese Ministers, Sir John Dick, Sir Joseph Banks, and Lord Macartney. Nor could he
resist writing a brief account of the occasion for the *Public Advertiser.*

At the end of the month, Boswell had the opportunity to shine at a much larger gathering—the annual dinner of the Royal Humane Society, an organization devoted to helping persons who had apparently drowned or otherwise suffocated. According to the *General Evening Post* of 1 April, the gathering was huge, the company was brilliant, and the many "loyal toasts" were "succeeded by an affecting procession of a considerable number of fine children and grown persons who had been restored by the exertions of this benevolent society." The entertainment included a song "written and sung by James Boswell, Esq., one of the Stewards." It is all terrible, but the second stanza is the funniest:

> Lo! a troop of grateful creatures
> Which our institution boasts;
> Dim, nay dead, were once their features—
> But for us they had been ghosts.

In the spring of 1790 various hints suggest that Boswell was also beginning, though cautiously, to entertain thoughts of a second marriage. In March he wrote to Miss Isabella Wilson of Newcastle—"an experiment" he termed it in his Register of Letters—recalling their meeting two years earlier and "begging to hear how she is [and] if she recollects me." Miss Wilson replied cordially, but for the moment he did not pursue the experiment. In the same month he wrote chivalrous verses to Lady Mary Lindsay, the daughter of the Countess of Crawford, and had these printed anonymously in the *General Evening Post* as well as in some Scottish newspapers.

Boswell seems to have engaged in a more serious flirtation as well. This is known only from the early April entries in his Register of Letters: "Rev. Mr. Temple a short note as to a fit of love of the most dangerous kind" and, a few days later, "Mr. Temple of my Rousseau-like confession."[8] Moreover, the entry for 15 April reads: "Countess of Crawford of my having been in a *dangerous* fever of love, entreating allowance for my *égarements.*[9] One maxim I am *sure* is solid: Let no man try *absolutely* to *change* his character. It is *impossible.* Let him make the *best* of it and *lessen* its evil as much as he can."

Lacking the texts of these letters, we are left to wonder why the fit of love was so particularly "dangerous" and who the lady in question might have been. The danger could hardly have been matrimonial. Perhaps the mysterious lady is the Mrs. F., soon called Mrs. Fox, who is mentioned in the notes beginning on 3 April. Nothing is known about

---

[8] A reference to Rousseau's intense subjective outpourings, characteristic of most of his writings and culminating in his *Confessions* (1784).
[9] Strayings.

her, but she must have been presentable, for Boswell included her with other invited guests. That she was also Irish may be inferred from the company in which she appears—Malone, John Clere Parsons, Robert Jephson,[10] and young Jephson's cousin Baker.

The notes that begin on 1 April are cryptic and noncommittal, no doubt because Boswell dictated them to Veronica. Although they are brief, they give an impression of the variety of Boswell's activities until the full journal resumes in mid-May.]

THURSDAY 1 APRIL. Dined at Sir Robert Strange's;[1] General Melville. Evening Sir Joshua's; Mrs. Gwyn.[2]

FRIDAY 2 APRIL. Good Friday. Breakfasted at home. Mrs. F. a minute. Ludgate Hill Church. Mrs. F. and Glover told me I had false spirits, though I did not know it. Akerman (Malone refusing) and Macklin.[3]

SATURDAY 3 APRIL. Pierrepont visited me.[4] Mrs. F., Seward,[5] Baker dined. Parsons [came for] coffee. Malone's to revise. She[6] and Baker came there. I very easy.

SUNDAY 4 APRIL. Easter. Chocolate, Chapter. St. Paul's, solemn service. Mrs. Gregg's. Dined at Lord Lonsdale's; Penn and the two dogs.[7]

MONDAY 5 APRIL. Dined at Lord Mayor's;[8] quite well. Read Mr. Dawes;[9] not drinking.

TUESDAY 6 APRIL. At home. Revised with Malone.

WEDNESDAY 7 APRIL. Pulteney breakfasted. Dined Sir Joshua: Planta, Barry,[1a] Malone.

---

[10]Robert Jephson, a moderately successful playwright and a friend of Malone's since they were schoolfellows in Dublin.

[1]A noted engraver, Strange was a Scots Jacobite, who had lived alternately abroad and in England. He eventually won the King's favour after engraving Benjamin West's *Apotheosis of the Royal Children* and was knighted in 1787.

[2]Mary Gwyn (also spelled Gwynn or Gwynne), who before her marriage, while still Mary Horneck, had been a great friend of Oliver Goldsmith's.

[3]Charles Macklin, the famous actor and playwright, now in his nineties.

[4]Charles Medows, whom Boswell had known since 1768 when he was a young naval captain; he had recently taken the name Pierrepont upon inheriting an uncle's estate.

[5]William Seward was a compiler of anecdotes and a fellow hypochondriac, described by Boswell as "well known to a numerous and valuable acquaintance for his literature, love of the fine arts, and social virtues" (*Life of Johnson*, 28 June 1777, note). A friend of Johnson's, he provided material for the *Life*.

[6]Mrs. F.

[7]Two of Lonsdale's henchmen.

[8]An unusually large and elegant assembly held by the Lord Mayor, William Pickett.

[9]Perhaps Manasseh Dawes, a barrister who wrote on legal and social subjects.

[1a]Joseph Planta was Keeper of Manuscripts and of Medals at the British Museum; James Barry was a painter of ambitious historical subjects and Professor of Painting at the Royal Academy.

THURSDAY 8 APRIL. Dined at Mrs. Buchanan's; Palmer. Humane Society.

FRIDAY 9 APRIL. Breakfasted with Mrs. Scott. Dined Malone.

SATURDAY 10 APRIL. Lord Lonsdale; two dogs.

SUNDAY 11 APRIL. Prayers, sermon at home. Dined at Lord Lonsdale's; proposal for history of Carlisle.[2] Two dogs dined.

MONDAY 12 APRIL. Breakfasted and dined at home. Revised at Malone's.

TUESDAY 13 APRIL. Called at Sir John Dick's. Breakfasted with Sir Archibald Campbell. Talked of Hastings and the slave trade.[3] Governor Penn called. Dined at Club with Lord Palmerston, Lord Lucan, Sir W. Scott, Windham, Dr. Fordyce, Sir Joshua, Courtenay, Malone.

WEDNESDAY 14 APRIL. Dilly breakfasted with me. Attended at the Old Bailey. Dined with the sheriff. Called on Madame Fox.

THURSDAY 15 APRIL. Old Bailey. Dined at Mr. Dilly's with Reed,[4] Braithwaite, Mayo, etc. Whist. Night there.

FRIDAY 16 APRIL. Old Bailey. Dined at Sir Joshua's. [Saw] *Beggar's Opera* complete.[5] Full of enjoyment of London. Home quiet.

SATURDAY 17 APRIL. Old Bailey. Dined Parsons with Mlle. d'Eon, Sir W. Young, Seward, Greatheed, Gregg, Marchese di Piedmonte.[6] Stayed till two in the morning.

SUNDAY 18 APRIL. Called at Mrs. Scott's with Veronica. Called at Rev. Mr. Wright's, who asked me to stay to dinner; refused. Eat beef with Veronica and Sandy. Dined at Mr. Malone's and revised a little.

---

[2]Boswell planned to write such a history.

[3]General Sir Archibald Campbell of Inverneil had been Boswell's client in earlier years. Having served as Governor of Madras from 1785 to 1789, he was no doubt interested in discussing the Hastings affair. The slave trade was also controversial, particularly since William Wilberforce had begun his campaign to abolish it by his May 1789 motion in Parliament.

[4]Isaac Reed, editor of the *European Magazine* and of Shakespeare, generally known as "steady Reed." Boswell credited him with an "extensive and accurate knowledge of English literary history" (*Life of Johnson*, beginning of 1781).

[5]When Boswell saw *The Beggar's Opera* in Edinburgh in 1780, he was irritated by some members of the audience and left at the end of the second act; the following year he missed the opening.

[6]The company included the Chevalier d'Eon, a former French diplomat and a notorious transvestite, whose sex remained a mystery until after his death; Sir William Young, formerly M.P., a Fellow of the Royal Society and of the Society of Antiquaries; and Henry Gregg, a barrister at Lincoln's Inn. The Marchese di Piedmonte has not been identified.

Jephson came with Mrs. Fox to tea. Shook hands with her, but took no further notice of her. Stayed all night at Dilly's to be ready for execution.

MONDAY 19 APRIL. Up a little after four; at Newgate by five. No appearance. To public house, got gin and water and a pipe. Akerman's; conducted to gaol. Hot port with Owen Sibbley and Billy Ward, etc. Sheriff, etc. came. Press-yard; talked with Masters, who beat his child to death, and Count Marini. Execution did not shock.[7] Talked with Rev. Mr. Hussey.[8] Breakfasted with the sheriff, etc. Old Bailey; made enquiries about James Boswell.[9] In sick ward with Gillespie. I dined at sheriff's table. Tea at Wrathall; oilman.[1] Went to Lord Lonsdale's; exulted in nominal and fictitious votes being abolished.[2] Home, dreary a little.

TUESDAY 20 APRIL. Plymsell breakfasted.[3] Old Bailey. Boswell had been acquitted. Long trial for forgery. Dined with Lord Lonsdale; two dogs. Home.[4]

WEDNESDAY 21 APRIL. David called, also Miss Carmichael.[5] Called at Governor Penn's. Went to Mr. Earle's. Wrote to Temple, Fergusson, and Grange's nephew.[6] Dined at home. Wrote to Lord

[7]Over the years Boswell had observed a considerable number of executions, drawn to them by a morbid fascination. Thomas Hewitt Masters was tried and sentenced the preceding Monday for killing the daughter of his mistress; Antonio Marini, self-professed son of a Venetian aristocrat, was convicted with two others of having murdered their companion. The press-yard—a courtyard in Newgate from which the prisoners left for the place of execution outside the prison walls—owed its name to the fact that until 1772 prisoners who refused to enter a plea were tortured there by having their bodies pressed by heavy weights.

[8]The Rev. John Hussey had been an acquaintance of Johnson's.

[9]Boswell's namesake, indicted for stealing an oil kettle and seven quarts of oil.

[1]Wrathall and Co. were tea-dealers in Tottenham Court Road. "Oilman" is perhaps a reference to the accused James Boswell.

[2]On this day the House of Lords, by reversing a decision of the Court of Session, dealt a death-blow to the practice in Scotland of allowing wealthy landowners to create voters without the normally required qualifications. Boswell consistently opposed such "nominal and fictitious" voters in Scotland; in England Lonsdale was one of the worst offenders in creating them in his constituencies.

[3]J. Plymsell was the compositor for the *Life of Johnson*.

[4]At this point two lines have been cut out of the manuscript.

[5]Poll Carmichael, one of several dependants whom Johnson had charitably taken into his house.

[6]Boswell was replying to the Rev. Joseph Fergusson's request that he help John Johnston, the nephew of Boswell's old friend John Johnston of Grange, to find a position as ship's surgeon. On Johnston's death in 1786, Boswell had become the nephew's trustee.

Lonsdale. Worked hard at *Life* all the rest of the day. Prepared for Southill.

[EDITORIAL NOTE. No record has survived of the next few days. As arranged beforehand by letter, Boswell apparently accompanied Charles Dilly on 22 April on a visit to his family home at Southill, Bedfordshire, owned by his older brother, Squire John Dilly. Quite possibly Boswell kept no notes of this visit. But he began them again with the new month.]

SATURDAY 1 MAY. Breakfasted Mr. Malone's as usual.[7] Dined and supped at Earle's; Mrs. and Miss Lister.[8]

SUNDAY 2 MAY. Jamie and I walked out to Chelsea and brought Betsy home to dinner. Jamie and I went to Trinity Chapel, near Brompton. T.D. and wife dined. Allan drank tea afterwards. Marched Jamie down to Westminster; introduced him to Dr. Vincent and was informed that the holidays began that week.[9]

MONDAY 3 MAY. Dined at Ayrshire Club. Sad hurly-burly.

TUESDAY 4 MAY. Chaplain's Table, Dr. Vincent, at four.[1] Revised.

WEDNESDAY 5 MAY. Eumelian.[2]

THURSDAY 6 MAY. Mr. Dilly's. Supped at Sir R. Strange's.

FRIDAY 7 MAY. Mr. Malone's with Mr. Courtenay.

SATURDAY 8 MAY. Mr. Nichols, Mr. Dilly, Mr. Malone, Molly Knowles.[3]

SUNDAY 9 MAY. St. Mary Woolnoth Church. Dilly's; Dr. Lettsom, Marquess Lansdowne.[4] Night, Mount.

---

[7]That is, on the first of the month, when they read over the just published monthly periodicals.

[8]Harriet Lister, an amateur painter of landscapes, was close to forty and wealthy; a few years later she married the painter Amos Green and returned to her native York.

[9]This was to be Jamie's first day at Westminster School, but when Boswell learned of the imminent vacation, he brought the boy home again. Dr. William Vincent was the Headmaster.

[1]Vincent was chaplain-in-ordinary to the King during May, presiding at the Chaplain's Table at St. James's Palace.

[2]A club that met at the Blenheim Tavern in Bond Street. It was named for its founder, Dr. John Ash, *Eumelian* being based on the Homeric epithet "armed with good ashen spear" (eu = well, melia = ash, spear). Two years earlier, Boswell had been admitted as an honorary member; Reynolds, Windham, and Burney also belonged.

[3]Mary Knowles, a Quaker, had provoked Johnson into denouncing a young woman for leaving the Church of England by becoming a convert to Quakerism. Boswell included an account of their spirited discussion in the *Life of Johnson*.

[4]John Coakley Lettsom, a prominent Quaker physician, had been a fellow guest at Charles Dilly's on previous occasions. Boswell knew William Petty, first Marquess of Lansdowne, as Lord Shelburne, the Prime Minister who had concluded the peace with America. His son was one of Sandy's classmates at Eton.

MONDAY 10 MAY. Mr. Hoole, Captain Farquharson, and Bruce Campbell breakfasted.[5] Went to the Duke of Leeds.[6] French ordinary.[7] Dined at Lord Lonsdale's.

[EDITORIAL NOTE. The full journal begins again here with the heading, "Journal from the time that my old friend Temple arrived on a visit to London and me in 1790." Boswell later explains that he began to write it only a few days before 29 May, so that the first entries must have been written in retrospect.

Boswell had not seen Temple since his stay in London in May 1783, followed by their brief trip north together in June. Their reunion after seven years had been planned for several months. Temple was bringing with him his oldest daughter Anne, called Nancy, who was just a year older than Veronica. Temple's journal and Nancy's letters complement Boswell's own record of the next few weeks.]

FRIDAY 14 MAY. Mr. and Miss Temple arrived at my house, no. 38 Queen Anne Street West. My brother T.D. was waiting with me, ready to receive them. It was very agreeable to me to perceive no alteration upon my friend. Veronica and little James were now in the house with me. Miss Temple, notwithstanding a defect in one of her legs and feet which made her walk lame,[8] was a pretty, elegant, accomplished girl. We had tea. The feebleness of Temple's manner was very apparent to me. I insisted that he and his daughter should be my guests.

SATURDAY 15 MAY. Lord Lonsdale sent for me in the forenoon, and when I went, I found it was to ask me to accompany him to his

[5] John Hoole was a translator of Tasso, Ariosto, and Metastasio. He had been befriended by Johnson, who wrote the dedications for two of his works, and he supplied Boswell with Johnsoniana both before and after this meeting. Gregor Farquharson, a captain on half-pay in a regiment of foot, had been instrumental in getting Boswell his first brief in London. Bruce Campbell of Milrig was Boswell's second cousin.

[6] Boswell appears to have requested this interview to discuss whether he needed the King's permission to include in the *Life of Johnson* the long letter Johnson had written in 1768 to Frederick Augusta Barnard, the King's Librarian, offering advice on how to acquire books in foreign countries for the royal library. Barnard was reluctant to agree to its publication. Francis Godolphin Osborne, fifth Duke of Leeds, who had held various offices at Court in earlier years and was now Secretary of State for Foreign Affairs, had been helpful in transmitting to Boswell the royal permission to use an account of the famous interview between Johnson and the King; he considered the publication of Johnson's letter to Barnard unobjectionable but suggested that someone closer to the King should broach the subject with him. However, in answer to Boswell's letter explaining Leeds's position, Barnard curtly refused to permit the Johnson letter to be published, and it is not included in the *Life*.

[7] A tavern serving meals at a fixed price.

[8] Nancy Temple was born with a deformed foot.

seat at Laleham in Middlesex, about seventeen miles from town. I represented the hardship of leaving my friend, who had only come to me the night before, all the way from Cornwall. But the Potentate pressed my going, said he did not know when he should be there again, and that he would bring me back on Monday before dinner. So I yielded; but when I came home and found Temple gone out, I was very uneasy, and apprehensive that he might be offended and leave my house. I left an earnest letter for him, and also one for Veronica to insist on his remaining. I dined at Lord Lonsdale's, and he contrived to put off time so, that it was almost dark when his coach set out, carrying his Lordship, Sir Michael Le Fleming, Colonel Lowther, and me. It was about two in the morning when we got to Laleham, where he had a small house on the banks of the Thames, with an old maidservant and a gardener as its inhabitants. I had some bread and milk, and went to bed.

SUNDAY 16 MAY. We walked out before breakfast, having crossed [by] the ferry, which belongs to Lord Lonsdale. The view from Laleham is beautiful: the silver Thames, its green meads, tufts of wood interspersed, St. Anne's Hill, and Cooper's Hill. It was a charming day. Saul and Squire Denton arrived, having been ordered to come down with a turbot and a couple of lobsters. After breakfast the same coachful as yesterday drove to Runnymede,[9] and having returned to Staines, took a boat and rowed down to Laleham. Our dinner was ill-dressed. Out of about a score of bottles of wine which were opened, there were but very few that were not spoilt, so that we had no comfortable regale,[1] and the Earl was violent and abusive, talking of what strange company I kept— Sir Joshua Reynolds, etc., etc., etc. I was quite indignant and said, "My Lord, it is company of which I am very proud, and think myself much honoured by being admitted into it." My feelings were so disagreeable that I inwardly resolved to withdraw myself from all connection with him.

MONDAY 17 MAY. We set out so as to reach London in time for me to dine at my own house with my friend and his daughter, whom I had the comfort to find not at all disobliged. They and my daughter had settled to go to Ranelagh,[2] and that I should accompany them. I felt great reluctance to it, my nerves being as usual irritated by the jaunt,

---

[9]The site of the signing of the Magna Carta.
[1]Repast.
[2]A fashionable place of amusement, famous for its rotunda, a large covered amphitheatre. Describing this visit to her mother in Cornwall, Nancy Temple gave her impression of Veronica: "You cannot conceive a more unpolished girl than Miss B. is. She is really vulgar, speaks broad Scotch, but appears very good-humoured. I am really surprised at Mr. Boswell's keeping her so secluded: he never scarce permits her to go out. She seems now like a bird got out of her cage" (*Diaries of William Johnston Temple*, ed. Lewis Bettany, 1929, p. 70).

and my temper ruffled by feeling myself, as I thought, degraded by Lord L.'s usage. However, after sitting a little while with Malone and his brother,[3] I agreed to go, and little James was so importunate that I took him with us. I got into good humour, and went through the evening very well. I joined Miss Lister and had a great deal of conversation with her, very frankly, and found her very intelligent. Mr. Campbell of Craigie[4] walked some time with me and my children, and was very agreeable. It was between one and two when we got home.

TUESDAY 18 MAY. I visited Miss Lister and saw her drawings of the Cumberland lakes, etc., remarkably well done.[5] My guests and my daughter and I dined at Mr. Hawkins's, Member for St. Michael's; nobody else there but Mr. Kerr, a self-sufficient, tedious Scotchman who had been tutor to Sir John St. Aubyn.[6] Hawkins and my people went to the play.[7] I repaired to Malone's and revised a small portion of my *Life of Johnson,* but was interrupted by his brother, etc.

WEDNESDAY 19 MAY. It soothed me always now in the mornings to find my friend and his daughter and mine at breakfast, so that I seemed not so destitute as I had been. Temple had talked to me of marrying a woman of fortune. I mentioned several, and had flattering notions that I might be successful; but I wavered so, and was so much satisfied that my attachment to my valuable departed spouse, and my habits of living without restraint, unfitted me for a fair connection with any woman, that I doubted if I could as an honest man marry again, besides the consideration that it would distress my children. However, I let the scheme float in my mind, and having confessed to my old friend my warm propensities, considered a contract with any decent woman as an insurance against some very imprudent connection. We went to the Exhibition of the Royal Academy, and all dined at home. They went to Astley's;[8] I went to Malone's, where I was asked to dine, and drank some wine. Kemble was there. I have omitted to mention that I this morning saw three men hanged before Newgate.[9]

---

[3]Richard Malone, a former M.P. in the Irish House of Commons, who was created Baron Sunderlin in the Irish peerage in 1785. He was Malone's older brother.

[4]William Campbell, an Ayrshire neighbour.

[5]Harriet Lister had shown one of her landscapes at the Royal Academy as honorary exhibitor in 1784.

[6]Christopher Hawkins, M.P. for Mitchell (St. Michael's), was a longtime friend of Temple's; St. Aubyn, M.P. for Penryn, a prominent Cornish landowner.

[7]At Drury Lane Theatre, where they saw Kemble and Miss Farren in Arthur Murphy's *All in the Wrong.*

[8]A popular equestrian circus. Its owner, Philip Astley, was the main attraction.

[9]Boswell added this sentence later. One of the men was executed for counterfeiting, the other two for robbery.

THURSDAY 20 MAY. I was now in absolute poverty. I had in prospect half a year's expense of Veronica, Sandy, and Betsy, say £150; my house-rent, £25; housekeeping (due), £25; in all £200, besides a number of bills due. I had only £62 in my brother's hands, and expected from Mr. Bruce Campbell[1] £50, so that there was a deficiency of £90, over and above the bills or accounts for a variety of articles, such as clothes, wine, fish, coals, butcher meat, etc. I had yesterday called on Mr. Forbes of Callendar to borrow £200 of him,[2] but he was gone to Scotland. I thought of several people, upon a curious principle that I would apply to such as I was little acquainted with, for if they refused me, there would be nothing lost; whereas if they behaved handsomely, I should gain a true friend or two more. But I could not bring myself to ask anyone. I walked this morning in Bond Street, meditating on my forlorn state at the time, and found tears in my eyes. I had however hopes of a remittance in June out of the money due to me by the Cuninghames. But being exposed in the mean time alarmed me. My guests and Veronica and I dined at Mr. Dilly's, where were Dr. Bush, an American physician, Mr. Justice Conant,[3] and Dr. Mayo. Steady Reed joined us after dinner.

FRIDAY 21 MAY. I this morning received from James Bruce[4] an unexpected receipt from the Ayr Bank for £80, which appeared to me a great relief, and my spirits were raised. My guests and daughter dined with Miss Palmer at Sir Joshua Reynolds's, and went to the play.[5] I dined at home, and went in the evening to a concert at Mr. Earle's, where I heard some very good music. There was a numerous and genteel company, and among them the Duchess of Bedford, with whom I had never before been in company. A Miss Wainwright sung charmingly,[6] and pleased me by a resemblance which I thought she had to Miss Wilson, my Newcastle flame. I had a great deal of conversation with Miss Lister in a still more frank style than at Ranelagh, showing

---

[1]Campbell helped to manage the Auchinleck estate in return for a small salary.

[2]An Aberdeen coppersmith, Forbes had made a huge fortune from Government contracts and had bought the estate at Callendar in Stirlingshire in 1783. Four years later he had married Margaret McAdam, a family friend of the Boswells.

[3]Nathaniel Conant, Justice of the Peace for Middlesex. He later became chief magistrate of the Bow Street public office and was knighted.

[4]The overseer at Auchinleck.

[5]At Drury Lane Theatre, where they saw *A Trip to Scarborough* by Richard Brinsley Sheridan and *The Devil to Pay; or, The Wives Metamorphosed,* an operatic version by Theophilus Cibber of Thomas Jevon's *The Devil of a Wife.*

[6]Perhaps Harriet Wainwright, who composed songs and later published a treatise on singing.

her my singular character. I was pressed to stay supper, which I did, and enjoyed it much. There were two-and-twenty covers,[7] and good entertainment in every respect.

SATURDAY 22 MAY. My life appeared both to myself and my old friend to be passed in a very idle and dissipated manner. He advised me to wait till the General Election, and if Lord Lonsdale did not then give me a seat in Parliament, to withdraw from him gradually. We all dined at home today. It was wet, and my spirits were depressed. I saw from my window Governor Penn trotting home. I followed him into his house. He said he was low. I made him come with me and we drank a bottle of madeira in a few minutes quietly, and then being better, went upstairs to tea. Mr. Hawkins came and stayed supper, Penn having gone away. We were very cheerful, and Hawkins talked away at a wonderful rate.

SUNDAY 23 MAY. My brother David came and went with Temple and me to the Neapolitan Minister's chapel, that Temple might hear High Mass for the first time. It was so crowded and hot that we stayed but a short time. I then took Temple to the Portuguese Chapel, which was not crowded, but High Mass was over.[8] I sat some time with Malone. My guests, my daughter, and I dined at Lord Lisburne's, a truly excellent dinner. No company there but General Vaughan[9] and Mr. Forster, son of the commissary at Berwick. My Lord talked well of public characters, etc. Veronica appeared as I could wish. Temple went with me in the evening to the Mount Coffee-house and sat some time with Sir Charles Farnaby, Governor Penn, etc.

MONDAY 24 MAY. My eldest son having been very earnest that I should come to Eton to be present at the ceremony of *montem*, that is, the procession of the school to a mount at Salt Hill,[1] I could not refuse; so went down today and put up in the evening at the Star and Garter at Windsor, a secondary inn, the great ones being all full. As I walked to Eton, Sandy, who was hovering about, joined me, and was very happy

---

[7]Place settings; that is, there were twenty-two at table.

[8]Although Catholic worship was officially forbidden in England, the public could attend Mass at the chapels attached to the embassies of Catholic countries; these chapels in fact served as missions.

[9]Wilmot Vaughan, first Earl of Lisburne, was a distant relation and early patron of Temple's; Lt.-Gen. John Vaughan, governor of Berwick, was Lisburne's brother.

[1]This traditional ceremony, held every three years, consisted of a colourful procession around the school and up Salt Hill. The students collected "salt" (money) from the spectators in exchange for a pinch of salt. The boy who was designated captain of *montem* had to pay the day's expenses but was allowed to keep the remaining funds, which could be substantial.

to see me, as I was to see him. I went with him to Mrs. Harris, his dame's,[2] where I saw he was quite at ease. She told me that she would not give me my bill till the next breaking up, 26 July. This was a relief to my mind, as it gave me more time to be ready. I called on Dr. Davies,[3] and left my name, he being not at home. I took my son and his companion, Vansittart, with me to my inn, where they and Dr. Lind, whom I had met in the street, supped with me. Lind's Scotch manner disgusted me somewhat.[4] I felt myself somewhat uneasy at being only one night out of London, and at an inn. There was a noisy club roaring in the next room to me. I however fell asleep, and observed next day that I had been *sung* to sleep, which was the earliest mode in which we obtained that repose.

TUESDAY 25 MAY. It was a very wet morning. I rose relaxed[5] and melancholy as in the country, and walked about an hour under cover, in the middle of the town; I thought under the Town Hall.[6] Then breakfasted, visited Mr. Goodall, my son's tutor, and drank some chocolade with him. Was much pleased to see my son smartly dressed in scarlet, etc., and appearing quite an Eton boy. Visited Mr. Baker, with whom I saw Mr. and Mrs. and two Miss La Touches, and liked the gentle Irish tone.[7] Saw the boys parade round the schoolyard, it being now fair, and marched a great part of the way with them towards Salt Hill. Returned to Windsor, got into the stage, and came to town in time to dine with Lord Lonsdale, who, I found, had done me the honour of a call the night before. This was creditable. I relished being with him again; only Colonel Lowther, Saul, Squire Denton, Rev. Mr. Fletcher. Was welcomed by my guests, Veronica, and Jemmy.

WEDNESDAY 26 MAY. Temple and I visited Malone, who had called on Temple. I dined at Malone's with Lord Sunderlin and the two Jephsons.[8] My guests dined at Sir Francis Blake's.

THURSDAY 27 MAY. Was at the printing-house some time. Temple and I dined at my brother David's, where was Tiberius Cavallo.

---

[2] Catherine Harris, matron of Sandy's boarding-house at Eton.

[3] Jonathan Davies, D.D., Headmaster of Eton College at this time.

[4] James Lind, M.D., an eccentric Scotsman who had settled at Windsor and had become physician to the royal household there. Boswell had known him earlier in Edinburgh. Years later, as an old man, Lind was celebrated by Shelley as "beloved friend" in *Prince Athanase.*

[5] Boswell means "enfeebled."

[6] Presumably under the recently renovated Guildhall, in an area used for Saturday markets and for the three annual fairs.

[7] Baker was private tutor to the sons of the Dublin banker John La Touche. Both sons were at Eton.

[8] Young Jephson and his uncle, Robert Jephson.

In the evening I had a long revise of part of Johnson's *Life* at Malone's.

FRIDAY 28 MAY. Went with Mrs. and Miss Lister and Miss Buchanan and saw Sir Joshua Reynolds's pictures. He was very polite and pleasing. Mr. Lumisden[9] and Mr. Tiberius Cavallo dined with us. Mr. Hawkins and my brother David could not come. My guests and daughter went to the opera.[1] Mr. Lumisden and I sat the evening together, and had a little punch.

SATURDAY 29 MAY. I awaked sadly dejected and under such a fit of hypochondria as I had not experienced for a considerable time. I despaired of doing any good myself, and timidly shrunk from the thought of little James being at Westminster School. I however rose, and went in the coach with my guests and daughter and saw them into Westminster Abbey to be present at the Grand Music.[2]

I grew a little better and paid a visit to Mr. Wingfield, undermaster of Westminster School, to whom Sir George Osborn[3] had given me a line recommending little James. I found him to be an intelligent, civil man; he told me that my son, whatever progress he had made, would be properly placed in the school; that a private tutor was of service to some boys and pernicious to others; and after a trial he would let me know whether my son should have that additional tuition. At the top of St. James's Street I met young Willes, whom I had not seen for several years, and was sincerely glad to find him pretty well. I remembered his father with real regard, for he was very kind to me.[4] Poor Ross, the player, who had lately come from Bath, breakfasted with me by appointment and talked of a history of the English stage which he was to publish by subscription.[5] I visited Penn and Malone. Courtenay came home with me, and we talked of my claim on Government. Courtenay

---

[9]Andrew Lumisden, a Scots Jacobite, had served as secretary to the Old Pretender in Rome, 1757–66; he returned to Scotland in 1773 and was pardoned in 1778. He was the brother-in-law of Sir Robert Strange. Boswell, who had met him in Rome in 1765, was interested in his writings.

[1]They heard Sebastiano Nasolini's *Andromaca* at the Haymarket Theatre.

[2]The second day of the Handel Commemoration, devoted to the *Messiah*. Temple and his party waited from eight in the morning to noon for the performance to begin. Probably Boswell did not remain because he had vowed, after hearing the work in June 1784, not to efface that impression by listening to it ever again.

[3]A London acquaintance, brother of Boswell's old friend John Osborn.

[4]Edward Willes's father, Judge Edward Willes, had gone out of his way to be friendly to Boswell during his first visit to the English assizes at Carlisle in 1778, had seen Boswell again at York the following year, and had invited him to dine in London in 1785.

[5]David Ross was an actor and theatre manager. In 1767 Boswell wrote a Prologue for the opening of the Edinburgh Theatre Royal, which Ross was managing, and they renewed their acquaintance in 1783. Ross did not live to write his projected stage history.

thought that as I had not supported Administration uniformly, I had no claim.[6] I felt myself now in a strange state. I saw no probable prospect of raising myself, or even of being easy in my circumstances. My friend Temple told me fairly that he had never seen anybody so idle as I was. I could scarcely take the necessary trouble of preparing my book for the press. I had kept no journal for a long time, till within these two days that I began it again, nor had I marked down my expenses. Still I dreamed of applying resolutely to the practice of the law, and of having it said, "He never took fairly to the English bar till he was fifty."

I was asked today to dinner both at Lord Lonsdale's and Mr. Metcalfe's. This made me seem to myself of some consequence. But I was engaged to the anniversary of Charles the Second's Restoration at Chelsea College, to which dinner I had an invitation from Sir George Howard, the Governor, for fifty years from 1785, having been introduced to it by Mr. Burke in 1783, when he was Paymaster of the Army,[7] and having been absent only in 1788, when I was in Scotland on account of my dear wife's illness. I wish I had kept a list of the company present each year. Dr. Monsey the physician, and Mr. Adair the surgeon, had been succeeded by Dr. Moseley last year and Mr. Keate this. Today the company was Sir George Howard, Major Bulkeley, Major Dawson, Dr. Burney, Mr. Keate, the Rev. Mr. Blayney, Mr. Graham of the establishment;[8] and of guests, Sir George Osborn, General Trapaud, General Pattison, Colonel Teesdale, Major Da Costa, Rev. Dr. Steevens, Mr. George Drummond, Captain Bulkeley of the Guards, and

---

[6]Boswell had attacked Henry Dundas and other Government supporters in his second *Letter to the People of Scotland* (1785); more recently, he had flaunted his support for the Prince of Wales, Pitt's enemy, just after the Regency crisis of 1778–1789 while George III was temporarily insane.

[7]Chelsea Royal Hospital for old and disabled soldiers, still called Chelsea College for the theological college that preceded it on the site, was founded by Charles II. Apparently General Howard had expressed the hope, in 1785, that Boswell would take part in the festivities for the next fifty years. Edmund Burke had introduced him while serving as Treasurer of the College, one of his functions as Paymaster General of the Forces, a position which he held briefly in 1782 and again in 1783.

[8]Organized as if it were a regiment of foot, Chelsea College was officially headed by General Sir George Howard, M.P., who had fought in most of the major battles of the century, and was run by Maj. William Bulkeley. Lt.-Col. Thomas Dawson became adjutant the following year. The medical staff consisted of the physician Benjamin Moseley, M.D. (replacing the eccentric old Dr. Messenger Monsey, whom Boswell had met in previous years and who had died in 1788 at the age of ninety-four), the surgeon Thomas Keate, and the apothecary Richard Robert Graham. The Rev. Robert Blayney, a Hebrew scholar, took the place of the two official chaplains on this day; Charles Burney was the organist and, as such, lived at the College.

myself. Poor Captain Grant was unable to attend.[9] There is generally a change of generals each year. It was an excellent dinner, as usual, and I drank of all the liquors: cold drink, small beer, ale, porter, cider, madeira, sherry, old hock, port, claret. I was in good spirits at the festival, talked well, and was pleased, as the table began to thin, to find Mr. Keate come and sit by me and carry on some intelligent conversation. Sir George was called away. Major Bulkeley took the chair, and we circulated the glass a long time. I never saw candles there before, I think.[1] Trapaud, Da Costa, and I drank a glass of cherry brandy at Dawson's and went to town in Trapaud's coach. I called at Metcalfe's. He and Malone were gone home with Sir Joshua. I foolishly followed, for I was much intoxicated, and I suppose talked nonsense. I played whist ill, and lost some shillings. I walked with Malone to his street, and then being restless, sauntered in Oxford Street and Bond Street till it was very late, or rather early. Very irregular this; but I thought the festival an excuse.

SUNDAY 30 MAY. Awaked somewhat feverish. My old friend and I attended morning service at St. George's, Hanover Square, and I experienced the tranquillity, the divine composure, which such a scene used to produce in my mind in the days of youth. Temple and I dined at Hawkins's, where were his brother Mr. John Hawkins, Mr. Zimmermann of Brunswick and his son, Mr. Wadström the Swede, Mr. Giddy of Pembroke College, Oxford, and his son Mr. Davies.[2] I was flat when I first entered. But a hearty dinner and a good deal of wine set me to rights. Mr. Wadström came home with Temple and me and supped. He entertained us with his curious notions of the Swedenborg kind, in which he was quite serious.[3] What a strange thing is the human mind!

---

[9]Capt. Lewis Grant, the adjutant of Chelsea College, was seventy-four years old and died the following year. He was the son of the minister of Auchinleck in Boswell's grandfather's time.

[1]Presumably because they had never stayed long enough to need candles. The festival dinners usually began at eleven in the morning and ended at three in the afternoon.

[2]Eberhard Zimmermann, Professor of Mathematics at the Collegium Carolinum in Brunswick; Carl Bernhard Wadström, traveller and abolitionist; the Rev. Edward Giddy and his son Davies Giddy. Young Giddy changed his name to Davies Gilbert upon inheriting extensive lands from his wife, Mary Ann Gilbert, and later became President of the Royal Society.

[3]The Swedish theologian Emanuel Swedenborg's idiosyncratic system included the belief that angels and devils were former human beings who had chosen the company most congenial to them and who continued to live as they had on earth. His followers had founded a Church of New Jerusalem in England in 1788. Wadström had recently returned from the interior of Africa, where, inspired by Swedenborg, he had hoped to find a Christian people; his observations were cited in Parliamentary debates on the abolition of slavery. Temple described him as fanatic.

MONDAY 31 MAY. My guests and daughter went to see sights. I went to my printer's and Mr. Dilly's, whom I engaged to dine with me, which he accordingly did. Counsellor Gregg drank a glass of wine and also tea with us.

TUESDAY 1 JUNE. Breakfasted with Malone as usual. I dined at home with my guests, and accompanied them and my daughter to Vauxhall.[4] In the course of some following days they saw several things. I went with them to Chelsea College, Lord Fife's house, the King's Library,[5] and the Tower. I was at Westminster Hall in my barrister's dress on the 4 June,[6] and sat in the Court of Chancery. I dined one day at Lord Lonsdale's. A fit of hypochondria, from which I had been pretty free, I may say entirely so, all winter, returned upon me, and I was in sad inquietude.

SATURDAY 5 JUNE. Sir Joshua Reynolds, his nieces Mrs. Gwatkin and Miss Palmer and nephew Mr. John Palmer, Lord Sunderlin, Mr. Malone, Mr. Jephson, and Mr. Courtenay dined with us. I wished to show Temple some really good society. In the state of mind in which I was, the entertaining of such a company appeared to me in prospect to be an arduous undertaking, but I soon got into a better frame and all went on well. Lord Sunderlin, Malone, and Jephson stayed supper. Betsy dined with us.

SUNDAY 6 JUNE. Temple and I walked about a little while. He and little James went to Lincoln's Inn Chapel. I attended evening prayers at Portland Chapel. I and my guests and daughter dined at Mr. Hawkins's. Mr. Douglas, a gentleman from Berwick, and Mr. Radcliffe, a gentleman from the west of England, were there. I became pretty hearty by means of turbot, venison, and a liberal dose of wine. In the evening little James called on me in a coach, and I accompanied him to Dean's Yard and left him with Mrs. Clough, at whose house he was to be boarded, that he might next day enter to Westminster School. I parted from him with tender concern.

---

[4]Popular pleasure gardens, older than Ranelagh. By the time of this outing, Nancy Temple had formed a hearty dislike for Veronica: "You cannot conceive how disagreeable Miss Boswell is at these places. She is so vulgar and uncouth and such a strange figure that she keeps one in continual dread of what she will say or do. Away she flies into the thickest of the crowd without any regard to herself or us. And then she is so fearful of getting into a carriage" (*Diaries of William Johnston Temple*, ed. Lewis Bettany, p. 71).
[5]Fife House, in Whitehall Yard near the Thames, was built twenty years earlier by Boswell's old acquaintance James Duff, second Earl Fife; the King's Library in Buckingham House was the site of a memorable meeting, vividly described in the *Life of Johnson* (February 1767), at which the King complimented Johnson on his work.
[6]The Monarch's official birthday.

MONDAY 7 JUNE. My brother T. D. and young Mr. Bruce Campbell dined with us. My guests and daughter went to the play.[7] I stayed at home, arranging Dr. Johnson's *Life*. The house seemed dull without little James.

TUESDAY 8 JUNE. My guests went to Mr. Claxton's, near Croydon.[8] I was as far as Mr. Sewell's in Cornhill to get some little information for Johnson's *Life*. Hundreds of such pieces of trouble have I been obliged to take in the course of the printing.[9] I went to Lord Lonsdale's a little before seven, intending to dine with him; but he, unlike his usual way, had been at table so long that I would not go in, so came home and had cold meat, and then went to Malone's and revised some of my work. On my return at night, I was distressed to hear from my servant, who had carried some things to little James, that some big boys had forced him the night before to drink burgundy till he was intoxicated.

WEDNESDAY 9 JUNE. Was restless. Took breakfast, partly at Sir Joshua Reynolds's, partly at Sir Joseph Banks's, where there is every day in the year an excellent breakfast of the best tea and the best bread and butter, whether Sir Joseph be at home or not, his librarian Mr. Dryander, a Swede, always attending.[1] Today there were only he and Tiberius Cavallo and another gentleman besides myself. My daughter and I dined at Sir Joshua Reynolds's with Mrs. Horneck and her daughters,[2] the Rev. Dr. Wynn, a reading, talking man, etc. I went in the evening to the Essex Head Club, the last meeting this season, and returned and supped at Sir Joshua's.

THURSDAY 10 JUNE. I dined with Sir William Scott, by appointment, to *sit* upon my record of the conversation between Johnson

---

[7]At Covent Garden, where they saw Joseph George Holman as Hamlet and James Byrn's *Nootka Sound; or, Britain Prepared,* a pantomime-opera about a current dispute with Spain concerning the possession of Nootka Sound on the west coast of Vancouver Island in North America.

[8]John Claxton, a barrister at Lincoln's Inn, was an old Cambridge friend of Temple's and, through Temple, of Boswell's. He had an estate at Shirley, near Croydon.

[9]John Sewell, a bookseller, was publisher of the *European Magazine,* which had printed several letters of Johnson's in 1787. Boswell recalled his efforts to gather material in the Advertisement to the first edition of the *Life of Johnson:* "Were I to detail…the inquiries which I have found it necessary to make by various channels, I should probably be thought ridiculously ostentatious."

[1]Jonas Dryander, a botanist, lived in Sir Joseph Banks's house in Soho Square and catalogued his remarkable scientific library.

[2]Mrs. Hannah Horneck and her married daughters, Mary Gwyn and Catherine Bunbury. Goldsmith, a close friend, had addressed the daughters in verse respectively as "the Jessamy [i.e., fashionable] Bride" and "Little Comedy."

and him.[3] Lady Scott, whom I had seen several times, but always reserved, was today exceedingly agreeable, in so much that I protested that I would take her directly if Sir William would part with her. I asked if she had a sister, and was informed she had one, Miss Fanny, four-and-twenty, not so good a size as Lady Scott and not so domestic, but a Ranelagh girl, as Sir William said; at the same time very good-humoured and very religious, in so much that she reads select prayers and a sermon every Sunday evening to her father's servants. "Let me see her," cried I. "This is the very woman that I should wish to have." Lady Scott told me that she had very lately refused a handsome young man. "I am happy to hear it," said I. "That is a proof what kind of man is agreeable to her. *I* shall have a good chance." In this manner we joked, I all the while considering that a daughter of the ancient family of Bagnall of Bagnall in Staffordshire, with £6,000 certain and to be probably a co-heiress of estates to the value of £2,000 a year, was a most desirable object. Lady Scott promised I should see her; but Sir William told me that at this moment a young gentleman who would one day succeed to a peerage was in suit of her, and I must wait the event.[4] My scheme was entirely *convenience* and *ambition*, being conscious that the loss I had suffered would ever cloud my mind. But I thought that I might take the chance of advantage, and being connected with Sir William Scott might be of essential service to me.

He talked to me in a very friendly manner when I complained to him in confidence of my situation and asked him if I should blame myself for having removed from the provincial court in Scotland to the wide field of London. He consoled me, saying, "You were in a state of relegation[5] there." "True," said I, "I continually languished to be here, and imagined I should advance myself. But what am I doing?" "Why" (said Sir William), "enjoying your existence, and in the way to get some promotion; and you will consider that at once you may obtain something that will make up for all." I told him that his brother, Sir John, had promised to do what he could for me when he was Chancellor, if that should ever happen. "I know" (said Sir William), "he is a

---

[3]As a result of this meeting, which Boswell later recalled as providing "one of the pleasantest days I ever passed in my life" (Boswell to Sir William Scott, 9 August 1791), he slightly revised his account of the long conversation that had taken place in Scott's chambers in the Middle Temple on 10 April 1778. Scott was a good friend of Johnson's and was one of the executors of his will.

[4]In 1793 Frances Bagnall married Thomas Windsor, who was the second son of Other Lewis Windsor, fourth Earl of Plymouth, but who did not succeed to the peerage.

[5]Exile or banishment.

very honest man now, and I hope will be the same then."[6] Sir William, upon my pressing him, owned that he himself was often so low-spirited that he would give up everything, did not his wife encourage him. I asked him if it was possible he could imagine himself an unfortunate man. He said yes. But how, I asked, could he think so and retain his senses, considering what great promotion he had obtained?[7] He told me that he thought thus: "How much more important would another man make himself if he had such promotion."

We walked to the other side of Blackfriars Bridge after our coffee. We had taken a bottle apiece of Newcastle port, which was so good that I said, "This is not *New*castle port. It is 'my *old* lad of the castle.'"[8] We revised my Johnsonian leaves, and I stayed supper and sat till the venerable St. Paul's had struck one. I walked home, it being quite light. Found little James at home, next day being a whole holiday.

FRIDAY 11 JUNE. Was not at all in good spirits. Intended to have dined at home with Veronica and little James, but an invitation from Malone took me out. Nobody but his brother with us. We revised a little. Little James went back to Westminster.

SATURDAY 12 JUNE. My spirits were very bad. It vexed me that poor Veronica should have a father so unable to be of use to her. She was sensible and cheerful. I dined with her and my son James, whose right it was to come home on Saturday to dinner and stay till Sunday evening. I was quite restless after dinner. I had resolved to go to Sir Joseph Banks's tea in the evening. But could not read, and was at a loss what to do in the mean time. I sauntered in the Strand, quite list-less. At last I called on Sir Joshua Reynolds, found him quite alone with his port before him, drank a few glasses, but was dull and quite languid. Then at Sir Joseph Banks's tea; saw variety of literary men, but had no animation. Talked with Mr. Paradise of my bad spirits. He said he was now much better, and counselled me not to seek for relief

---

[6]Sir John Scott was Solicitor-General; Sir William calls him "honest" in the sense of honourable, to be relied upon to keep his word. He became Lord Chancellor in 1801, far too late to help Boswell, and is now remembered as the notoriously reactionary first Earl of Eldon denounced by Shelley.

[7]In May, Scott had been appointed Master of the Faculties at Doctors' Commons, the combined admiralty and ecclesiastical court on which he served as judge.

[8]Multiple punning: Boswell plays *New*castle off against "old castle" and is probably also teasing Scott for being a native of Newcastle, a port on the River Tyne. The quotation, Prince Hal's phrase for Falstaff (*1 Henry IV*, I. ii. 47–48), aptly describes good port because Falstaff (called Sir John Oldcastle in Shakespeare's first version of the play) likes to drink good wine. But we do not know what is meant by Newcastle port and why it was considered inferior.

from excess of wine, as he had done, but found a moderate use of it much more efficacious.[9] Was glad to come home and get to bed.

SUNDAY 13 JUNE. My heart was sore for my son James, who complained of being very unhappy at Westminster School. Poor little fellow, on the Sunday when I first walked down with him to introduce him, he said to me, "Is it not hard that what should be the most agreeable part of life is made the most unhappy by being at school, and that to learn only the dead languages?" I could not *argue* against this, but insisted on that kind of education having formed the greatest men in this nation. He was much cast down as we walked, but when we got to Prince's Street, he said, "I find myself more composed." Last Sunday, which was the day on which he actually entered to the boarding-house, I was very anxious. I made him kneel with me in the forenoon, and I prayed aloud for him, that as he was now about to enter on a new situation in life, GOD would be pleased to bless him and preserve him from the temptations to which he would be exposed. This day Veronica and he and I went to evening service about four o'clock: prayers and sermon in our parish church of Marylebone. My spirits were sadly depressed. I dined tête-à-tête with Malone and revised forty-six pages of my *Life of Johnson*.

MONDAY 14 JUNE. The Parliament being dissolved,[1] the hurry and agitation hurt my weak nerves. I breakfasted with honest Baldwin, my printer, and concerted that in case I should be called away for some weeks, my compositor, Plymsell, an intelligent and accurate man, should have other employment that he might leave, and resume my book on my return. I went to Dilly's and was so ill that I could scarcely articulate. His kindly expressions consoled me somewhat. I resolved that as I had no chance for success in Ayrshire, not to go to the election but write to my friends that I declined to stand.[2] My servant James found me here, Lord Lonsdale having sent twice for me and having desired that I should be inquired for wherever I might be supposed to be. I was sorry that I had been found, for Colonel Lowther had told me that when he suggested my coming in for Carlisle, the Earl disapproved and said, "He would get drunk and make a foolish speech." This, if fairly reported, was an absolute proof that his Lordship had no con-

[9]John Paradise, a scholar and linguist, had recently signed an agreement with his creditors. He had been in severe financial straits and had had distressing personal problems with his erratic, violent-tempered wife, Lucy Ludwell of Virginia.
[1]On Friday, 11 June, in preparation for the General Election.
[2]The Ayrshire election was set for 19 July. Boswell had known since the preceding August, before the by-election, that he had no chance of succeeding (see above, p. 10).

fidence in me, and indeed his not employing me in Westminster Hall[3] might show this. I could not bear the thoughts of being engaged by him in some of his political jobs.

I came home and found Temple and his daughter returned. I was against going to Lord Lonsdale's and saw him now in such a light that I declared I would not accept of one of his seats in Parliament. However, Temple urged me to go to him, which I did, and found him at dinner though it was but about three o'clock; indeed dinner was almost over, and he had drunk a good deal of wine. He said he had not seen me for a long time. I said that I supposed he would be very busy, and was unwilling to intrude. He told me that the King's Bench had nearly been moved against me because, the mayor being at the same time one of the senior aldermen, there were at present but three Justices of Carlisle, and by his Lordship's own absence and mine the order of poor's rates could not be made, and a complaint was to have been made against the Recorder for not being there.[4] Therefore it was necessary for me to go down directly, and the Recorder must also be present at the election. He talked meanly of this being all I had to do for my £20 salary. This sudden requisition[5] vexed me not a little. I mentioned my worthy old friend having come all the way from Cornwall chiefly to see me, and endeavoured to evade the shock; but I found him determined, and was obliged to engage to go with him to Lancaster in my way[6] next day at twelve. Penn, whom he had set up at Lancaster and said he would spend £50,000 rather than not have a seat there for him,[7] was ready to set out, accompanied by Colonel Lowther. Both of them talked to me, as it were, in half hints, that I must not hang back *now*.

I hastened home and lamented to Temple my unfortunate situation. He was friendly and soothing. I had eat and drunk a little at Lord Lonsdale's. I was heated.[8] I rashly went three times in the course of

---

[3]That is, in legal cases. The law courts sat in Westminster Hall.

[4]By statute two Justices of the Peace were required to determine the poor's rates—the annual assessments for the support of the poor. The Carlisle charter specified that the mayor, two senior aldermen, and the Recorder were *ex officio* J.P.s. Both Boswell, the Recorder, and Lonsdale, a long-time alderman, were in London and hence unavailable. The precise nature of the problem remains unclear, however, because the mayor and the second alderman were presumably able to function in Carlisle.

[5]Demand.

[6]On Boswell's way to Carlisle.

[7]Penn lost in Lancaster but won another Parliamentary seat controlled by Lonsdale a few months later.

[8]Boswell has inked out the following sentence in the manuscript (see Statement of Editorial Practices).

this day to a stranger. I was feverish. My brother T.D. and his wife dined with us. Both Temple and he thought that I should write to Lord Lonsdale resigning the Recordership. I accordingly had a letter sketched. But I went to Malone, who insisted that as I had asked the office, I should go down, resolutely discharge the duty, see whether it was meant to bring me into Parliament or not, and if not, to resign some time afterwards and withdraw from so disagreeable a connection. I came home and on many accounts was in a wretched state.

TUESDAY 15 JUNE. Had rested very ill; hot, feverish, tossing. My dear friend Temple was quite uneasy to see the state in which I was. It hurt me particularly that my dismal hypochondria had returned at the time when he had kindly come to see me after a seven years' separation.[1] I was so troubled in thought that I absolutely groaned. About half past eleven I went to Lord Lonsdale's. He was not stirring. I came home and wrote a letter of earnest expostulation against being obliged to quit London at this moment, declaring at the same time that if really necessary, I would go.

[Boswell to Lonsdale]

Queen Anne Street West, 15 June 1790
MY LORD,—I am persuaded your Lordship would not intentionally distress me, which my quitting town at this moment would do very much on account of circumstances in my private affairs with which it would be improper to trouble your Lordship.

I should at any rate be very unwilling now to go so near my own county as Carlisle because I have resolved to withdraw myself as a candidate upon finding that I should only discover[2] my weakness; and it would, I fear, have an awkward appearance to be almost in the neighbourhood and not go to the election. The real truth is that my views now are such that my want of success is no disappointment to me, but I would avoid any disagreeable circumstance.

If it be really necessary that the Recorder should be present at the election at Carlisle, I shall certainly be there at the time of which I can have due notice, for while I hold that place I shall be faithful to its

---

[1]While Boswell experienced these warm feelings towards his old friend, Temple was becoming increasingly critical of Boswell and dissatisfied with his stay in London: "Never thinks of anyone but himself; indifferent to other people's feelings or whether they are amused; envious...no command of his tongue; restless, no composure....Could not bear the confinement of a town....The noise and roaring of the coaches dreadful both by night and day." (*Diaries of William Johnston Temple*, ed. Lewis Bettany, p. 79).
[2]Expose.

duties. But I earnestly request that your Lordship may not ask me to go down sooner. I have the honour to be with great respect, my Lord, your Lordship's most obedient, humble servant.

I sent this, and said I would call directly. I did so and found him alone and stated to him all my unwillingness. He talked of the importance of preventing complaints, and said that I must go unless I resigned the office of Recorder so that another might be appointed. I jumped inwardly at this, but calmly said, "I rather would resign." Finding this, he began to mutter that reflections would be thrown out,[3] etc., etc., etc. "My Lord," said I, "your Lordship shall have no reflections on my account. I'll go directly, do the business handsomely, and then resign with a good grace." I was happy to think that I had announced my resignation before the subject of my not being brought into Parliament had been in question.

I should have mentioned that I called this forenoon on Sir Michael Le Fleming, who told me that he had pressed on the Earl my being elected for Carlisle, and urged that having a man who was known might even have *some* influence on the minds of a Committee;[4] but that his Lordship had resolved to set up two blackguards.[5] Sir Michael said that in short Lord Lonsdale liked my company much and wished to have me go with him, and being not perfectly decided in his own mind, might wish to have me ready as a stopgap if it should so strike him. I told Sir Michael warmly that this was quite unsuitable to me, that I was as proud as Lucifer, and that I would have no connection with Lord Lonsdale farther than paying my respects to him as an independent gentleman. I dined with some satisfaction with my guests and daughter. After dinner Temple and I sauntered in Wimpole Street, and he advised me to return to the Scotch bar, as he saw no prospect of my getting any *advantage* by being in London. I could not bear the thoughts of sinking so, and said I would try one other winter and attend Westminster Hall and apply to the Lord Chancellor. In short I was quite dislocated.

The Earl had told me that, if he could, he intended to set out at four or five in the morning. Knowing how uncertain he was, and dreading the torment of waiting, I settled with him that he should send and

[3]That he, Lonsdale, would be criticized, presumably for having appointed a Recorder unwilling to attend to his duties.
[4]A Parliamentary committee.
[5]Lonsdale backed two of his faithful followers, Edward Knubley and James Clarke Satterthwaite, as M.P.s for Carlisle.

let me know when he was ready. In the evening Temple and I had a little cold negus as in old times, after our daughters had gone upstairs. I revived somewhat. I went to bed with the stillness of a desperate man, ready to be called at four, at the same time supposing that perhaps the Earl might not go till next evening.

WEDNESDAY 16 JUNE. I stayed at home all day in a strange state of mind, to be ready at a call. My dear friend Temple did all in his power to console me. Malone, upon a message from me, came, and we settled that my *Life of Johnson* should go on at press a certain way[6] during my absence. About eleven at night came a note from Lord Lonsdale summoning me to breakfast with him next morning at half past eight, and then proceed to the north. This was now a distressing knell. I considered that the time was when I should have been elated by such a message. But now all ambitious hopes were gone.

[EDITORIAL NOTE. The journal continues without a break from this point to 16 July, but on separate leaves headed "The diary of my wretched life till my return to London."]

THURSDAY 17 JUNE. Rose in very bad spirits. A little conversation with my dear friend Temple, and parted cordially. At nine, L.'s. No appearance. Waited almost two hours. Went home. All gone out. Returned. He at breakfast. Irritated at my going. Jackson with him.[7] Before whom and Robinson his servant (when I represented how hard it was on me to go), he was in a fury, and said, "You have some sinister motive." "How can your Lordship say so?" "Because I know the man to whom I speak. I suppose you want to have a large fee." "Did your Lordship ever see anything in my conduct to make you think so?" "You asked the Recordership of me. I did not wish you should be Recorder. But you were so earnest, I granted it. And now when duty is required, you would give it up.[8] What have you done for your salary? I will advise the Corporation not to accept your resignation till you have attended the Midsummer Sessions as well as the election. I suppose you

---

[6]To a certain extent.

[7]Richard Jackson was an alderman and former mayor of Carlisle.

[8]Boswell had requested the position with great formality in a letter of 1 December 1787: "The office of Recorder of Carlisle which he has presumed to solicit would put him in a situation for which he most earnestly wishes.... He begs leave to suggest that the appointment of a gentleman of family and fortune would be creditable for that ancient Corporation, and that he would feel it in such a manner as to make him do his duty not only with fidelity but with a warmth of zeal." But as early as on the first trip north with Lonsdale, from 21 December 1787 to 7 January 1788, relations between the two were tense.

think we are fond of your company. You are mistaken. We don't care for it. *I* should have heard of no difficulties. It is your own concern. I suppose you thought I was to bring you into Parliament. I never had any such intention. It would do you harm to be in Parliament." This was a full discovery. I had leave of absence for an hour; went to Malone, and told him. He advised me to go in apparent good humour and get away as soon as I could. It vexed me that I was dragged away from the printing of my *Life of Johnson,* and that perhaps Malone might be gone to Ireland[9] before I could get back to London.

At L.'s again. Time was trifled away till the afternoon, I am not sure what hour. L. took me under the arm, and we walked by Grosvenor Square to Oxford Street, near Hanover Square, to get into his coach. As we walked, the bringing into Parliament was resumed, and he showed his poor opinion of me, saying I would get drunk and make a foolish speech. I talked too freely of my liberal and independent views, and of their inconsistency with being brought in by him unless special terms were granted. He was provoked. In the coach the same subject was unfortunately resumed, and I expressed myself, I do not recollect exactly how, but so as to raise his passion almost to madness, so that he used shocking words to me, saying, "Take it as you will. I am ready to give you satisfaction." "My Lord," said I, "you have said enough." I was in a stunned state of mind, but calm and determined. He went on with insult: "You have kept low company all your life. What are *you,* Sir?" "A gentleman, my Lord, a man of honour; and I hope to show myself such." He brutally said, "You will be settled when you have a bullet in your belly." Jackson sat silent.

When we came to Barnet and entered the inn, I told him he had treated me very ill and very unjustly. He said, "I will give you satisfaction *now.* I have pistols here." "If you please, my Lord; and I will be obliged to you for pistols." "What, Sir, against myself? Certainly not." I went out and inquired if there was any regiment quartered there, thinking that I might get one of the officers to lend me pistols and be my second. There was none. I returned to him and said I would go back to London and find a friend, and let his Lordship know when we could meet. We had a cold dinner, during which he said it would seem strange to me when the friend I should bring would say that his words to me were warranted; that I was the aggressor, and ought to ask pardon; that I had attacked his honour. Looking on him really as a madman, and wishing upon principle never to have a duel if I could avoid

---

[9]Malone was completing his great edition of Shakespeare, begun in 1783, and planned to go to his family home in Ireland as soon as his work was done.

it with credit, I protested that I had no such intention as he supposed; and then in order to give him an opportunity to have the matter adjusted, I asked his pardon for using expressions which his Lordship had imagined attacked his honour, but which I solemnly declared were not so meant by me. He then said he would not have used such words to me if he had not thought that my expressions were meant as he had supposed. Then we drank a glass of wine.

Captain Payne joined us and sat some time. After he was gone, and I was walking before the door of the inn, L. sent for me, and when I came, held out his hand and gave it me, saying, "Boswell, forget all that is past." Jackson said to me that the affair had been very well settled, and not a syllable about it should ever transpire. He said L. was interested in not mentioning it. After this we travelled on socially enough, but I was inwardly mortified to think that I had deceived myself so woefully as to my hopes from the GREAT LOWTHER, and that I was now obliged to submit to what was very disagreeable to me without any reward or hope of any good, but merely to get out of the scrape into which I had brought myself. We travelled all night, and on *Friday*[1] lay at Doncaster.

SATURDAY 19 JUNE. With a very uneasy mind I was wheeled on to Lancaster, where I left L. at Mr. Watson's, one of his friends, and went to the New Inn, where I found Captain Satterthwaite entertaining some of L.'s political people.[2] Went early to bed.

SUNDAY 20 JUNE. Breakfasted at Mr. J. Satterthwaite's after having seen Colonel Lowther and Mr. Penn, to the latter of whom I mentioned my intention to *be off* from L., but with caution. When I waited on L., he gave me his hand, but took notice that I was not merry. I repeated how hard it was upon me to be obliged to be absent so long from London. But he seemed to be quite callous. Jackson and I went to Carlisle in the mail-coach and arrived at midnight. I hated to think of all my idle bustle here.

MONDAY 21 JUNE. Mr. McDowall of Garthland and his brother from India visited me.[3] Waited on the mayor.[3a] Had the poor's-rates orders all signed. Dined with him. Was quite weary. Drank coffee at

---

[1]The italicized *Friday* serves as a substitute for an entry for Friday 18 June.

[2]James Clarke Satterthwaite, captain in the 30th Regiment of Foot, was until now the Lonsdale-controlled M.P. for Cockermouth.

[3]After defeating Boswell and two other contestants in the 1789 by-election, McDowall had served only a few months as M.P. for Ayrshire and had just won a safer seat in the General Election. His brother, Hay McDowall, was a major in a regiment that had been stationed in the East Indies.

[3a]This year's mayor was Jeremiah Wherlings, the postmaster.

Alkin's.[4] Had a most discouraging letter from Temple that he understood I could not succeed in the law either in England or Scotland,
and advising a retreat to Auchinleck.[5] My ambition and projects and
all the animation with which my mind used to be kept afloat were
checked. But I had still hopes that something fortunate would start
up. I had a very sensible letter from Veronica, which consoled me. I
supped alone at my inn. I was not at all well either in body or mind.
Either this or next day I wrote to Veronica[6] and to Mr. Alexander of
Ballamyle about a toll on my church road.

[EDITORIAL NOTE. On 21 June Boswell also poured out his heart to
Temple in a long letter, beginning with the outburst, "My dear Temple,—At no period during our long friendship have I been more unhappy than at present." After reviewing the events of the preceding
days in great detail, Boswell concluded: "O my old and most intimate
friend, what a shocking state am I now reduced to. I entreat of you, if
you possibly can, to afford me some consolation directed to me here,
and pray do not divulge my mortification. I will endeavour to appear
indifferent, and as I now resign my Recordership, I shall gradually get
rid of all communication with this brutal fellow. How much does it distress me to think that I should have had a return of dire hypochondria
at the very time when you and your amiable daughter were with us,
and then that I should have been compelled to leave you. As to making provision for your amusement from my friends, alas! the selfish-
ness of London is too great. I look up to GOD for relief to my mind,
and I have this *real consolation* that we have met after a long absence
the same friends as when we parted. My kindest compliments to Miss
Temple. Ever most affectionately yours, James Boswell."]

TUESDAY 22 JUNE. I lay till twelve, merely to get time over. Sir
James Johnstone and I drank our coffee together. I read a little in
Terence. I had many wavering schemes: to go into the mayor's house;

---

[4]Alkin's Coffee-house in Castle Street, Carlisle.
[5]Temple wrote: "I much fear you will not succeed in the law either here or at
Edinburgh. Auchinleck should be your haven, port, and resting-place, with occasional
visits to this busy, bustling, trifling scene." In addition, Temple complained about his
own stay in London: "I have nothing to do and hardly know how to amuse myself. My
few friends are gone, and you have made no provision for my entertainment by means
of yours" (19 June 1790).
[6]Boswell has crossed out the rest of this sentence, having later fixed the date of the
letter to Claud Alexander as 24 June. "Ballamyle" was Alexander's euphemistic change
from the original place-name "Ballochmyle," which Boswell mocked in his verse
the Attempt to Change the Good Old Name of Ballochmyle to Ballamyle."

to go to Newcastle and be under Mr. Leighton's care; to go to Mr. Senhouse's; to go to Springkell.[7] My having no servant with me and being in bad health made it awkward for me to go to any gentleman's house. The mayor and I took a short saunter. Walking was painful to me. He dined with me at my inn. I had drunk very little wine since I left London, so that I was low; but that was better than being heated. I drank tea with the Rev. Mr. Carlyle in his study, and had really a glimpse of satisfaction. He was translating an Arabian history,[8] and his books and literary conversation relieved me somewhat. I came again to my inn, dejected and insignificant, and having lain till twelve, went to bed again at eight. I shrunk from the thought of having to waste time here for about three weeks. I recollected my valuable wife with most affectionate regret, and felt how helpless I was when deprived of her. I endeavoured to cherish the hope of meeting her in a better world. I thought how unlike I now was to the father of five children: a son at Eton, a son at Westminster, etc., etc.

WEDNESDAY 23 JUNE. Captain Knubley had come the night before. He came to me; said, "L. had a most tyrannical temper and not a spark of gratitude." Yet he was going to Lancaster to him upon a message.[9] I wavered miserably. At last I thought I would go to Longtown[1] and be nursed, and write to Sir William Maxwell to come to me. So I set out with a Paisley manufacturer and a London rider,[2] the latter of whom I envied for his smartness and self-complacency. Neither Mr. nor Mrs. Black were at home at Longtown,[3] so I resolved to proceed to Ecclefechan, and from thence to Springkell in a post-chaise. There I learnt that Sir William Maxwell and his family were gone to the west country.[4] I resolved to wait for the mail-coach in the morning at three. I had tea and oatcakes and honey, and *felt* being in Scotland,

[7]John Leighton was a Newcastle surgeon who cared for Boswell's brother John; James Senhouse, a Carlisle surgeon; Springkell, the home of Boswell's distant cousin Sir William Maxwell in Dumfriesshire, a few miles north-west of the Scottish border.

[8]A distinguished orientalist, the Rev. Joseph Dacre Carlyle was translating the work of Abū al-Mahāsin Yūsuf Ibn Taghrībirdī, a fifteenth-century Arab; it was published in 1792 with the title *Rerum Aegyptiacarum annales*.

[9]Thanks to Lonsdale, Knubley had been Sheriff of Cumberland in 1785–86. He had also won the November 1786 election as Lonsdale's candidate, only to be unseated by a Parliamentary Committee three months later. On first acquaintance, Boswell had found him a "pleasant young man but rustic" (Journal, 25 Nov. 1786).

[1]A town in Scotland nine miles north-west of Carlisle.

[2]A manufacturer from Paisley, Renfrewshire, and a commercial traveller (American: travelling salesman).

[3]Black was the postmaster of Longtown.

[4]The west of Scotland.

but Oh! how inferior. Without my expecting it, came the Edinburgh and Carlisle diligence. I took a seat in it to Longtown. I shrunk from the solitude there, and resolved to go on to Carlisle and resume my own room at the Bush, which was comparatively a kind of comfort. A coarse north-of-Scotland man, who had been ten years in London without acquiring a single English accent, was with me in the diligence and disgusted me. When I arrived at the Bush, the house was crowded and my room taken up, and I was obliged to take a bed in the room with Knubley. I was quite feeble and dejected. I had spent about a pound on an idle excursion. I did not taste fermented liquor today.

THURSDAY 24 JUNE. Had slept unsound, dreaming a great deal, in particular that Veronica approached me suddenly, saying, "Now my mother's disease is come at last—a consumption"; and she looked ill, and when I took her hand, there was a clammy sweat upon it. I awaked much affected. I began to think, to recollect my worthy, rational, steady father. What was I doing here at Carlisle? In what a scattered state was the Family of Auchinleck? I was very sad. Scarcely had I any hope. I had yesterday received a letter from my brother David communicating from Lady Auchinleck Euphemia's uneasiness at staying longer at the Edinburgh boarding-school. I resolved to relieve her. I rose a little after eight. Walked out at the Scotch Gate weary and uneasy. Came to Jollie's shop. Tried various books; could fix to none except the "Life" of Dr. Leechman by Wodrow; not well done, and the group of Glasgow College ideas made me dreary as in my youth.[5] Called on Hodgson, surgeon-apothecary, once my landlord at the assizes. Breakfasted with him, his wife, and a widow who boarded with them. Felt myself a man troubled in mind. Wished to lodge at his house. But it was now full. Went to the mayor's and settled to have a room at his house at night. Felt an alarm as to my local complaint, as if inflammatory and tending to mortification.[6] Wrote letters to Lady Auchinleck, Euphemia, Mr. Robert Boswell, and Mr. Alexander of Ballamyle. Said to Lady Auchinleck that I was unhappy here, but it was but a variation of uneasiness; that I could be of no service to my daughters, but I feared the contrary; prayed GOD to bless my children and make them happier than their father. I was much relieved by writing with great kindness

[5]James Wodrow's biography of William Leechman was prefixed to the latter's recently published *Sermons*. While Boswell was at the University of Glasgow in the winter of 1759–60, Leechman was a popular Professor of Divinity (he became Principal of the University in 1761); his biography reminded Boswell of his dull and lonely life in Glasgow, where his father had sent him to remove him from the temptations of Edinburgh.

[6]Putrefaction. Boswell's complaint seems to have been a local genital abscess.

to Euphemia. I dined at the Bush on a roast chicken and drank about a pint of port, and felt a certain degree of animation and some glimmering of hope that I might still have some enjoyment in life. I read some in Terence with satisfaction. I went to the coffee-house and drunk coffee and read newspapers for a long time. Then went to the mayor's, Mr. Wherlings the postmaster's, where I had settled that I would lodge. I sat an hour or two very dully with him and his daughter, and then took possession of a good room, well furnished.

FRIDAY 25 JUNE. Had enjoyed a good night's rest and dreamed none. When I rose, was alarmed with the pain of my local complaint, which I had mentioned to Knubley yesterday, and this morning mentioned to my barber,[7] that I might inquire who were the best surgeons here. Resolved however to wait some time before calling one, as I hoped to cure myself. It was a rainy day. I did not stir out, but finished reading the *Andria* of Terence, and read Mountfort's comedy of *Greenwich Park*. Wondered at its gross licentiousness being allowed on the stage.[8] Was weakly dejected and could hardly think it possible that I could ever be able to do any good. Was as low as I had ever been in the country. But felt that the mind will acquiesce wonderfully in any situation. Resolved that I never again would allow my spirits to exult. Yet had an unwillingness to think that I should have no more enjoyment in life. Notwithstanding the reconciliation and shaking hands with L., had a certain uneasiness as if I had not been spirited enough with him, and felt a strange regret that I had not had the *éclat* of being in the field against the GREAT LOWTHER. But the *serious* apprehension that I might have been cut off by *violence* from my young family, and my *magnum opus*, the *Life of Johnson*, left unfinished, weighed on the other side. I breakfasted, dined, and drank tea with my landlord and his daughter, both good-humoured and obliging. Took only two glasses of wine. I eagerly counted the hours.

SATURDAY 26 JUNE. Had not rested very well. Had dreamed disagreeable Edinburgh dreams. It was still rainy weather. I read a great part of Waller's poems, which I had never read before but very imperfectly. Did not think so very highly of them as I supposed I should. But this was probably owing to my unhappy state of mind. I read a part of Terence's *Eunuchus*. It had strangely happened that I had never

---

[7]The rest of this sentence has been scored out in the manuscript.
[8]William Mountfort's 1691 play featured seduction scenes, breeches parts for the two main actresses, and dialogue with coarse language and sexual innuendo. It was last performed in 1741.

read more than one, or at most two, of his plays. I resolved to read them all. I borrowed a Delphin edition[1] from a bookseller's and made a study of Terence, whose mode of writing I found difficult to me. I read some in old volumes of magazines, which gave me dull and dreary impressions of the nothingness of human affairs. I weathered out the day stupidly and uneasily. No company but the mayor and his daughter. Drank two glasses of wine.[2] My complaint was no better. The precept[3] for election came today. It was a *degree* of consolation that it *must* begin in eight days. I wrote to Mr. Earle for advice, and I wrote a very earnest letter to Governor Penn, stating my wretchedness and entreating that if he could prudently venture it, he would intercede with the Earl to let me go, as everything might now be done without me. I was sensible that I *deserved* that part of my unhappiness[4] occasioned by my complaint, for *what* can be more culpable at my time of life, and in my situation as the head of a family, than the wild conduct of a licentious youth? I was now incapacitated from taking the relief which exercise and society might perhaps have afforded. I had a poor, selfish comfort in a good bed. I was a despicable being.

[Boswell to Penn]

Carlisle, 26 June 1790

MY DEAR SIR,—I cannot express to you how very miserable I am. In the first place, some time before I left London I was afflicted with a return of the bad spirits to which I am subject, which have continued in a sad degree and been much increased by the mortifying discovery made to me by Lord Lonsdale—not that his Lordship was not to bring me into Parliament, for you and everyone who ever mentioned that subject to me can attest that I declared I did not expect it—but that he had formed such an opinion of my character as I am conscious I do not deserve, so that an ambitious hope which I had cherished of being connected with and patronized by one of the greatest men in this country is utterly blasted....

I have not stirred out for two days. To confess the truth, I am ill, painfully ill, as I deserve to be, and dare not, nor will not trust to any practitioner here. I am therefore following the method of Mr. Earle but, as you may imagine, am very anxious to be with him. When you

[1]One of a series of annotated editions published in Paris during the reign of Louis XIV, ostensibly for the Dauphin.
[2]The following sentence has been scored out in the manuscript.
[3]The order authorizing the election.
[4]The next four words have been scored out in the manuscript.

consider the complication of evils to which I am now subjected without having a soul with whom I can communicate, I am sure you will feel for me. Let Lord Lonsdale think of me as he pleases, there is not a man alive who would with more zeal have laboured to assist in establishing his real consequence, or one who is more gratefully sensible of any favour done to him. All *that* is now out of the question. But surely his Lordship would not wish to afflict one who never intentionally offended him. For GOD's sake, then, my dear Sir, if you can possibly do it without my incurring his Lordship's displeasure, be so good as to represent to him my unhappy state more or less as you may think prudent, and asking his pardon for my weakness, entreat of him to let me have his permission to leave Carlisle....

I have applied to you in my distress, conscious that were you to apply to me in a like situation, I should be earnest to assist you. I depend on your not mentioning a word of what I write except to the Earl himself if you think you may venture, and that you will burn this unhappy scrawl when you have read it. At any rate, I trust that you will by Monday's post let me have the consolation of hearing from you. I am, dear Sir, yours most sincerely.

P.S. You cannot imagine how it vexes me to be forced to write thus. But I suffer severely. Pray forgive me.

SUNDAY 27 JUNE. Awaked miserably relaxed.[5] It was a wet day. Went to St. Cuthbert's Church and heard Rev. Mr. Carlyle preach very well, but was devoured by hypochondria. Had a long rational letter from Veronica. Saw how bad a father I was. Had a letter from Sir John Scott, in a friendly manner recommending a quiet resignation and not to contend with L. Dined as dully as I had ever done at Glasgow or anywhere. Went to the Cathedral at four. All was dull and dead within me. I was convinced that true religion is the gift of GOD's grace. A weary evening. Read today some more of Waller, part of Miln the dissenting teacher's lectures on the Creation, the Deluge, etc., of which he could tell nothing.[6] Was sick of his speculations. Read some of the *Spectator* and had a faint relish of it. But I was quite depressed. Of what avail were all the happy days I had ever enjoyed with *the Gang*,[7] etc.? Was it *possible*, I thought, that I could ever again enjoy such? Dr. Warren some

[5]In the sense of enfeebled.
[6]The scope of Robert Miln's work is suggested by its title: *A Course of Physico-Theological Lectures upon the State of the World from the Creation to the Deluge* (1786).
[7]That is, Reynolds, Malone, Courtenay, and Boswell.

months ago told me that a change of spirits would come, and cautioned me against imagining that I never could be well again. But alas! as I then told him, that very thought is the worst part of the disease. I could not conceive at present how mankind in any situation could for a moment be deluded into a feeling of happiness, or even of quiet. I was *sure* that if I were at *Edinburgh* all the despicable dejection of my early years would return. I dreaded that in a moment of desperation I might go thither. But I trusted that I should have as much firmness as to keep myself between London and Auchinleck.

MONDAY 28 JUNE. Awaked much in yesterday's state. Authority from L. to proclaim the election to begin on Saturday was a small relief, as it in some degree limited my sufferings. Had an answer from Euphemia, very happy. A large packet as to the debt due to me from the Cuninghames came from Mr. Robert Boswell.[8] When "the grasshopper is a burthen"[9] a large packet is grievous. I could scarcely attend to it, and I was so dim that I understood £10[1] per cent on £500 to be only £10 a year, and wrote so to him. My landlord's daughter, being used to computation in the post office, set me right in the evening. I wrote also to Mr. W. Brown at Kilmarnock, a debt of whose I had unwarily allowed to be conveyed in trust to me; and though James Cuninghame wrote to me that my settling my debt independent of Brown's could not hurt Brown, I was in such delicate doubt that I delayed signing the agreement till I should hear from Brown.[2] I finished the reading of Waller, also *Eunuchus,* and began *Heautontimorumenos.*[3]

I had been three whole days with only the mayor and his daughter. I went this afternoon to the coffee-house and had coffee and newspapers and a little trifling conversation with one or two people. Whiled away about three hours very insipidly. The Scotch papers affected me strangely with disgusting sensations. The Rev. Dr. Grisdale[4] sat a little while with us in the evening at the mayor's. What a life do I now lead! Mrs. Johnston, a poor old woman past sixty, niece of Lord Kames by a sister who made a low marriage, visited me tonight. I had obtained

[8]Robert Boswell, Boswell's first cousin, was taking care of Boswell's financial affairs in Edinburgh.
[9]Ecclesiastes 12: 5.
[1]Boswell accidentally inserted an extra £ sign here.
[2]Boswell's loan to the Cuninghames was linked to a loan of £134 which William Brown had made to Mrs. Boswell's deceased nephew Alexander Cuninghame and which Brown had assigned to Boswell in 1780. Boswell now wanted to be sure that he could be repaid without damaging Brown's claim.
[3]*The Self-Tormentor,* another comedy by Terence.
[4]Brown Grisdale, D.D., schoolmaster at Carlisle.

for her £5 a year from her cousin, Mr. Drummond of Blair, on which, and the profits of a school (2/- a quarter each scholar, by which she might earn £8), she supported herself decently.[5] She told me that when she had her health she was quite happy, but that sometimes she was ill and had to hire a woman to take care of her. I was struck with this account. I wished that I could procure some addition to her.

TUESDAY 29 JUNE. After a disturbed night, rose sad. Received a letter from Penn that they were to be at Carlisle the end of the week, and advising me to stay. I could perceive that he was afraid to interfere. It was however some consolation that I was to see him soon. I sauntered a little after breakfast and then read some more of *Heautontimorumenos*. I could eat very little. Yet meals were a kind of amusement. I had coffee to breakfast. We dined at half past two, drank tea about six, and at night I had a basin of boiled milk with biscuit or toast. I could with difficulty walk. The mayor had more discernment than I supposed. He mentioned to me confidentially how Lord L. gradually modelled the Corporation so that it is now absolutely and entirely at his command, and all the expense occasioned by his political operations is paid out of their funds. I was vexed that I had ever had any concern with it or him. So silly[6] was I that it was a kind of relief to go after dinner to old Potts's shop and buy raisins, and eat some and give some to children. I went to bed a little after ten.

WEDNESDAY 30 JUNE. With difficulty could I get up at nine.[7] I had suffered great pain in the night from my complaint, and been sadly apprehensive of its growing very bad. I experienced a very singular thing: the recollection of one dream in the course of a following one. I had first dreamed that I was accompanying my dear M.M. through a wood. I had then another dream which I do not remember; but in the midst of it I was thus struck: "Stay, I am forgetting a former dream" (for I was conscious that I was then dreaming), and by degrees I recalled it. During these wretched nights I have had variety of dreams; one of last night was that I visited Mr. Langton at Oxford, and saw his numerous family.[8]

---

[5]On the death of Henry Home, Lord Kames, Boswell had persuaded George Home Drummond of Blair-Drummond, Kames's son, to continue the modest annual allowance granted Mrs. Johnston by his father. At the two-shilling rate, she was earning £8 per annum, not per quarter, from her pupils.

[6]Feeble or sickly.

[7]The following sentence has been scored out in the manuscript.

[8]Bennet Langton, an original member of The Club and a close friend of both Johnson's and Boswell's, was the fond father of ten children. Boswell had been corresponding with him since March, drawing on his extensive knowledge of Johnson.

I wrote after breakfast a long letter to Mr. Bruce Campbell as to the embarrassed state of my finances, trying if he could suggest how I could go on; that I doubted if I could live cheaper at Auchinleck, and that I could not support a country life; desiring in confidence to have from him information and advice as to the Ayrshire election, for if the coalition for Sir A. F. was stronger than the interest of the other three candidates united, why make a struggle?[9] And as for myself, why stand alone merely to show how few supported me? It might appear spirited in England, but would do me no service in Scotland. Better address the real freeholders and mention that so many were engaged on the side of supposed power (before the nominal and fictitious votes were declared bad) that I found it in vain to stand now, but there being a fair field opened, would hope for success on a future occasion.[1] I wrote to Colonel Montgomerie at his desire (mentioned to me by Veronica, who wrote me the substance of letters which came to me), authorizing him to prosecute two men who had robbed my hawk's nest, which I had given to him.

I dined with the mayor and some more members of the Corporation at the Bush, to talk over some of the business of the city. I felt a short relief in change and being at an inn; but it soon went off, and the vulgarity of the company was worse than my daily dullness. I drank five or six glasses of wine. Was feeble. Went to bed early. Had in the forenoon made some extracts from Waller. Wrote to Malone a long complaining letter, anxious lest he should be gone, or his Shakspeare[2] ready before my return.

[Boswell to Malone]

Carlisle, 30 June 1790
MY DEAR MALONE,—I do not think it is in the power of words to convey to you how miserable I have been since I left you....You have had distress of mind. But your active spirit never failed within you. I have heard you say that you never sat listless by the fire. I have during these wretched days sat so, hours and hours. Everything that ever vexed me has returned. I feel myself a poor, forlorn being, with no permanent

---

[9]Sir Adam Fergusson had the support of Lord Eglinton; the three opponents were Sir Andrew Cathcart, Sir John Whitefoord, and Boswell himself.
[1]The *Scots Magazine* reported that in March of this year Ayrshire had 86 bona fide freeholders and 119 nominal ones. Boswell was basing his hope for future success on the House of Lords' recent decision to bar the nominal and fictitious votes.
[2]Boswell deliberately uses the spelling of the name adopted by Malone, who believed that this reflected the pronunciation of Shakespeare's own time.

vigour of mind, no friend that can enable me to advance myself in life. A fortune sadly encumbered—children whom I can with difficulty support and of whom I am at a loss how to dispose with advantage and propriety—such is the general prospect. And *for immediate* feelings, added to *ennui* and self-upbraiding, I am again unfortunate enough to have *one* sore of a certain nature contracted, I think, Monday forthnight,[3] which *alone* gives me more pain and alarm than *several* which I had lately....

How shocking is it to think that I was dragged away from my friend Temple, who came from Cornwall almost on purpose to see me and saw me so little—and was forced to interrupt my *Life of Dr. Johnson*, the most important, perhaps *now* the only concern of any consequence that I ever shall have in this world. And what galls me and irritates me with impatience is the thought that I lose those hours which you could now have given me for revising my manuscript and that perhaps you may be gone before I get back to town. Even the fear of not being in London when at last your Shakspeare comes out is shocking. My dear friend! for God's sake if you possibly can, let me have some consolation. The melancholy to which I am subject I know cannot be helped. But I beseech you try to alleviate such of my sufferings as can admit of soothing.

THURSDAY 1 JULY. Awaked ill and so miserable that stupefaction seemed desirable; lay dozing till near one. Was the worse for this. Rose with a headache. Had another sensible letter from Veronica; also one in course[4] from Mr. Earle with advice which somewhat soothed me. Had no breakfast. Eat very little dinner. Sauntered a little while. Went by chance into the shop of Mr. Blamire, surgeon, to get medicines ordered by Mr. Earle; found him an intelligent, clever man, which pleased me; but did not consult him. Dr. Heysham, physician, who sat some time at the mayor's in the evening with his worship and me, told me that Blamire had been surgeon to a military hospital in Germany during the war, and had taken his degree at Leiden;[5] so I found I might, if very uneasy, apply to him. Dr. Grisdale also sat awhile with us. I had lounged and had coffee at Alkin's, where as usual I had a little conversation with a Captain Stordy. I read a little more of *Heautontimorumenos* and compared some of it with Dacier's translation,[6] lent

---

[3] An older form of fortnight.
[4] In turn; that is, in answer to Boswell's request for advice on 26 June.
[5] Thomas Blamire had presumably taken part in the War of the Bavarian Succession (1778–79). The University of Leiden had long been renowned as a medical school.
[6] Anne Dacier's French translation, published in 1688.

me by Dr. Grisdale. Kept up tonight till between eleven and twelve; heard that Lancaster election was over, and that Lord Lonsdale would perhaps come tonight; he certainly would come next day. Shrunk from the thought of noise and exertion. Hoped that by quiet solicitation I might obtain a speedy release.

FRIDAY 2 JULY. Much as yesterday. Wrote a long letter to Sir W. Forbes.

[EDITORIAL NOTE. In this letter, after dwelling on his "state of mortification," Boswell expressed his anxieties about his future: "What, then, is now to be done? I have no chance in Ayrshire. I have not money to purchase a seat.[7] I see no prospect of success at the English bar. I could not bear to stand again at the Scotch bar. A country life would be insupportable. I have still a friend or two in the south by whose influence I may obtain some promotion, and of them I must earnestly endeavour to avail myself. The consciousness of having a mind subject to the saddest fits of melancholy is a deplorable circumstance. Yet even with that I am ready to go either to the East or West Indies." He then complained: "It was particularly hard upon me to be taken from the printing of my *Life of Dr. Johnson,* of which 300 quarto pages are done, making about a third of the whole, and the press must stop till I return. But what vexes me more is that I lose all this time the hours which Mr. Malone could have given me for the revisal of my manuscript, more than 350 pages of which are yet unconsidered by his acute and elegant mind....I heartily wish the book were fairly *in boards,*[8] for in my desponding hours, I am apt to imagine with a *blue* apprehension that I shall die before it is concluded." The journal for 2 July now resumes.]

Had an answer from Mr. Brown at Kilmarnock that I might settle without him, and one from Mr. Robert Boswell setting me right.[9] I wrote to him and sent the agreement signed. In answer to a sentence in his, "To Auchinleck you must at last come," I answered, "So I must, alive or dead; but if I come alive, I will bring some addition to what I now have." A number of vexing thoughts crowded upon me. I recalled all the ambitious flutterings which I had experienced from my youth, notwithstanding miserable occasional depressions of spirit. I figured myself retired to the country without having attained any one object of advancement—and brooding over that consideration, fancying myself

[7]In Parliament.
[8]Bound.
[9]That he would be paid £50 per annum (ten per cent of £500) by the Cuninghames, and not £10 as he had initially thought on 28 June.

despised by others, and undoubtedly being so in my own eyes. In that frame, how could I bear to drag on a life of vexation, and while inwardly gnawed by mortification, how could I entertain company and make any creditable appearance? No, I should never do this. Rather let me hide myself in London, or go to some distant corner of the globe. It made me sick when I imagined myself returned to Edinburgh no better than when I left it, after the enjoyment of London society. I however brought myself to think that I might do very well if I had a seat on the bench, maintained a creditable character as a retired judge, and passed part of the year in London, part at Auchinleck. But how could I obtain this? It was wildness to think that Dundas would *really* act with liberality towards me, and my expectations by a resolute application to the Chancellor, or by soliciting Sir William and Sir John Scott, could not be considered as solid.[1]

Yesterday and today I wrote a long letter to Veronica. I had received a letter from Colonel Wemyss reminding me of my declaration in his favour at the next Fife election, which I saw from the newspapers was to be on the *22 July*.[2] I was timidly anxious lest he should charge me with behaving unhandsomely if I did not go to it. I wrote to him today that it would be almost impossible, and at any rate distressingly inconvenient, for me to attend, regretting my embarrassment, and begging that he would set my mind at rest as to any imagination of his not having a considerable majority. I speculated on contrivances to disentangle myself from such a vexatious circumstance should he request me to come, but hoped he would not. However, it was plain I could not but be uneasy till I heard from him. My own frank declaration for him brought me into this scrape. I shall on every other occasion leave myself explicitly at liberty not to attend an election if very inconvenient.

In the evening I had a message from Colonel Lowther that he was come to the Bush and wished to see me. I went and met him and Satterthwaite and Knubley and Denton and Counsellors Hubbersty and Ainslie. I was feeble and low, and their spirits surprised me as a kind of novelty. I could not however resist some effect from them. I perceived human nature to be a strange, fluctuating, inexplicable thing. I came early home in quiet.

---

[1] Boswell frequently thought about becoming a judge of the Court of Session, as his father had been before him. At times he hoped for but more often he dreaded such an appointment. In any case, he had already been warned by Thurlow four years earlier that the appointments to this court were controlled by Dundas.

[2] Because his father had acquired voting rights in Fife through his land-holdings there, Boswell was eligible to vote in this election.

SATURDAY 3 JULY. Lord Lonsdale had come late last night to the Bush. A message came for me this morning. I went and was received politely and breakfasted with his Lordship, who talked to me, seemingly confidentially, as to the mode of conducting the election, and I really thought was desirous to make up to me. I went up to Penn in his bedchamber, and being told by him that he had shown my melancholy letter to the Earl, was amazed that it had not made his Lordship relent and allow me to go. He is certainly the most *cruel* man upon earth. It was a little provoking to be told by his Lordship that my looks were improved, and that I would be the better for having been quiet here. I went into the Town Hall with the mayor, and felt a dead indifference as to the election, now that all prospect of ambition by means of Lord L. was cut off. The preliminary forms were gone through, the candidates on each side proposed, and a poll demanded. It was proposed by Satterthwaite and acceded to that both sides should meet and adjust regulations for ease and expedition, and Curwen[3] having civilly suggested that it should be where I lodged, they came to the mayor's, and I assisted to contrive it so that there should be such terms as that the poll, I thought, could not last many days. I dined at the Bush with Lord Lonsdale, a large mixed company. I drank six or seven glasses of wine, to appear not out of humour very much, and was fatigued by huzzaing. Stole away to Alkin's and had coffee and heard the opposite party very violent. I was calm and steady. But was secretly struck when I heard a Scotchman, a Mr. Elliot, agent to the Duke of Norfolk, who had remembered my father so respectable on the bench, regretting that I should appear in the train of a tyrant.[4]

SUNDAY 4 JULY. Awaked rather easier; walked out in fine air. Went to my barber's[5] and performed a medical operation on my sore, which visibly did good. Lord L. had gone home for this day. Was at St. Cuthbert's Church forenoon, and had better feelings than last Sunday. I had all this dreary time regretted that I was not able to pay a visit to the hospitable Mr. Richardson at Rickerby, whose pretty Place is a short walk along the river-side.[6] I took resolution and went today. Nobody

[3]John Christian Curwen, one of the two anti-Lonsdale candidates, had been Boswell's companion during his 1778 visit to Carlisle. Fletcher Christian, the *Bounty* mutineer, was his first cousin.

[4]Charles Howard, eleventh Duke of Norfolk, a long-standing rival of Lonsdale's, was supporting his opponents. Boswell had liked him greatly when they had met at Carlisle in 1778.

[5]The rest of this sentence has been scored out in the manuscript.

[6]William Richardson had built his villa about one mile north-east of Carlisle.

with him but the two Miss Simpsons, daughters of an old and intimate friend of his, whose circumstances, from benevolence to others, got into such disorder that he was obliged to retire to France. A good family dinner well served, consisting of excellent things, with a choice dessert, was a reviving novelty to me. I told him that I could only drink a few glasses of port. But he insinuated his light French white wine, champagne, and claret, over and above, and I could not resist sharing of all in moderation, but so as to raise my spirits. I communicated to him my resigning the Recordership, and why. He thought me quite right; wondered at the conduct of L., but prudently advised me to say as little as might be; that I would be courted by the other party. But if I behaved generously, it was not impossible but L.'s mind might be impressed so as to act in a liberal manner. He thought my having made a trial was natural and had probability in its favour. *Now* I was to be independent. How striking was it to find such sentiments in a man who had risen from nothing to a great fortune, as a dry-salter[7] in London. I respected him. After tea and coffee I returned to Carlisle. Sat awhile with Penn, etc., at the Bush. Went home, and early to bed.

MONDAY 5 JULY. What a wretched register is this! "A lazar-house it seemed."[8] It is the journal of a diseased mind. I had passed a very uneasy night. The good cheer at Rickerby had been too much for my relaxed[9] organs. I awaked in great concern about my son James, who I feared might be ruined at Westminster School. I called out piteously, "O my poor son!" During all this time the loss of my valuable wife, who from my earliest consciousness had been my agreeable and confidential cousin and my cheerful comforter in all difficulties, was perpetually recurring upon my wounded spirit. I had eager vain stretchings of mind towards her. Alas, I could do nothing but lament. I thought that an earnest kind attention to her children would be the best exercise of my affection for her.

I waited on L.; found him in violent anger that it had been agreed that if the long oaths were demanded, they should be put to five freemen at a time.[1] In vain did I state that the mayor by my advice insisted to know what was agreeable to both sides, and fixed this accordingly. I now saw a specimen of Satterthwaite, who had told me before that he

---

[7] A dealer in a variety of products, including drugs, dyes, gums, oils, pickles, and chemicals used in paint.
[8] Adam's vision of the fallen world in *Paradise Lost* (xi. 479).
[9] Weakened.
[1] The taking of oaths was part of the tedious process of admitting voters to the poll. Freeholders could be required to swear to the nature and value of their estates as well as to take general oaths of allegiance.

had not mentioned the five at a time to L., that it might not be opposed, and the poll might be hastened. He now said that he had left it
to the mayor.[2] I insisted that the other party having proposed the five
at a time, it was twice put to him if he had any objection, and he said
he had none. It was then fixed. L. had a furious look, and referring to
me, said, "A friend may do more hurt than an enemy. He wants to get
to London, and does not care a farthing how the election goes." He
and I talked a little while by ourselves. He was base enough to try to
have the agreement of both parties, confirmed by the mayor, rendered
ineffectual. He said to me, "You are in very bad humour. But let us
part handsomely"—as if I could handsomely break a fair stipulation.
He had said in his vile passion, "You shall have a fifteen-days' poll."[3] I
knew that was in his power. I told him calmly that I was now not impatient, that I had arranged my affairs; that I begged his Lordship
would do me justice; and I expressed a desire that we should not part—
which I am sorry I did, but my conduct shall demonstrate to his penetration my opinion of him. I left him and was vexed to find that even
Hubbersty, the counsel who was present at the agreement, was not *firm*
as to the fact. Satterthwaite, when again with me alone, said, "It *was* an
agreement, and I will sooner lose my right hand than go back from it."
When fairly in court, Satterthwaite and Curwen settled that this day
each party should poll only fifty; so time was given to bring L. to reason. The crowd and noise and heat were very offensive to me. But
time was allowed between the tallies, when I went out and had broth,
and a walk on the walls and without the English Gate in the sun, so as
to feel a certain degree of soothing.

I had today a letter from Mr. Bruce Campbell deciding me as to
declining any appearance in Ayrshire at this time, but no clear light as
to finances. Something, however.[4] One from Aird of Crossflat,[5] as a
cunning, interested freeholder, to which I instantly gave a very short
answer, showing that I understood him and would be rid of him. One
from Veronica with sensible accounts of herself and of Mrs. Macbride's
kindness to her,[6] and mentioning that little James plagued her for

---

[2]Once before, Boswell had observed Satterthwaite, like other Lonsdale followers,
"creeping before Lord L. and abusing him behind his back." Boswell had also, however, credited him with "a certain depth of shrewd sense" (Journal, 5 January 1788).
[3]Since 1785 the maximum time permitted for the poll.
[4]Perhaps promising at least some financial relief.
[5]Robert Aird owned a farm near Auchinleck. Boswell wrote "Corseflat" in the manuscript.
[6]Ursula Macbride's husband, Capt. John Macbride, R.N., M.P., was an Irish cousin of
Margaret Boswell's.

money and that she was afraid Westminster was very expensive. In his handwriting was subjoined this paragraph: "Pray, Sir, is not Veronica to give me some money, as, if I am at Westminster, I must not be a miser?" This little characteristical trait revived me immediately, after having been so sad about him. But I could not help being apprehensive of danger to his morals. I had also a kind, elegant, spirited letter from Temple, feeling for my situation at present, exhorting me to quit all connection with L., and asking me to come to him and "soothe myself with the affection of one who truly loved and valued me." This was an animating consolation which I felt at my heart. I dined quietly with the mayor and sat at home, except going to my barber's and performing the operation. As I had not been asked to L.'s dinner, I kept aloof, and besides was much easier at my own quarters.

TUESDAY 6 JULY. Was rather easier. It was a fine, bright day. I recalled early *English* sensations of *Carlisle*.[7] But they were darkened by gloom, and *now* I felt that Carlisle was no better to me than any Scotch town, such is the effect of habit. I felt myself patient in the Town Hall, and the great question as to the legality of the honorary freemen having occurred, I rose and delivered a firm and decided opinion for them in clear and nervous[8] terms, which I inwardly wondered at my being able to do, my mind being so weak and depressed. I spoke too in a conciliating manner for the mayor, representing the uneasiness of his situation, when the honorary freemen were so unpopular. But that he must do his duty according to his opinion as an honest man. I gave a short history of the proceedings concerning the question, with remarks showing myself master of it.[9] I found that my speech was highly approved, and had been reported to L. Satterthwaite told me that L. had inquired for me yesterday and wondered I had not dined at his table, so he engaged me to dine today. I went down to the garrison, where L. keeps his people at an election,[1] and waited on him. He was

[7] Boswell had always had warm feelings about Carlisle, the first English town he saw when, at sixteen, he rode over from Moffat, where he was recovering from a nervous breakdown.

[8] Forceful.

[9] Wherlings was again recognizing as voters the unpopular honorary freemen—Lonsdale's "mushrooms"—whom the Carlisle Corporation had enfranchised at Lonsdale's behest in October 1784 and January 1785, and who had temporarily elected Lonsdale's candidates in the by-elections of April and of November–December 1786. After each of these elections, Select Committees of the House of Commons had unseated the Lonsdale candidates but had not ruled on the Carlisle Corporation's right to create honorary freemen. Boswell was restating the position he had taken on behalf of his patron in December 1786.

[1] Lonsdale was Colonel of the Cumberland and Westmorland Militia.

polite, and made me walk with him in the garden in presence of his numerous myrmidons. He then expressed a wish that I should return to the Hall, which I instantly did. We sat about seven hours and a half, and there being a hundred on each side polled today, it was now absolutely certain that the business would be over in a few days. I went to the Bush about half past five and found dinner would not be till six. I tired[2] and sauntered; and in short he put off time, *occupatus nihil agendo,*[3] till seven, when we sat down, a company of twenty-eight. He whispered me at table that he would give me a glass of his own madeira and of his own claret. It was a very dull day. There was no circulation of the bottle with any briskness. But this was better than the turbulence of Saturday. He fell asleep after dinner, and they all sat humdrum around him. When he awaked he asked me to breakfast with him next morning in private. I got home about eleven.

WEDNESDAY 7 JULY. I went to breakfast in private with L. and did imagine that in consequence of the handsome appearance I had made as counsel for the mayor, his Lordship meant to show some substantial mark of his approbation and thanks. But all that this *confidential* breakfast meant was to communicate a confused, sulky intention of having the Justices who licensed Carlisle publicans irregularly brought under prosecution before the mayor and me at the City Sessions on Monday.[4] I took occasion to mention something that I had said in delivering my opinion in court on the question concerning the honorary freemen. He cut me short, saying, "I hear you did vastly well." This day in court Satterthwaite talked to me of L.'s strange conduct, and said that I, who had sentiment and expression, should write down just one day. I said it would not be believed. "Oh," said he, "I and others will underwrite it." It amused me to think how much I *had* written down. Satterthwaite said that if the success of the election had anyhow depended on the agreement as to putting the oaths to five at a time, L. would have broken through it.

I went, after the poll was over, to L.'s rendezvous in Fisher Street, being told that he was fond of having attendance paid there.[5] The election for the county of Cumberland was to be next day; and he had ordered dinner at three for himself and Penn and a Mr. Hinde, that

[2]That is, he was bored.
[3]"Occupied with doing nothing."
[4]Three innkeepers had been licensed to sell ale by the Duke of Norfolk and John Christian Curwen, both county Justices, but apparently a technical irregularity could be shown. The City Sessions were the municipal court proceedings.
[5]Lonsdale apparently had the use of rooms in Redness Hall on Fisher Street, the headquarters of the Carlisle guilds.

they might go that night to Whitehaven Castle,[6] and come next morning to Cockermouth to the election. It was now however near six; and he was sitting in a ruinous room, hot and fetid, with a parcel of clerks round him, arranging his new-made freemen of Carlisle. Penn, etc., etc., etc., sat silent and dull at some distance, *in waiting.* Penn said he was well in body but in mind miserable. It was shocking to see him such a slave, but he had informed me that he was under *great pecuniary obligations* to L. About seven we got to the Bush, pained with fasting. L. then said that he would not go to Whitehaven, but would set out very early in the morning for Cockermouth; therefore he and the two gentlemen who were to go with him would dine in private and go to bed soon. Thus he got rid of the large table where I dined, Colonel Lowther in the chair. He had said to me that he would see me before he went to bed; so I was obliged to make a bow to him after I had left the large company. He stopped me, and I was obliged to stay an hour and a half, till it was past eleven. He snored part of the time and Penn and Hinde sat mutes. This was his "going to bed soon." He had dined snugly and had his own wine and fine fruit. I shared of both, but was grievously tired. At last I got home.

I had today consulted Mr. Blamire, whom I found to be an intelligent, sensible surgeon, who had attended a military hospital during the German war. I was cheered somewhat by this. I was now less impatient and wretched. I received a letter from Lady Auchinleck, very judicious and kind, recommending that Euphemia should come to Carlisle and go with me to London. I should a few days ago have shrunk from the charge of a daughter, but I was now so well that I accepted of it, and wrote to Lady Auchinleck accordingly. Her steady good sense gave me a better view of existence. What a weak mind is mine! There had not been in it for a fortnight even a glimpse of the possibility of any enjoyment till Sunday morning last, when there started up a fancy that I should have some satisfaction if I lived at Dulwich, and now and then associated with Lord Thurlow.[7] Even a possibility in imagination was a relief. What sunk me very low was the sensation that I was precisely as when in wretched low spirits thirty years ago, without any addition to my character from my having had the friendship of Dr. Johnson and many eminent men, made the tour of Europe, and Corsica in particular, and written two very successful books. I was as a board on which fine figures had been painted, but which some corrosive application had reduced to its original nakedness.

---

[6] A favourite seat of Lonsdale's, about forty miles south-west of Carlisle.
[7] Thurlow had a cottage, known as Knight's Hill Farm, near Dulwich.

THURSDAY 8 JULY. It was considered as a holiday when L. was at a distance. We had dinner at a reasonable hour. Colonel Lowther was in the chair, and the company were at their ease and made mellow; indeed rather too much so. I had as yesterday some comfortable negus, and took steady care of myself. The poll had been conducted without disturbance. I had not been many hours in court. A letter from Mr. Bruce Campbell informed me of £70 or £80 being to be lodged on my account at Ayr by James Bruce, who it seems was ill with rheumatisms. Luckily my heart had warmed while here, and I had written him a kindly letter, ordering him four dozen of London porter.[8] I found it much better to breakfast and dine at L.'s inn as formerly on such an occasion, so as to appear on the same footing with him as formerly.

FRIDAY 9 JULY. Breakfasted with the mayor, but was sent for to the Bush, L. having returned last night. I found him in violent indignation that the oaths had been given to Dr. Coulthard yesterday to affront him, as he had been violent for the old freemen, and had now returned to L.'s party, to which he had formerly been attached.[9] He was a sad, profligate fellow and ought not to have been countenanced. L. was now determined that all the oaths should be given to the opposite freemen one by one. This occasioned a great uproar in court. I was appealed to for the terms of the agreement as to this, and I declared that I understood the *principle* was to prevent delay, and therefore that it was understood the oaths should be put to five at a time, or, in effect, only twice to each tally.[1] The counsel for Satterthwaite and Knubley contended that the agreement was broken by *one* having been sworn. I was fretted amongst them, and left it to the mayor to do as he pleased, and he, poor creature, I saw would not hold to the agreement when he found L. was for infringing it. At last it was settled (after swearing two singly) that each should poll only twenty this day, and so we had quietness and a great deal of vacant time, the mayor and clerks, etc., being only obliged to continue in court to keep the poll open seven hours.[2]

I went today again to L.'s committee-room and sat a long time *patiently*. It was rumoured that Curwen was to be chaired[3] next day. I

[8]Although he always treated Bruce considerately, Boswell had made derogatory remarks about him in some of his last letters to Margaret Boswell. Bruce seems not to have pressed the tenants sufficiently to fulfil their obligations to Boswell and had become slow in presenting the estate accounts.

[9]A few years earlier Dr. Maurice Coulthard's name had been signed to an attack on the "mushroom" voters.

[1]Each tally consisted of ten voters.

[2]By law the poll had to be open at least seven hours between 8 a.m. and 8 p.m.

[3]Carried aloft as a sign of being the victorious candidate.

considered this as an insult to the *prima facie* legal majority, and L. was indignant against it. I offered if his Lordship would be one magistrate to stop it, I would be another; but I found that he did not incline to stand forward. So I was indifferent. When we got to the Bush, he continued in his room talking with me a long time after dinner was upon the table and the company waiting. I relished this somewhat maliciously. I found that he would not let the poll close next day, so I proposed to adjourn it to twelve on Monday, that there might be time to hold the City Sessions previously. The thought that I should be free on Monday was a cordial to me. Yet I had some weak fears that he might harshly insist on some longer delay.[4] My complaint was now greatly better. My mind had a considerable degree of soundness. I sat next to Major Clarke, the town-major,[5] a decent veteran, and took wine and negus only to do me good and not to excess. Eating more liberally made an alteration on me to the better. How mechanical is man! I received a note from Mr. Allason of Cowdam, an Ayrshire freeholder, asking me to come to the King's Arms, where I found him and his wife and a young lady. They had taken a short jaunt. I drank a glass of wine and saw them sup, and was as polite as I could be; mentioned the state of politics in Ayrshire, my withdrawing, and hopes that on another occasion things would be better. I had today written to Mr. Bruce Campbell and to all the gentlemen who had promised me their support, to the above effect. I sat up till near one, writing to Temple, Veronica, Mrs. Macbride (who had been very kind to her), and my brother T.D., who was truly affectionate.

[Boswell to Veronica]

Carlisle, 9 July 1790

MY DEAR VERONICA,—Let me apologize to you for being so long without writing. My depression of mind made me avoid it as much as I could. But it gives me real concern to find that you have entertained any doubt of my loving you as much as your brothers. What, my own Ve, could you seriously entertain such a notion? Be assured you have no reason. I blame myself for having *talked laxly*, as Dr. Johnson used to say,[6] and said that I did not like you very much. But my dear Veronica, your conduct since you came under my Queen Anne Street West roof, and your sensible and affectionate attention during my absence

---

[4]The following sentence has been scored out in the manuscript.
[5]John Clarke, the chief executive officer of the local garrison.
[6]In one instance, of himself: "I may, perhaps, have said this, for nobody at times talks more laxly than I do" (*Journal of a Tour to the Hebrides*, 24 October 1773).

and in my distress, have endeared you to me very much. So depend upon it that you have a truly affectionate father, which you shall see, and no uneasy apprehension shall remain....

You must resolve to be on the best terms with Euphemia, and *on my assurance* have no jealousy. We shall have Betsy to dinner when I come. I am a good deal better, and am at all times, my dear Veronica, your affectionate father,

JAMES BOSWELL.

My love to my dear little James if you see him before I come.

SATURDAY 10 JULY. L. had gone to the election for the county of Westmorland, carrying Colonel Lowther, Penn, and Hinde with him.[7] I breakfasted at the Bush, and was tolerably easy. I got another letter from Lady Auchinleck, informing me that Euphemia was to be at Carlisle on Sunday evening, and relieving me from any apprehension as to my having a call to the Fife election.[8] The poll went on without disturbance till Curwen and his colleague[9] had exhausted their number, and then Curwen speechified, having introduced a circle of ladies to hear him. After which he and his friends withdrew, and the other candidates were to continue polling on till five. I went to the Bush a little before five, and there I found that L. had left orders that *the chairing should be prevented;* that his men in garrison *should be let out,* but had said nothing *direct*. Satterthwaite and Knubley kept themselves safe. Wheatley, one of his stewards, and Thompson, adjutant of the Westmorland Militia, had received the orders, imperfect as they were. It was suggested that I should swear in a number of constables to keep the peace. I however first wrote to Curwen as follows:

"Sir:—As I consider chairing a candidate, before the poll is declared, to have a tendency towards a breach of the peace, I request of you not to attempt it. But in case the attempt should be made, I think it my duty, as one of the magistrates of this city, to swear in a number of additional constables to prevent unhappy consequences. I am, Sir, your most humble servant.

To John Christian Curwen, Esq.
    Carlisle, 10 July 1790."

[7]Le Fleming and Lowther were returned. Lonsdale controlled both Westmorland seats, and there was no contest.
[8]She wrote that Henry Erskine, who had solicited Boswell's vote, had withdrawn from the Fife contest.
[9]Wilson Gale Braddyll, the other Parliamentary candidate.

Captain Walker of the Cumberland Militia carried this, and I went with Wheatley and Thompson to the garrison and was preparing to swear in constables, when Captain Walker and Mr. Strong, an attorney of L.'s party, came along with Mr. Jackson and Mr. Losh from Mr. Curwen's committee-room, to communicate that their party were resolved not to give up their design of chairing, but they would do it in the most peaceable manner without any insult to the other party, and would not come near either the Bush or the house in Fisher Street; that they therefore hoped the men in that house would be kept in, as they were under command, which the people on the other side were not. Jackson said that my note would be considered as inciting disturbance. Losh said they had a thousand men armed. "O Sir," said I, "it seems then you have been prepared." He said the people in the stamperies[1] and many others were armed with sticks to support them. I said all the concern that I took in the matter was to swear in constables in order to keep the peace; that I wished they would not persist in what was provoking to the honorary freemen and an insult to the returning officer; and I proposed that Captain Walker should return with them to their committee-room, and that I would go to the Bush and talk with the gentlemen there, whom I should advise to permit the chairing as a childish, ridiculous thing, rather than have mischief in the city from a contest about it. That the attempt should be delayed in the mean time. To this they acceded, and they, Walker, and Strong went away. I then swore in constables, five and five, and was proceeding to swear in a third five, when I all of a sudden heard the noise of a mob and saw numbers of Lord Lonsdale's garrison men rushing into the house. At the same time I heard the glass of the windows shivering, and showers of stones rattling, and many of them coming into the house, some into the room where I was. Lord Lonsdale's men wanted to have orders to sally out and attack the mob, but I would not suffer them. I was in great apprehension that the mob might break in, and that I might be killed. I went out twice, making signals to desist, and they seemed not hostile to me. But stones flew about, thrown from a distance, and I retired into the house, taking care however to appear undismayed. Curwen at length came and dispersed the mob. About six-and-thirty of Lord Lonsdale's people were wounded, some of them pretty severely. When I got to the Bush, I was somewhat provoked to find the candidates, etc., had dined quite unconcerned. I drank more wine than I had done for some time, and played whist and lost, and supped at the Bush.

[1] The local calico-printing works, called stamperies because in them cloth was block-printed or "stamped."

SUNDAY 11 JULY. My barber not having come in time to shave me, I did not get to church. I had another good day as last Sunday at Mr. Richardson's, who recommended to me to get good City acquaintances. Mr. Mounsey, the attorney, who had dined at Naworth Castle,[2] joined us at tea. He led his horse and walked with me to Carlisle, and I supped at his house.

MONDAY 12 JULY. Euphemia had arrived the night before in the Edinburgh diligence. I had a bad cold and did not sit up till she came. I found her this morning at the King's Arms, where she was to stay till I got a release. L. was now returned. I apprehended that his ferocious caprice might find fault with my having restrained his men from sallying out, but he said not a word. I hinted going away.[3] He said that some innkeepers were to be convicted of selling ale without being duly licensed, having licences only from the Duke of Norfolk and Mr. Christian as county Justices, and I must stay to do that business. I was vexed to be thus detained, and to be made an instrument of his resentment.[4] But I could not avoid it. I breakfasted and dined with Euphemia, and tried to amuse her as well as I could. But my melancholy was visible. A letter from Lady Auchinleck informed me that there was no contest in Fife, which relieved me.[5]

TUESDAY 13 JULY. L. still continued the poll of his honorary freemen, and I was in a shocking uncertainty when he would end it. I attended on Euphemia as yesterday, played at draughts, and shifted tolerably; but was indignant that a gentleman's daughter should be thus imprisoned, and that L., to whom I mentioned her being here, never minded it. I had a message in the evening to come to the Bush, and found arrangements prepared for convicting the innkeepers next morning. I went by invitation of L. and joined his company and drank a glass or two.

WEDNESDAY 14 JULY. I convicted three innkeepers, declaring the licences which they produced to be in my opinion of no avail.[6] I was

[2]An estate belonging to the Earl of Carlisle.
[3]This day Boswell's resignation as Recorder was to have taken effect.
[4]The complaints against the innkeepers Robert James, Thomas Norman, and Thomas Head were all signed by Lonsdale's henchman George Saul. Boswell wrote "Christian" for "Curwen" because he had changed his name only three months earlier, to perpetuate the highly respected family name of Isabella Curwen, his second wife and cousin, whom he had married in 1782.
[5]This was the second letter from Lady Auchinleck to reach Boswell within two days. Only the first informed him that he was not needed in the Fife election, but he had apparently forgotten that he had already recorded this news in his entry for 10 July.
[6]Boswell imposed a fine of forty shillings and costs on each of the accused.

pressed by Alderman Jackson, etc., aided by old Harrison[7] the lawyer's opinion, to seize and detain the licences, in order that they might be produced as evidence in an indictment against the Justices who granted them; and it was keenly urged that it was my *duty* to do this, in the same manner as it is the duty of a magistrate to detain a forged note, that it may be given in evidence of the crime. But I did not think I had power to do this, more especially as the Court of King's Bench had refused to grant informations against the magistrates, which I thought took criminality out of the case. I had stated a doubt to Harrison whether I could legally act as Recorder after the time at which I had intimated that my resignation was to take place. He said that I was Recorder till my resignation was accepted. The old mischief-maker had mentioned to L. my having thus consulted him, and a bad construction was put on it. For after the business was over, L. and Penn and I were in a room together, and L. again attacked me passionately; said I had consulted Mr. Harrison with a view to get off; that I had sent for my daughter for a pretence; that he had been told by a person whom he believed that before I was acquainted with him, I had said that I should have one of his seats in Parliament, and that when I got the Recordership, I had said I had now got one step. I in vain assured him that I never had talked in that manner, and I appealed to Penn that I had uniformly declared, whenever the subject of L.'s bringing me into Parliament was mentioned, that I had no claim on him, and did not expect it. Penn confirmed this. L. renewed his upbraiding me for soliciting the Recordership and then throwing it up. I defended myself calmly, but he said I had done everything wrong since I left London; that I had done wrong this very morning (alluding no doubt to my refusing to seize the licences), and that when it should be observed that I was not at his house as usual, he would say that I had earnestly asked the Recordership, and thrown it up in the most unhandsome manner. It was difficult to be patient under such savage injustice. But I was quiet, and Penn afterwards told me he was glad I was. I left the room, and went to Euphemia and fretted.

The poll at last was concluded, and L.'s candidates returned.[8] (By the way, they were chaired before it was concluded, which was an irregularity, and sanctioned that of the other candidates.) I went into the court where L. sat as chairman of the County Sessions. After all that had passed, he waved to me to come near to him, and asked if all was well ended, and to all appearance was confidential with me. I then

[7]The blind lawyer Myles Harrison, now seventy-six years old.
[8]As in the two previous Carlisle by-elections, Lonsdale's candidates were later unseated on petition to the House of Commons. This time the Select Committee explicitly ruled that only bona fide freemen had the right to vote.

ventured to ask his commands. He said, "You won't go before dinner?" I bowed. Penn had advised me to stay and dine with him, and he considered that I was now invited. What a strange madman is L.! I saw Colonel Lowther to be a fallacious fellow, for he had told me in London that L. had said I would get drunk and make a foolish speech, were I in Parliament, which convinced him that he did not approve of me as a Member; but today he said L. had said it with perfect good humour, so that he had drawn no unfavourable conclusion. I could not believe anything he said.

I eat some dinner early with Euphemia, and then had a message that I was wanted at the Bush. I went and found L. sitting alone, with papers before him. He said he was very busy. I begged pardon, but said a message had come that his Lordship wanted me. "Will you dine with me?" said he. I said I would have the honour to wait on him. I accordingly dined, and he appeared quite as he used to do, and was hearty (as far as he can be who never was seen to laugh fairly), had many songs sung, and kept us sitting till between eleven and twelve. He had asked me to go to his private dining-room and eat fruit. I played the game all through and went, hugging myself in the thought of being free from him and setting out early next morning. Penn, Captain Walker, etc., etc., were at this repast, which was crowned with L.'s own old wine. I said not a word when we separated, for fear that some other crotchet for delay should come into his head. I had drunk so much wine as to have a headache. It was near two in the morning when I got to my lodgings.

THURSDAY 15 JULY. Set out with Euphemia in the mail-coach, in which we went as far as Ferrybridge, and lay there some hours and reposed. In the morning,[1] went into the York coach called high-flyer; went all night, which was hard work, but London was in prospect; breakfasted next day at Hertford, and liked to see again a Home-Circuit town.[2] Arrived in London safely.

[EDITORIAL NOTE. With the comment "After this, my journal is written in a book," Boswell now returns to the bound notebook containing the entries for 1–19 January and 14 May–16 June 1790.]

SATURDAY 17 JULY. Having been driven all night in the stage-coach, I was somewhat confused, and my mind was so sore from the severe bruise it had suffered that I could not at once relish the comfort of London fully. However, I did feel it pretty well, having come in by Shoreditch Church and through the City. When I got to my own house I

---

[1] That is, on 16 July.
[2] Boswell had been a counsellor on the Home Circuit, covering the counties near London, as well as on the Northern Circuit.

found that my son James had been ill of a fever for a week. How lucky was it that this additional unhappiness had not reached me at Carlisle! He was however better. Dr. Warren and Mr. Devaynes both called when I was at home, and to see them again raised my spirits somewhat. I found a cordial reception from Malone and dined with him; only Jephson there.

SUNDAY 18 JULY. Stayed at home in the forenoon. Sir Joshua Reynolds came and invited me and my two daughters[3] to dinner next day. I dined at Malone's; Reed and Jephson there. Found myself growing better. James advanced in recovery. I was part of the morning service at St. George's, Hanover Square. Met Sir W. Lowther there.

MONDAY 19 JULY. Had found that by my kind and active friend Malone's aid my book had gone on in my absence five sheets.[4] I was quite pleased to see another *proof* and to be put in train again. I and my daughters dined at Sir Joshua Reynolds's with Lord Eliot, his son Mr. John,[5] Mr. Devaynes, Malone and Jephson and Metcalfe, an excellent day, and Devaynes asked all the gentlemen to dine at his villa,[6] the *prospect* of which enlivened the *present conviviality*. My health was now about restored. I lived generously. My daughters behaved very well. Only the sad recollection of my irreparable loss hung at my heart. I had a kind of feeling that it would be unkind should I not still be pained by it. My daughters and I and most of the company passed the evening, played cards, and supped. I lost too much at whist, betting keenly as I am apt to do.

TUESDAY 20 JULY. Was restless, and sauntered about a good deal. Found old John Ross Mackye at home[7] and wished for his soup today, but he asked me for Thursday. Dined quietly at home.

WEDNESDAY 21 JULY. Forced myself to stay at home most of the day. Either today or yesterday, had a long revise of Johnson's *Life* with Malone, and I think called today on Mrs. Macbride and sat some time with her.

THURSDAY 22 JULY. Either yesterday or today, breakfasted with Sir William Lowther in Dover Street, as I had met him twice and he had both times said he would be glad to see me. I told him enough of my

[3]Veronica and Euphemia; Betsy was at school at Blacklands House in Chelsea.
[4]That is, forty pages.
[5]Edward Craggs Eliot, a wealthy Cornish landowner and a prominent M.P. for many years until he was created first Baron Eliot of St. Germans, was a close friend and patron of Reynolds's and member of The Club; his son, the Hon. John Eliot, M.P., had been called to the English bar together with Boswell in 1786.
[6]Called "The Bush," near Hyde Park Corner.
[7]Mackye, a Scots advocate and former M.P. who had held several political offices in England, was Lord Auchinleck's sole surviving friend in London.

story with L., and he told me that L. had left him out of the county of Cumberland at the General Election, without any reason that he could find out and without ever signifying any offence.[8] He was of opinion that L. was mad. Lady Augusta Lowther, sister of Lord Westmorland,[9] Sir William's lady, was very civil. I wished to guard myself against appearing all at once quite out with L. I dined at Ross Mackye's with Col. Charles Stuart, General Vernon, Laird Heron, and his brother the Major.[1] To see a man upwards of eighty enjoying sociality was encouraging,[2] but there was no animating conversation, and the Scottish feelings raised in my mind by the two Herons disgusted me, and I figured myself doomed to pass my days with such feelings were I to live in Scotland. We drank rather too much wine.

FRIDAY 23 JULY. Dined really in social glee at Mr. Devaynes's beautiful villa with the gentlemen who had been at Sir Joshua Reynolds's on Monday, with the agreeable addition of Courtenay. Passed the evening at Sir Joshua's and played whist.

SATURDAY 24 JULY. Went to Baldwin's printing-office, where I was happy to find myself again, though I found neither my friend Baldwin the master, Selfe the corrector, nor Plymsell the compositor. Advanced to Dilly's and was comforted by his cordial friendship. Dined with him tête-à-tête, and partook liberally of old hock and mountain. Was warmed, and wished to have a social evening at a coffee-house. Tried the Grecian, Temple, and George's, Temple Bar; hardly a soul there or at Nando's. Read the Scotch newspapers at Peele's, which was pretty full. But I knew nobody. The Bedford was empty, and one solitary gentleman sat in the Piazza.[3] I had a small but disagreeable loss tonight, my pocket having been picked of a proof-sheet of my *Life of*

[8]While M.P. for Cumberland during the preceding six years, Lowther had not always voted with Lonsdale and thereby no doubt incurred his displeasure. Although now out of favour, he eventually inherited most of Lonsdale's titles and estates, being the closest surviving relation in a collateral line of Lowthers.

[9]John Fane, tenth Earl of Westmorland, was Lord Lieutenant of Ireland at this time.

[1]Col. Charles Stuart, fourth son of the former Prime Minister, the Earl of Bute; General Charles Vernon, Lieutenant of the Tower; Patrick Heron of Kirroughtrie, and Maj. Basil Heron.

[2]Mackye was eighty-three years old.

[3]Well-known coffee-houses, close to each other, located between the Inns of Court and Covent Garden: the Grecian at the Temple (the Middle and Inner Temples) on the Strand; George's at Temple Bar, a gateway to the City designed by Wren in 1672 to commemorate the great fire of London and situated where the Strand joins Fleet Street; Nando's also at Temple Bar and Fleet Street; Peele's, noted for its files of newspapers, further on in Fleet Street; the Bedford and the Piazza in the Piazza adjacent to Covent Garden Theatre.

Johnson, with the manuscript belonging to it. But this could not be remedied, and luckily all was secured in print but two lines which I could supply. Came to Sir Joshua's; found Malone there; played whist and supped.

SUNDAY 25 JULY. Dined tête-à-tête with Malone and had a revise of my book. In the forenoon I had been at St. George's Church, Hanover Square, Veronica with me.

MONDAY 26 JULY. Was quiet at home. Colonel Craufurd drank tea with us, and revived not unpleasing feelings.[4] Sandy came home from Eton for the long vacation. I was glad to see him improved, but thought the vacation by much too long[5] and a great disadvantage.

TUESDAY 27 JULY. Lord Palmerston had last week sent me a message by Sir Joshua Reynolds inviting me to dine today at his villa at East Sheen.[6] I went in Sir Joshua's coach with him and Miss Palmer. The day was fine, the Place pretty, the company Mr. Cholmondeley, whom I had never seen before but whom I thought very agreeable; my old acquaintance his mother; Mrs. Gwyn and Mrs. Bunbury, and Dr. Blagden.[7] I was charmed with Lady Palmerston's gentle, elegant appearance and manner. My Lord made an apology for having invited me without first waiting on me, but said he would certainly do it soon, and he was much obliged to me. The respectable old rooms, which belonged to his Lordship's great-grandfather Sir John Temple, brother of Sir William,[8] the portraits, the very complete dinner and wines and attendance, pleased me highly. I was actually in one of the scenes which I figured in a letter to the Hon. A. Erskine.[8a] Dr. Blagden went with us to Sir Joshua's; whist and a bit of supper.

[4]Lt.-Col. John Walkinshaw Craufurd, an old friend, had repeatedly offered to support Boswell's political candidacy in Ayrshire.
[5]It was more than six weeks.
[6]Henry Temple, second Viscount Palmerston, M.P. and member of The Club, owned a magnificent house and extensive grounds near Richmond.
[7]The guests included George James Cholmondeley, a Commissioner of Excise, remembered also because Johnson was once rude to him but then apologized handsomely; his mother, Mary Cholmondeley, described by Johnson as that "very airy lady" (*Life of Johnson,* 23 September 1773), sister of the great actress Peg Woffington; and Charles Blagden, M.D., Secretary of the Royal Society.
[8]Sir William Temple was the statesman and writer who had been the patron of the young Swift.
[8a] Boswell is recalling his youthful reverie, described to his friend Andrew Erskine: "How many parties of pleasure shall I have in town! How many fine jaunts to the noble seats of dukes, lords, and Members of Parliament in the country!" (8 May 1762, *Letters between the Honourable Andrew Erskine and James Boswell, Esq.,* pp. 104–105).

WEDNESDAY 28 JULY. Sandy walked out with me to Blacklands House to conduct Betsy home. I had today for the first time these many months all my children together. My brother David and his wife dined with us, and Mrs. and Miss Buchanan were to have been of the party, but were prevented by Miss Buchanan's being indisposed. I was delighted with Betsy's speaking English,[9] and resolved that she should not be a night from Blacklands for years. I was invited to dine at Sir Joshua's with Courtenay, Malone, etc. My company having dispersed early, I went to Sir Joshua's, but Courtenay was gone, and instead of a *comfortable* party for whist, I found Mrs. Cholmondeley, Mrs. Gwyn, Mrs. Bunbury; in short a *lady* society, and I now find that I dislike that unless where there is something to *interest* me. I wished to steal away, but was asked to join at whist, which it seems I reluctantly and with a bad grace consented to do. I was really in ill humour, and did not stay to supper, but walked home, with a strange feeling that I did not like London. Sir Joshua and Malone afterwards showed me that I was in the wrong to be so uncomplying, the very essence of politeness, by which society gains so much, being to do what we do not like, that we may please others.

THURSDAY 29 JULY. Dined at Mr. Dilly's with Captain Walter, steady Reed, Dr. Lettsom and his son; was easy in mind and social. Drank rather too liberally. Stayed and played whist.

FRIDAY 30 JULY. Colonel Arabin had written to me to fix a day for dining with Mrs. Fitzgerald, a lady who wished to have my advice as to obtaining a divorce against her husband for infidelity, the marriage having been in Scotland.[1] A new acquaintance, especially when there is anything of an *adventure,* always pleases me. At five o'clock I repaired to no. 82 in Piccadilly, close by Clarges Street. Not to detail the history minutely, there was a pretty numerous company, two *genteelish* ladies and their husbands, one a clergyman of *buckish* cast,[2] Colonel Arabin and a natural son, and a Captain Davids of the marines, who seemed to be some connection of the house and called for more wine after dinner. The lady herself, I found, was the wife of Mr. Fitzgerald, an elegant Irishman of about £5,000 a year, younger than herself and given to gallantry, so that they had lived separate for some time,

---

[9]That is, without a Scottish accent.
[1]Lt.-Col. William John Arabin had written to Boswell, asking him to advise Mary Fitzgerald on whether she could obtain a divorce in Scotland even though her husband's transgressions were taking place in England. Arabin considered the outcome very doubtful because the woman was bringing the suit. When Boswell had met Arabin in 1785, they had discussed Arabin's own wish for a divorce because of his wife's infidelity.
[2]Foppish appearance.

having been married eleven years; he had now a girl who had been her servant who lived with him and had five children by him. We dined in a room on the third floor, commanding a view of the Green Park, St. James's Park, the Queen's House,[3] Westminster Abbey, the Surrey hills, etc. I said I never before had dined in a room with such a prospect, and I exclaimed, "How delightful it is to see the country and be sure you are not in it. Piccadilly is between us and it!" We had an excellent entertainment in every respect, and I was fond of the gay and fashionable manners of my hostess, with whom I had a private consultation. I stayed till eleven, and really felt this as a day of enjoyment.

SATURDAY 31 JULY. Had a most hearty day at Sir Joshua Reynolds's, Miss Palmer being in the country. He had at dinner Lord Eliot, Mr. Agar, Malone, Courtenay, Jephson, Batt,[4] Langley, and myself. Some of us remained, played whist, and supped. Agar entertained us with the most extravagant fictions of vanity.

SUNDAY 1 AUGUST. Stayed at home, and read one of Dr. Johnson's sermons to my children.[5] My sons and I drank tea at my brother David's. In the forenoon I visited Mrs. Buchanan with my daughters.

MONDAY 2 AUGUST. A very bad, rainy, dull day. Insisted on Malone and Jephson dining with me, which they did at six, and we forgot the weather. In the evening it was better and we went to whist at Sir Joshua's.

TUESDAY 3 AUGUST. Dined at Sir Joshua Reynolds's with Lord Eliot, Malone, and Jephson, and played whist. Sir Joshua was to go next day to Mr. Burke's in the country.

WEDNESDAY 4 AUGUST. Walked into the City to visit Captain Preston, but he was gone back to Woodford.[6] Came in upon my good friend Baldwin the printer's family dinner, which I took cordially.

---

[3]Another name for Buckingham House (later Buckingham Palace), at the west end of St. James's Park. It was called the Queen's House because George III had settled it on Queen Charlotte, and it was known for its delightful location, offering views of both the town and the nearby countryside.

[4]Welbore Ellis Agar, Commissioner of Customs, and John Thomas Batt, a barrister and government auditor of Irish accounts.

[5]One of the sermons Johnson had written for his friend Dr. John Taylor of Ashbourne, which were published in 1788–89 as *Sermons, on Different Subjects, Left for Publication by the Reverend John Taylor, LL.D.* Johnson's authorship of these sermons, though not acknowledged, was widely recognized.

[6]Capt. Robert Preston, M.P., was a first cousin of Boswell's mother but the same age as Boswell. A former captain and now an East India Company shipowner, he had a country-house in Woodford, north-east of London.

THURSDAY 5 AUGUST. Courtenay and his son dined with me. Jephson came after dinner and Malone in the evening, and he and Jephson and Veronica and I played whist. We had some supper.

FRIDAY 6 AUGUST. I think I revised some of Johnson's *Life* at Malone's one of the evenings of this week, I am not sure which. I think I dined at home today.

SATURDAY 7 AUGUST. Walked into the City; met Sir Michael Le Fleming, who asked me to dine with him, and he by chance found Penn also disengaged. There was only a young Senhouse from Barbados[7] besides, and Sir Michael soon dismissed him. So the Baronet and Penn and I had a cordial meeting. It was pleasant to me to be well with them notwithstanding L.'s strange conduct. They went to ride in the evening, so we did not sit late. I was however so much intoxicated with good wine in a warm day that I could not rest, and sauntered in a kind of drowsy dissipation, and very foolishly——[8]

SUNDAY 8 AUGUST. My two sons went to Oxford Chapel, Sandy in the morning and he and Jamie in the afternoon. I and my daughters went in the afternoon to St. George's, Hanover Square, I having dined quietly at home. I heard my children say sacred lessons in the evening.

MONDAY 9 AUGUST. Had settled that I was to go to Woodford and wait on Captain Preston and his new-married lady. Rose between six and seven; breakfasted with Dilly and intended to go down in the Woodford coach, but found walking so pleasant that I continued it all the way.[9] Felt a kind of strange sensation on being again in coloured clothes.[1] Mrs. Preston was a well-looking, good-humoured young woman. No company there but a Mrs. Jones, a widow, and Mr. Constable, the surgeon. I was entertained heartily, and the strong common sense and prosperity of Preston drove away low spirits. He said, "A country gentleman's life is no better than that of one of his horses; he gets his dinner, and he gets his supper." He told me that Captain Cotton, who is sometimes so low-spirited as to cry like a child, was very well handled by Captain Sealy one day. "Now," said he, "Cotton, you are a rich man, your family is amply provided for. You have two very fine girls for your daughters, and your two sons are doing as well as

[7] One of the sons of William Senhouse, surveyor-general of Barbados and the Leeward Islands, and nephew of Humphrey Senhouse, one of Lonsdale's M.P.s.
[8] At this point the entry breaks off with a dash.
[9] Preston had recently married Elizabeth Brown. Boswell must have walked over six miles from Dilly's house in the Poultry to Woodford.
[1] Apparently on this day Boswell stopped wearing mourning.

you could wish. Yet you are very low-spirited. How can this be accounted for? Here is nobody but your friend Preston and myself. If you have committed murder, confess it at once, and be hanged." This showed Cotton how unreasonable he was.[2] Preston and I walked round his Place, and I enjoyed that fanciful pleasure which I have always in the county of Essex. He told me that Pitt had broken his word to him repeatedly, but that he continued to support him for his own credit in being uniform and not swayed by interest, and he trusted that Pitt would feel how much he had been in the wrong to him, and would provide for his brother, Sir Charles.[3] I perceived in Preston a kind of sound understanding better than talents.

TUESDAY 10 AUGUST. I had enjoyed an admirable repose, and rose really well, but soon felt relaxation.[4] Preston rode to town. I was offered a seat in his coach with the ladies; but they were not to go for some hours, and my impatience could not brook waiting, so I walked away, intending to relieve my fatigue in one of the numerous coaches which pass that road. But I found walking so beneficial, and had such a pride in the vigour of it, that I persevered as I did yesterday. I dined at home, and after dinner went to Malone's, who had sent me a note that Sir Joshua Reynolds was arrived and wanted us at whist in the evening. We went and I won. The heat of the weather and various draughts of wine and water had thrown me into a fermentation, so that in walking home I did not shun a very fine object and——[5]

WEDNESDAY 11 AUGUST. Dined at Sir Joshua Reynolds's with Lord Eliot and his son John, Malone, and Jephson, and played whist. I lost a good deal. Drank too liberally. Wandered absurdly before going home.

THURSDAY 12 AUGUST. Sir Joshua Reynolds and I dined with the Stationers' Company in their Hall. It seems we were the first guests whom they had ever invited, but as I had resolved to exert myself in procuring a fulfillment of a wish that Sir Joshua and I had formed of dining with all the City Companies of London (he having carried me to the Painter-Stainers'), I had applied to Dilly, and Baldwin, being now one of the wardens, had proposed an innovation in order that we should be invited, which was carried by an unanimous vote and entered

[2]This anecdote concerns Capt. John Sealy and either Capt. Joseph Cotton or Capt. John Cotton, all three having commanded East India Company ships at about the same time. Cotton had visited Auchinleck with his friend Preston in 1783.

[3]Sir Charles Preston, Bt., was, in fact, appointed Commissioner of Customs for Scotland in 1798, later in Pitt's ministry.

[4]A lack of energy.

[5]As on 7 August, Boswell's entry breaks off with a dash.

in their books; so I said to Sir Joshua that now he and I were *entered at Stationers' Hall.*[6] Dinner was at half past three; there were fifteen haunches of venison and as many pasties, with other good substantial dishes. It was for the credit of literature to see such a feast and so numerous a company, 225 present; but I did not like many being of it who were not actual booksellers, printers, or stationers. Sir Joshua and I were placed on the right hand of Mr. March,[7] the Master for this year, at the table at the top of the room for him and those of higher rank, and there were three long tables in our view, as the form is in all Halls according to ancient form. In a lofty gallery at the foot of the room was a good band of music, which enlivened us greatly. I enjoyed a *"City feast"* fully. After a few general toasts we retired into a handsome room, where we had our wine coolly: port, sherry, and mountain. I observed to Sir Joshua that it was agreeable to hear names resounding which we had been used to read on title-pages from our earliest years: Mr. Dodsley, Mr. Rivington, Mr. Longman, Mr. Crowder,[8] etc.:

And still I seem to tread on classic ground.[9]

We had tea and coffee and then whist. Sir Joshua and I beat Aldermen Wright and Gill, of which I boasted, they having both been Mayor of London.[1] Sir Joshua wisely went away, but I, being full of wine, stayed, played another rubber, which I luckily won, and then supped and drank more, but was very much intoxicated and could not recollect much of what passed. Wandered absurdly.

[6]Boswell and Reynolds were not actually the first guests of the Stationers' Company, the old-established guild of printers and booksellers, but they may have been the first since an order of 1754 barred strangers from the August dinner. The phrase "Entered at Stationers' Hall" meant registered for purposes of copyright, but unfortunately for Boswell's witticism, no record of the special vote of invitation exists in the company's books. On the contrary, the order of 1754 was reaffirmed annually; Baldwin, as a member of the guild's governing body, must have made special arrangements to bring his guests. Reynolds had taken Boswell to the Painter-Stainers' guild, which included artists as well as craftsmen, in October 1786.

[7]John March was a respected printer with premises at George Street, Tower Hill.

[8]Hearing the names of the current guild members—James Dodsley, John Rivington, Thomas Longman—Boswell is recalling some of the great names of the past: Robert Dodsley, who had been associated with Pope, Swift, and Johnson as friend or publisher; Charles Rivington, who had encouraged Richardson to write his first novel, *Pamela;* Thomas Longman, uncle of the present Longman, who had founded the publishing-house of that name and co-sponsored Johnson's *Dictionary.* Stanley Crowder, in business since 1755 and publisher of Gay, was still alive.

[9]Joseph Addison, *A Letter from Italy,* l. 12.

[1]Thomas Wright had been Lord Mayor from 1779 to 1780; William Gill, from 1788 to 1789.

FRIDAY 13 AUGUST. Awaked very ill and lay till it was far in the forenoon. Went to Sir Joshua, and he walked with me to Hatchett's and saw a splendid chariot or car, made for the Empress of Russia.[2] I had resolved to dine quietly at home, but Courtenay had called and left a note that he was to dine at Malone's; upon which I wrote to Malone that if it was not an invited company, I would come. It was not; and I was as usual received with most agreeable hospitality, and by good cheer and good conversation was soon revived and had a very pleasant day. After Jephson went to bed,[3] I talked with Courtenay and Malone of L.'s shocking conduct to me. They both thought that I was well rid of such a connection, for that I must have had a quarrel with him if I had been one of his Members and refused implicit compliance. Malone said that both L. and I had been deceived: he had concluded that a man who had praised him so highly, when all the world abused him, was willing to be his dependant, and would think it an honour; and therefore he had sent me a card of invitation to dine with him, without being acquainted with me or having called on me, thus treating me as an inferior character;[4] and I had flattered myself that this powerful lord would exert his influence particularly to promote me. We talked of the great advantage of keeping a journal so as to preserve conversations in which knowledge and wit and anecdote occur. I do not find that any particulars of this day's conversation start out.[5] But it was in general most agreeable.

SATURDAY 14 AUGUST. Dined at Sir William Scott's with Sir William Wynne, the Attorney- and Solicitor-General, Mr. Bernard, Under-Secretary of State, Dr. Fisher,[6] Sir Joshua Reynolds, and Mr. Malone; a very good, agreeable day, rational and easy, without much exertion. Malone and I went home with Sir Joshua, played whist, and supped.

SUNDAY 15 AUGUST. Having engaged to dine again with Preston at Woodford, did not get to church except for a few minutes to one in the City. Mr. Grindall, the surgeon,[7] carried me there and back again

---

[2]John Hatchett was coachmaker to the King and Queen.

[3]Apparently Robert Jephson was staying with Malone at this time.

[4]Because Lonsdale had not observed the usual courtesies, Boswell had declined the invitation with an excuse, but he had subsequently cultivated Lonsdale's acquaintance.

[5]Stand out.

[6]An impressive company, including Wynne, the head of the ecclesiastical courts; Sir Archibald Macdonald, the Attorney-General; Sir John Scott, the Solicitor-General; and John Fisher, LL.D., who practised law in the ecclesiastical and admiralty courts.

[7]Richard Grindall of the London Hospital, who specialized in treating patients associated with the East India Company. Earlier Boswell could not resist the witticism, "he cut nabobs for the stone and found diamonds"—nabobs or nawabs being those who had returned from India with great wealth—but thought him "a fine, frank, sensible, jolly Englishman" (Journal, 8 April 1781).

in his chariot. I liked much Mr. Brown, a ship-broker, Preston's brother-in-law, a very sensible and genteel young man. I passed the day cordially, and in the evening sat an hour with Mr. Dilly.

MONDAY 16 AUGUST. Had at dinner with me, by invitation some days before, Lord Eliot and his son John, Sir Joshua Reynolds, Mr. Jephson; Mr. Malone had forgotten his invitation and gone to search old registers, so did not come to us till after dinner. I had met Lord Ossory in the forenoon, who had come to town occasionally.[8] I asked him to dine with us, and he obligingly came. We had a very good day and all drank tea and coffee, so that my daughters had the advantage of good company. Sir Joshua, Malone, and Jephson stayed till late and played whist, and the two last supped. I was struck to observe how Westminster scholars, however different in age and rank,[9] draw to one another. Lord Ossory and my little James got into close conference, and his Lordship was pleased to say, "He is the finest boy I ever saw in my life." It seems he gave James half a guinea, saying, "I must tip you. I never see a Westminster but I tip him."

TUESDAY 17 AUGUST. My brother David and his wife and mother-in-law, Major Green, Mr. Bosville of Yorkshire,[1] and Mr. Lumisden dined with us, and drank tea and coffee. We were very social. My mind was now in a pretty tranquil state.

WEDNESDAY 18 AUGUST. My daughter Betsy dined with us. I was quite pleased with her English accent. Her brothers and I went home with her in the evening.

THURSDAY 19 AUGUST. Dined at Sir Joshua Reynolds's with Lord Eliot, his son John, Mr. Malone, Mr. Jephson, Mr. Metcalfe, Mr. Hoole, Mr. Edward Gwatkin.[2] Not much discussion but cheerfulness enough. I played one rubber at whist and won, and then being cut out, went away and passed half an hour in Old Burlington Street.

FRIDAY 20 AUGUST. Was strangely restless. Went to Baldwin's printing-house; called at Sir Joshua's, intending if at home to dine with him, but he was gone to Metcalfe's. Did not choose to appear obtruding myself at one place when another had failed. It was too late for my dinner at home. Took bread and cheese and cider at the Bear and

[8] By chance. John Fitzpatrick, second Earl of Upper Ossory, was a member of The Club.

[9] Lord Ossory had been at Westminster School in the 1750s.

[1] William Bosville, whom Boswell regarded as a kinsman and—despite Bosville's demurrer—as the current "chief" of the Boswell "clan," succeeding his father, Godfrey Bosville.

[2] Gwatkin was the brother-in-law of Reynolds's niece Theophila, "Offie," the older sister of Mary Palmer and her predecessor as Reynolds's companion.

Rummer in Mortimer Street, corner of Wells Street. I came home and drank tea with Euphemia, Veronica being at Mrs. Wood's and my sons at Astley's.

SATURDAY 21 AUGUST. Mr. Dilly and I dined with Dr. Lettsom at his charming villa at Camberwell Grove. A Mr.———, an old gentleman of Aberdeen who had lived long at Santa Cruz and had been thirty-six years without being in Britain, dined there, as did Dr. Sims, the Irish City physician.[3] We played at bowls both before and after dinner, two gentlemen of Camberwell, whose names I forget, having joined us. I relished the amusement much, and was conscious of being carried along the stream of life with no steady direction but without positive pain, for which I am so framed as to think that I may compound.[4]

SUNDAY 22 AUGUST. Euphemia, being lame, kept the house. I took Veronica and my sons to St. George's Church in the morning, dined at home, and took Veronica and Jamie there again in the afternoon, Sandy having a headache. Veronica and I drank tea at my brother David's, where was Mr. Cleghorn, formerly a merchant at Benicarló, who had embraced the Roman Catholic faith and now lived in the College at St. Omer's, where he assisted in educating the youth.[5] Mr. Bosville also was here. We had much conversation of what was done at St. Omer's, and of the manners of Spain. I felt realities amuse my wavering mind.

MONDAY 23 AUGUST. I dined quietly at home. In the evening late I waited on Mr. Agar to talk with him concerning some trinkets of Signor Mischi from Parma which had by mistake been sent to the custom-house. The pomposity and splendour of Agar diverted me. I had need of diversion today, for I had received accounts that poor James Bruce died on the 18th. He had been ill a considerable time, but I did not apprehend he was in danger. Some nights ago, but before

[3]Lettsom had made his estate of Grove Hill in the south of London into a showplace with a small museum of natural history, an outstanding library, and a botanical garden. His guests on this occasion included the Aberdeen gentleman, who had lived in St. Croix in the Virgin Islands, and the Irish-born Dr. James Sims, for more than twenty years President of the London Medical Society.

[4]An allusion to the end of Johnson's *Rasselas,* which shows the characters "contented to be driven along the stream of life without directing their course to any particular port." Boswell suggests that he might come to terms with ("compound") such an aimless life so long as it was without great pain.

[5]Presumably T.D. knew Thomas Cleghorn from his years as merchant in Valencia, which is eighty miles south-west of Benicarló. St.-Omer was a famous school in northern France for the sons of English Catholics. It was founded by English Jesuits in the late sixteenth century, but since the Jesuits' expulsion from France in 1762 it was run by the clergy of the English College at Douay.

his death, I awaked in a fright, having heard his voice distinctly pronouncing these words: "Health, health, amen." To hear that an old servant to whom I had been habituated from my infancy, or rather indeed a kind of friend and tutor with whom I had in my early years confidentially associated, who was born at Auchinleck, was a most knowing and ingenious man and seemed in imagination to be an inseparable circumstance about the Place[6]—to hear that he was gone was a sad memento of the transitory nature of human life. I felt however a certain degree of that indifference which comes upon the mind as we advance in years, compared with the lively impressions in youth.

TUESDAY 24 AUGUST. Dined at Malone's with only Courtenay, and in the evening read my journal at Ashbourne with Dr. Johnson in 1777[7] and heard their remarks.

WEDNESDAY 25 AUGUST. Dined at home. Was always doing a little towards the correction and improvement of my manuscript or *copy*, as it is called, of Johnson's *Life*.

THURSDAY 26 AUGUST. Dined at Mr. Dilly's with Dr. Mayo, Mr. Sharp, and the Rev. Mr. Townshend, brother of the late alderman. We had good talk, and after Dr. Mayo went, played two rubbers at whist and supped and had punch.

FRIDAY 27 AUGUST. Courtenay and Malone dined with me, and we passed an agreeable day, of which, however, nothing remains upon my memory.

SATURDAY 28 AUGUST. Dined at the house of Forbes, the great copper-smith, in Primrose Street off Bishopsgate Street, his brother being entertainer.[8] The company was all Scotch except one Barnes, who had been a Quaker. Perry and Gray, the editors of the *Gazetteer*, were of the party.[1] I was disgusted by the reviving in my mind of forward, coarse, north-of-Scotland manners. We drank a considerable quantity.

SUNDAY 29 AUGUST. Poor David Ross, the actor, from whom I had a little before received a melancholy note that he was not able to

---

[6]The estate proper.

[7]A record of Boswell's experiences in Ashbourne, Derbyshire, where he had joined Johnson on a visit to his friend Dr. John Taylor. Boswell included this lively, fully written journal for 14–24 September 1777 in the *Life of Johnson* with only minor stylistic changes; presumably he read the version that would appear in the *Life* to his friends.

[8]William Forbes of Callendar and his brother David, who served as host.

[1]James Perry had founded the *European Magazine* and had become editor of the *Gazetteer*, a staunchly Whig paper, in 1783. His friend and co-editor James Gray was a former schoolteacher.

walk, and could not afford coach-hire, had (wonderful contrast, characteristic of the man) written to me a second note inviting me with other friends to dine with him today at the Thatched House Tavern[2] on a haunch of venison. I had sent my excuse as being engaged to dine in the country, but the curiosity of the scene so played upon my mind that I yielded to it. When I got into St. James's Street, I felt myself uneasy that I had not been at church, and half resolved not to go to Ross. But I perceived him walking slowly, and could not resist, so came up to him, saying, "*Video meliora proboque.*"[3] I found that I had half an hour, so went to St. James's Church and had a part of the evening service. Not one of Ross's guests came but myself; so we had the haunch at his lodgings in Thatched House Court, just behind the tavern. He had porter, port, and sherry, and I *floated* the haunch with three bottles of claret. A low-bred, obliging girl whom he called Mrs. Ross[4] dined with us. What we talked of I do not recollect, but we sat till about eleven. A strange day.

MONDAY 30 AUGUST. I took Baldwin's family dinner; only he and I and his son, the printer. Settled that two compositors should be put upon my *magnum opus* so as that it might be dispatched faster by almost a half.[5] Mrs. Baldwin came home and gave us tea.[6] I passed the evening at Sir Joshua's. Played both whist and brag[7] and lost a good deal; was vexed. Paid a visit in Old Burlington Street.

TUESDAY 31 AUGUST. The last part of yesterday as marked should have been ascribed to this day.

WEDNESDAY 1 SEPTEMBER. Breakfasted at Malone's as usual on the first of the month. Dined at home. In the evening had a party at tea, cards, and supper: Mr. and Mrs. Wood, Mr. Lumisden, T.D., his wife and Mrs. Green, and Miss De Camps.[8] We were very cheerful; at least the company was, and I appeared to be so.

THURSDAY 2 SEPTEMBER. Dined at home. My daughters drank tea at their uncle's. Little James made it for me. I was busy preparing a quantity of *copy* for my two compositors.

---

[2]An old establishment in St. James's Street, frequented by Swift. Ross walked with difficulty because he had broken his leg about twelve years earlier.

[3]Ovid, *Metamorphoses*, vii. 20, trans. F. J. Miller, Loeb ed.: "I see the better and approve it."

[4]Boswell had known Ross's first wife, Fanny Murray, who had died in 1778. She was a famous courtesan before her marriage but apparently a good wife to Ross.

[5]Baldwin asked a compositor named Manning to join Plymsell in working on the *Life of Johnson.*

[6]A short vertical line in the manuscript indicates that from this point Boswell is recording the events of the following evening.

[7]A card-game similar to poker.

[8]The final *s* shows that the reference is to two young women of this name.

FRIDAY 3 SEPTEMBER. It had been for some time settled that my brother T.D. should go down to Auchinleck with a commission or power of attorney from me to collect my rents and arrange my affairs. It was comfortable to me to think that he would put all things in good order. I dined at home. I had in the forenoon seen Tassie's collection of imitations of gems,[9] along with Mr. Lumisden and Sandy. I attended my daughters to Leicester Square, where they were to drink tea with Miss Douglases, and having met with Col. Phillips Glover,[1] who told me he was going to Bow Street to hear a noted bruiser[2] accused of an assault, examined by Justice Addington,[3] I went with him, but was not much amused. I then visited old Macklin, and sat with wonder hearing him talk distinctly of old stories. I drank tea at the Mount Coffee-house.

SATURDAY 4 SEPTEMBER. Dined at home. In the evening at Malone's revising Johnson's *Life*.

SUNDAY 5 SEPTEMBER. Had little Betsy brought home to breakfast. Took all my children with me to St. George's, Hanover Square, in the forenoon. Mr. Dilly and T.D.[4] dined and drank tea with us. I had of late dined very frequently at home. I was asked today to dine at Sir Joshua's. I went in the evening, played whist with some compunction as *contra bonos mores*[5] in this country, and supped.

MONDAY 6 SEPTEMBER. Dined at Malone's, a dinner made for my brother T.D. We had Sir Joshua Reynolds, Dr. Burney, Mr. Langley, Mr. Kemble, and Mr. Reed. An excellent day. T.D. was much pleased. I played whist and supped.

TUESDAY 7 SEPTEMBER. Went with T.D. and saw him into the Princess Royal stage-coach, which was to carry him to Carlisle. His steadiness and accuracy pleased me much. I dined at home.

WEDNESDAY 8 SEPTEMBER. Sandy returned to Eton. It vexed me to see him unwilling to go. I dined at home. I had now found that my *magnum opus* must be in two volumes.

---

[9]A huge collection of about 15,000 impressions of ancient and modern gems made and exhibited by James Tassie, a fellow Scotsman. Boswell was a subscriber to the printed catalogue, which appeared in 1791.

[1]A colonel of the North Lincolnshire Militia and deputy-lieutenant for Lincolnshire; he was a cousin of the poet Richard Glover.

[2]A prize-fighter.

[3]William (later Sir William) Addington, Justice of the Peace for Middlesex and magistrate of the public office in Bow Street.

[4]Boswell has inked out a few indecipherable words between "T.D." and "dined" in the manuscript.

[5]"Contrary to good morals." Card-playing on Sunday was frowned upon in Britain; it was condoned on the Continent.

THURSDAY 9 SEPTEMBER. Dined at Mr. Dilly's with Mr. Syms, Rev. Mr. Jones, Rev. Mr. Belsham, Dr. Gillies, Mr. Graham who married Mrs. Macaulay,[6] and I think three West Indians. A hearty day as usual at honest Dilly's table. I played two rubbers at whist and neither lost nor won. Then went to Sir Joshua's; played whist again, won, and supped. He entertained Dr. Laurence and Malone and me with a dialogue which he had composed between himself and Dr. Johnson.[7]

FRIDAY 10 SEPTEMBER. Dined at home. How the rest of the day was passed I do not recollect. My life at present, though for some time my health and spirits have been wonderfully good, is surely as idly spent as can almost be imagined. I merely attend to the progress of my *Life of Johnson*, and that by no means with great assiduity, such as that which Malone employs on Shakspeare. I am losing for myself and children all the enjoyment of a fine Place in the country. I am following no profession. I fear I am gradually losing any claim to preferment in the law in Scotland. But with the *consciousness* which I have of the nature of my own mind, I am sure that I am escaping innumerable hours of uneasiness which I should have were I in Scotland. I am in that great scene which I have ever contemplated with admiration, and in which there are continual openings for advantage.

[EDITORIAL NOTE. The journal, which ends here, does not mention that in late August, despite his negative feelings about Scotland, Boswell was attempting to make a major acquisition there. John Boswell of Knockroon, who had been involved in the failure of the banking-house Douglas, Heron, and Co. eighteen years earlier, was finally forced to sell his estate. This property had once been part of the lands of Auchinleck, and Boswell was determined to bring it back. On 25 August he approached William Forbes of Callendar for a loan. Knowing that Lord Dumfries, his powerful neighbour, was also interested in acquiring Knockroon, he declared that he would "give £500 more than its value rather than suffer it to go to a stranger." Besides, Knockroon had been "a patrimony to a younger son," and Boswell intended to follow this tradition by bequeathing the estate to Jamie.

Boswell had no liquid funds at this time, and his debts were considerable. Forbes of Callendar refused his request. But his helpful

---

[6]William Graham had married Mrs. Catharine Macaulay, twenty-five years his senior, in 1778. She was well-known for her *History of England* and also for her egalitarian views, which provoked Johnson to suggest that they ask her footman to dine with them.
[7]A brief parody in which Reynolds praises Garrick while Johnson—known for allowing no one to praise or blame Garrick without contradiction—criticizes him. In a subsequent companion piece, Reynolds has Gibbon attacking Garrick while Johnson—known also for freely contradicting himself—praises him.

Ayrshire neighbour Alexander Fairlie of Fairlie agreed to lend £1,500, and in mid-October Boswell was able to acquire the property, though at the very high price of £2,500.

Only brief notes cover the period from 11 September to 2 October.]

SATURDAY 11 SEPTEMBER. Sir Joshua's with Lord Eliot. Whist.

SUNDAY 12 SEPTEMBER. Home. Mrs. T.D. and mother.

MONDAY 13 SEPTEMBER. Intended Hicks's Hall[8] but found *Life* took up all time. Not well; dined home.

TUESDAY 14 SEPTEMBER. Ross's death; agitated. Busy. Dinner, home.

WEDNESDAY 15 SEPTEMBER. Settling Ross's funeral.[9] Jamie's birthday, dined home.

THURSDAY 16 SEPTEMBER. Dined home. Mr. and Mrs. and Miss Corri[1] and Jephson and Miss Douglases.

FRIDAY 17 SEPTEMBER. Ross's funeral. Printing-house. Dined Malone. Whist, Sir Joshua's: Lord Eliot, Langley, Laurence.

SATURDAY 18 SEPTEMBER. Walked into City; met Baldwin, asked to dine, comfortable. First sheet, two volume.[2] Sir Joshua's, whist: three hand;[3] then Malone.

SUNDAY 19 SEPTEMBER. St. George's service. Dined home. Malone's evening with Bourne, Jephson, etc.

MONDAY 20 SEPTEMBER. I and daughters dined Sir Joshua's. Malone, Mr. and Mrs. Kemble, Drs. Blagden and Laurence. Cards.

TUESDAY 21 SEPTEMBER. Dined home. Tea, music, etc., [at] Corri's.

WEDNESDAY 22 SEPTEMBER. Called at Sir Joshua's, asked to dine. Brocklesby, Malone, Laurence, Blagden.*.[4]

THURSDAY 23 SEPTEMBER. Dined home.

FRIDAY 24 SEPTEMBER.*. Found Dilly, dined with him; Syms came in. Sir Joshua's, cards, Laurence.

SATURDAY 25 SEPTEMBER. Walked out; called Sir Joshua's, asked to dine, only family. Cards. Miss A. Kirby and Malone.*.

SUNDAY 26 SEPTEMBER. St. George's forenoon; Miss Upton.[5] Jamie and I Chelsea in morning. Oxford Chapel afternoon. Mrs.

---

[8]The Middlesex Sessions House in Clerkenwell.

[9]Boswell made the arrangements, invited whatever friends of Ross's he could think of, served as chief mourner, probably wrote the obituary in the *Gentleman's Magazine*, and advanced £15. 3s. 3d. to cover the costs of the funeral.

[1]Domenico Corri, Italian musician and the Boswell girls' music-master, had just moved to London from Edinburgh, where Boswell had attended his concerts.

[2]Boswell was seeing the first sheet of the second volume of the *Life of Johnson*.

[3]Three-handed whist—a special form of the game usually played by four.

[4]A private symbol.

[5]Jane Upton, whom Boswell was beginning to admire in church.

Boswell, Mrs. and Major Green dinner and tea. Sleepy at night; bathed feet[6] and to bed.

MONDAY 27 SEPTEMBER. Dined home. Malone's evening, revised; very agreeable.

TUESDAY 28 SEPTEMBER. Dined home. Great company evening.

WEDNESDAY 29 SEPTEMBER. Dined home; Mr. Crawford from Ireland.[7] Evening, cards Sir Joshua's. Intoxicated a little.*.

THURSDAY 30 SEPTEMBER. Awaked very ill. Lay long. Dined Sir Joshua's: Malone, Laurence, Humphry. Cards.

FRIDAY 1 OCTOBER. Breakfasted Malone as usual. Printing-house. Dined Kemble: Sir Joshua and Miss P.,[8] Malone. Mr. and Mrs. Siddons[9] supped. Intoxicated somewhat.*.

SATURDAY 2 OCTOBER. Printing-house. Then to Westminster and took Jamie to Chelsea College and had a most comfortable dinner with Captain Grant; Dr. Burney and little Betsy there. Then Mrs. Hockley's.

[EDITORIAL NOTE. The notes end at this point, and so we must rely on letters and other accounts to follow Boswell's experiences between 3 October 1790 and 31 January 1791. These reveal that the printing of the *Life of Johnson* was progressing satisfactorily, if slowly, and that Boswell was coming to feel more confident, for the moment, both about the value and the financial possibilities of his work. He was pleased by a recent offer of £1,000 made by an unnamed bookseller but believed he could do better. Reporting that the first quarto volume was now printed, he wrote to Robert Boswell on 28 September: "I am a bold man to have refused *a cool thousand*. But my work may be called a view of literature and literary men in Great Britain for half a century.[1] His Majesty's gracious permission to publish the conversation with which he honoured Dr. Johnson is of great consequence. In truth, my work will contain several *morceaux* of uncommon value." A week later he was able to write to Sandy that fifty-six pages of the second volume were printed. He would

[6]One of Boswell's favourite indulgences.
[7]Recommended by Boswell's Irish cousin Margaret O'Reilly, Richard Crawford called, hoping that Boswell would provide introductions and other help to start a career in the East India trade.
[8]Miss Palmer.
[9]William Siddons, a minor actor, and his wife Sarah Siddons, the greatest actress of her time, who was painted by Reynolds as *The Tragic Muse*. She was Kemble's sister.
[1]Boswell later used this description on his title-page.

have to postpone his promised visit to Eton: "My *magnum opus*...requires my presence much." Still more optimistically, he declared to Sir William Forbes in a letter of 11 October: "I would not now accept of £1,500 for the property. Mr. Malone tells me I would get that but is clear I should refuse it. You cannot imagine what a rich and varied treasure it will contain." And in answer to Forbes's praise of life in the Scottish countryside, he added: "Pray do not blame me too much that I as yet shrink from quitting this great ocean,[2] on the surface of which I still see visions of hope."

When Boswell visited Sandy at Eton later in October, he again seized the opportunity to collect material for the *Life of Johnson*—this time from the well-known novelist Fanny Burney. A favourite of Dr. Johnson's, whom she had revered and who, in turn, admired her as the author of *Evelina* (1778) and *Cecilia* (1782), she was as indefatigable as Boswell in recording daily life in diaries and letters. At this time she was living at Windsor with the royal family as Second Keeper of the Queen's Robes. Boswell approached her at the gate of St. George's Chapel.

[From Fanny Burney's Diary, October 1790]

[BOSWELL.] "You must give me some of your choice little notes of the Doctor's; we have seen him long enough upon stilts; I want to show him in a new light. Grave Sam, and great Sam, and solemn Sam, and learned Sam—all these he has appeared over and over. Now I want to entwine a wreath of the graces across his brow; I want to show him as gay Sam, agreeable Sam, pleasant Sam; so you must help me with some of his beautiful billets to yourself."

I evaded this by declaring I had not any stores at hand. He proposed a thousand curious expedients to get at them, but I was invincible....

He then told me his *Life of Dr. Johnson* was nearly printed, and took a proof-sheet out of his pocket to show me; with crowds passing and repassing, knowing me well, and staring well at him; for we were now at the iron rails of the Queen's Lodge.

I stopped; I could not ask him in: I saw he expected it, and was reduced to apologize, and tell him I must attend the Queen immediately....But finding he had no chance of entering, he stopped me again at the gate, and said he would read me a part of his work.

[2]A reference to London.

There was no refusing this, and he began, with a letter of Dr. Johnson's to himself. He read it in strong imitation of the Doctor's manner, very well, and not caricature. But Mrs. Schwellenberg[3] was at her window, a crowd was gathering to stand round the rails, and the King and Queen and royal family now approached from the terrace. I made a rather quick apology, and, with a step as quick as my now weakened limbs have left in my power, I hurried to my apartment.

You may suppose I had inquiries enough, from all around, of "Who was the gentleman I was talking to at the rails?" And an injunction rather frank not to admit him beyond those limits.

However, I saw him again the next morning, in coming from early prayers, and he again renewed...his petition for my letters of Dr. Johnson.

I cannot consent to print private letters, even of a man so justly celebrated, when addressed to myself; no, I shall hold sacred those revered and but too scarce testimonies of the high honour his kindness conferred upon me.[4]

Boswell attracted public notice in a very different forum when he performed his own ballad, "William Pitt, the Grocer of London," at the Lord Mayor's Feast in the Guildhall on 9 November. At this elaborate celebration honouring the newly elected Lord Mayor, John Boydell, the chief guest was the Prime Minister, who had just managed to end a major international crisis. For several months, the dispute with Spain about Nootka Sound and British trading rights on the north-west coast of America had seemed to be leading inescapably to war. But then Pitt's envoy persuaded Spain to agree to a Convention that granted Britain the contested trading rights, and the text of the agreement was made public on the morning of Lord Mayor's Day. To mark the occasion, Boswell hastily composed a ballad, set to the tune of Charles Dibdin's "Poor Jack," in which he extolled the Prime Minister as "The Grocer of London," Pitt being an honorary member of the Grocers' Company.

---

[3]The tyrannical Elizabeth Juliana Schwellenberg, First Keeper of the Queen's Robes and Fanny Burney's immediate superior.
[4]*Diary and Letters of Madame d'Arblay,* ed. Charlotte Barrett and Austin Dobson, iv. 431–33. True to her convictions, Fanny Burney did not provide Boswell with any Johnson letters.

WILLIAM PITT
THE GROCER OF LONDON

Fell[5] faction be silent, and clamour no more
    Against Government, laws, and the times,
Our glory triumphant from shore sounds to shore,
    There's both reason and truth in my rhymes.

Let no dark suspicion our bosoms invade,
    And make gloomy November more dull;
There's a GROCER of LONDON who watches our trade,
    And takes care of th'estate of JOHN BULL.

There's a Grocer of London,
A Grocer of London,
A Grocer of London who watches our trade,
And takes care of th'estate of JOHN BULL.

Though fleets in vain-boasting hostility ride,
    Still BRITAIN is queen of the main;
The secret well kept now comes forth with due pride;
    And lo! a Convention with Spain!

Too noble to brag, as we're never afraid,
    'Tis enough that we've had a good pull.[6]
There's a GROCER of LONDON who watches our trade,
    And takes care of th'estate of JOHN BULL.

There's a Grocer of London,
A Grocer of London,
A Grocer of London who watches our trade,
And takes care of th'estate of JOHN BULL.

Although Pitt appears to have left before the singing, Boswell's presentation of his ballad was clearly one of the high points of the evening.
The *Public Advertiser* of 11 November, which published the ballad, mentioned several encores as well as the fact that "the author's health was
twice drunk with three cheers standing."

In this instance Boswell was trying to do more than merely entertain. Still eager to serve in Parliament, he apparently hoped that his
laudatory ballad would win him Pitt's support if, as was rumoured, Sir
Adam Fergusson would give up his seat as M.P. for Ayrshire and ac

[5]Fierce.
[6]A trial by strength.

cept a Government post. But Pitt was not inclined to be helpful, and then Fergusson did not relinquish his seat after all.

Boswell's life of pleasant sociability continued, as is revealed in a series of informative letters to Malone, who left for Ireland in early December after finally completing his Shakespeare edition. On 4 December Boswell reported: "I have dined with Jack Wilkes at the London Tavern after the launch of an Indiaman—with dear Edwards[7]—Dilly—at home with Courtenay—Dr. Barrow—at the mess of the Coldstream—at The Club—at Warren Hastings's—at Hawkins the Cornish Member's—and at home with a colonel of the Guards, etc." At these dinners he had kept the promise he had made to Courtenay that until the first of March—that is, when the *Life of Johnson* would be completed—he would not drink more wine than "four good glasses at dinner, and a pint after it." He was pleased to have received long letters from Bennet Langton describing Johnson's visit in 1778 to the militia at Warley Common and offering other Johnson material. He was also pleased by a return visit from Warren Hastings, from whom he had finally received the promised Johnson letters and, better still—indeed, setting "the diamonds in pure gold of Ophir"—a letter from Hastings about Johnson as well. Boswell could furthermore tell Malone that he and Burke were on easier terms again. On the other hand, he was embarrassed to find that General Burgoyne, veteran of the American war[8] and successful dramatist, whom he had proposed for membership in The Club, was blackballed by three members.

Still, Boswell seems to have been in an exceptionally good mood at this time. "I am in great spirits," he wrote to Temple in a brief note of 24 November, in which he also advised his friend not to let his daughter Nancy refuse the seemingly advantageous match being proposed by the Rev. Charles Powlett, whose father was the illegitimate son of the late Duke of Bolton and the actress Lavinia Fenton, the original Polly in Gay's *Beggar's Opera*. Boswell himself was still thinking of matrimony, and was clearly unwilling to accept Temple's recent warning that he should "abandon the thoughts of a union with some female, young, fair, and wealthy." As Temple had

---

[7]Almost certainly Oliver Edwards, a lawyer and college friend of Johnson's, remembered for explaining that he had tried to be a philosopher, "but, I don't know how, cheerfulness was always breaking in" (*Life of Johnson*, 17 April 1778).
[8]Boswell prided himself on having interviewed Gen. John Burgoyne in May 1778 immediately following his return to England after capitulating to the Americans at Saratoga.

asked pointedly on 18 October, "Where will you find such an one, who will resign herself to fifty and a family of almost grown men and women? It is in vain to dream of the northern charmer;[9] she has far different ideas, and even success with her would be misery. Would it not be more advisable to continue to amuse your girls and endeavour to procure them suitable husbands?" Undaunted, Boswell now indulged in romantic fantasies about Miss Upton, whom he knew only from sitting near her at St. George's, Hanover Square, during Sunday morning services. In December he wrote to Sir Michael Le Fleming, reminding him of a promise to arrange an introduction. He was also inspired to write an elegant little poem, undated but very likely of this period:

LOVE AT CHURCH

When in St. George's hallowed dome,
Upton, thy pleasing form I see,
My fluttering thoughts, too apt to roam,
Are wholly fixed on heaven and thee.

And let not cold, censorious age
Call me irreverent and light;
Read we not in the sacred page
That duty should with joy unite?

In grateful notes my voice I raise,
And earnestly beholding you,
While chanting my Creator's praise,
Creation's fairest work I view.

Devotion thus my love can raise,
In this I trust there is no sin;
As marriages in heaven are made,
A courtship may at church begin.

Such sentimental fancies did not, however, prevent Boswell from paying attention to more practical matters. On the recommendation of T.D., now at Auchinleck, Boswell appointed a well-meaning young man, Andrew Gibb, to succeed James Bruce as overseer of the estate. Boswell insisted on frequent reports from Gibb, as he had earlier from Bruce, and in return sent full instructions concerning all aspects of estate management.

[9]Isabella Wilson of Newcastle.

ANDREW:—From the account which my brother gives me of you, I am hopeful that you will act faithfully and diligently in my service....I expect to receive a letter from you at least once a week, informing me what you and others employed by me are doing. And as you have now a considerable charge for so young a man, you must endeavour to show yourself worthy of it, and to make yourself more and more fit for it.

I am very anxious that all things about Auchinleck should be kept in good repair and not suffer by my absence. You must therefore be particularly careful to stop all persons who attempt to pass through my parks and plantations...but see that they keep to the patent public roads. If any persons insist to pass and accordingly do so, let me have a list of their names and I will order them to be prosecuted.

You must also frequently visit the different farms upon the estate and mark down whether the tenants have managed them according to their leases; and when you see the houses or fences in any degree of disrepair, give notice to have them made sufficient in the space of a week, and if the tenants fail to comply, do you get it done and take receipts from the workmen that the expense may be paid along with the next term's rent. Lay down a determined resolution to act without partiality or love of popularity except what you may acquire by being just between man and man.

These admonitions were followed by specific instructions about payments to be made to and by Gibb, about a tenant's request for grazing privileges, and even about a carpet to be brought from the church to the house to prevent its being ruined by dampness.

Moreover, Boswell was active in support of friends and acquaintances. He translated General Paoli's speech to the General Assembly of Corsica for the 30 November issue of the *London Chronicle*. And he had himself quoted in the *Public Advertiser* of 9 December on the regrettable public indifference to the plight of Warren Hastings, whose trial was dragging on.

Yet Boswell's mood was changing. In January, his zestful good spirits, which had been with him ever since he recovered from his break with Lonsdale, gave way to increasing gloom. He was finding his work on the *Life of Johnson* interminable, and he missed Malone's help, advice, and restraining influence. Although the printing had been progressing at a steady rate—to page 216 of the second volume by 4 December, page 256 by 16 December, page 376 by 18 January—the material was expanding in Shandean fashion as new information had to be inserted. "I have yet near two hundred pages of copy besides letters and *the death,* which is not yet written," he complained to Malone on the 18th. "Your absence is a woeful want in all respects....My spirits are at present bad." On 29 January he wrote to Malone in still deeper depression: "You will find this a most desponding and disagreeable letter, for which I ask your pardon. But your vigour of mind and warmth of heart make your friendship of such consequence that it is drawn upon like a bank. I have for some weeks had the most woeful return of melancholy, insomuch that I have not only had no relish of anything but a continual uneasiness, and all the prospect before me for the rest of life has seemed gloomy and hopeless."

Apart from reflecting Boswell's general frustration—his feeling that he was going nowhere on all fronts—these letters to Malone also reveal a further cause of Boswell's despondency: his pressing financial problems. Payment of the £500 he had borrowed in 1781 to lend to Bruce Boswell, a former East India captain, was now due. His cousin was as insolvent as ever, but Boswell had to repay his own loan in instalments starting in 1791. In addition, he had to raise £1,000 immediately in part-payment for Knockroon. So disturbed was he by these claims that he considered selling the copyright of the *Life of Johnson* for 1,000 guineas, the more so as the profits from this work were coming to seem uncertain. But he could not make up his mind and begged Malone for advice: "Pray decide for me....In my present state of spirits, I am all timidity. Your absence has been a severe stroke to me. I am at present quite at a loss what to do."

Amid these anxieties, Boswell signed a lease for modest chambers in the Inner Temple to have a base for the law practice he still hoped to develop. In addition, he moved himself and his family from 38 Queen Anne Street West to new quarters at 47 Great Portland Street. Jamie liked it[1]—especially the closet space—but Boswell found it less comfortable. Complaining to Sandy on 31 January about "such bad spirits that I know not what to do," the burden of working on the *Life of Johnson,* and the absence of Malone, he added: "I get

---

[1]Euphemia, too, appears to have been happy in Great Portland Street. She returned to the neighbourhood after being confined in an asylum for many years, spent her last days at no. 48, and died there in 1837.

hardly any sleep, which is hard. I am still in the front parlour, and it is very noisy." He was to live at Great Portland Street for the rest of his life.

Boswell resumed the journal on 1 February 1791 with the following note: "After a long cessation, I now endeavour to resume keeping a journal at a time when my spirits are very bad. I shall begin with the first day of this month."]

1791

TUESDAY 1 FEBRUARY. Felt myself quite dejected and fretful. Sat awhile with Seward and heard his nephew talk of the manner in which his mother (Seward's sister) was affected with hypochondria. I had the week before dined at Sir Joshua Reynolds's, Lord Falmouth's, and the Bishop of London's[2] without much relief; so thought today of sending an excuse to Lord Lucan's, where I was engaged. Went, however, and was pleased (so far as I was capable) with Lord and Lady Lucan and Miss Bingham. The other guests were Lord Mulgrave, Sir Joshua Reynolds, and Mr. Craufurd of Auchenames and the Bishop of Clonfert (Marlay).[3] I could only force a decent appearance. I went home with Sir Joshua and played whist; Dr. Blagden and Metcalfe there. Lost a guinea, which in my poor state vexed me. Went to sleep tonight in my back drawing-room, having been harassed with noise in the front parlour where I had slept hitherto.

WEDNESDAY 2 FEBRUARY.[4] Had rested better. After breakfast

[2]George Evelyn Boscawen, third Viscount Falmouth, was a member of an ancient, wealthy Cornish family and a friend of Temple's. Beilby Porteus, D.D., had been Bishop of London since 1787; he was known for favouring strict religious observances and for opposing both slavery and the French Revolution.

[3]Apart from the Lucans' daughter, the Hon. Anne Bingham, the company included old acquaintances: Constantine John Phipps, second Baron Mulgrave, M.P., who in 1773 as a naval officer had headed an expedition that tried to find a northern passage to India; John Craufurd, nicknamed "Fish" since his Eton days, until recently M.P. for Glasgow Burghs; and Richard Marlay, D.D., a long-time member of The Club, now Bishop of Clonfert and later of Waterford. Boswell expressed his appreciation of Lord and Lady Lucan in the *Life of Johnson* (preceding 22 June 1784), noting that at their house Johnson had "found hospitality united with extraordinary accomplishments, and embellished with charms of which no man could be insensible."

[4]Boswell inadvertently dated this entry 3 February and the next entry 4 February.

called on Kemble to get a note of Johnson's conversation with Mrs. Siddons.[5] Talked of my bad spirits. He kindly asked me to dine quietly with him. I went to the printing-house, a cold, raw day; had no pleasure from my book. Had in the morning visited Paradise and compared notes with him on hypochondria, which he said I described perfectly;[6] also sat awhile with T.D., whose steady sense pleased me. I had a comfortable though sick-minded day at Kemble's; only Mr. Siddons there. Was very sober, and played two rubbers at sixpenny whist. Came home about ten and sat an hour and a half with Mr. and Mrs. Wood, who were with my daughters.

THURSDAY 3 FEBRUARY. Kemble came to me in the morning and made out a note of Dr. Johnson's conversation with Mrs. Siddons for my book. He encouraged me to hope that there would be a great sale, of which I now was despairing. Sat at home and laboured at *Life* all the evening.

FRIDAY 4 FEBRUARY. Walked about in dejection. Happened to meet Dr. Blagden, and went home with him and made my complaints of *tedium* and unhappiness. I found he had been affected in the same manner. He had *provincial* notions, and advised me to go and live at Auchinleck. Talking with him insensibly did me some good, and I came home rather better. Sat again at home all the evening, getting a good deal of Johnson's *Life* (now advanced to its last year) ready for the press. For the first time these several weeks felt some degree of comfort when I went to bed.

SATURDAY 5 FEBRUARY. Courtenay had been in town some days, and I had called on him twice, but did not see him till today when I met him in the street. He gave me *some* animation. I went early to Sir William Scott and settled with him how I should mention Lord Thurlow's application to the King to enable Johnson to go abroad, and its failure.[7] I *groaned* to Sir William. He said he wished he was free as I

[5]When Mrs. Siddons visited Johnson in October 1783, they talked amiably about plays and acting. Boswell reproduced Kemble's note in the *Life of Johnson* (October 1783).

[6]In some of Boswell's anonymous essays, entitled *The Hypochondriack*, published in the *London Magazine* (1777–83).

[7]In his last year, Johnson, feeling unwell, thought he might prolong his life by spending the winter in Italy. A group of his friends, headed by Boswell and Reynolds, approached the King through the Lord Chancellor, Lord Thurlow, asking for an augmentation of Johnson's pension. When the King rejected their plea, Thurlow tactfully offered a "loan," actually a gift, out of his own pocket to pay Johnson's expenses. Boswell reprinted the letter in which Johnson gratefully declined Thurlow's offer, and commented only: "Upon this unexpected failure I abstain from presuming to make any remarks or to offer any conjectures" (*Life of Johnson*, 9 September 1784).

was; he was tired of business. All seemed dark. I found Dilly at breakfast in his kitchen and shared with him. He did not raise my hopes high of the sale of my book. I called on Mr. Forbes, who was ill of the gout and confined to his room, and sat a good while with Mrs. Forbes.[8] Went to Johnson's in St. Paul's Churchyard,[9] and saw two publications to quote from in Johnson's *Life*. Wright, the printer, happened to come in and named me,[1] and afterwards Johnson asked me when my book was to be ready. I told him in about a month, but that there would be too much of it. "Oh no," said he, "it will be very entertaining." I was twice at the printing-house. I hastened home to dress to dine at Cator's,[2] but found the card was for next Saturday. Being agitated for going out, I could not stay at home, and sallied forth. I went to Sir Joshua's, but he was gone to dine out. I then sauntered into the Park, and walked down to Dean's Yard and inquired for my son James. But he had gone home some time before. This was lucky, for I did intend to have taken him with me to some coffee-house or eating-house to dinner, which was teaching him a bad custom. I hesitated where to go, and at length satisfied myself with drinking tea at the Hungerford Coffee-house,[3] a very comfortable one where I had never been before. I whiled away time, called on old Macklin and missed him, went to Sir Joseph Banks's Conversation;[4] soon tired, came home (after sitting some time with my brother, who had this evening at last a letter from Dundas telling him that he was to have the vacant place of a clerk in the Navy Pay Office);[5] found Mrs. Paradise with my daughters; was in bad humour and too violent with Veronica. A sad life. Seeing my son James now quite reconciled to Westminster School was some comfort to me.

[8]John Forbes, a banker, and his wife Joanna were both related to Boswell: Forbes was a cousin on the Boswell side; one of Mrs. Forbes's grandmothers was a half-sister of Boswell's mother, Euphemia Erskine.

[9]Joseph Johnson was a well-established bookseller and publisher. The centre of a group of social reformers including William Godwin and Mary Wollstonecraft, he published Blake—a friend whom he helped to establish as a writer—Cowper, and Wordsworth but withdrew from the printing of the second part of Paine's *Rights of Man* when that appeared too dangerously radical.

[1]Addressed him by name. Thomas Wright was a printer in Essex Street, the Strand.

[2]John Cator was a wealthy timber-merchant, rough and pompous in manner. Johnson praised his business sense and Boswell his hospitality.

[3]In the Strand.

[4]One of the daily gatherings at which the hospitable Banks, as President of the Royal Society, encouraged scientists and other socially prominent guests to mingle.

[5]A modest position with a salary of about £100 a year. Dundas was finally making good the promise to take care of T.D. that he had made to the dying Lord Auchinleck in 1782.

SUNDAY 6 FEBRUARY. Veronica went to Fitzroy Chapel with Mrs. Wood. Euphemia and James and I tried to get a seat in St. George's, but could not, and they were equally unsuccessful in the afternoon. I sat awhile with Seward. It made me uneasy when he asked whether I did not go to church now; was my faith wavering? I dined at Earl Fife's, where were Lord Kellie, Lord Torphichen, the young Laird of Grant, Colonel Colquhoun, and Mr. Bosville. It was dull work, and Scottish sensations disgusted me.[6] I was quite as if dining in Edinburgh. I for the first time was at Lady Lucan's tea, and saw a great deal of good company, but had little enjoyment.

MONDAY 7 FEBRUARY. Not at all well. Dined at home. Went in the evening to the Free and Easy Club at the Thatched House. Played whist and came home at eleven. Lost only a shilling.

TUESDAY 8 FEBRUARY. Was at printing-house. Dined at Literary Club. It was "stale, flat, and unprofitable."[7] Charles Fox was there, and my gloom made even him appear insipid.[8] Went home with Sir Joshua, and appeared so dull that Dick Burke addressed me in a line which I do not recollect:

Shake off this vile disease, etc.[9]

I played whist and lost nineteen shillings. Felt myself shrink from London and all its society. I believe I should have stolen away to Auchinleck had I not recollected the ambitious thoughts which I had all my life indulged, and which seemed now to be totally blasted.

WEDNESDAY 9 FEBRUARY. Intended to have worked hard at my *Life*, but called on Courtenay, and he prevailed with me to saunter about with him. We called on Wilkes but did not find him. I could not go home to dine, being once set agog. Found Sir Joshua and Miss Palmer by themselves. Had some degree of relief, but it did not last. They went to Mr. Burke's and I to the Essex Head Club, which was more numerous than usual.

THURSDAY 10 and FRIDAY 11 FEBRUARY have escaped my recollection.

---

[6]The company consisted almost entirely of Scotsmen: Earl Fife; Archibald Erskine, seventh Earl of Kellie, the brother of Boswell's old friend Andrew Erskine; James Sandilands, ninth Lord Torphichen; Lewis Alexander Grant; and Lt.-Col. William Colquhoun.

[7]*Hamlet*, I. ii. 133.

[8]Charles James Fox, leader of the Opposition, was known for his great wit and charm.

[9]Richard Burke, Edmund Burke's brother, was an acquaintance from Reynolds's dinners. His quotation has not been identified.

SATURDAY 12 FEBRUARY. Dined at Mr. Cator's in the Adelphi[1] with a numerous company: Sir Lionel Lloyd; Mr. Duncan Davidson,[2] wife, son, and two daughters; Dr. Vincent, Master of Westminster School, and Mrs. Vincent; Mr. Seward, etc. Large rooms, many servants, a plentiful board and all its concomitants, dispelled the black vapours for some time. Dr. Vincent's tranquillity and steady conversation pleased me. I played whist and lost seventeen shillings. Seward and I sat some time after the company was gone.

SUNDAY 13 FEBRUARY. My two daughters and little James and I went to Portland Chapel; found it comfortless. T.D. dined with us on beef and pudding and porter. I went in the evening again to Lady Lucan's. Had no relish of it. Was however soothed by a good deal of conversation with Sir Harry Englefield about painting and Sir Joshua and Dr. Johnson.[3]

MONDAY 14 FEBRUARY. My worthy printer Baldwin endeavoured to cheer me with hopes that my *Life of Johnson* might be profitable, though Steevens had thrown cold water on my hopes.[4] He kindly gave me his family dinner and some mountain, and I was somewhat cheered. I drank tea by appointment with the corrector of his press, Mr. Tomlins, who, having contracted debt, was obliged to quit the bar, and was now honestly getting his livelihood by *certain* diligence.[5] He showed me a good part of an index to my *Life of Johnson,* which he had offered to make, and offering to do it very reasonably, had been desired by me to go on with it. I intended to *prefix* it as an *Alphabetical Table of Contents* to make my first volume more equal with my second, which had swelled much beyond my computation.[6] I talked freely with him of my yet endeavouring to get into practice at the bar. He advised

[1]One of the best addresses in London—a terrace of elegant houses built by the Adam brothers and located between the Strand and the Thames.

[2]Duncan Davidson of Tulloch was Justice of the Peace and Deputy-Lieutenant for Ross and Cromarty; he had just been elected M.P.

[3]A man of fashion still in his thirties, Sir Henry Charles Englefield—an antiquarian and writer on scientific subjects—had recently become a frequent companion of Reynolds's.

[4]"Steevens *kindly* tells me that I have overprinted, and that the curiosity about Johnson is *now* only in our own circle" (Boswell to Malone, 29 January 1791). George Steevens, who had re-edited Johnson's Shakespeare, was known for his spitefulness and anonymous attacks in print on his friends.

[5]Thomas Edlyne Tomlins had been a barrister of the Inner Temple and had written two legal works. A few years after this meeting his fortunes improved; he served as counsel to several Government officials and was subsequently knighted.

[6]Even though the Alphabetical Table of Contents takes up fifteen pages, the first volume is fifty-two pages shorter than the second.

me as soon as my great work was published to have it understood that I was now to apply closely to business, and to prove this by a constant attendance in Westminster Hall; and he said that by reading the recent reports and books of practice, I might be in condition to do very well. I *yet* was somewhat encouraged, though I *now* shrunk from all labour. Found Murphy at Elmsley's shop, who had written a concise *Life of Johnson* to be prefixed to his works.[7]

TUESDAY 15 FEBRUARY. I was still sadly ill. I went between three and four and called on Wilkes, who was not yet come from the City. I said I would look for him, and I luckily spied him in the Park, walking home. When I joined him near to the passage up to his house in Prince's Court, he kindly said, "Come along," and asked me where I dined today. "With you," said I, "if you'll give me leave." He made me very welcome. I told him and Miss Wilkes of my being in bad spirits, and that I wished to try if he could animate me. I soon felt *some* relief. There was nobody there. I had a dispensation from Courtenay, to whom I had promised in December to restrict myself till the first of March to drink no more than four glasses and a pint of wine a day. I took today about a bottle and a half. I had a momentary elevation. The perpetual gaiety of Wilkes amazed me. But the inarticulation both of him and his daughter *strained my ears*.[8] His love of books and prints seemed as eager as ever. He told me one of his lively sayings lately. He complimented Rose, the Recorder of London, on being made a Knight: "For," said he, "your wife will be a Lady, and we shall have young Roses—*Quocunque calcaveris Rosa erit*—wherever you *tread*."[9] A young upholsterer from the Isle of Wight came in the evening and drank a glass or two with us, and then we drank tea with Miss Wilkes; and I was asked to come again on Friday and dine at *three*[1] and meet this upholsterer, a smart little fellow. I came home heated.

WEDNESDAY 16 FEBRUARY. Was no better.

THURSDAY 17 FEBRUARY. As before, still sore and fretful. Wet weather. In the evening had a pretty little cold *souper* at Seward's with Madame Boissac, who had been a singer at the Opera at Lyons, a little

[7]Murphy's *Essay on the Life and Genius of Dr. Johnson* appeared in the 1792 edition of Johnson's *Works*. Peter Elmsley was a bookseller and publisher in the Strand.

[8]Mary ("Polly") Wilkes, who was her father's closest companion, was suffering from extreme hoarseness that lasted for several months. In what sense Wilkes, too, suffered from "inarticulation" is unclear.

[9]Sir John William Rose had been knighted the preceding November. Wilkes was quoting Persius, *Satires*, ii. 38: "Quidquid calcaverit hic, rosa fiat: Wherever he treads, may roses bloom" and punning on "tread" in the sense of "copulate."

[1]An old-fashioned time for dining; most people dined closer to five o'clock.

neat Frenchwoman with animal spirits and rapid talk that seemed wonderful to me in my present state, and M.———, a French painter and engraver. A little eating and wine and talk and singing gave me a slight respite.

[EDITORIAL NOTE. Courtenay, who was present at this party, wrote to Malone on 22 February: "Poor Boswell is very low and dispirited and almost melancholy mad—feels no spring, no pleasure in existence—and is so perceptibly altered for the worse that it is remarked everywhere. I try all I can to rouse him but he recurs so tiresomely and tediously to the same cursed, trite, commonplace topics about death, etc.—that we grow old, and when we are old we are not young—that I despair of effecting a cure. Dr. Warren and Devaynes very kindly interest themselves about him, but you would be of more service to him than anybody is....Seward gave B. a supper t'other night (a French pie)—the company an opera-singer and a young French architect—yet it did not do. He complains like Solomon that "all is vanity.""[2]]

FRIDAY 18 FEBRUARY. Old Mr. Ross Mackye having asked me for today to meet the Hon. and Rev. W. Stuart, I sent an excuse to Wilkes and had a tolerable day, just we three. I drank about a bottle and a half. But there was no real or permanent relief. Stuart told me Lord Macartney had taken notice how changed I was.[3]

SATURDAY 19 FEBRUARY. Dejected and miserable.

SUNDAY 20 FEBRUARY. Had dreamed that my little daughter Betsy was dead, and I awaked half crying. I had not seen her for a long time, not since I moved into my house in Great Portland Street. I sent out for her directly and, when she came, was pleased with her appearance and English accent. I took her and little James with me and paid a visit to Lady Strange.[4] There I met my friend Dilly, and took a walk with him into Lincoln's Inn Fields, being in great despondency as to *Life of Johnson*. He told me that Stockdale[5] told him it had been depreciated and, on being pressed, owned that Steevens had

[2]Ecclesiastes 1: 2.

[3]The Hon. and Rev. William Stuart, vicar of Luton, Bedfordshire, described by Boswell as "an exemplary parish priest" (*Life of Johnson*, 10 April 1783)—he later became Bishop of St. David's and then Archbishop of Armagh—was Macartney's brother-in-law. Stuart was the fifth son of the Earl of Bute.

[4]Isabella, Lady Strange was the wife of the engraver Sir Robert Strange and the sister of Andrew Lumisden. Boswell had consulted her frequently in 1786 about moving to London, and he had then lived near the Stranges in Great Queen Street for almost three years.

[5]John Stockdale, a bookseller and publisher in Piccadilly.

talked against it. It vexed me to think that this malicious man had, I feared, access to it at the printing-house. Good Dilly advised me to accept of the £1,000 which I was now informed by a letter from Malone had been talked of for it by *Robinson*.[6] I apprehended Malone had been too sanguine in imagining it had been *offered*. I was unwilling to separate myself as an author from Dilly, with whom my name had been so long connected, though he in the most friendly manner pressed it, notwithstanding he should lose seven and a half per cent agency on publication.[7] My great tribulation was being *obliged* to lay down £1,000 for Knockroon more than the £1,500 which I was to have from Mr. Fairlie upon its security; which, if I failed to do, I should be disgraced and vexatiously lose the purchase. Yet Malone had raised my hopes high of the success of my work, and if it did succeed, the quarto edition alone would yield me above £1,200.

I went with my three daughters and little James to Portland Chapel. I was in wretched spirits. I dined at Dr. Warren's. His lady was ill and remained in the drawing-room, and the company was his two daughters, five of his sons, and a Captain Maude[8] of the Horse Guards. It was not a vivid day. I was *not myself*. I had only two Boswellian fancies.[9] Warren told that the Chancellor had taken a fancy that he was fond of music and understood it, and went to the Ancient Music. But that he had got no farther in the knowledge of sounds than to distinguish between the braying of an ass and the bleating of a sheep. "Well," said I, "*that* is *ancient* music." It was said that the King's being such a patron of it might make the Chancellor seem to like it. "Then," said I, "he has not only the King's *conscience*, but his *ear*."[1] We did not dine till past six. I eat and drank of too many things, which disturbed my stomach, and I was ill when I came home.

[6]George Robinson, a prominent bookseller and publisher, who bought up copyrights and was said to pay his authors well.

[7]Boswell had been associated with Charles Dilly and his older brother Edward since 1768, when they had published the *Account of Corsica*. Agency here means commission.

[8]A phonetic spelling; Collett Mawhood was captain in the 2nd Regiment of Life Guards.

[9]*Bons mots.*

[1]Between February and May twelve Concerts of Ancient Music were performed under royal patronage at the New Rooms in Tottenham Street. Boswell's witticism about ancient music depends on the Biblical association of the braying of the ass and the bleating of the sheep, perhaps recalling I Samuel 15: 14: "What meaneth then this bleating of the sheep in mine ears, and the lowing of the oxen which I hear?" The second witticism depends on the traditional view of the Chancellor as "the keeper of the King's conscience," perhaps because in earlier times he had also been the King's chaplain.

MONDAY 21 FEBRUARY. During this dismal mist of mind, I one day sat a part of the morning with Mrs. Fitzgerald. I several times sat a little while with my brother T.D., whose good sense and orderly activity consoled yet mortified me. Courtenay was truly friendly and showed me much kindness. He now lodged within a few doors of me.[2] I was very ill today. The embarrassed state of my affairs overwhelmed my spirits. Yet here was Courtenay with a wife and seven children, and not a shilling. But the blasting of all my ambitious hopes was galling. I however still had glimpses of hope. I abhorred my new house, from my having been dismal ever since I came into it. My two daughters who were with me seemed in so ill-governed a state, and with so little prospect of being in a better, and they both, but especially the second, had so little respect for me (as indeed how could they for a sickly-minded wretch?) that I was irritated by their behaviour and wished earnestly to have them stationed somewhere with propriety at a distance from me. I was at home all day.

TUESDAY 22 FEBRUARY. Though resolved against entertaining for a long time, I had fixed to give Courtenay some hodgepodge[3] today. I had a note from him that he would be kept late in the House of Commons, so I should not wait. His son and T.D. dined with us about half past six. Mrs. Sharp, a maiden lady, great-granddaughter of the Archbishop of St. Andrews,[4] drank tea with us. After she and the two others were gone, Courtenay came about ten and had his hodgepodge and bit of roast beef, and obligingly assisted me in *lightening* my animadversions on Mrs. Piozzi in my *Life of Johnson*[5]—for my own credit. His manly mind conveyed to me some sympathic force.

WEDNESDAY 23 FEBRUARY. Not at all well. At home till the evening, when Courtenay sent for me to come and sit with him and not mope by myself, when my daughters and his son were at Signor Corri's. I went, but for a time was quite ineffective and could hardly speak. I became somewhat easier, and drank a little mountain. I contemplated his firmness with wonder. He insisted that my daughters should eat oysters with him, and accordingly his son brought them to

---

[2]Courtenay had recently moved from Bryanston Street to Great Portland Street.

[3]A stew consisting of mutton and vegetables.

[4]The Archbishop, James Sharp, had been murdered in 1679 by Covenanters, Presbyterian extremists whose activities he had tried to limit. In calling his great-granddaughter "Mrs." Boswell uses the courtesy title for unmarried women of a certain age.

[5]Boswell toned down his criticism of Mrs. Piozzi's *Anecdotes of the Late Samuel Johnson* by concentrating on her inaccuracies (*Life of Johnson*, 1 July 1784) and by omitting the passages in which he had accused her of dishonesty, social climbing, and reaping financial profit from her publication of Johnson's letters.

us about eleven, and I felt myself a little cheered. He had suggested that I should ask the Chancellor to make me a Commissioner of Bankrupts, and was for my trying Westminster Hall resolutely; and, on my mentioning it, thought Hamilton might introduce me to the Chief Baron, Eyre.[6] So here were schemes.

THURSDAY 24 FEBRUARY. The day was fine. I felt a respite. An invitation came to dine next day at Mr. Dance's.[7] I dined at home. Little James was with us, it being a whole holiday. He went in the evening. I became suddenly so well that I wished to go into company and be gay. But restrained myself and laboured at *Life*.

FRIDAY 25 FEBRUARY. Not quite so well. But a letter which I had, I think yesterday, from my dear and valuable friend Temple animated me by suggesting that my friends would at last do something for me; advising me to cultivate them, and let *hope travel on*.[8] I dined at Mr. Dance's with his brother the City architect, Sir Joshua Reynolds and Miss Palmer, Serjeant Rooke and his lady and a young lady, her relation, Hon. Mrs. Boscawen, Laundress to the Queen,[9] and Mr. Drew the attorney. It was a curious scene to me to behold Dance, whom I had known at Rome in 1765 by no means in a great situation, now married to a lady of a jointure of £10,000 a year (Mrs. Dummer), a genteel, well-bred, agreeable woman, with all the magnificence of wealth.[1] I looked back also to my old friend his brother, Love the player,[2] and I now for the first time met George the architect, of whom I had heard Love often speak. It was not pleasing to find that Sir Joshua had all this time known that I was in sad spirits, and never once called or sent to inquire about me. We must take our friends as they are. "Courtenay has a *heart*."[3] I enjoyed the good things and the *English conversation* of

[6]Sir James Eyre was Lord Chief Baron of the Court of Exchequer. There were more than sixty commissioners of bankrupts, and two vacancies at this time.

[7]Nathaniel Dance was a successful portrait-painter. He later assumed the name of Holland and was created Baronet.

[8]Pope, *An Essay on Man*, ii. 274: "Hope travels thro', nor quits us when we die."

[9]The guests included George Dance, architect and clerk of the City Works, who had redesigned Newgate prison and other public buildings; Giles Rooke, a serjeant-at-law (a high-ranking barrister); and Anne Boscawen, niece of Adm. Edward Boscawen and first cousin to Viscount Falmouth, at this time Sempstress and Laundress to the Queen, who had earned the style "the Honourable" when serving as one of the Queen's maids of honour.

[1]As a young man Nathaniel Dance had studied art in Italy; he had just married Harriet Bishopp, the widow of Thomas Dummer and first cousin to Mrs. Boscawen.

[2]James Dance, whose stage name was James Love, had been Boswell's close friend as well as debtor in their early Edinburgh days (he had died in 1774). His wife, Mrs. Love, had been Boswell's mistress.

today a great deal better than I expected to do. In the evening played whist and lost 15/-.

SATURDAY 26 FEBRUARY. There had fallen a great quantity of snow, and the weather was windy and very cold. I was engaged to dine at Mr. Dilly's with Mr. Cumberland[4] and Dr. Mayo. I hesitated whether I should go. But thought Cumberland's conversation might do me good. So boldly marched. The other guests were Mr. Graham, husband of Mrs. Macaulay, and the Rev. Mr. Alison from Barbados. I had told Cumberland before dinner of my bad spirits. He said, thank GOD he himself had not that complaint; but he had seen his wife suffer a great deal from it, and he had observed the best remedy was change of place. We had a warm room, a good dinner and good wines, and I grew wonderfully easy. Mr. Sharp joined us after dinner. He was acquainted with Cowper, the poet, his account of whom was frightful, for with a great deal of genius and even pleasantry, he has at bottom a deep religious melancholy, to divert the shocking thoughts of which he is now translating Homer. He has been woefully deranged—in a strait waistcoat—and now is sometimes so ill that they take away his shoe-buckles, that he may have nothing within his reach with which he can hurt himself. It seems he apprehends himself to be in a state of *reprobation,* being impressed with the most dismal doctrines of Calvinism.[5] I was quite shocked to hear of such a state of mind. My own was good by comparison. Sharp gave me hopes of a great sale for my *Life of Johnson.* He said there were so many people in both the universities, etc., etc., who expected to see themselves, or those whom they knew, in it that they would be eager to have it. We played whist; I won. We supped, and I felt my gloom much lightened.

Cumberland carried me in a hackney-coach as far as Charles Street, St. James's, where he lodged. I talked to him of the sad loss which I had suffered by the death of my excellent wife. He said if he should have that misfortune, he would request some amiable woman to marry him and comfort him. And now, though he had denied it before dinner, perhaps from want of recollection, I found that he was subject to

[3]Perhaps an echo of Pope, *Epilogue to the Satires,* ii. 71: "Secker is decent, Rundel has a heart."

[4]Richard Cumberland, the prolific popular dramatist, to whom Dilly had introduced Boswell a few years earlier.

[5]According to Calvinist teachings, "reprobation" means being excluded from the salvation reserved for those whom God has elected. William Cowper had undergone a terrifying religious conversion in 1763–64 after feeling cursed and damned by God. He was now England's most famous living poet; his blank verse translation of *The Iliad* and *The Odyssey* appeared in this year.

mental affliction; for he told me that sometimes when he awaked in the night, his thoughts were terrible, and his relief was to wake Mrs. Cumberland and be soothed by a soft female voice speaking tenderly to him. I mentioned the dangers of not finding a woman attached to one as a second wife, and of the discord which such a connection often produced in a family. Nevertheless I allowed myself to imagine I might possibly form a fortunate union.

SUNDAY 27 FEBRUARY. Do not recollect how the forenoon was passed. Dined at home. Went with my daughters and little James to St. George's Church in the afternoon. At Lady Lucan's in the evening. Talked with Lady Lonsdale a good deal and with Dr. Burney. Was in indifferent spirits. Dr. Warren felt my hand cold, and said, "You have not taken a bottle of wine today." I went with him in his chariot to be carried to the first stand of hackney-coaches, as it was a wet night. Missing them in a long drive, I had time for a good long conversation with him. He told me that some people had a power of inspiring cheerfulness instantaneously; that when I was myself, I was one of those, and that for some time he had missed the effect which I used to have upon him; that I *must* drink more wine, for having been used to it, I required it, especially when low. When my spirits were better, I might take less. I said it was humiliating that man should be dependent on such material circumstances. "Sir," said he, "such is his nature. Man is naturally a timid animal. The savages skulk and venture into danger by a kind of force. They must rouse themselves by noises, or by the use of something which intoxicates, and the great Ruler of the World has contrived that something of that nature is everywhere to be found. In this town we see people with all the advantages of rank and fortune who yet are uneasy, and must have recourse to wine, and that pretty liberally." I went with him as far as George Street, Westminster, where he went to his brother the Bishop's,[6] and proposed that I should sit in the carriage till he came out; but as he was to be some time there, I came out and walked home in the rain, the hardship of which I felt brace me.

MONDAY 28 FEBRUARY. This day was the anniversary feast of the Humane Society, at the London Tavern. I had nominated Sir Joshua Reynolds my successor as one of the stewards and had engaged to accompany him; but I felt myself so weak and sore that I shrunk from it and thought of sending an excuse. There however came so pressing and so flattering a letter from Dr. Hawes[7] that I could not

---

[6]John Warren, D.D., Bishop of Bangor.
[7]William Hawes, M.D., was the founder of the Royal Humane Society.

resist, so I went with Sir Joshua; but experienced all the sickliness of hypochondria and, as on such occasions, wondered how all whom I saw could exert themselves. I could not have even an *imagination* of enjoyment. However, Dr. Finch, one of the prebendaries of Westminster, between whom and Sir Joshua I sat, insensibly pleased me as a new acquaintance and a respectable, courteous, conversable man,[8] and I became gradually better, so as not to suffer much, but rather have some degree of satisfaction; but I could only be *quiet* and not at all *conspicuous* as last year.[9] I went home with Sir Joshua and had tea with Miss Palmer, and we played three-hand whist.

TUESDAY 1 MARCH. By some unaccountable change either in my body or in some mysterious department, I awaked free from that miserable relaxation and gloom under which I had been, I think, for ten or eleven weeks. Instead of a horror at getting up, I felt an alacrity and, what is truly *amazing*, my mind viewed without depression the very circumstances which had appeared ready to sink me in ruin. In the night I had been favoured with a benignant dream of my dear wife, who distinctly pointed out in her own handwriting the propitiation of our Saviour. I told this to Courtenay, who, though unhappily a disbeliever, has no effect in shaking my faith. I dined at Sir Joshua Reynolds's. I relished exceedingly my relief from melancholy, but had no exuberant spirits. Before dinner I talked of bad spirits with Lord Eliot (who I was informed had suffered from that complaint) but without reference to himself. He was clear for the use of opium when there was a want of sleep, and maintained that it might easily be left off when there was not occasion for it. There was too numerous a company, as is almost uniformly the case at Sir Joshua's: Lords Eliot and Sheffield; Drs. Laurence and Blagden; Mr. Knight;[1] Mrs. Burke, her son, and Mr. Burke's niece, Miss French, true Irish. Mr. Burke did not come till after dinner. We were then in all fourteen. There was not much *good talk*, as Johnson would say.[2] In the evening we had Lord Inchiquin,

---

[8]Robert Pool Finch, D.D., rector of St. John the Evangelist, Westminster, was a well-known preacher, who had published many sermons and a widely read treatise on oaths and perjury.

[9]See p. 44 above.

[1]The company included John Holroyd Baker, first Baron Sheffield, an authority on agriculture and commerce and also Edward Gibbon's intimate friend and literary executor; and presumably Richard Payne Knight, M.P., the classical scholar whose *Worship of Priapus* (1786) had caused a stir of disapproval and whose *Analytical Essay on the Greek Alphabet* was published in this year.

[2]Boswell seems to be recalling Johnson's description of a dinner: "We had *talk* enough, but no *conversation;* there was nothing *discussed*" (*Life of Johnson*, 1783, iv. 186).

the Bishop of Clonfert, Mr. and Mrs. Weddell,[3] etc. This was the first day of my being free from my engagement to Courtenay not to drink more than four glasses in the time of dinner, and a pint after it. I did not too wantonly use my liberty. I played whist and betted foolishly, and lost £1.16, which vexed me. A number stayed supper, many of whom could not get to the table; so I, who had a place, observed there were some sitting Members and some petitioners.[4]

WEDNESDAY 2 MARCH.[5] Being now in good spirits, I had resolved to try fairly if I could see Miss Upton, and had yesterday called again, and not finding Mrs. Upton or her at home, had left my cards a second time. Today I sent a note in these words: "Mr. Boswell presents his compliments to Mrs. and Miss Upton. Having been so long their next neighbour at church, and having at last fortunately had the honour of being introduced to them by his friend Sir Michael Le Fleming,[6] he took the liberty twice to call at their door. If he has presumed too much, he is very sorry, and requests they may have the goodness to forgive him." I dined today at Mr. Gregg's in the City, where were Mr. ——, his brother-in-law, Dr. Bever, and Mr. Caleb Whitefoord;[7] a hearty day, but not too much so. In the evening Miss Gregg played both on the harpsichord and harp and sung admirably well. But I felt none of the fondness for her which made me once rave,[8] and it seemed awkward to me. I stole away in time to be at the Essex Head Club, and not be obliged to *act* also at supper. When I came home I found an answer to my note: "Mrs. and Miss Upton present their compliments to Mr. Boswell, are sorry they were not at home when he did them the honour to call, but hope to be more fortunate another time." This pleased me much; and I found I was known to the ladies, for their note was addressed "J. Boswell, Esq."[9] How many *adventures* do I meet with or contrive! But to be *capable* of any at all, after my late wretchedness, is a wonderful change.

THURSDAY 3 MARCH. Dined at W. G. Hamilton's, who had fantastically insisted that some passages in my *Life of Johnson* relative to him should be cancelled, and Courtenay and I were with him some

---

[3]Murrough O'Brien, fifth Earl of Inchiquin, was a friend of Reynolds's; William Weddell was M.P. for Malton, as was Burke.

[4]As in the House of Commons, where petitioners sought to oust sitting Members on appeal after a disputed election.

[5]On this date and the two following, Boswell inadvertently wrote "Feb."

[6]Miss Upton's father had preceded Le Fleming as M.P. for Westmorland.

[7]Thomas Bever, LL.D., was a legal scholar; Whitefoord a diplomat who had been one of the negotiators of the peace settlement with the Americans.

[8]This is the sole reference to Boswell's earlier fondness for Miss Gregg.

[9]An acknowledgement of his style as a landed gentleman.

time before dinner to talk of this. Courtenay had been plagued with tedious consultations about it, from the anxiety of Hamilton's vanity. I did not like it, but yielded to a certain degree.[1] Penn dined with us, and we four had a good *repas*. Penn and I drank an additional bottle of claret by ourselves, and I went with him to the Mount Coffee-house, where I had not been for a long time, and drank some negus. Upon the whole I had too much, though not greatly intoxicated.[2] I however walked too long in the streets. In the forenoon went to Mrs. Upton's; was received and found her to be a good, plain, north-of-England lady, and she and I conversed very well. But my dear *incognita* did not appear.

FRIDAY 4 MARCH. Lord Kellie had paid us a visit on Tuesday morning, and yesterday came unexpectedly worthy Langton and his daughters Diana and Jane. He had come suddenly to town upon business, and went off again yesterday. I was glad to be able to relish him, and he always raises me in my own opinion. This was a charming day. I walked to Islington, where by kind invitation I dined with the Rev. Mr. Strahan and talked of Dr. Johnson's last illness.[3] Mrs. Strahan was a pleasing woman, and I had really a good day. I indeed had some uneasiness when I set out about nine to return to town, but I luckily got a coach which took me to Smithfield. I sat awhile with Dilly and walked quietly home, tired enough.

SATURDAY 5 MARCH. [No entry for this day.]

SUNDAY 6 MARCH. At home in the morning, and suddenly resolved to go and bring Betsy to dinner. Jamie went with me. Was at St. George's in the afternoon. Evening quiet.

MONDAY 7 MARCH. Had met M. A. Taylor[4] yesterday on horseback, and he asked me to *take my chance* with him at dinner today, which I did, and found an excellent dinner; just he and his wife and Mr.

---

[1]"That *nervous* mortal W. G. H. is not satisfied with my report of some particulars *which I wrote down from his own mouth,* and is so much agitated, that Courtenay has persuaded me to allow a *new edition* of them by H. himself to be made at H.'s expense" (Boswell to Malone, 25 February 1791). Hamilton appears to have objected to being identified as the source for several pieces of Johnsoniana. Boswell was no doubt irritated because he regarded the naming of his informants as an important feature of the *Life of Johnson*. He did, however, remove Hamilton's name in several passages even though they were already in print, and Hamilton eventually paid for the cancels.

[2]The following sentence has been inked out in the manuscript.

[3]The Rev. George Strahan, vicar of St. Mary's, Islington, had been a great favourite of Johnson's and had been with him during his last days; he had also edited and overseen the publication of Johnson's *Prayers and Meditations* after his death. Strahan was the son of Johnson's old friend William Strahan, the printer of many of his works.

[4]Michael Angelo Taylor, a barrister and M.P., was one of the managers of Hastings's impeachment.

Campbell, brother to John at the bar, the company.[5] His purse-pomp-
ousness amused me. I said I had had a pleasant day. "It will be your
own fault," said he, "if you have not many such." I then walked stoutly
to the London Tavern, and in vigorous spirits supped with the stewards of the Humane Society, and remained at the bottle and glass till
I believe past two. Walked home.

TUESDAY 8 MARCH. Awaked not well; could not rest. Went into
the City. Dined comfortably with Dilly on his family dinner and took a
cheerful glass, but not too much. It was Shrove Tuesday.[6]

WEDNESDAY 9 MARCH. [No entry for this day.]

THURSDAY 10 MARCH. Dined at Dilly's with———.[7]

FRIDAY 11 MARCH. [No entry for this day.]

SATURDAY 12 MARCH. [No entry for this day.]

SUNDAY 13 MARCH. Went by appointment to dine at Woodford
with Mr. Preston, having met Surgeon Grindall at Batson's[8] and been
carried by him in his chariot. Had a jovial day, and came home at night
competently well.

MONDAY 14 MARCH. Dined at Mr. Deputy John Nichols's, a most
hearty City dinner, more solid victuals upon the table than I almost
ever saw at a private house. The company: Alderman Wilkes, Town
Clerk Rix, Comptroller Bushnan, Deputy Birch, Common-Councilman
Syms, Rev. Mr. Pridden and wife, Miss Nichols,[9] Rev. Mr. Beloe, steady
Reed. A capital day. I hugged myself in the thought of being so well in
the City, and Syms actually made me hope that I might one day be
Common Serjeant.[1] Eat and drank well. Stayed the evening; had cof-
fee, tea, whist, at which I won £1.8. Punch, porter, and sandwiches.
Walked home.

[5]William Henry Campbell of Liston Hall was the brother of John Campbell, who had
served as fellow counsellor with Boswell on a case heard at the bar of the House of
Commons while Boswell was visiting London in 1778. At that time John Campbell, a
Scotsman who had established himself in London, gave an account of English legal
practices that increased Boswell's eagerness to try the English bar.
[6]The day before Ash Wednesday, the beginning of Lent, and also the day on which
Boswell had wished the *Life of Johnson* to be published.
[7]Writing to Malone on 12 March, Boswell mentions some of the other guests:
Cumberland, Sharp, and Reed.
[8]A coffee-house in Cornhill.
[9]John Nichols was deputy of Faringdon Without, the ward of which John Wilkes was
alderman. Nichols was the printer of Johnson's *Lives of the Poets,* the editor of the
Gentleman's Magazine, and later the compiler of *Literary Anecdotes of the Eighteenth Century.* Mrs. Anne Pridden and Sarah Nichols were his daughters.
[1]The second-ranking legal officer for the Corporation of London, the first being the
Recorder.

TUESDAY 15 MARCH. Dined at Mr. Osborn's,[2] an elegant repast in quite a different style from yesterday; the company: Sir Joseph Banks, Mr. Agar, Sir W. Musgrave, General Rainsford, etc., etc., etc. My daughters (it being Veronica's birthday)[3] had this evening, for the first time, a *small party*. I came home soon on purpose to be at it; but I should have been ready to receive the company, and felt an awkwardness at going into the room. There were about thirty ladies and gentlemen—Mrs. Bosville and the Colonel,[4] Sir Joshua Reynolds, Chevalier Freire the Portuguese Minister, and M. Allo the Spanish Secretary, who played on his guitar—and Veronica played and sung. There was a whist-table. Major Green stayed and had some wine and water.

WEDNESDAY 16 MARCH. I should have mentioned a curious dream some nights ago. I thought I was in company with Mr. John Wesley, who said, "You will not see me standing with the rest of you at the Last Day." "How so, Sir?" said I. "Because," said he, "I am to be received into the immediate presence of GOD." "Have you, Sir," said I, "had that revealed to you?" He answered, "I have."[5] This day I felt myself restless, so walked about a good deal and at four called on Wilkes with intention to dine with him, and was accordingly asked. We had Miss Wilkes, the Rev. Mr. Beloe, and the Rev. Mr. Stockdale, who was now a water-drinker and talked of it with a vain ostentation.[6] Though wild in his manner, he had a good deal of literature, and his reminding me of my dear friend Temple pleased me. Wilkes was, as he never fails to be, very pleasant. I drank liberally, and first went to the Essex Head Club and then to Admiral Lloyd's *late party* at the Somerset.[7]

THURSDAY 17 MARCH. Dined at Sir Joshua Reynolds's, Euphemia with me; Veronica, being a little indisposed, did not go. Company: Dr. Farmer, Sir John and Lady Doyly and a clergyman, a friend

[2]Boswell had met John Osborn, former British Envoy Extraordinary to the court of Saxony, in Marseilles in 1765 and had visited him several times since then.

[3]It was her eighteenth.

[4]Diana Bosville, widow of Squire Godfrey Bosville, and her son, Col. Thomas Bosville. Regarding them as his kinsmen, Boswell had warm feelings towards both.

[5]Wesley, the evangelist and founder of Methodism, had died two weeks earlier in his eighty-eighth year. During the conversion he had experienced in 1738 he had felt that Christ was saving him from sin and death, and thereafter his teachings emphasized a profoundly personal relationship with God.

[6]The Rev. Percival Stockdale, author of poems, essays, and translations, was a self-styled genius known for his egotism. Boswell, who repeatedly called him a "strange mortal" (Journal, 21 March 1772, 6 April 1788), had met him through Temple.

[7]The Somerset coffee-house in the Strand.

of Sir John's; Mr. Vachell[8] and two others; quiet day. In the evening, whist. I won a little. Mrs. Hastings came and was charming,[9] and we had our cold supper and were very pleasant. Only the recollection of my dear valuable wife came painfully across me. It is impossible to describe fully what I suffer on that account. My thoughts are agitated with gloom and regret and tender sensations. The consideration of the happiness I enjoyed with her, the steady support which her good sense afforded me, the recollection of my improper conduct on many occasions, all crowded upon my mind, seem to overwhelm it; and the dismal circumstance that I am *never again* to have her cheering and affectionate society in this world is so afflicting that I am amazed how I can for a moment forget it, or ever be in the smallest degree easy. O merciful GOD, be pleased graciously to shed consolation upon my wounded spirit!

FRIDAY 18 MARCH. Had slept pretty well. But, as usual, when I had taken my scanty breakfast, I was unhappy. My idleness at present is extreme. I have no plan, no object. My *Life of Johnson* being nearly finished, I once thought of asking Robinson fairly as to the offer which he, through Mr. Malone, made for the copyright, which Mr. Malone understood to be £1,000; but apprehending that I might give occasion to its being slighted, I resolved to take the fair chance of the public. Dr. Milman, physician in Argyll Street,[1] whom I had met a few times, had politely called on me about a week ago and paid me the compliment of an invitation to dine with him today. I accepted, and found there Sir George and Lady Collier, Mr. and Mrs. Lutwidge, Dr. Russell,[2] Mr. Seward. We had a noble dinner. Mrs. Milman was very attentive, and he himself a sensible, gentleman-like man, and his wines—madeira, sherry, port, vin de graves, claret, burgundy, and champagne—were all excellent. Though not in exquisite spirits, I acquitted myself pretty well and relished much my good cheer, wondering at the general

[8]The guests included Richard Farmer, D.D., Master of Emmanuel College, Cambridge, a Shakespeare scholar and member of The Club, and William Vachell, High Sheriff of Cambridgeshire in 1790.

[9]Boswell had admired Anna Maria ("Marian") Hastings at an earlier meeting at Reynolds's house in March 1787. She had married Warren Hastings in 1777 after being divorced from Karl Imhoff, a German painter.

[1]Francis Milman was physician to the royal household.

[2]Sir George Collier had distinguished himself as a naval commander during the American war and had been appointed Captain of the *St. George* in 1790. Patrick Russell, M.D., had recently returned from India, where he had served as naturalist to the East India Company and had organized a collection of botanical specimens; his influential treatise on the plague was published in this year.

expense of living in this great metropolis. We had whist in the evening after our tea and coffee, and I won a trifle. I liked a new scene. When I came home I found a kind note from Lord Rockville that he was come to London, and wishing to know when he could call on me next morning.

SATURDAY 19 MARCH. Went to General Gordon's to breakfast and met Lord Rockville, who lived with him. He seemed a good deal older than when I saw him five years ago. I felt a temporary uneasiness at seeing him a Lord of Session and contrasting this with my bad success.[3] We however were cordial.

SUNDAY 20 MARCH. It was a wet day, so I and my children stayed at home and read the Bible.

MONDAY 21 MARCH. General Gordon sat with us while his brother Lord Rockville breakfasted. I then walked out with them, made some calls, and visited Sir John Dick. I felt a superiority over Lord Rockville, notwithstanding his office. He seemed to have provincial narrowness. Having gone to the printing-house, I dined at Baldwin's.

TUESDAY 22 MARCH. Did not go to The Club. Dined at home, I think.

WEDNESDAY 23 MARCH. Went to Westminster and talked with Mr. Dodd, the usher, as tutor to my son James, and also put him to Mr. Pierce the writing-master.

[EDITORIAL NOTE. At this point in the journal there is a gap of ten days, during which Boswell seems to have felt particularly despondent. On 2 April he confided to Temple: "I get bad rest in the night, and then I brood over all my complaints—the *sickly mind* which I have had from my early years—the disappointment of my hopes of success in life—the irrevocable separation between me and that excellent woman who was my cousin, my friend, and my wife—the embarrassment of my affairs—the disadvantage to my children in having so wretched a father—nay, the want of *absolute certainty* of being happy after death, the *sure prospect* of which is *frightful*."

Towards the end of March Boswell had to deal with a special problem that arose with regard to the *Life of Johnson*. Bishop Percy, anxious as usual, asked to see the passage on the late James Grainger's *Sugar-Cane*, assuming that Boswell would have reported one of Johnson's favourite stories about how he, Reynolds, and other friends had heard

---

[3]"Sandy" Gordon, an old friend and a fellow advocate in Edinburgh, was made Lord of Session in 1784 and, as such, had taken the style Lord Rockville. Boswell had last seen him at a party in Edinburgh in March 1785. He was staying in London with his older brother, Maj.-Gen. William Gordon.

a manuscript version of this poem read aloud by Thomas Warton. The company had laughed about the line "Now, Muse, let's sing of *rats*"— and Grainger had eventually compressed a sixteen-line section on these pests infesting sugar-cane into the notorious two-line circumlocution, "Nor with less waste the whisker'd vermin race / A countless clan despoil the lowland cane." Johnson had furthermore cast aspersions on Grainger's character, and Percy, a friend of the family's, feared that an account of these incidents would embarrass the surviving daughter. Although the passage in question was already in print, Boswell responded to Percy's concern. He cancelled Johnson's derogatory comments about Grainger's character, apparently recognizing that these might have been overstatements, and added Percy's praise of Grainger in a long footnote. However, Boswell retained several witticisms that Johnson had made at the expense of Percy, who was deeply offended when he saw the published *Life of Johnson*.

The journal resumes with the comment: "My life passed on with various sensations unrecorded for some time."]

SUNDAY 3 APRIL. Went to Portland Chapel in the afternoon with my children. My brother and his wife and Major Green dined and drank tea with us.

MONDAY 4 APRIL. Dined at Sir Joshua Reynolds's with Mrs. Moore,[4] Lord Eliot, Mr. E. Gwatkin, Mr. Johnson. In the evening came Mr. and Mrs. Burke and their son, etc., etc.

TUESDAY 5 APRIL. Dined at home, and in the evening my daughters had a *small party,* as it is called; music and whist.

WEDNESDAY 6 APRIL. An excessive wet day. Did not stir out. Was low-spirited.

[Boswell to Temple, 6 April 1791]

My *Life of Johnson* is at last drawing to a close. I am correcting the last sheet and have only to write an advertisement, to make out a note of errata and to correct a second sheet of contents, one being done. I really hope to publish it on the twenty-fifth current. My old and most intimate friend may be sure that a copy will be sent to him. I am at present in such bad spirits, that I have every fear concerning it—that I may get no profit, nay, may lose—that the public may be disappointed and think that I have done it poorly—that I may make many enemies and even have quarrels. Yet perhaps the very reverse of all this may happen.

[4]Presumably Jenny Hamilton Moore, widow of the dramatist Edward Moore and long a favourite of Reynolds's.

When my book is launched, I shall, if I am alive and in tolerable health and spirits, have some furniture put into my chambers in the Temple,[5] and force myself to sit there some hours every day, and to attend regularly in Westminster Hall. The chambers cost me £20 yearly, and I may reckon furniture and a lad to wait there occasionally £20 more. I doubt whether I shall get fees equal to the expense.

THURSDAY 7 APRIL. Dined at Sir William Scott's to meet his sister-in-law Miss Bagnall, of whom we had talked in a kind of jest as one to whom I should make love.[6] She proved to be a fine girl enough, but did not please me much. Her father was there, and Sir Joshua Reynolds, Sir John and Lady Turner, and Dr. Fisher. I drank too liberally. Sir Joshua and I stayed and played whist and I had some supper.

FRIDAY 8 APRIL. Was restless and could not dine at home. Baldwin asked me, and I drank a good bottle of wine, which warmed me a good deal; and then I went to Dilly's and had ham and porter, and then concluded the night at the club of "All Friends round the Globe." Sat next Mr. Akerman; drank two tumblers of port negus. Came home feverish. In the forenoon I had witnessed a loan to Courtenay by Sir Joshua of £200, which indeed I had chiefly negotiated. A policy of assurance[7] to that extent on Courtenay's life was assigned. I had then gone with them to see the wonderful optical exhibition, where by means of several mirrors a variety of objects were brought to all appearance fairly out, such as a hand holding a bunch of grapes, yet when you tried to touch it, there was nothing. Lord Eglinton joined us in the street and came up to me and shook hands with an air of great ease, saying he had not seen me. Ungrateful fellow, he had never called on me since my wife's death.[8]

SATURDAY 9 APRIL. Was heated and restless. Langton breakfasted with me. He and I paid a visit to Lord Macartney. Lord Mountstuart came in. I had not seen him for years. My heart warmed towards him, and I regretted that politics had made him keep aloof from an

[5]The chambers in the Inner Temple for which Boswell had signed a lease in January. He was pleased that they were "in the very staircase where Johnson lived" (Boswell to Malone, 12 March 1791).

[6]See above, 10 June 1790.

[7]Insurance.

[8]Although they were temperamentally unsympathetic, Boswell had once regarded the powerful Eglinton as his political leader in Ayrshire. But after Eglinton struck a deal in the 1784 Ayrshire election with his former opponent, Sir Adam Fergusson—a man whom Boswell hated—Boswell declared his political independence. Since he also regarded Eglinton as the Chief of the Montgomeries, his wife's family, he particularly resented Eglinton's neglect of her during her time in London.

old friend.[9] I was really inwardly affected, but gave no signs of it. I walked with Langton as far as Brompton, and then returned to town to attend another meeting upon Johnson's monument, when it was resolved to call the subscribers together to decide between Westminster Abbey and St. Paul's.[1] I wished to dine with somebody, but knew not with whom. Sir Joshua dined out. Jack Devaynes dined out. I came to Seward's a little before five, hoping that he and I might dine somewhere, but he was engaged. I sauntered hastily in the streets, feeling a sad state of restless dependence. Honest Governor Penn luckily asked me into his house, which was cordial, and I had a hearty family dinner from him, and a good deal of excellent port, of which I drank about twice as much as he, as he was not well. I finished the evening at Sir Joshua's, where were Glover (young *Leonidas*)[2] and Seward.

SUNDAY 10 APRIL. Breakfasted at the Gloucester Coffee-house[3] with Langton.

[EDITORIAL NOTE. The journal stops here close to the top of a page. For the long period from 11 April 1791 to 16 August 1792 only a few notes and snatches of journal have survived. Some of Boswell's activities can, however, be reconstructed from other sources.

His correspondence with Andrew Gibb, for instance, shows that a small drama was playing itself out at Auchinleck. When a former tenant, Andrew Dalrymple, refused to pay his debts, Boswell, as Laird, showed himself fair-minded but firm. On 12 February he had written to Gibb that if Dalrymple did not pay at least ten shillings in the pound, he should be imprisoned. "I am very unwilling to proceed to extremities, but an example must be made in such a case." The culprit was not to be found in March, tried to negotiate in April with an offer that

[9]John Stuart, styled Lord Mountstuart, the oldest son of the Earl of Bute, had invited Boswell to be his travelling companion in Italy in 1765. Boswell, who considered him his patron, found him alternately friendly and cold in later years. Their relationship ended when Boswell, in his *Letter to the People of Scotland* (1783), opposed Fox's East India Bill, which would have limited the rights of the East India Company and which led to the fall of the Fox-North Coalition, while Mountstuart took the other side and cut off all contact with Boswell.
[1]Reynolds wished to have the Johnson monument placed in St. Paul's Cathedral, rather than in Westminster Abbey as previously arranged, on the grounds that the Abbey needed no more monuments whereas St. Paul's would benefit from having its empty spaces embellished. Although Johnson was already buried in Westminster Abbey, the advocates of St. Paul's carried the day at the subscribers' meeting on 16 April. Malone and Boswell disapproved of the change of plan.
[2]So called because of his father Richard Glover's popular epic poem *Leonidas*.
[3]In Piccadilly.

Boswell found unacceptable, and by the end of May was indeed in prison in Ayr. From there, on 28 May, he wrote a penitent letter pleading for release, offering at least a partial repayment of his debt, and admitting that he deserved his punishment for having opposed Boswell "through the foolish advice of self-designing lawyers." Boswell agreed to the release with the comment, in his 4 June letter to Gibb: "He is the first of my tenants that I ever imprisoned, and I hope he will behave better in time to come."

For Boswell, however, the main events of the spring were the publications of several of his writings. The first to appear, in mid-April, was his verse pamphlet *No Abolition of Slavery,* opposing the bill to abolish the slave-trade that Wilberforce was introducing in Parliament. Of interest chiefly as an unabashed statement of the pro-slavery position, the verses are a bizarre combination of political and amatory themes. The speaker is a slave of love, he enjoys being so, and he ends with the peculiar argument that abolishing slavery, whether in society or in personal relations, "would be in vain / Since love's strong empire must remain."

In the passages on love, which are undoubtedly autobiographical, Boswell presents himself as a fierce black—an allusion to his dark complexion—who is captured and taken on a long voyage by a tyrannical mistress and eventually brought to the island of Venus, where he enjoys his blessings all the more after his trials. These effusions, which appear at the beginning and end of the poem, were in all likelihood written a year earlier; Boswell had sent the Countess of Crawford specimens of his "Slavery and Love" poem in April 1790. The completed piece, subtitled "The Universal Empire of Love," is addressed to "Miss ———, most pleasing of thy sex," presumably the mysterious lady who had inspired him with "the dangerous fever of love" at that time.

The political passages, which were composed more recently, are entirely in keeping with Boswell's general conservative outlook. Considering even the limited abolition of the slave-trade a dangerous attack on vested property rights, he mocks the "noodles" who would surely oppose reforms that threatened their own possessions but favoured reforms that threatened other people's property in distant lands.

> At your own cost fine projects try;
> Don't *rob*—from *pure humanity.*

Boswell then introduces a series of sarcastic verse paragraphs attacking the supporters of the anti-slave-trade Bill, among them Wilberforce, Windham, Courtenay, Burke, Pitt, and Fox.

Defending the institution of slavery, Boswell puts forward the traditional argument that slavery is part of "God's system" and is ac-knowledged in the Bible. He also argues that the current system was the blacks' best hope of progressing from savagery to civilization. In-spired by paintings belonging to Sir William Young, whose family owned estates in the West Indies, he proceeds to present a highly ide-alized description of the slaves on their "fragrant isle," living a care-free and protected life. In his anti-abolitionism Boswell was certainly opposed to the best minds of England—Burke, Fox, and Pitt united in supporting Wilberforce's Bill—but he stood with the majority of Par-liament, including most of the bishops. Although the poem was pub-lished anonymously, Boswell made no secret of his authorship, sent copies to his friends, and was proud of it.

Meanwhile, the publication of his great work had been delayed so long that the *Oracle* quipped that his own biography might have to be written before his *Life of Johnson* appeared. Now it was imminent. Last-minute correspondence with Malone about the precise wording of the title-page reveals that Boswell's worry over its every detail persisted. The Advertisement, dated 20 April, stressed his "labour and anxious atten-tion" in collecting material as well as his efforts to authenticate the in-numerable details. "I have sometimes been obliged to run half over London, in order to fix a date correctly." The work itself, in two quarto volumes, officially appeared on 16 May—a significant date since it was the twenty-eighth anniversary of Boswell's first meeting with Johnson. It opens with a long Dedication to Sir Joshua Reynolds, who is extolled for excellence not only in art but also in philosophy and literature, and who is honoured as "the intimate and beloved friend" of Johnson as well as of Boswell himself. To protect copyright, two passages of special in-terest—Johnson's letter to Lord Chesterfield indignantly rejecting him as a patron and the King's flattering conversation with Johnson—were published separately a few days before the book as a whole.

The success of the *Life* surpassed all expectations. On 13 May Bos-well could already report to Forbes: "My *Life of Dr. Johnson* is at length fairly launched, though the formal day of publication is not till Monday. Considering that *two volumes quarto, price two guineas*, must give pause, I have no reason to be discouraged. *This day* my volumes are purchased by *forty-one booksellers of London*, to the amount of *upwards of four hun-dred*, and one of them who received twenty sets in the morning has sent word that they are all sold and has got ten more." Of a total of 1,750 sets printed, 800 were sold in one or two weeks, 1,200 by the end of August, 1,400 by December, and 1,600 by August 1792.

Boswell's friends and acquaintances, to many of whom he sent com-plimentary copies, were enthusiastic in their praise.

[Temple to Boswell, 4 July 1791]

Perhaps no man was ever so perfectly painted as you have painted your hero. You have given us him in every point of view and exhibited him under every shade and under every colour. We think we see him and hear him and are equally entertained whether he contend for truth or for victory. You used to say that I did not know him, and your dialogue proves that I did not. Your book must greatly raise and diffuse your reputation, as it also abounds with many ingenious observations of your own, shows your familiarity and acceptance with persons of the finest discernment and how eminently you were regarded and loved by such a judge as Johnson. Indeed, I can hardly express the pleasure I feel in considering the fame and the profit it must procure you.

[Dr. Charles Burney to Boswell, 16 July 1791]

I believe it may be said with truth, that it is impossible to open either of your two volumes without finding some sentiment of our venerable sage worth remembering. His wit and his wisdom are equally original and impressive; and I have no doubt but that both will become proverbial to Englishmen, and long continue to direct their taste as well as morals. For my own part, I think myself infinitely obliged to you for embalming so many of his genuine sentiments which are not to be found in his works. Indeed if all his writings which had been previously printed were lost, or had never appeared, your book would have conveyed to posterity as advantageous an idea of his character, genius, and worth as Xenophon has done of those of Socrates.[4] I have often found your own reflections not only ingenious and lively but strong; and the latter part of your narrative, though I already knew its chief circumstances, has in it so much pathos that it renovated all my sorrows[5] and frequently made me weep like a tender-hearted female at a tragedy.

Burney suggested that Boswell take on the task of writing the memoirs of other deceased members of The Club and declared him henceforth The Club's official representative of Biography.

---

[4]No writings by Socrates have survived, but his thoughts and personality are known not only through Plato but also through Xenophon, who studied under him and later wrote an admiring memoir that included personal anecdotes and conversations.

[5]Virgil, *Aeneid*, ii. 3: "renovare dolorem: revive the sorrow." Burney is suggesting that his renewed sadness in reading about Johnson's last days resembles Aeneas's grief over the fall of Troy, which he is about to describe to Dido.

A few friends expressed reservations about the *Life*, several urging, for instance, that the next edition soften or omit references to those who felt injured by Boswell's frankness. Hugh Blair raised a different objection in an undated letter presumably written in the summer of 1791. After a long passage of praise he remarked: "I am not sure whether you have not depicted yourself sometimes too graphically and unnecessarily in your work. To me, who know you so well and so long, the impression these passages leave is no way unfavourable. But it is always a dangerous experiment for a man while he is living to exhibit himself too nakedly to the world." Although Blair had discussed the usefulness of a naïve narrator in his lectures on rhetoric, he was apparently oblivious to the fact that Boswell had deliberately presented himself as an ingenuous foil to Johnson.

Letters about the *Life of Johnson* continued to arrive all summer. Those who had received favourable treatment—Warren Hastings, the actress Frances Abington—were especially appreciative. And Boswell wanted the praise he was reaping to endure to posterity. He asked Wilkes to write down his compliments and Burke to record the King's laudatory comments so that these could be preserved in the Auchinleck archives. Apparently the King had agreed with Burke that the *Life* was the most entertaining book he had ever read. But Burke, in his reply of 20 July, claimed that he could not recall the King's praise in any further detail; in addition, he suggested that Boswell might have omitted many of the particulars in his work and would do well to publish no further anecdotes. His elaborately polite but chilly letter brought their personal relationship to an end.

As for the newspapers, they gave the *Life of Johnson* the same mixed reception as they had given to the *Tour to the Hebrides* six years earlier. Much depended on whether they admired Johnson and on whether they approved of Boswell's use of minute particulars.

[Excerpt from the *Gentleman's Magazine,* May 1791]

"As our magazine announced to the world the rapid sale of Dr. Johnson's *London*,[6] it is with equal pleasure and propriety that we now mention, as a proof of the lasting fame of that great man, that his *Life* by Mr. Boswell has been received by the public with extraordinary avidity. Long has the public expectation been raised by Mr. Boswell, and eagerly have the numerous admirers of Dr. Johnson looked forward

---

[6]The *Gentleman's Magazine* of May 1738 announced that a second edition of the poem was needed within a week of its publication.

towards the completion of this arduous task. Yet, great as these expectations may have been, they are at length, we may assert, completely gratified. A literary portrait is here delineated, which all who knew the original will allow to be the MAN HIMSELF...."

[Excerpt from the *St. James's Chronicle,* 16 May 1791]

"Mr. Boswell's *Life of Johnson* must certainly be allowed, on the whole, to be peculiarly authentic, very amusing, and in general...very interesting. We cannot, however, help being of opinion that there are a few superfluous pages. In saying this, we by no means wish to detract from the merit of the work, which contains a surprising quantity of Dr. J.'s original *conversation* and *correspondence,* and displays his real and unbiased opinions on a vast variety of subjects, many of considerable importance and general utility, and which, from the acuteness of his observations and exactness of manner, independent of his high character, carry with them considerable weight and conviction. This, we understand, is the part on which Mr. Boswell more particularly prides himself, and with great justice esteems the preservation of these relics a service done not merely to the admirers of Johnson but also to the republic of literature, of which he was so distinguished a member....

"An astonishing variety of anecdotes and circumstances are introduced respecting a vast number of well-known characters in many spheres of life....In this very wide and extended range of persons and materials, the whole is related with that vivacity and *naïveté,* which, whatever else may be objected to Mr. Boswell's style and manner, must be allowed to be his peculiar excellence."

[Excerpt from the *English Review,* July 1791]

"When these memoirs were first promised to the lovers of light literature, we well remember how the certain hopes of a full banquet of amusement lighted up every countenance. The effect of Mr. Boswell's *Tour* was the same as that of Sancho Panza's speeches: all eyes anxiously watched when he should unclose his lips again. His silence has been long; attention has been almost fatigued; but it will infallibly be again engaged. The variety of anecdotes, the notoriety of personages, and, above all, the airy garrulity of the narrative, will effectually recommend these volumes to volatile and desultory readers; and we own we should not envy, in the gravest student, that fastidiousness which should disdain the entertainment here provided for him. Johnson is allowed to have been a striking phenomenon in the moral and intellectual world; this phenomenon is described with a degree of minuteness of which there has been no example. Mr. Boswell claims this praise; and it must be allowed that no disciple has exceeded the zeal, or equalled the success, with which he has preserved the fleeting passages of his master's life...."

But Boswell did not abandon his work to chance and the opinions of others. He kept up an anonymous barrage of comments in the newspapers. The *Public Advertiser* of 18 June, for instance, reported that "Boswell, when he speaks of his *Life of Johnson*, calls it my *magnum opus*, but it may more properly be called his *opera*, for it is truly a composition founded on a true story, in which there is a *hero* with a number of *subordinate characters*, and an alternate succession of *recitative* and *airs* of various tone and effect, all however in delightful animation." Two days later, a paragraph in the same paper turned the ironic observation that one ought to live twice to benefit from experience—but unfortunately cannot do so—into a compliment: "Mr. Boswell, however, would persuade us that he is able to make Dr. Johnson live over again, and gravely tells his readers that by perusing his quarto volumes, they may '*live with him.*'"

Inevitably, some negative reviews also appeared. The *Oracle* of 23 June, judging by the neoclassical preference for generality, found the *Life* as a whole "infinitely too minute," many of the anecdotes "frivolous," and the "biographer's zeal...blind and undistinguishing." More damaging because it was funnier was an elaborate anonymous parody, presumably written by Boswell's acquaintance Alexander Chalmers, that appeared in the 5 July issue of the *Morning Herald* and was soon reprinted in other newspapers. Its general tenor can be grasped from its title and opening:

LESSON IN BIOGRAPHY
OR
HOW TO WRITE THE LIFE OF ONE'S FRIEND

(An Extract from the LIFE OF DR. POZZ, in ten volumes folio, written by JAMES BOZZ, Esq.; who flourished with him near fifty years).

We dined at the chop-house. Dr. Pozz was this day very instructive. We talked of books: I mentioned the history of *Tommy Trip*.[7] I said it

---

[7] A popular children's story about little Tommy Trip and his dog Jouler, published by John Newbery forty years earlier in *A Pretty Book of Pictures for Little Masters and Misses*.

was a great work. Pozz. "Yes, Sir, it is a great work; but, Sir, it is a great work relatively; it was a great work to you when you was a little boy; but now, Sir, you are a great man, and Tommy Trip is a little boy." I felt somewhat hurt at this comparison, and I believe he perceived it; for, as he was squeezing a lemon, he said, "Never be affronted at a comparison, I have been compared to many things, but I never was affronted. No, Sir, if they would call me a dog, and you a canister tied to my tail, I would not be affronted."

Cheered by this kind mention of me, though in such a situation, I asked him what he thought of a friend of ours, who was always making comparisons. Pozz. "Sir, that fellow has a simile for everything but himself; I knew him when he kept shop; he then made money, Sir, and now he makes comparisons: Sir, he would say that you and I were two figs stuck together, two figs in adhesion, Sir, and then he would laugh." Bozz. "But have not some great writers determined that *comparisons* are now and then *odious?*" Pozz. "No, Sir, not odious in themselves, but odious as comparisons; the fellows who make them are odious. The Whigs make comparisons."[8]

Soon after the publication of the *Life of Johnson* Boswell had an opportunity to present a more dignified view of himself in the "Memoirs of James Boswell, Esq.," published in two parts in the May and June issues of the *European Magazine.* Although these memoirs give the impression of having been written by a sympathetic observer, some of the phrasing marks them as Boswell's own. The concise chronological account reviews his birth, education, varied early experiences in Scotland, London, and abroad, marriage, and legal career, as well as his beliefs, hopes, and disappointments in politics. Throughout, Boswell's writings in both prose and verse receive particular attention. The account is brought down to the present with the report of Mrs. Boswell's death and his great sense of loss. It concludes: "He however did not resign himself to unavailing grief but endeavoured to dissipate his melancholy by occupation and amusement in the metropolis, in which he enjoys perhaps as extensive and varied an acquaintance as any man of his time.... His attention to the business of Westminster Hall has been chiefly interrupted by his great literary work in which he was engaged

---

[8]The parody here ridicules the serious discussion of a platitude (the odiousness of comparisons had been noted since the fourteenth century), Johnson's idiosyncratic associative thinking, his specious reasoning, and his perennial dislike of the Whigs.

for many years, *The Life of Dr. Johnson,* which he has at last published, in two volumes quarto, and which has been received by the world with extraordinary approbation."

Indeed, the publication of his *magnum opus* gratifyingly increased Boswell's social prominence. A paragraph in the *Public Advertiser* of 27 May announced that "Boswell has so many invitations in consequence of his *Life of Johnson* that he may be *literally* said to *live* upon his deceased friend." Early in June he took part in the gala Royal Academy Dinner given annually on the King's Birthday. According to the *Public Advertiser* of 7 June, he was invited as a fellow artist even though his art could not be exhibited by the Academy, and he sat on Reynolds's right. On this occasion Boswell undertook to translate the Swedish love-song with which the eminent architect Sir William Chambers, who was born in Göteborg, entertained the company. In high spirits, Boswell accompanied his rhymed version with "some sounds which he called a Swedish chorus." The *Public Advertiser* found it "truly pleasing to see the great architect of our time and the biographer of Johnson thus united in playful gaiety." But Boswell was drinking heavily again—so much so that his Quaker friend Dr. Lettsom felt compelled to write a letter warning him that excessive drinking could induce depression, undermine his health, and possibly shorten his life.

Later in June Boswell maintained his contacts with the City by contributing an original song to the anniversary celebration of Alderman Curtis's election to Parliament. The song reaffirmed his enthusiasm for the British monarchy:

> Time has been when the City and Court used to jar,
> Our days are, thank heaven, more propitious by far.
> Now both with the warmest affection unite
> In support of our Monarch's just, limited right....

In keeping with the royalist sentiments expressed in these lines as well as in his earlier "Death of Favras," Boswell strongly disapproved of another anniversary about to be celebrated—that of the taking of the Bastille. News from France had been disquieting, for riots, pillaging, massacres, and mutinies had taken place in Paris and in the French provinces both before and after the attack on the Bastille on 14 July 1789. Opinions in England differed sharply between those who deplored this violence and feared that it might spread to Britain, and others who sympathized with the French republicans and began to call for government reforms in their own country.

When Boswell heard that the Rev. Andrew Kippis, a respected Presbyterian clergyman with whom he had been corresponding, planned to attend the 14 July celebration of the Friends of the French Revolution at the Crown and Anchor Tavern, Boswell did his best to dissuade him in a letter of 11 July that expressed his own opinion of the events in France: "No man is a warmer and more determined foe to despotism and oppression than I am or could more sincerely rejoice at a rational and temperate reformation of the abuses of the French government, a reformation of which I with great pleasure observed the progress in a constitutional meeting of the states of that kingdom under their monarch as a free agent. But when seditious and unprincipled spirits violently overturned that constitutional system, destroyed all limits, trampled upon all establishments, let loose the wild fury of a multitude amounting to twenty-four millions and, in short, produced all the horrors of a barbarous anarchy, it appeared to me that the change was infinitely for the worse."[9] Kippis was not to be swayed and, expressing the point of view of many British republicans at this time, explained that he found no inconsistency in sympathizing with the French people who were being freed from a despotic government while supporting the limited monarchy of England. But Boswell need not have worried; the 14 July meeting passed off quite peacefully, without provoking the civil unrest that the anti-republicans had feared.

During the summer Boswell also indulged in a new amatory diversion. On a weekend jaunt to Windsor, he met a "gay little Parisienne," as he called her in his 1 July letter to Lord Eliot. Mlle. Divry appears to have been the mistress of an English nobleman, who monopolized her evenings but left her the opportunity for clandestine meetings in the daytime. Boswell's advances were prompt and successful; their affair continued for about two months. Her brief notes, in illiterate French with a sprinkling of English, asked for bottles of wine, urged patience, and reproached Boswell for becoming too demanding: "Nous nous sommes vue comme amis, cenet pas pour nous tiraniser."[1] Subsequent notes requested the renewal of pawn-tickets and money for her lawyer's expenses. But Boswell could not afford to support her. On 15 August she wrote from Newgate and, receiving little sympathy, shortly

[9]In May 1789 the States General (the elected representatives of the clergy, nobility, and third estate or commoners) had been invited to Versailles by Louis XVI to serve as a legislative body. But the co-operation among all these groups that Boswell favoured had never come about because most of the clergy and nobility would not agree to work with the third estate. Boswell's impression that France was in a state of anarchy was surely heightened by the news that the royal family's attempt to flee the country had just been foiled when they were arrested at Varennes on 22 June.
[1]"We have considered ourselves friends and should not tyrannize over each other."

thereafter sent him the following undated note: "Comant pouves vous conter sur moi d apres la manière donte vous vous ete comporter avec moi. L on conois ses amis lor ce quil nous le prouve. Voici votre conger, ne me troublé pas davantage—je suis heureuse cet asé vous andir."[2]

At precisely the same time Boswell was thinking once more about matrimony. One possible candidate was Miss Harriet Milles, whom he described to Temple in a letter of 21 August as "daughter of the late Dean of Exeter, a most agreeable woman *d'une certaine age*, and with a fortune of £10,000." He wrote to her first on 2 July in a gallant tone, asking permission to call the next day with his little daughter—a nice touch. She replied that she would be out but that he might call on an old lady of her acquaintance who wished to discuss his book. While Miss Milles continued to put off a meeting, Boswell drafted an extraordinary letter, full of conflicting emotions. He confessed that he had walked her street for hours to see her leave for the country, asked whether her affections were engaged, but declared that he could not commit himself. Miss Milles replied coldly.

Boswell had greater satisfaction on another front. On 2 July, at Reynolds's suggestion, he was elected Secretary for Foreign Correspondence of the Royal Academy. He was extremely proud of this honour and wrote model letters in French and Italian to demonstrate his fitness for the position.

But then, in early August, Boswell's recent success as biographer brought about an awkward social situation. Having invited himself to dinner at Sir William Scott's house, he was chagrined to hear from his host that some of the guests were uneasy about his presence, fearing that their conversations might be published without their consent. Boswell replied sharply on 5 August: "I should be curious to know *who* they are that are conceited and absurd enough to imagine that I could take the trouble to publish *their* conversation because I have recorded the wisdom and wit of Johnson." He declined the invitation Scott now extended and persisted in his resolution after Scott sent a second note. When Scott wrote for a third time, Boswell took a more conciliatory tone and explained that he had stayed away not from pique but from the fear of dampening the company's spirits. He also, however, emphasized in this letter of 9 August that recording Johnson's conversations "was a *peculiar* undertaking, attended with much anxiety and

[2]"How could you expect anything from me after the way you behaved? One knows one's friends when they prove it. Go away! Don't bother me any more. I am happy—that's all you need to know."

labour, and that the conversations of people in general are by no means of that nature as to bear being registered."

In August Boswell once more turned to the law, as he had promised himself he would after completing the *Life of Johnson*, and went on the Home Circuit. He was welcomed back warmly by his fellow lawyers, who toasted him as a returning prodigal son. At Chelmsford Boswell took part in two cases and had the pleasure of having his lively presentation reported in the press. He proceeded south to Lewes, where he wrote a few pages of journal, which are headed simply "Lewes."]

[FRIDAY 12 AUGUST.] On Friday 12 August 1791 I breakfasted here, it being the first time I had ever been in the place. Happening to go into the shop of ——, the barber at whose house I had taken lodgings, I began to talk of my going on to Brighthelmstone, and that I would have a full crop of folly by seeing men run in sacks, etc. "I hope not, Sir," said a steady man who was all in a lather in the act of being shaved. "Why so, Sir?" said I. "Because, Sir," said he, "it is to be hoped that the young gentleman" (meaning the Prince of Wales) "as he grows older may grow wiser."[3] This and some other pleasantries passed.

[SATURDAY 13 AUGUST.] Next day I returned from Brighthelmstone and dined at the White Hart Inn with Silvester, Runnington, and Knowlys.[4] They went to Brighthelmstone. I then walked out. A decent man accosted me and named me. Wonderful as it may be (since seeing a man in lather is like seeing a country in snow), I knew him, and he carried me directly through his house where the bank of which he is chief proprietor is kept, and showed...[5] At Lewes Mr. Harben to his garden; asked him to sup. [HARBEN.] "Very busy but come in course of the evening." [BOSWELL.] "Is there here any good, agreeable clergyman who would have the charity [to talk with me]?" [HARBEN.] "Yes, Sir, Mr. Gwynne." Sent his man to desire Mr. G. to

[3]George Augustus Frederick, Prince of Wales, later George IV, was turning the fishing village of Brighthelmstone into the fashionable resort of Brighton; his residence there, the exotic Pavilion, had been completed five years earlier. He was notorious for his love of amusements, many of them extravagant and some childish. Boswell visited Brighton later on this day, as planned, and although he did not manage to see the Prince, he attended a ball.

[4]John Silvester, Charles Runnington, and Newman Knowlys were all London barristers on the Home Circuit.

[5]The statement breaks off here, at the end of the page; the next page begins with an elliptical third-person summary. Boswell's host, whom he had met at the barber's shop the previous day, was Thomas Harben, an important citizen in Lewes and the neighbouring town of Seaford.

walk out on the bank.[6] Introduced to him. Stout man with a gentle voice and smiling air. It seems a great assistant to Harben at Seaford. I had six wheatears.[7] He let me have them all. Good cider, porter, port. He gave me Harben's history. Risen from nothing. Illiterate watchmaker, ironmonger, and great shop for hardware. But able in Seaford politics. Now has bank here and at Brighton. Supposed worth more than £10,000. His sons each a place as good as £800.[8] He came and drank brandy and water. Heard of Serjeant Kempe. Wrote letter to go early.[9]

SUNDAY [14 AUGUST]. Very well. Called on Harben. Went with Gwynne to his church, St. Anne's, the oldest. Thin congregation. Good sermon on "Pure religion," etc., and verse preceding.[1] Asked by Gwynne to dine next day. Thought once of going to Seaford. Met Palmer and Adam and Langridge, a genteel attorney.[2] Walked with him. Was much pleased with the square flints.[3] Thought of getting them and a builder to make me a Sussex summer-house at Auchinleck. As we passed under Mr. Shelley's summer-house, he asked if we would not walk into the garden. Obliged to him. Charming view of old castle and his fine field, etc., etc. After polite reception Adam *fully* announced Mr. Boswell. He gave a spring.[4] We were carried into the house to see

[6]Presumably Boswell meant to write "to the bank." The Rev. William Gwynne was the rector of St. Anne's, a church dating back to the twelfth century, and also headmaster of the Free Grammar School.

[7]Small birds, which were considered a great delicacy.

[8]Identifying him as "Harben, of upstart notoriety," the *Universal British Directory of Trade* (1791, iii. 746) claimed that he profited from having the taxes paid into his bank, that he swelled the rolls with his workers to ensure the election of his candidate, and that he had obtained a position worth £600 for his oldest son, another worth £200 for his second son. He was rumoured to have become wealthy by buying gold treasure as base metal from a wrecked ship.

[9]Boswell asked to dine with William Kempe, whom he had known on earlier Home Circuits. Kempe was also Recorder of Lewes.

[1]"Pure religion and undefiled before God and the Father is this, to visit the fatherless and widows in their affliction, and to keep himself unspotted from the world." The preceding verse focuses on the man who is not genuinely religious (James 1: 27).

[2]Arthur Palmer and William Adam, London barristers. Adam was also a prominent M.P., who was currently devoting more time to the law than to politics because of pressing financial problems. William Langridge was a Lewes attorney.

[3]Square flint-work is traditional in Sussex architecture. Flints, which are hard grey stones, are usually round.

[4]Henry Shelley presumably leaped up with pleasure on learning his guest's identity from Adam's full introduction. Justice of the Peace for Sussex, Shelley had a house and garden next to the playground of the Free School. He came from an old Lewes family but appears to have acquired his wealth through his wife, an heiress.

drawings of buildings, etc., near Lewes made by Lambert by direction of Mr. Elliot of the Temple, who left them to Mr. Shelley.[5] Sir ——has collected largely for history of Sussex.[5a] Shelley a great friend of Thrales. His lady sister to Sir R. Cotton, a cousin of Signora Piozzi, but quite *off*.[6] She and three daughters came in but went before we had done with our drawings. At dinner several. Hurst a hard-headed, well-informed fellow.[7] Walked quietly to Mr. Shelley's to tea; bold front. Still in dining-room. I walked on. He sent a servant after me. I returned. Elegant house. Fine dessert. Good wine.

[EDITORIAL NOTE.] A few days later, still on the southern part of the Home Circuit, Boswell made an impromptu jaunt to Portsmouth. Sponsored by his friend and kinsman Captain Macbride, he viewed the fleet and inspected the convicts at work on the fortifications. He returned to London on 20 August and two days later summed up his experiences in a letter to Temple: "Though I did not get a single brief, do not repent of the expense as I am showing myself desirous of business and imbibing legal knowledge."

At the end of August he went to Auchinleck, his first visit since Margaret's death. Sandy had arrived three weeks earlier for the grouse shooting. Now that the excitement following the publication of the *Life of Johnson* had worn off, Boswell suffered a serious let-down. The house seemed deserted, and he was haunted by memories of his wife. To escape, he paid a great many visits in the neighbourhood. "But, alas," he confided to Temple in retrospect on 22 November, "I could not escape from myself."

Still, Boswell took care of family obligations by increasing the annuities to be paid to his daughters after his death. And he must have been pleased by his success at the Michaelmas Head Court at Ayr, which reviewed the eligibility of Ayrshire voters each year. He spoke forcefully against accepting the nominal and fictitious voters, many of whom

---

[5]Nine years earlier Shelley had inherited the drawings made by James Lambert, Jr., a minor Sussex painter, from John Elliot, a London barrister who was the only son of a Lewes brewer.

[5a]Sir William Burrell, whose researches were never published but are now in the British Library.

[6]Shelley's wife Philadelphia was the daughter of Sir Lynch Cotton, Mrs. Piozzi's uncle, and was as much a cousin as was her brother Sir Robert Salusbury Cotton, but perhaps he is mentioned here because he had been particularly friendly with Mrs. Piozzi in their youth. Mrs. Shelley had apparently broken off relations with Mrs. Piozzi after her marriage to Gabriel Piozzi.

[7]Robert Hurst was another London barrister on the Home Circuit.

had been added to the rolls in recent years by Eglinton and by Boswell's long-time enemy Sir Adam Fergusson. After the debate, in which Boswell opposed Fergusson, over a hundred voters were struck from the rolls, and the *Edinburgh Advertiser* of 7 October reported triumphantly: "Thus the great county of Ayr has set a noble example of public spirit and patriotism in securing the freedom of election and destroying the *Parchment Barons* of Scotland."

Boswell left Auchinleck on 18 October, but his return to London did not relieve his depression. His attempts to practise law were fruitless. And when he tried to renew his acquaintance with Miss Milles, he was finally and totally rebuffed.

Boswell's low spirits were intensified by the rapidly failing health of Sir Joshua Reynolds, whom he visited frequently. Reynolds, already blind in one eye, feared that he was losing the sight of the other one and was also becoming despondent. Boswell encouraged him to talk about his childhood and first artistic efforts. Obviously preparing for a new writing project, Boswell set down these recollections with the heading "Notes for a Life of Sir Joshua Reynolds."

Reynolds's illness worsened and was finally diagnosed as a severe liver ailment. Two weeks later, on 23 February 1792, he died. His funeral was a grand affair: his body lay in state in the Royal Academy's rooms in Somerset House and was then carried to St. Paul's Cathedral for burial. In the elaborate procession Boswell, as Secretary for Foreign Correspondence, walked with the Royal Academy rather than with The Club. Among Reynolds's legacies were £200 for Boswell to enable him to buy a memento at the projected sale of Reynolds's collection of paintings. Boswell felt his loss keenly. "This sad event damps the spirits much," he wrote to Sandy on 25 February. "We never shall have his place supplied." Reynolds was, in fact, the last of the older generation of Boswell's friends who had made London so attractive a place for him.

In March 1792 Boswell's mood improved and he once more looked for new opportunities. For one wild moment, he seems to have considered making a proposal to Mary Palmer, who had just inherited more than £30,000 from Reynolds. Temple, writing on 11 March, pointed out the obvious objections: "How can you think of Miss Palmer? Don't you imagine she will aspire to a title?...However, there is no harm in trying; but would she not suspect you of mercenary views? Will she not expect love and rapture?...Perhaps, before you venture to say anything, you should be able to read her wishes in her eyes. Indeed, I am afraid to advise." At the same time Boswell played with the idea of accompanying Lord Macartney, who had just been appointed England's first ambassador to Peking.[8] Temple was aghast: "I trust you are not in earnest in what you say of going to China with Lord Macartney," he wrote on 30 March. "At our time of life the climate would kill you either there or here." And, indeed, nothing came of either of these schemes.

All this while letters concerning the *Life of Johnson* continued to arrive. Most were favourable, but a few suggested changes or drew attention to inaccuracies. Boswell incorporated such suggestions into the text or footnotes of the second edition, on which he began to work in a desultory fashion in February and which Baldwin started to print in April.

Although he accomplished little work, Boswell's social life flourished. On 13 June he confided to his cousin, Robert Boswell: "I *enjoy* a good deal in somewhat a feverish manner." A week later he went on a jaunt to Margate for the opening ceremonies of the Margate Infirmary for Sea Bathing, founded for the poor and sick of London by his friend Dr. Lettsom. On 25 June he gave a dinner and musical party for Veronica that was attended by Franz Joseph Haydn and Johann Peter Salomon, the impresario who had arranged Haydn's highly successful London concerts in 1791–92.

But Boswell's high spirits repeatedly led him to embarrassing excesses. For instance, he became overly enthusiastic at the celebration on 26 June of the second anniversary of Alderman Curtis's election to Parliament, attended by 250 guests at the London Tavern. Eager to keep up with the politics of the City, he not only repeated the song in praise of Curtis that he had composed for the 1791 anniversary, adding new lines, but also mounted a chair to present it and then launched into an unwelcome political speech until he was cut short by the chairman, Alderman George Mackenzie Macaulay. At first, Boswell seems to have found the episode amusing, as seen in the punning paragraph he contributed to the *Public Advertiser* soon after the festivities: "Alderman Macaulay and Mr. Boswell may be truly styled Alderman Curtis's *chairmen,* one *in,* the other *upon* his chair." But other newspaper comments must have troubled him. The most unfavourable notice appeared in the 26–28 June issue of the *St. James's Chronicle: "Notoriety.*—Nothing, says a literary friend, can be a stronger evidence of the force of

---

[8]Although Chinese goods—especially tea, silk, and chinaware—had been popular in England since the early eighteenth century, the Chinese had not granted European nations diplomatic recognition and had severely restricted trade with foreigners. Macartney was being sent to Peking to try to establish diplomatic relations and to improve the privileges of the East India Company, which controlled the China trade but was permitted to function only in Canton and there only for part of the year.

this passion than that a man of real wit, learning, and genius, endowed with qualities to ensure him the respect of the wise and the worthy, should court popularity by what might be almost called gross buffoonery at a City feast.—What would Dr. Johnson have said to see his friend and *biographer*...mounted on a stool for the entertainment of an electioneering meeting?" Nor could Boswell have ignored the anxious letter Sandy sent from Eton on 4 July: "You have been attacked in one of the papers for 'standing on a stool, descending to gross buffoonery that you might gain popular applause.'" Boswell never made such a public spectacle of himself again.

Yet in private he continued to experience embarrassments. After a convivial dinner at John Cator's house in Kent he sent off to his host— and immediately regretted sending—some ribald verses composed with his fellow guests Parsons and Seward. In late June he wrote penitently to Mary Palmer, who had just married the Earl of Inchiquin, asking her pardon for unspecified offences—presumably some belittling verses he had composed and circulated about her.[9] His visit to the Inchiquin estate at Taplow, near Windsor, seems to have restored the friendship. Early in August Boswell also sent more formal apologies to Lord and Lady Salisbury, whose mansion at Hatfield he visited for the first time while in the neighbourhood for the Hertford Assizes. He regretted his indecorous behaviour, explaining that three days of feasting just prior to his visit had made him unwell. Clearly, he was drinking heavily again.

Taking part in the assizes was only one of Boswell's legal activities in the spring and summer of 1792. He took up the cause of an extraordinary group of prisoners—four men and one woman—who had escaped from Botany Bay, Australia. This region, which had been discovered by Capt. James Cook in 1770, had quickly replaced the American colonies as a dumping-ground for criminals sentenced to transportation. About 750 convicts, more than 200 of them women, had arrived in the new colony in January 1788 with such inadequate supplies that they were soon on the edge of starvation. In the spring of 1791 William Bryant, a Cornish fisherman who had been transported for smuggling, conceived the desperate plan of escaping in a small boat, an open cutter with one sail and six oars. At ten o'clock on the night of 28 March Bryant set out in this boat, equipped only with a chart, a quadrant, a compass, and a limited supply of food. He was accompanied by his wife,

[9]Mary Palmer, by now in her early forties, had married Inchiquin, a widower in his seventies, five months after Reynolds's death. On this occasion Boswell had written "Palmeria it seems will be wedded at last," a series of witty couplets about her disappointed suitors, and a suggestive quatrain of advice to her husband.

Mary Broad, whom he had married in Australia; their one-year-old son and her three-year-old daughter; and seven men, only three of whom knew anything about the sea. Heading for the island of Timor in the Dutch East Indies, more than 3,000 miles away, they sailed along the east and north coasts of Australia and then across the Gulf of Carpentaria. As described in the surviving "Memorandums" of James Martin, one of the members of the expedition, they found nourishment in turtles and unfamiliar local fruit while near land, mended their leaking boat with beeswax or soap, and repeatedly repelled attacks by unfriendly natives by firing a musket over their heads. Since the fugitives had started out at the beginning of the monsoon, the wind was against them, the seas were so rough that they were frequently in danger of capsizing, and for the first five weeks the rain left them constantly wet. Miraculously, they reached Timor on 5 June 1791 after a ten-week voyage.

At first their escape seemed to have succeeded. They were treated well by the Dutch Governor, who believed their story that they had come from a shipwrecked English vessel. But then their identity was discovered. They were immediately imprisoned and a short time later sent off on the same ship that held the mutineers of the *Bounty* recently captured in Tahiti. At the Cape of Good Hope they were transferred to another ship and brought back to England. On the way, at Batavia in Java, William Bryant and the older child died of fever. Then one of the convicts drowned in an attempt to escape, and two others died of infection. Then Mary Bryant's other child died. In short, although all the fugitives had withstood the hardships of the dreadful voyage from Botany Bay to Timor, six perished once they were back in British hands.

The survivors were brought before a magistrate at the Bow Street public office on 30 June 1792. All had originally been sentenced to seven years at Botany Bay: Mary Bryant for a street-robbery in Plymouth and stealing a cloak (she had escaped capital punishment by agreeing to transportation); James Martin for stealing sixteen-and-a-half pounds of old lead and four-and-a-half pounds of old iron; Nathaniel Lilley for stealing a fish-net, a watch, and two spoons; John Butcher for stealing three small pigs; and William Allen for stealing twenty-six handkerchiefs. The story of their escape and their present plight aroused immediate sympathy. The *London Chronicle* of 30 June–3 July 1792 concluded its account of their experiences by stating: "They declared they would sooner suffer death than return to Botany Bay. His Majesty, who is ever willing to extend his mercy, surely never had objects more worthy of it. These poor people being destitute of necessaries, several gentlemen gave them money." Early in July all five were sent to Newgate under an indeterminate sentence—a relatively lenient penalty since the usual one for escaping from transportation was death.

Soon after their arrival Boswell exerted himself on behalf of these unfortunate convicts. On 10 August, he requested a brief interview with Henry Dundas, who was now Home Secretary and, as such, responsible for deciding their fate. Six days later Boswell wrote again, complaining that Dundas had not kept the appointment and asking that at least no harsh measures be taken against the prisoners while Boswell was away from town. He had, in fact, delayed his departure for his long-projected trip to visit Temple in Cornwall in order to plead for the fugitives.

As he set out on his travels, Boswell was thinking about new writing projects. He was weighing the pros and cons of writing the life of Reynolds, perhaps encouraged by the thought that he might gather material from the members of Reynolds's family who lived in Cornwall. Boswell seems also to have considered writing the history of his own family. Sandy, who was just completing his studies at Eton, wrote to him on the subject with touching modesty on 13 July: "I am happy that you intend compiling *the memoirs* of *the Family....* Although it cannot but please me that after-ages should see a memorial of me, yet such a memorial cannot please them, such a memorial cannot do me credit. I hope that during the course of my life I may have it in my power to do something (however little prospect I now have) which may...show me not unworthy of you."

On the trip to Cornwall, the first long one that Boswell had taken in several years, he was accompanied by Veronica and Euphemia. Sandy had gone to Scotland, having received his father's permission to study at Edinburgh in the autumn. Jamie remained in London, and Betsy was visiting friends in Badshot. Perhaps the same impulse that was making Boswell think of other writing projects now made him take a new notebook and resume his journal.]

FRIDAY 17 AUGUST. Set out from my house, no. 47 Great Portland Street, with my daughters Veronica and Euphemia in a postchaise, about a quarter before eight in the morning. The weather was fine. As we drove through Oxford Street, we felt the love of London strongly. Having seen by the book of roads that it was not more than eleven miles about to go by Badshot, where my daughter Betsy was at the seat of Mr. Williams, we went there, and found a most agreeable reception.[1] Mr. Williams walked about his grounds with me and my three daughters. I admired much his hop plantations, which were more

[1] Boswell almost certainly consulted Daniel Paterson's *New and Accurate Description of All the Direct and Principal Cross Roads in Great Britain*, a popular guide known as Paterson's *Roads*, which gave the distances between towns. Boswell's host was John Williams, the father of one of Betsy's schoolmates.

beautifully regular than any I had ever seen. His Place is within two miles of Farnham, and the hops of the district round it, called "Farnham hops," sell higher than any other, because they pick them more nicely and never let leaves mix with the fruit, as is the practice in other places. When the hop is ready, is known by its size and flavour. He pointed out to us a distemper pretty frequent, of which many accounts are given but none satisfactory, which is a kind of mouldiness which comes upon the hop and quite destroys it. We had a good view of part of Surrey, particularly Farnham and its ancient castle. Mr. Williams is a jolly, sensible English Squire; Mrs. Williams, sister of Sir George Thomas,[2] a pleasing, elegant woman. A friend of hers, Mrs. Yeldham, a widow lady, was here on a visit. Betsy seemed to be quite at home, and treated with the greatest affection. When I asked her if she would go with us, she said, "No, I thank you, Sir." Her English language and manner quite delighted me.[3] I felt somewhat awkward and uneasy from knowing that her companion at Blacklands boarding-school, Mr. Williams's only daughter, only about fourteen, had complained to her and the boarding-mistress that I had been rude to her when she was last at my house. It seems after dinner, when I had taken too much wine, I had been too fond. Betsy told me the particulars, of which I had no distinct recollection, but I was vexed that such a thing should have happened, which might easily be exaggerated into very bad usage of the child of those to whom my little daughter is under great obligations. I was however glad to believe that she had not mentioned it to her father and mother, for their behaviour to me could not possibly have been what I found it today unless they had extraordinary good sense and liberality indeed to make allowance for me. But it is a sad degradation of character to require allowance to be made; and let me be on my guard, first, against intoxication, and, secondly, at least against its improper effects. I wondered at Betsy's judgement and prudence,[4] who, when I talked of what Miss Williams had complained of, said she would do what she could to make her forget it, and desired I would not speak of it to her, for she would be very angry if she knew it had been repeated to me. Surely girls are more forward in understanding than boys in general. We had a good dinner and good wines, and I had the discretion to stop after Mr. Williams and I had taken a glass or two out of the second bottle of port after dinner, as we had drunk liberally in the time of dinner. Euphemia, who had been but a little while in bed the night before, was

[2]Thomas, an M.P., chaired a committee to assist French *émigrés*.
[3]Boswell has inked out the long passage from "I felt" to "boys in general" in the manuscript.
[4]Betsy was only twelve years old.

much fatigued and grew so ill that she was obliged to lie down. I however resolved not to stay here all night if possible, though we were much pressed to it, for we were asked to be at the Bishop of Salisbury's[5] to dinner next day at four, which we could scarcely make out from hence. Euphemia grew better, and a post-chaise which we had from Farnham conveyed us to Basingstoke, where we found an excellent inn.

SATURDAY 18 AUGUST. It rained very hard, but we set out, and it was fair by the time we reached Andover. We arrived at the Bishop's Palace of Salisbury in good time to dinner. Our company was the Bishop, his lady, son, and daughter; Miss (say Mrs.)[6] Rooke, Mrs. Douglas's sister; Mr. Hudson, the Bishop's secretary; and Dr. Ash, the physician, and his niece Miss Bishop, who had been making a tour for some weeks and were going to Weymouth. The Palace was large, and elegantly repaired by the late Bishop (Barrington), who laid out upon it and the grounds about it seven thousand pounds.[7] The furniture, which Bishop Douglas bought of him, cost £1,500. Mr. ——, apothecary, played a rubber of whist with us in the evening. Dr. Ash and his niece left us.

SUNDAY 19 AUGUST. After breakfast Dr. Ash and his niece came, and they and the Bishop's son and daughter, Miss Rooke and I and my daughters went and saw the Cathedral, which had been repairing and was not yet opened for service. I was not sensible of any alteration, as I recollected only the beautiful light Gothic pillars.[8] Dr. Ash and his niece parted from us, and we attended morning prayers in the Bishop's Chapel, his son officiating, after which Mr. and Miss Douglas and I and my daughters took a walk and saw Mr. Douglas's house at St. Nicholas's Hospital, to the Mastership of which he was appointed by his father.[9] There is in the close and near to the Palace a foundation by Seth Ward, Bishop of Sarum, for ten widows of clergymen of the diocese.[1] The estate was originally £200, which produced £20 each.

---

[5]Boswell's old friend John Douglas had become Bishop of Salisbury in 1791.

[6]JB's reminder to address this mature single woman as *Mrs.*, not *Miss.*

[7]Shute Barrington had been recently translated to the richer see of Durham. During his nine years at Salisbury he had greatly embellished his palace and gardens.

[8]The renovations, begun in 1786 and directed by the architect James Wyatt, were more extensive than Boswell realized. The belfry and two small chapels were demolished, stained-glass windows were taken down, many monuments were moved, and the interior was whitewashed. However, Boswell rightly remembered the pillars, part of the cathedral's elegant English Gothic style. He had previously visited Salisbury while staying at Wilton in April 1775.

[9]William Douglas had earned a B.A. at Oxford in 1789 and had just been appointed to St. Nicholas's Hospital, a religious community for a small number of needy men and women, founded in the thirteenth century.

[1]Known as the College of Matrons, the home was founded in 1682 and was the greatest public benefaction of Bishop Seth Ward. Sarum is the old name for Salisbury.

A CARICATURE OF JAMES LOWTHER, 1st Earl of Lonsdale (1736–1802), engraving published in 1786. This print satirizes the corrupt method of electing M.P.s to represent Carlisle by packing the rolls with "honorary freemen," unqualified voters known as Lonsdale's "toadstools" or "mushrooms."

Edmond Malone (1741–1812), painted in his later years by Sir William Beechey. This undated portrait may be from the period when Malone was assisting Boswell with his *Life of Johnson*.

I send a Revise

THE

L I F E

OF

SAMUEL JOHNSON, LL.D.

COMPREHENDING

AN ACCOUNT OF HIS STUDIES AND NUMEROUS WORKS,

IN CHRONOLOGICAL ORDER;

A SERIES OF HIS

EPISTOLARY CORRESPONDENCE AND CONVERSATIONS
WITH MANY EMINENT PERSONS;

ALSO,

VARIOUS ORIGINAL PIECES OF HIS COMPOSITION,
NEVER BEFORE PUBLISHED,

THE WHOLE EXHIBITING

A VIEW OF LITERATURE AND LITERARY MEN
IN GREAT - BRITAIN,

FOR NEAR HALF A CENTURY, DURING WHICH HE FLOURISHED.

BY JAMES BOSWELL, ESQ.

In Two Volumes

Quò fit ut omnis
Votivâ pateat veluti deſcripta tabellâ
Vita ſenis.———   HORAT.

VOL. I

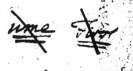

LONDON,
PRINTED BY HENRY BALDWIN;
FOR CHARLES DILLY, IN THE POULTRY.
MDCCXCI.

PROOF OF THE TITLE-PAGE of the *Life of Johnson*, 1791, showing Boswell's corrections.

WARREN HASTINGS (1732–1818) with his wife Anna Maria ("Marian"), an ayah, and their house at Alipore. This painting by John Zoffany was begun about 1783 while Hastings was still Governor-General of India and was completed about 1787. Boswell supported Hastings during his trial for malfeasance in office and was charmed by his wife.

MARY PALMER O'BRIEN, Countess of Inchiquin (1750–1820), painted by Sir Thomas Lawrence about 1794. Sir Joshua Reynolds's niece and companion, she was admired by Boswell as "the fair Palmeria."

THE DOUBLE CUBE ROOM at Wilton House, where Henry Herbert, 10th Earl of Pembroke (1734–1794), entertained Boswell and his daughters Veronica and Euphemia in August 1792.

THE LAST KNOWN SELF-PORTRAIT of Sir Joshua Reynolds (1723–
1792), painted in 1789. Boswell saw it in Cornwall at the seat of
Robert Lovell Gwatkin, husband of Reynolds's niece Theophila,
and called it "the best representation of my celebrated friend."

"The Royal Academicians in General Assembly," painted by Henry Singleton in 1795, shows many of the figures mentioned in these journals. Benjamin West, President of the Academy, wearing a ceremonial hat, is in the centre. Ozias Humphry faces him on his right; Sir William Chambers sits below him on his left. Joseph Farington, looking towards West, stands below a plaster cast of the *Laocoön*. The absence of Boswell, who served as the Academy's Secretary for Foreign Correspondence, suggests that this group portrait was painted after his death.

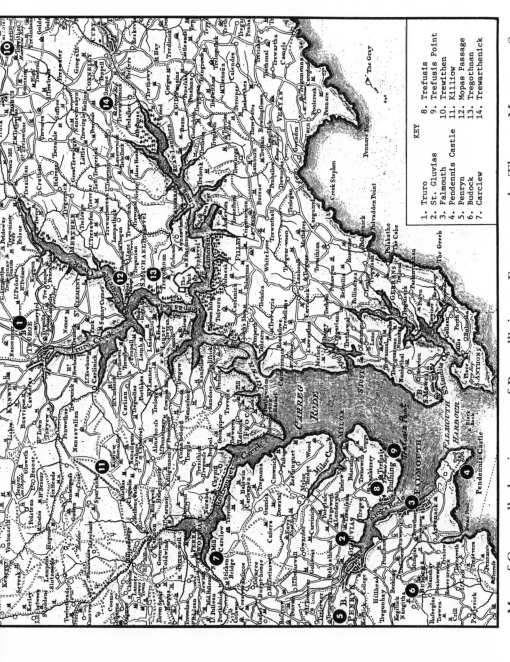

KEY

1. Truro
2. St. Gluvias
3. Falmouth
4. Pendennis Castle
5. Penryn
6. Budock
7. Carclew
8. Trefusis
9. Trefusis Point
10. Trewithen
11. Killiow
12. Mopas Passage
13. Tregothnan
14. Trewarthenick

Map of Cornwall, showing part of Boswell's jaunt. From a map by Thomas Martyn, 1784.

EDMUND BURKE (1729–1797), painted by John Hoppner about 1795. Burke wears the splendid gown of the LL.D., awarded him in 1790 by his Alma Mater, Trinity College, Dublin, which commissioned this portrait and still exhibits it in the Public Theatre.

It is now £270. But the increase in money is not equal to the increased price of provisions. They have however pretty good accommodation, having each a kitchen and two other rooms; and such as have an additional income may live very well. Indeed I believe all of them have; for the Bishop, who did not give the due praise to the legal fund for the widows of ministers in Scotland, to which all the clergy are compelled to contribute,[2] told me that the voluntary charities in England were sufficient. Of this I have some doubt, because I have often heard of the widows of clergymen in England being in great distress. But I did not dispute with my worthy friend the Bishop, who was now old, he having entered at Oxford in 1736, and from the gout flying through his body had an irritability which occasioned a perpetual fretfulness, which, without any real bad humour, was for ever showing itself in trifles, particularly towards his son, who however was to blame in *answering;* so that I applied to him in a light sense *improbus ille puer.*[3] It is striking to observe how peevishness will lessen the most respectable character till *reflection* brings it up again to its proper level.

Six of the aforesaid widows dined with us today, it being the custom for them to dine with the Bishop once a year. Six were all who could come. They were very decent matrons. The Bishop modestly said, "They are just such as my wife would have been if I had not obtained preferment." His Lordship observed to me that it was wonderful both that he was not made a bishop long before, and that he was made one at the time when it unexpectedly happened. He was not in the humour for much conversation; but he set me right as to his exhibition to Balliol College, Oxford, which was not from Glasgow, as has been generally supposed, for he never studied there, but from ——. I wished to get from him the particulars of his life. Perhaps I may in time. He was chaplain to the third Regiment of Foot Guards, and was at the battle of Fontenoy.[4] We were treated here with the greatest hospitality, and my daughters were very happy, which they from some erroneous no-

---

[2]Legislation to provide the widows of Scottish clergymen with annuities had been enacted several times during the previous fifty years, most recently in 1779.

[3]Virgil, *Eclogues,* viii. 50: "Heartless is the boy."

[4]Douglas had been appointed to his first bishopric, of Carlisle, in 1787 when he was already sixty-six years old. In his youth, he had studied at Balliol on two separate exhibitions (scholarships) reserved for Scottish students, one beginning in 1738, which enabled him to earn a B.A. and M.A., the other seven years later. His second exhibition, the respected Snell, was normally reserved for a student of the University of Glasgow, but Douglas was chosen by Balliol, perhaps because the Glasgow authorities had not named a suitable candidate. Before returning to Oxford, Douglas was present at Fontenoy, a major battle of the War of the Austrian Succession fought on 30 April 1745, at which the British and their allies were defeated by the French.

tion did not expect to be. My servant James Ross came on Saturday by the coach. I found a kind letter from Lord Pembroke in answer to mine from London. I sent James today with a note to him. He sent back word "he would be glad to see us; he would not ride out, on purpose that he might be at home to receive us. I must not talk of hours, nor be in such a hurry as I was last time."[5]

MONDAY 20 AUGUST. I find I *journalize* too tediously. Let me try to abbreviate. We got to Wilton in good time to breakfast, and met with the politest reception from Lord Pembroke, who attended us in person while we viewed his noble house and statues and pictures and magnificent seat. He directed our attention to a wood of three thousand acres, to various prospects, to Sir Philip Sidney's Walk, whose *Arcadia* however he frankly avowed he thought a strange performance[6]— I forget the word he used, but it was a well-chosen one, I think synonymous to rhapsody.[7] I not having read *Arcadia* sheltered my ignorance under the trite observation that it was in the taste of the age. His Lordship's gentleness to all the animals in his park was very pleasing. A ram from Constantinople of a large size and black and white wool was remarkably tame. He told me he had disposed of the patronage of a Welsh living,[8] as he never could give it to a friend, the Welsh language being necessary, and with the price was to take in a considerable addition to his park, which he pointed out. I was glad to find him making several improvements at his family seat. The *approach,* which was formerly so ugly that the Duchess of Queensberry used to call it "the *re*proach," was now formed with elegant taste, and an elegant lodge was built; and he was fitting up a large library in a part of the house which had remained unfinished. He took the trouble to show us his *manège* and made some of his horses stand upon steps, and pick up a handkerchief, and in short exhibit specimens of that docility which he himself has improved.[9]

After having been many years without seeing him except for a few minutes occasionally, I was delighted to find him walking about

[5]Henry Herbert, tenth Earl of Pembroke, was urging Boswell not to be afraid of staying too long at Wilton. The last time Boswell had visited him, together with Paoli in 1775, they had left after three days, feeling gloomy and somewhat neglected by their host.

[6]Sidney wrote his pastoral romance *Arcadia* at Wilton in the 1580s while staying with his sister, the Countess of Pembroke.

[7]In the earlier sense of miscellany or medley.

[8]A clergyman's position with a guaranteed income.

[9]Wilton House, rebuilt in the mid-seventeenth century after the earlier Tudor mansion burned down, had had a notoriously awkward entrance on the east side. Pembroke, who is still known as the Equestrian Earl, not only trained his horses in his new *manège* or riding-school, designed by Sir William Chambers, but also wrote an influential treatise on horsemanship.

with me familiarly arm in arm and chatting freely as formerly. I saw that nothing was wanting but opportunity to keep up our gay friendship.[1] But he is, like many others, and those very amiable too, an out-of-sight out-of-mind man. I thanked him for thus gratifying my daughters, and apologized for their not being fine ladies. I reminded him of the loss they had suffered of a valuable mother, whose worth he knew. He said it was so much the better they were not fine ladies, and observed that Scotch girls could take better care of themselves than mothers in England. There is to be sure a general *prudence* among them. He asked us very kindly to stay till next day; and on my telling him I could not, as a gentleman (the Rev. Mr. Phillipps near Torrington) was engaged to meet me at Exeter, he insisted we should dine, to which I agreed; and he courteously said, "You shall have it at any hour. I will order it *now*" (not yet three, though five was his time). We actually had it at four. When I looked at him, I perceived his figure and gait older. But when he talked, his countenance and manner were as lively as ever. My daughters were quite charmed with him. I felt it strange, and regretted it, that so amiable a man should have contracted such dissolute habits, and at this very time, instead of living respectably with his charming Countess, had Baccelli, the superannuated dancing courtesan, in a *casino* in the neighbourhood.[2]

His company were Sir John Blaquiere and his son, Mr. Staples a young surgeon, and Sperati the violoncello player,[3] with whom Veronica was acquainted. *Travelling* Coxe (an epithet of mine for him which made the Earl laugh, who justly observed that he was a bad writer, his style being harsh, and that he was *le plus grand questionneur du monde*)[4]

---

[1]Boswell and Pembroke had been acquainted since 1768, when Pembroke wrote to ask for an introduction to Paoli in Corsica. After meeting Pembroke a few years later, Boswell had enjoyed his hospitality in London and had, in fact, hoped for preferment through him.

[2]The Italian dancer Giovanna Francesca Antonia Guiseppe Zanerini, who used her mother's name, Baccelli, was ensconced near Wilton House. For twenty years she had been the mistress of John Frederick Sackville, third Duke of Dorset, with whom she had lived both in Paris, where he had been the British Ambassador, and in his family mansion at Knole. They had separated just before his marriage in 1789. Elizabeth, Countess of Pembroke, had suffered from her husband's infidelity before; in 1784 she was apparently left in the South of France with their dying daughter while he went to Florence with an opera-girl.

[3]B. Sperati was the first violoncellist at the Concerts of Ancient Music and at two London theatres.

[4]The Rev. William Coxe, Pembroke's appointee as rector of Bemerton, had written several accounts of his travels on the Continent; we do not know why the Earl considered him the most inquisitive person in the world.

and Mr. Turner, Clerk of the Peace,[5] joined us at dinner. We lived well and with perfect ease. His Lordship drank a little wine, but chiefly toast and water with lemon juice. But he made burgundy, champagne, hock, port, claret, etc., circulate liberally; and Sir John Blaquiere said pleasantly to me after dinner, from his Irish convivial habits, "GOD bless you. For till today I believe we have seldom done more than finish one bottle." I was amused by Sir John's imagining that he and I were old acquaintance in Scotland. He was thinking of somebody else. But it did very well, as I did not contradict it. I had dined with him winter before last at Courtenay's, when he had the same fancy.[6] Tea and coffee were ordered, and Lord Pembroke went to the *ladies*. In a few minutes we followed; and it was truly a *sight* to me, a man of *multitudinous imagination*, to behold *my daughters Veronica and Euphemia* sitting with the Earl of Pembroke in his immense drawing-room, under the family picture by Van Dyck, undoubtedly the most capital work in portrait-painting that the world has to show.[7] How many *Scotch lairds* are there whose daughters could have such an honour? They behaved very well. We went at night to Shaftesbury, the Angel but a secondary inn where post-chaises were not kept; but the landlady was a decent, very old woman about fourscore, very civil, and the bill reasonable.

TUESDAY 21[8] AUGUST. We continued the road by Shaftesbury, which Lord Pembroke had recommended as seven miles shorter. The inns however were not so good as on the Dorchester line, which we did not get upon till we came to Honiton. We reached Exeter at night and put up at Thompson's Hotel, a good house. Here James Ross was waiting for us, having come by the coach.

WEDNESDAY 22 AUGUST. I found my cousin and old acquaintance, Maj. Daniel Hamilton, who having married a Devonshire lady, has for many years been Receiver of Land Tax for one half of the county, and is also a partner in the Exeter Bank. He has a house in Exeter, and one also at ———, about a mile out of town. He explained to me our relationship. His grandfather was a son of the family of

[5] A Clerk of the Peace was an officer who kept the county records and helped Justices of the Peace in drawing up Indictments and issuing other legal documents.
[6] See above, 28 November 1789.
[7] Sir Anthony Van Dyck's largest family group, painted c. 1635–36, consists of ten full-length portraits of Philip Herbert, fourth Earl of Pembroke, his six surviving children, a son-in-law, a daughter-in-law, and his second wife. Boswell saw it in the magnificent double-cube drawing-room especially designed by Inigo Jones for this and Pembroke's other Van Dyck portraits.
[8] Boswell inadvertently wrote 20, and 21 at the beginning of the next entry.

Dalzell and brother to Anna Hamilton, my great-grandmother.[9] He and my father therefore were second cousins. He went with me to call on Mr. Jackson, the organist here. He was out of town, but we saw Mrs. Jackson and his daughter, some landscapes painted by him, and his portrait and several pictures, particularly landscapes, by Gainsborough, with whom he was very intimate.[1] The Major then went with me and Euphemia (Veronica staying at the inn) and showed us what is called the *Ditch,* being the fossé and ruinous banks of the old castle, which the late Mr. Patch, a ——, brother to Patch the caricature-painter, having obtained a lease of, formed with wonderful taste into a garden varied with walks and shrubbery in an extraordinary and beautiful manner.[2] We then looked at the courts of justice where the assizes are held. It rained, and Euphemia went to her sister. The Major and I had patience till it grew fair, and then surveyed the public walk and the high street. He dined with us, and after dinner came the Rev. Mr. Phillipps of ——[3] near Torrington, a lively, well-informed man whom I had met at Miss Palmer's since Sir Joshua Reynolds's death, and who had engaged to meet me here and give me directions for travelling in the west, which he did in writing. There came also my old acquaintance Dr. Daniel, who had studied physic at Edinburgh.[4] So we had a goodly society. Mr. Jackson came in the evening, and he and Mr. Phillipps supped with us. The Major went to his country-house, and Daniel, I suppose, to his patients. Jackson was a man of stately figure and address, but was too opinionated. He drank no wine, which had been his practice all his life.

THURSDAY 23 AUGUST. Having risen early by mistake, I did not go to bed again, but read Mr. Jackson's two little volumes of *Letters, Being Essays on Various Subjects,* which I had bought the day before. I was disappointed, for in some review I had seen an account of them

[9]Hamilton's house was at North Brook, near Exeter. His grandfather, John Hamilton, was one of the Hamiltons of Dalzell, and Anna Hamilton was Lord Auchinleck's paternal grandmother.

[1]William Jackson was not only the organist at Exeter Cathedral and a composer but also an amateur artist. Gainsborough, a close friend for twenty years, had painted his portrait—perhaps the one Boswell saw—and had exhibited it at the Royal Academy in 1770.

[2]John Patch, a surgeon who had died five years earlier, had converted the fosse or moat of Rougemont Castle, built by William the Conqueror, into a garden and had also built a house on the grounds. One of his brothers was the painter and engraver Thomas Patch, a student of Florentine art who had spent most of his life in Italy.

[3]The Rev. John Phillipps lived in Mambury.

[4]Boswell had met George Daniel frequently while he was studying medicine at Edinburgh in 1780–81.

which made me think them better than I found them. I thought them now flimsy and conceited. I own however that his arguments for sponta-neous generation, which form by much the most ingenious of his letters, puzzled me.[5] I must find a refutation of them, for I am sure they are not solid. Mr. Phillipps and Dr. Daniel and his lady came to us at breakfast, after which Mr. Phillipps accompanied my daughters and me to the Ca-thedral, where we heard morning service performed and Mr. Jackson play on the noble organ. There was an anthem of his composition which I thought remarkably sweet. Major Hamilton came to town before we set out, which [we did] about twelve. I felt a curious sensation on entering Cornwall, of which I had thought so long. The country had quite the ap-pearance of many of the bad parts of Scotland. We got at night to Bodmin.

FRIDAY 24 AUGUST. The country from Launceston to Bodmin and onwards till we came within view of Truro seemed as dreary as any I had ever seen. It had the wildness of our Highlands without the grandeur. About Truro the scene changed much for the better; but a little way from it the desert began again, and I wondered that my friend Temple should have praised Cornwall. However, when we approached his vicarage of St. Gluvias, and saw Falmouth and the adjacent lands and the bay, we were agreeably surprised. I found the vicarage pret-tily situated on a bank which my friend had dressed and planted with real taste. Under the bank flowed an arm of the sea, and on an emi-nence opposite stands Penryn, a borough built of stone[6] and contain-ing two thousand people. It is not above half a quarter of a mile from the vicarage, and is in the parish, so the church, which is close to the vicarage, though pretty well concealed by trees, though a spacious build-ing, has a goodly congregation, and there is not the dispiriting sensa-tion of a *country parish* which I apprehended. We saw at first Mrs. Temple, two daughters, and four sons, Robert, the second, being at a school in Devonshire.[7] By and by my friend returned from his ride, and I had the satisfaction of at last embracing him on this spot. It seemed quite a dream to me being at last *in Cornwall!* We dined and walked, and Miss Temple and Veronica gave us some music, and we supped, and then evening prayers were read.

[5]In "Of Self-Production," Letter xxiv of his *Thirty Letters on Various Subjects* (1782), Jackson argues that only the principle of spontaneous generation can explain how cer-tain plants and animals originally came into existence in places cut off from the rest of the world.

[6]Penryn is famous for its granite.

[7]Boswell met Temple's wife Anne; the daughters Anne (called Nancy), who had ac-companied Temple to London in 1790 and was now twenty years old, and Laura, aged eleven; and the sons Francis (called Frank), twenty-two; John James, fifteen; Frederick, thirteen; and Octavius, eight. The absent son, Robert George, was seventeen.

SATURDAY 25 AUGUST. After breakfast I walked with Mr. Francis Temple to Penryn and surveyed it from one end to the other. My servant came by the Falmouth coach. My friend and I rode out, but the rain of this climate soon drove us home. The time passed much in the same way as yesterday.

SUNDAY 26 AUGUST. I was pleased to witness my friend's performing divine service in his church here. He has another, two miles off, called St. Budock, where he does duty every Sunday afternoon, and Mr. Beverley, schoolmaster of Penryn, a true Yorkshireman, officiates here. We had two Miss Coodes, Penryn young ladies, to drink tea with us.[8]

MONDAY 27 AUGUST. My friend and I rode to Pendennis Castle. It was a fine day, and I liked the prospect of Falmouth Bay,[1] and the various branches or *rivers,* as they are called, issuing into the country. We walked quite round the Castle, and returned by Falmouth. The sight of a town and harbour animated me, though the town is in general composed of narrow streets. It is but about two miles from Penryn. My friend and I congratulated ourselves on our friendship being now the same as ever.

TUESDAY 28 AUGUST. We went with Miss Temple, my daughters, and Mr. Francis Temple about two miles off to Carclew, the seat of Sir William Lemon, Member for the county, and viewed his house and Place, for which, in consequence of a letter from Temple, leave had been obtained, and my friend and I invited to dine there next day. It is a substantial house, much improved by its present owner, the rooms large and comfortable.[2] There are a few good pictures. The Place is well planted, and a good view from it of an arm of the sea. None of the family appeared. Sir Christopher Hawkins came to dinner, and stayed till late in the evening. He politely engaged us to come to his house at Trewithen on Friday, and that we should meet him at his house at Trewinnard[3] on Thursday sennight in our way to the Land's End, to which he agreed to accompany us.

WEDNESDAY 29 AUGUST. Temple and I dined with Sir William Lemon. His lady, a sister of Justice Buller's, had quite the quickness

---

[8]Two of the seven daughters of Edward Coode. Their grandfather had been Temple's predecessor as vicar of St. Gluvias.

[1]Pendennis is a fortified castle noted for its spectacular location on a rock atop a three-hundred-foot hill, overlooking Falmouth harbour on one side and the English Channel on the other.

[2]Sir William Lemon, M.P., owed his wealth to his grandfather, who had made his fortune in copper-mining.

[3]The Hawkins family, which had settled in Cornwall in the mid-sixteenth century, had owned Trewinnard since the 1630s and had acquired the estate of Trewithen, where Hawkins was born, in the early eighteenth century through Hawkins's grandmother.

and penetration of her brother.[4] I perceived that she would like to have my friend Sir Christopher Hawkins as her son-in-law. I said, "Madam, I'll send him to you in a box; and as he is a *delicate* gentleman, I'll write upon it, *Glass*." She humoured the fancy and added in the *waggon* or other *carriage* style, "*Keep this side uppermost.*" Everything at this house was as became a Member for a county. The company besides ourselves were the Rev. Mr. Sandys and his lady and Captain Williams of Truro. Sir William's second daughter, Miss Maria, seemed to be a charming woman. When we went to tea, I in my way *attached* myself to her, keeping up conversation wonderfully. I was struck by a new instance how generally I am known. She told me she stood next me at Mrs. Broadhead's masquerade when Mr. Broadhead talked to me of having me with him to a snug party.[5] I exclaimed, "Why did you not speak to me? What, Miss Maria Lemon, of whom I had heard so much?" Mamma was ready again with her smartness: "What! would you have had her speak to the *great Boswell?*" I observed at dinner a kind of apprehension that I might make a *book* of my tour in this country; for when Lady Lemon called to Sir William, "You don't observe Mrs. Sandys making love to you," and I said, "Is this your way in Cornwall, to prompt your husbands to gallantry?" she answered, "Pray don't insert this." I laughed and said, "No, no." Yet travellers have drawn conclusions upon as slight a foundation. "It is a custom in Cornwall"—and so they will gravely remark from superficial, hasty ignorance. This was a good day as days go *in the country*.[6]

THURSDAY 30 AUGUST. A showery day. Temple and I rode to Trefusis, about two miles off. We there met Sir William Lemon and the Rev. Mr. Sandys, riding on the same errand, to look at the prospect from the Point, which is indeed very fine: Falmouth, Pendennis Castle, the bay with arms extending into the land, the ocean, and the village of Flushing under the eye, beneath the hill or bank. Sir William proved himself to be a truly courteous man, for he was as eager to show me this Place as his own. His lady and eldest daughter and Mrs. Sandys were paying a visit to Mrs. Trefusis, a Swiss lady from

---

[4]Lady Lemon's brother was the formidable Sir Francis Buller, Judge of the King's Bench, whom Boswell had observed in 1786 presiding in his London courtroom.

[5]On 11 May 1792 Boswell had attended the fashionable subscription masquerade for about 600 guests held annually at Mary Broadhead's home in Portland Place. Her husband, Theodore Henry Brinckman, who had changed his name to Broadhead, had been Sheriff of Surrey in 1786.

[6]Boswell's characteristic doubts about the pleasures of life in the country—an echo of Johnson's comments on the subject, such as, "They who are content to live in the country, are *fit* for the country" (*Life of Johnson*, 30 June 1784).

Lausanne.[7] We met them coming out, and we went through the house, a parcel of old-fashioned, musty rooms. But we saw a chimney-piece curiously carved, and some good pictures.

FRIDAY 31 AUGUST. Miss Temple and my daughters in a chaise, and Temple and his son Francis and I on horseback, went to Trewithen to visit Sir Christopher Hawkins. It was still Cornish weather, showery and fair successively. But it is necessary in this country to have a great deal of rain, the soil is so dry and it soon is absorbed, so that it is not so incommodious as in Ayrshire, though it is bad enough. Trewithen is situated on a bleak eminence, without much shelter except that of some plantations of Scotch firs. The house is built of stone, large and roomy. The dining-room is spacious. I liked to see a good number of family portraits, for this is an English family of ancient standing in Cornwall, but not of eminent distinction for wealth till this gentleman's grandfather, who[8] was called *Ironspurs,* saved a great deal of money, in which course he was followed by his son and afterwards by Sir Christopher's mother during a long minority; and now the present representative goes on accumulating. He is said to be exceedingly rich, and he lives on a very economical plan, and very retired, though he has contrived to negotiate with Lord Falmouth for a seat in Parliament for the borough of St. Michael, and thus has been made a Baronet.[9] We passed the time well enough with eating and drinking and a rubber at whist, and some conversation. At Trewithen there is a very good picture of Charles the Second by ———. It belonged to the family of Granville, Lord Lansdown, after the wreck of which their house was pulled to pieces, and everything was sold.[1]

---

[7]Trefusis is the name both of a place, near Falmouth, and of a family which had lived there since Norman times. The family representative at this time, Robert George William Trefusis, was married to Albertina Marianna Gaulis, the daughter of a Lausanne magistrate.

[8]At this point Boswell has inked out one line, which is indecipherable.

[9]Hawkins's grandfather, also called Christopher Hawkins, briefly outlived his son, Col. Thomas Hawkins, M.P., who died in 1766, leaving the eight-year-old Christopher to be brought up by his mother, Anne. An M.P. for the past eight years, he had been created Baronet in July 1791.

[1]The painting presumably came from Stow House, a magnificent mansion in Kilkhampton, Cornwall, built in 1680 by John Granville, Viscount Lansdown and Earl of Bath, who had been a strong supporter of the monarchy before and after the Restoration and had been ennobled by Charles II in 1661. The dissolution of the family occurred in 1711 with the death of his grandson at the age of nineteen. At that time, the Granville estates were divided among three surviving aunts, and objects from the house were sold to many Cornish gentlemen. The family of Granville to which Boswell refers is either Viscount Lansdown's or that of his nephew, the poet George Granville, Baron Lansdown.

SATURDAY 1 SEPTEMBER. We came to Killiow, two miles nearer Penryn than Truro, and dined at Mr. Gwatkin's, where were Mr. Vivian, mayor of Truro, and his lady, and Messrs. Powlett and Walk, officers of the 25 Regiment, a company of which, detached from headquarters at Plymouth, was quartered at Truro.[2] I saw here the last picture Sir Joshua Reynolds did of himself. It has a sort of *pulled-up* look,[3] and not the placid gentleness of his smiling manner; but the features, though rather too largely and strongly limned, are most exactly portrayed, and the dress in every respect being such as he usually wore, I think it the best representation of my celebrated friend.[4] We got into a jolly frame here, and I drank rather too freely. It was not agreeable riding home at night.

SUNDAY 2 SEPTEMBER. After we got into church there was as heavy a rain as I think I ever saw. It being the first Sunday of a month, the Holy Sacrament was administered, and I received it from the hands of my old and most intimate friend. The weather, as is customary, changed after dinner, and the evening was fair, so that several young people sung sacred music in the churchyard at night, which it seems is an usage here.

MONDAY 3 SEPTEMBER. It rained heavier and more continued than any day I had yet seen in Cornwall; not but it was as violent a rain, perhaps more so, the day before, but it did not last so long. During my visit here, my friend's third son now alive, John James, so named after John Claxton, Esq., of Shirley in Surrey and me, read to me every morning a lesson both in Greek from Homer's *Iliad*, book 5, and from the 2 and 3 orations of Cicero against Catiline. I felt this refreshing, and had sensations as in my early years, and was pleased to think that I might recover my learning whenever I should force myself to apply again. What a difference would it make on my existence should I do so! I trust I shall. Temple and I had recourse to one of the best modes of relief in rainy weather, which is to do something that occupies without straining or at all fatiguing the mind. We sorted according to years the large mass of letters of mine to him

[2]Killiow was the seat of Robert Lovell Gwatkin, Sheriff of Cornwall in 1789 and the husband of Reynolds's niece Mary Theophila. The guests consisted of John Vivian, vice-warden of the Cornish tin mines and this year's mayor of Truro; his wife, the former Betsy Cranch, known in her youth for her beauty and many suitors; Lt. Thomas Norton Powlett and very likely Lt. William Barry Wade, there being no Walk in the 25th Regiment.

[3]See the illustration in this book.

[4]This painting remained in the Gwatkin family for many years and is now in private hands.

since our first correspondence in 1757.[5] He was afterwards to arrange them according to their dates. As I looked into several of them at different periods, I had curious sensations. However, amidst all the changes and varieties, and those pretty strong ones too, I could still trace enough of personal identity: warmth of heart and imagination, vanity and piety. My friend agreed with me that it was wonderful I had made myself the man I was, considering the extreme narrowness of my education; for he remembered me the most puritanical being, and the most timid in society; and now there was no man of more elevated ecclesiastical notions, more liberal views, and perhaps none so universally easy and of more address in social life. We laughed confidentially at my wonderful art of displaying extraordinary symptoms of learning and knowledge, when I had read so little in a regular way. Yet I had, as the French say, *feuilletté* a great many books, and had, like Johnson, the art of quickly seizing a general notion from perusing a small part.[6] I here read only Moseley's *Treatise on Coffee,* in which there is a ludicrous affectation of learning, probably all borrowed without his understanding it, and not much actual information, though it indeed brings together a great deal in recommendation of a favourite liquor of mine;[7] and a small portion of the first volume of *Les Confessions de J.-J. Rousseau.*

It grew fair in the evening, and I walked with my daughters and Mr. Francis Temple (to whom, being a midshipman, I gave the title of Captain[8]) to Falmouth, and carried them to the play. The House was very mean, being two rooms at a low inn. But the performers acted *Which is the Man, The Wapping Landlady,* and *The Padlock* (of which we stayed the first act) really very well. The company belonged to young

---

[5]Temple had presumably collected about 200 of Boswell's letters. Of these, 116 have survived, the earliest dated 29 July 1758. Nancy Temple and the Rev. Charles Powlett destroyed some of Boswell's letters soon after Temple's death, and more were lost on the Continent, where Powlett, by then Nancy's widower, lived after 1827. The total surviving Boswell-Temple correspondence consists of about 460 letters.

[6]Boswell notes that Johnson "had a peculiar facility in seizing at once what was valuable in any book, without submitting to the labour of perusing it from beginning to end" (*Life of Johnson* i. 71).

[7]Dr. Benjamin Moseley's *Treatise Concerning the Properties and Effects of Coffee,* first published under a slightly different title in 1785 and in its fifth edition in 1792, gives a history of the uses of coffee and recommends it as a cure for a multitude of diseases.

[8]Ironic teasing: for almost two years Frank had hoped to become a lieutenant, and Temple had pressed Boswell and other friends to use their influence with anyone who could arrange his promotion.

Hughes, son to one of the proprietors of Sadler'sWells.[9] My mind *rusts* very soon in the country, especially in damp weather. I felt *strange* even in this little theatre, though the music was only two fiddles, played one by a white and one by a Negro, who sat in a little recess close by one side of the stage, and the *boxes* were a small division on each side of the *pit*, which was an even floor. In one of the boxes I was surprised to perceive,[1] with three foreign gentlemen, the little French mademoiselle whom I knew for some time in London by the name of Divry. We took no notice of our ever having been acquainted. She had come down with one of the foreigners to stay with him till he sailed. I felt a little of

> *Je reconnais les atteintes*
> *Qui m'ont autrefois charmés,*

as the French song goes.[2] But I checked such feelings at once by recollecting what a mercenary and base creature she was. Notwithstanding all the rain of yesterday and today we walked without wetting our feet to Falmouth and back again. We enjoyed some supper and punch on our return.

TUESDAY 4 SEPTEMBER. I was engaged to dine today with Mr. Gwatkin and meet Sir Christopher Hawkins at night at the Truro Whist Club. I had engaged to dine at Truro yesterday with a club called the Four Burrow Club (from four *burrows* or ancient *tumuli*[3] in a field where they hunt). It meets at the members' houses alternately. But as it is famous for hard drinking, Temple very properly made me send an excuse. Today the morning was fair, but I had some rain in my way to Gwatkin's, whom I met near his house in the carriage with his lady. They took me in, and told me the plan was altered, for M. Depont, the

---

[9]The performance took place in the local inn because the Falmouth theatre had burned down two weeks earlier. The programme consisted of Hannah Cowley's ten-year-old comedy *Which is the Man?*, with the alternative title *The Cornish Romp*, no longer on the London stage; the twenty-year-old but still popular ballet-pantomime *The Wapping Landlady;* and Isaac Bickerstaffe's equally old comic opera, *The Padlock*, intended as an afterpiece. The theatre's manager was Richard Hughes; his father, of the same name, owned several theatres in the vicinity and had taken over a quarter share of the Sadler's Wells Theatre a year earlier, saving it from failing and becoming a Methodist Chapel.

[1]Boswell has inked out most of the following passage, to "base creature she was," in the manuscript.

[2]"I feel again the spells that once enchanted me"—a song Boswell had learned as a young man in Berlin.

[3]Burial mounds made of earth, which abound in Cornwall.

gentleman to whom Mr. Burke's celebrated *Letter* on the French Revolution was addressed,[4] was that day to dine with Mr. Vivian, the mayor of Truro, and we were to be of the party. M. Depont was a very genteel, pleasing young man, and spoke English well. We had there also Mr. Daniell, a rich merchant in the town,[5] and his lady. There is good living at Truro, there being a number of wealthy people in it. Both Vivian and Daniell were stately fellows, and vin de graves, sherry, and port circulated heartily, but not to excess. I drank here some Cornish cider, remarkably good, which I am told it seldom is. After tea and coffee all the gentlemen went to the club. M. Depont stayed a short while. Twenty-one supped, the greatest number ever known, a compliment to me, as I was informed. I played two rubbers at whist, half a crown the rate, and I betted two crowns each rubber. I won two guineas. The supper and wine and negus or punch, which each man drank as he chose after supper, was only eighteen pence. Mr. ———, the apothecary, was in the chair. He told me it was a very old club, having lasted above fifty years. It meets every Monday. I recollect three physicians, Drs. ———, Captain Reynolds of the navy, two Mr. Nankivells (a singular name, as to which Mrs. Gwatkin told me that someone observed there were strange names of *men* in Cornwall: *Nan*kivell and *Pol*whele), also Mr. Enys, a half-pay officer, uncle to the representative of that ancient family. The two officers of the 25 were here. They showed me the tallest man in the regiment, *Jamie Buchanan,* born near Stirling, who had been five-and-twenty years in the regiment, and was still a private. I asked him why he was not a sergeant? He said he had been a little wild. Poor fellow, though but four-and-forty, he was much broke. But he had been ten years at Gibraltar. There was no hard drinking at this club tonight. I liked it very well. But I was told the *genius* of it is to *badger* each other, as it is called; that is to say, to have a great deal of coarse raillery, which I was glad to be told my presence restrained. Hawkins was as good as his word, and met me here. Mrs. Gwatkin waited at Mr. Vivian's, and her husband and I went home with her in the chaise.

[4]Charles-Jean-François Depont, a young idealist who strongly supported the French Revolution, had been entertained by the Burke family when he and his father, a magistrate in Metz, had visited England in 1785. His admiration for Burke's earlier speeches had led him to ask Burke in 1789 to set down his thoughts on the French Revolution. The reply, the *Reflections on the Revolution in France,* published in November 1791, was far longer and more critical of the events in France than Depont had expected.

[5]Ralph Allen Daniell owed his wealth to his father's and his own successful mining operations. He was named after his granduncle Ralph Allen of Prior Park, Bath, the friend and patron of Pope and Fielding.

WEDNESDAY 5 SEPTEMBER. After breakfast Mr. Gwatkin accompanied me through a pretty waste country to view some of the riches of Cornwall, the mines. We went to one called *Poldice*[6] and some others near it. There we found William Murdoch, son of my tenant John Murdoch in Bellow Mill.[7] He is settled in Cornwall very advantageously as a superintendent of Messrs. Boulton and Watt's engines, and has shares in a number of mines. He showed us some of the engines, the contrivance and power of which is wonderful. But I had seen some before. The tin and copper often lie very near together. They call a course or vein of metal a *lode*. Some of the mines are of an immense depth.[8] The miners go down sometimes perpendicularly in iron buckets, sometimes by steep ladders from one depth to another, descending transversely. I did not go down. I was surprised to see the miners look so well, even when just come out of the pits, and the men, women, and children employed in beating and sorting and otherwise preparing the ore and stone seemed active and cheerful. The heaps of earth thrown out of the mines seem like huts at a distance; and as Mr. Gwatkin observed, the country has a more waste appearance by the soil being pared[1] for fuel, of which stacks are to be seen standing thick everywhere except in cultivated spots, which I observed produce richly. Mr. Gwatkin and I rode to St. Gluvias through a part of the country I had not yet seen, in which I observed one or two pretty good seats of gentlemen who seemed comfortable. Mrs. Gwatkin was at Temple's before us, and we had a capital dinner, more company having been expected. Mr. and Mrs. Gwatkin left us in the evening.

THURSDAY 6 SEPTEMBER. Mrs. Temple and my daughters and my friend and I and Francis on horseback (James my servant being understood as always attending me) set out for the Land's End. We had a fine day, and passed through Helston; then took a slight view of the ancient seat of Godolphin, now belonging to the Duke of Leeds.[2] Little to be seen. Then passed through the village of St. Erth and came to Trewinnard, the oldest seat of the Hawkins family, where Sir Christopher had engaged to meet us at dinner, which he accordingly

[6]A profitable tin- and copper-mine.
[7]Bellow Mill was situated in Lady Auchinleck's jointure lands on the Auchinleck estate.
[8]The steam-engines developed by the firm of Matthew Boulton and James Watt had replaced the manual pumps used to drain water from the mines—some of them almost 2,000 feet deep—and had revolutionized tin- and copper-mining in Cornwall in the past two decades.
[1]Sliced off and cut up.
[2]The Duke of Leeds had come into possession of Godolphin through his mother, the daughter of Francis, second Earl of Godolphin.

did. I liked this Place much better than Trewithen. It is situated in a better part of the country, and there is an air of antiquity and cultivation about it. The house is indeed a collection of strange rooms huddled together with a number of inconvenient passages and narrow staircases. In the evening we left the Baronet and proceeded to Penzance. It had rained again today several times. Sir Christopher had given us a letter to Mr. Price, a rich Jamaica planter here. So after putting up at the hotel, an awkward inn, I called on him and found him a contemporary of Beauclerk and Langton at Trinity College, Oxford, and a man of reading and animation, but a kind of humourist.[3] He would not sup with us, but promised to come to breakfast next day.

FRIDAY 7 SEPTEMBER. Mr. Price breakfasted with us, and talked a great deal and in true Tory style. He carried me and Temple and Frank to see a collection of fossils belonging to Mr. Giddy, surgeon here,[4] consisting of specimens of tin, copper, lead, the soapy rock, and a few pebbles. It was a very good collection of its size. It rained sadly. Hawkins came to us—a strange man to have a large fortune, for he rode without a greatcoat, and was much wet. He and Temple, on account of the badness of the day, resolved not to go to the Land's End. The ladies, in the chaise which we had from Falmouth, and Mr. Francis Temple and I in a Penzance chaise drove to the Land's End. I had amused myself during this jaunt with remarks on the inhabitants of the country, whom I called Cornish *clouts,* from Spenser's *Colin Clout.* I talked of them as wild animals; and that droves of them might be seen running about with bare legs, some with shoes, some without. One of them yesterday gaped and laughed like a fool when I said to F. Temple, "There's one that is *shod.* But he must have been *worked.*" They truly reminded one of Yahoos.[5] It was so dark from the rain that we did not go to see the Logan Stone.[6] But it luckily grew fair, though not

[3] An eccentric. Although John Price was born in Penzance, most of his family had lived in Jamaica ever since one of his forebears had commanded the British capture of the island from the Spanish in 1655. His father had returned to England, had settled in Penzance for reasons of health, and had married Margery Badcock of that town. But Price appears to have lived on the family's Jamaica estates for a time and had married there. Topham Beauclerk, like Bennet Langton, had been a friend of Johnson's and an early member of The Club.

[4] Thomas Giddy, a respected magistrate as well as surgeon in Penzance.

[5] Boswell likens the local people to the shepherd boy in Spenser's pastoral poems (with a pun on "clout" in the archaic sense of "clod"), suggests that the man with shoes is like a work-horse, and compares them to the brutish creatures in Swift's *Gulliver's Travels.*

[6] A sixty-five-ton stone that could be rocked with little effort—one of the local sights.

clear, as we reached the Land's End, which our chaises could not approach nearer than about a quarter of a mile's distance on account of immense stones, which I observed peculiarly scattered over the country of Cornwall in firm, separate masses. Most of them are what is called moorstone, a kind of granite, but which is so damp that it must, when built in the wall of a house, be lined with brick or other stone. We walked to the extreme point, projecting in an immense rocky neck of land into the sea. The clustering rocks had the BOLDEST APPEARANCE I EVER BEHELD, but the sight of the tremendous elevation above the ocean was horrid. Veronica (as we were told by one of three *clouts* who left the harrows to attend on us) went nearer to the edge of the precipice than any lady or gentleman had ever done. My head half turned at seeing her, and I roared out in shocking agitation. I now at last felt the sensation, which I had long imagined, of being at *the Land's End of England,* about six hundred miles from Auchinleck or Edinburgh.

We returned to Penzance to dinner. Hawkins and Temple had dined, as we were not expected till six; and indeed it was half past five before we returned. I had in the morning eat some fresh pilchards, broiled. I liked them exceedingly. They were fatter and more savoury than herrings. I eat two more before dinner. Fish is very cheap at Penzance. A large cod's head and shoulders which we had for dinner cost only ninepence, and half a glass of brandy. I was at a loss in Cornwall for butter, having unluckily been informed that their method of making it is to boil the milk and then stir it about with their hands. This, though to be sure in reality not less cleanly than the way in which bread is baked everywhere, affected me with a prejudice against it which I could not overcome, and I never tasted butter but at Gwatkin's, where I was told a churn was used. After dinner we all repaired by invitation to Mr. Price's, where we found a grand dessert: pineapples, grapes, pears, plums, preserved ginger, tamarinds, macaroons (biscuits of almonds), etc., etc. He gave us admirable madeira which had been in the ——Indies,[7] and rich punch, but I stuck to the former, except tasting one glass of the punch. Mr. Giddy and a Captain ——, a strange sort of a gentleman born at Pinkie House near Edinburgh,[8] were of the party. Price harangued away at a great rate. He had his room hung with pictures, particularly portraits, some very good ones by Opie before he went to London.[1] He showed us two beautiful enamelled minia-

[7]The East or West Indies; the traditional method of aging and flavouring fine madeira was to send it on a long voyage.
[8]An estate east of Edinburgh.
[1]Price had encouraged John Opie, the son of a local workman, to take up painting; he had settled in London in 1780 and had become a successful portrait-painter.

tures of Mary, Queen of Scots, and Prince Charles Stuart, and a medal of his brother under the name of Henricus IX, for our host was a warm friend to the old House.[2] He showed us also a miniature picture of Marshal Saxe[3] and a large gold box with a beautiful painting in the lid, a kind of *monument* of several of his mother's relations. But what we admired most was a beautiful small cabinet, embroidered in a charming manner on satin in the finest colours of silks, silver, and gold, with fruits and flowers. The wooden corners were of ebony, and the drawers of cedarwood. Coffee and tea were served about. In short, it was a fine repast. But we were told his ordinary course of living was very penurious. This was truly a curious scene, and I perceived myself much improved by the genuine good wine. Sir Kit went home tonight.

SATURDAY 8 SEPTEMBER. It was a fine day. We proceeded to Marazion and crossed in a boat to St. Michael's Mount, so well known by various accounts and descriptions that I need not say much here. Though the town built at the harbour be no doubt profitable, it is a disgusting nuisance to have a parcel of low, dirty people collected there, and a vile smell of spoiled fish and garbage lying about. The Mount formerly belonged to the Basset family. It is now the property of Sir John St. Aubyn, who has fitted up and ornamented the rooms in the Castle with taste and expense, and would he but remove the *town*, might make a charming residence of it.[4] We went with difficulty up the narrow, winding staircase to the top of the tower, the prospect from which, both by sea and land, is very fine. The ladies and Frank went to St. Gluvias. My friend and I, having had a polite invitation from Sir Francis Basset, went to his seat at Tehidy Park, about fourteen miles off, and there indeed we found *life:* a seat of an ancient family, the ground prettily varied by rising and falling; a great deal of wood; a large and splendid house; table, servants, everything in style. Lady Basset was a charming little woman with that elegance of look, manner, and address which is very rare, but which is enchanting when we see it. She, I found, was sister to the learned Mrs. Buller,[5] of whom she talked to me as one of my acquaintance and engagingly asked, "Where is our friend General Paoli?" thus politely introducing something in common

---

[2]Henry Benedict Maria Clement, Cardinal York, might have become Henry IX of England if the House of Stuart had retained the throne.

[3]Maurice, Comte de Saxe, was a famous French general, victor at the battle of Fontenoy.

[4]The St. Aubyn family had purchased the Mount, a picturesque island of granite only one mile in circumference, from the Bassets more than a hundred years earlier.

[5]Boswell commented on Mary Buller's learning whenever he recorded their infrequent meetings. She was proficient in French and Greek, interested in poetry, and widely travelled.

between her Ladyship and me; adding, "You have made us all well acquainted with Corsica." I soon therefore had easy conversation with her. Sir Francis courteously met us on the stairs before his house. I had never before seen him. He is a genteel, smart little man, well-informed and lively, so that we had no languor. There were at table two Miss Bassets, his sisters, two little girls, his daughters, and their governess and Mr. Enys, whom I had seen at Truro. Two soups, fish, venison, and a great variety of other excellent dishes, an admirable dessert, burgundy, champagne, vin de graves, two kinds of madeira, sherry, port, claret delighted me, and his high Tory talk crowned my satisfaction. He had three granduncles killed in battle for Charles I. His blue-and-buff dress and attachment to Charles Fox seemed not quite consistent with all this old aristocracy.[6] But in the present reign, *party* and not principles has been the band of political union. He did not press the bottle, and I was politely moderate, so that I was not at all flustered, which was more agreeable than if I had. His coffee was excellent, and then came a case of *liqueurs,* noyau both red and white, etc. In short (as Gwatkin predicted to me) there was everything here as at Twickenham, where it seems Sir Francis has a house. He was pleased to say he hoped we should meet in London. I should have observed that there are here some good pictures, particularly some portraits by Van Dyck.

Temple and I, after taking leave of the ladies, rode placidly along and enjoyed the scene which we had seen, and joined in support of subordination of rank, by which all the elegance of life is produced. We stopped at Redruth and visited William Murdoch at his own house, who showed us some curious specimens of Cornish minerals, and produced a bottle of port; but I chose *mahogany* (two parts gin and one part treacle, which Lord Eliot made us at Sir Joshua Reynolds's as a Cornish liquor,[7] but it seems they make it also with brandy, and often add porter to it). It was a curious sensation to me to find a tenant's son in so good a state. Temple asked him to dinner next day, but he did not come. We got home in safety.

[EDITORIAL NOTE. On this day Nancy Temple gave a more jaundiced view of the Boswells' stay at St. Gluvias in a letter to a friend.]

---

[6]Sir Francis Basset's family—and their ownership of Tehidy—went back to the twelfth century. In spite of his Tory sympathies for his seventeenth-century forebears, Basset was a staunch Whig, as a sign of which he was wearing the Whig colours. He had been M.P. for Penryn for the past twelve years.
[7]On 30 March 1781, the first time Boswell met Eliot.

[Nancy Temple to Padgy Peters]

These girls are so boisterous and unpleasant that I think the strongest
nerves would feel a shock from being with them. I went to Trewithen, as
I told you I intended, and I then promised myself it should be the last
time I would ever go anywhere with them. Our first plan was to go thither
by water, at least as far as Mopus[8] where Sir Christopher Hawkins's carriage was to take us up, but Euphemia Boswell's fears and the badness of
the weather obliged us to alter our scheme. So we hired a chaise and got
to Mopus by land instead of water. Here a new difficulty arose. Miss
Euphemia, to be sure, could not possibly cross the Passage; however, partly
by entreaty and partly by almost scolding we made her get into the boat,
and all the way over she blubbered and sobbed like a child. Can you conceive anything more ridiculous and absurd than a woman almost six foot
high behaving in this manner?

When we got to the opposite shore, I thought it reasonable to expect that no more frights would throw us all into consternation; but
no such thing, I assure you. Miss Boswell[9] must likewise show her timidity and delicacy. The bad road near the Passage prevented the carriage from coming close to the water, so we were obliged to walk up
the hill to it, my father following us very leisurely on horseback. Imagine Miss Boswell, all terrified and alarmed, dart through a gate into a
field, tearing her gown to tatters every step she took. What could all
this be for, you naturally exclaim! Why, my dear? For the just and well-
grounded fear that my father would ride over us....

Mr. Boswell is a curious genius, too. He is perpetually falling in love,
as he calls it, and then he can do nothing but talk of the angelic creature. In a man of more than fifty such behaviour is folly. In short, I
am truly weary of them all, and if the truth were known, I believe they
are full as weary of this (to them) stupid place.

SUNDAY 9 SEPTEMBER. Attended divine service at St. Gluvias,
and after dinner rode with my friend to his other church at Budock.
The retirement of it, a small congregation of vulgar only, the view of
Falmouth Bay from the windows, the old-fashioned appearance, in
short the *tout ensemble*,[1] soothed my mind, and I romantically speculated on living out of the world—at Budock. As my friend and I rode

---

[8]Now Malpas.
[9]Veronica.
[1]The general effect.

calmly between his churches, I observed that he held a creditable actual station in society, whereas I held none. Yet we both agreed that I was better as the distinguished biographer than as a Lord of Session. We recollected Dundas when our companion at college,[2] when we thought him much our inferior, and wondered at his great preferment. When I talked of *insisting* on having some promotion through Dundas, Temple advised me never to ask any little place, but to assume it as my right to have a considerable one. On our return to Penryn we by appointment visited Mr. George, the attorney, who is married to a rich old woman who has built him a very large house and makes him lead a very strange life with her, turning night into day. He showed us a great collection of fossils and one of prints, particularly everything concerning Shakspeare.[3] I was heartily tired. In the evening we had Miss Sukey Frood, the mantua-maker, to sing sacred music to us.[4]

MONDAY 10 SEPTEMBER. The dampness of the climate and the want of variety of objects to engage and agitate, and a certain unfortunate association of melancholy with the country, especially about the fall of the leaf, now affected me sadly. Today arrived the Rev. Mr. Whitaker, the historian of Manchester, the defender of Mary, Queen of Scots,[5] etc., who had expressed an earnest desire to see *the Great Biographer*. His strong animal spirits, fulness of knowledge, and impetuosity of talk, almost overpowered me; but I roused myself so as to keep my ground wonderfully for a day. There came also the Rev. Mr. Trist, an amiable, pleasing man, "of manners gentle,"[6] who had put off a journey on purpose to see me; and I *acted a part* with so much address that Temple told me I appeared a most lively and happy man. In the evening we all danced, Whitaker for the first time in his life. I took the aid of wine today in my colloquial warfare, and of brandy and water at night, so *kept it up*. We sat till near two in the morning, and Trist thanked Temple for this *charming* day.

[2]All three had studied at the University of Edinburgh while in their teens.
[3]George Chapman George owned a collection of nearly 4,000 prints illustrating scenes from Shakespeare.
[4]This is the only appearance in the journal of Sukey (Susan) Frood, a young dressmaker who was to play a major part in a drama of passion in the Temple household less than a year later. Following Mrs. Temple's sudden death in March 1793, Temple fell desperately in love with Sukey, who kept house for the family for several months until forced to leave by the disapproving Nancy. The malicious assertion by Nancy and her suitor, Charles Powlett, that Frank Temple had seduced Sukey eventually shamed Temple into resigning himself to a more permanent separation.
[5]The Rev. John Whitaker, rector of the nearby parish of Ruan Lanyhorne, was the author of the *History of Manchester* and of *Mary, Queen of Scots, Vindicated;* at this time he was working on a new interpretation of Mary. Boswell had met him in London in 1772.
[6]The opening line of Pope's epitaph on Gay: "Of manners gentle, of affections mild."

TUESDAY 11 SEPTEMBER. This day we were to set out in our progress towards London. The thought was a little sad, from the principle, so well illustrated by Johnson in the *Idler, the horror of the last,*[7] as I was probably never to be here again. But the *relief of change* and varied views predominated. Trist had gone to Penryn last night, and set out in the morning. Whitaker was with us and displayed the same coarse abilities as yesterday. I was glad I had not long to bear up against him, nor much occasion to be tried. The Rev. Mr. Baron from Lostwithiel[8] came to breakfast, a learned and decent elderly man. Gwatkin politely sent his chaise for me and my daughters. They and young Temple went in it. My friend and John James and I rode. It was a pretty good day. I was glad to turn my back on Mrs. Temple, whose meanness of dress and manner and peevishness of temper quite disgusted me.

At Gwatkin's we were met by Lord and Lady Falmouth. I had written a note to my Lady, understanding my Lord not to be in the country, that we would wait on her Ladyship on Wednesday. My Lord having arrived, he before my note came had written to me inviting us for that very day. Mr. and Mrs. Daniell of Truro also dined with us today. I drank rather too liberally and pressed the bottle too much. Lady Falmouth and Mr. and Mrs. Daniell went home. My Lord stayed with us and we played whist, and I called him *Lieutenant Boscawen,* by which name I had known him at Edinburgh,[9] and he took it with perfect good humour. Temple's sons went home. I made time pass[1] tolerably by means of exciting animal heat.

WEDNESDAY 12 SEPTEMBER. I rose with feelings just as I should have had at a gentleman's house in Scotland. We sauntered about awhile after breakfast, looking at Gwatkin's embryo improvements,[2] of which I had no relish. Then he and I and Lord Falmouth and Temple rode to Truro, and having seen that town fully, I was pleased with the appearance of business and wealth. We visited Mr. Daniell's father, a respectable old gentleman of seventy-six, who has been very successful

---

[7] An allusion to the last *Idler,* in which Johnson writes movingly of the endings of various periods of life, such as leaving a place or losing a friend—significant in themselves and as foreshadowings of death.

[8] The Rev. John Baron had been vicar and alderman of Lostwithiel for many years.

[9] Falmouth was still Ensign Boscawen when Boswell knew him in 1776. He inherited his title from his uncle in 1782.

[1] Boswell has inked out the remaining words of this entry in the manuscript.

[2] Presumably an allusion to the changes, in their early stages, that Gwatkin was making on his estate.

in the mines and has built a large and excellent house.[3] We there saw a very good picture by Opie of this gentleman holding a rich piece of ore, the importance of which, as evidence of a newly discovered treasure, seems to be eagerly pointed out by a miner in his proper dress, done from the life, a man very eminent.[4]

Our ladies were to go round in the chaise. We crossed at Mopus (the Passage rougher than Lord Falmouth or Gwatkin ever remembered it) and rode to Lord Falmouth's seat of Tregothnan. The weather being fair, I begged not to dismount but to be shown a part of the Place. His Lordship obligingly rode with us, Mr. Daniell having now joined, and here I was unaffectedly in admiration of grand banks of wood with valleys between, many noble old trees, extensive young plantations made by his Lordship,[5] bold views of arms of the sea, particularly where...; variety of excellent farming carried on by Lady Falmouth. Mrs. Crewe of Cheshire, her Ladyship's mother, accompanied by a Miss Townshend (a humble friend whom she called sometimes *Town* sometimes *Towy*) arrived just as we came. The house is a strange old building but large and roomy, with halls and passages and a staircase gutting it.[6] There are however two very good public rooms on the ground floor, and our entertainment was in a capital style. I need not specify particulars.

Lord Falmouth being my old acquaintance, having drunk jollily in my house at Edinburgh and having the reputation of a good bottle-companion, I was resolved to have a bout with him, though he, I know not for what reason, seemed slow today. I pressed bottle after bottle, I think three; and then being too much elevated, exclaimed what a strange country Cornwall was; that I had never had my fill, and that what I had got at all to inspire jollity I had owed to myself. This was not well, and in the drawing-room I was by no means so decorous as is fit for the company of ladies, being noisy and rattling. His Lordship was a good deal intoxicated. After supper he proposed a bowl of punch, of which I accepted, and when it was done, insisted on having another,

[3]Thomas Daniell had been chief clerk of Sir William Lemon's grandfather, William Lemon, who founded the family's mining fortune. Daniell, having married the wealthy Ralph Allen's niece, was able to buy out Lemon's business after his death. His house, said to be the finest in Truro, was made of stone shipped to him by Ralph Allen from Bath.
[4]The distinguished man in Opie's painting is not Thomas Daniell but his son, Ralph Allen Daniell; he is shown seated and holding a specimen of copper ore, with the miner standing beside him. The painting had been exhibited at the Royal Academy in 1786.
[5]Boswell inserted the next few words as an interlinear addition and, in spite of a fingerpost pointing to the margin, did not complete the phrase.
[6]Breaking it up into narrow passages.

so that I did not well know how I got to bed. My worthy friend Temple was uneasy at all this.

THURSDAY 13 SEPTEMBER. I rose considerably disturbed, but walked out and got better. Mr. Gwatkin had idly insisted on our going to the Truro assembly in the evening, which disconcerted my plan of *quartering* another night at *Trewithen*, which Sir Christopher by a letter to me on Tuesday at Mr. Gwatkin's had endeavoured to *evade*, pressing this Truro assembly. I was pleased this morning to perceive no symptom of displeasure in Lady Falmouth at my riotous conduct. She politely showed Temple and me a valuable collection of minerals. My Lord gave us a long walk and showed us different parts of his seat and entertained us with grapes. I said quietly to Temple that if we had been told when at *Edinburgh College* that we should be thus treated at the grand seat of a great English nobleman, we should have looked forward with high expectation. But how short is reality of imagination! However, we had here substantial enjoyment. I notwithstanding felt myself weary, and thought his Lordship must be so too. But one man cannot judge of the feelings of another. I have been for weeks *interested* and *happy* at Auchinleck, when, had I *described* the sources of my enjoyment, very few could have conceived them. Temple and I had a chaise from Truro and went by appointment to ——, the seat of Mr. Gregor, one of the Members for the county, that I might have it to say I dined with both.[7] He seemed to be a civil, sensible young man. Mr. Glanville, who married Mrs. Gregor's sister whom he had lately lost, was here, and the rest of our company was Mrs. Gregor and two other ladies. There were some good portraits. Our dinner was very well, and I drank in moderation. I should have mentioned many good portraits at Lord Falmouth's: several by Kneller; Lord Keppel and Captain Buckle (Admiral Boscawen's Captain) by Sir Joshua Reynolds, done a great many years ago and in excellent preservation.[8] There is a curious family piece of the last generation entitled "The half of Lord and Lady

[7]Francis Gregor and Sir William Lemon were both M.P.s for Cornwall. Gregor's seat, on the banks of the River Fal, was called Trewarthenick.

[8]We do not know which of the many portraits painted by the German-born Sir Godfrey Kneller during his career in England from 1676 to 1723 Boswell saw at Tregothnan. We do know, however, that Falmouth owned Reynolds's portrait of Adm. Augustus Keppel, painted c. 1759, and Reynolds's portrait of Capt. Matthew Buckle, painted in 1760. Both Keppel and Buckle distinguished themselves in naval encounters against the Spanish and the French in many parts of the world, and Keppel became a *cause célèbre* in 1779 when, as Commander-in-Chief of the Grand Fleet, he was accused of neglect of duty, subjected to a court martial, and acquitted. Earlier, Buckle had apparently served under Adm. Edward Boscawen, Lord Falmouth's father, a naval hero famous especially for his determined attacks on the French in North America.

Falmouth's children," being *nine*, so that they were *in all eighteen*.[9] To Hawkins's *evasive* letter I had sent a verbal answer that we should be with him on Thursday; so he was *fixed* by my resolute address, and actually sent his chaise to Mr. Gregor's. But I returned it with a note that we were to be at Truro assembly, where we hoped to meet him. Mr. Gregor went with Temple and me in our chaise to that same assembly, which occasioned no small trouble in unpacking, that my daughters might appear. It was a very thin one. I admired Miss Clutterbuck, sister of an attorney, whose fine figure and pleasing countenance engaged me not a little. But the *name* (though an ancient one in Devonshire)[1] was very uncouth. Lady Falmouth showed the most polite attention to my daughters. I was quite out of spirits, and to shun sleeping at an inn and riding next morning, I went to Trewithen with Hawkins in his chaise. My daughters were most civilly entertained at the house of Mr. Daniell, and Temple lay at the inn.

FRIDAY 14 SEPTEMBER. Some warm negus and a bit of dry toast at two in the morning and a warmed bed had proved very comfortable, for when my daughters and Temple arrived near eleven, I was *not yet stirring*. I was *physically* much better, and after breakfast set out on horseback. It rained very hard, and I felt myself by no means in good humour. I rode briskly on, and at St. Austell got myself dried, and having borrowed a thick greatcoat of my landlord and put it above my own, I kept out the rain. Before we reached Lostwithiel it grew pretty fair. I was struck with the poor appearance of Grampound, a borough from whence Lord Eliot sends two Members, and not much less so by Lord Mount Edgcumbe's Lostwithiel,[2] three miles beyond which we came to the parsonage of Temple's friend, the Rev. Mr. Forster at Boconnoc, which is beautifully situated in a valley in Lord Camelford's magnificent park, through a considerable part of which we passed; and the rain having ceased, I had a disposition to be pleased. We were hospitably received by a lively old bachelor, a man of literature and taste in all its varieties, but who had unfortunately been for some time almost deprived of his eyesight, so as not to be able to read or to distinguish faces. But the defect was not perceptible to us, and his conversation was animated. We had here his curate, Mr. Furley, who had been nine years chaplain to the English factory[3] at St. Petersburg, and Messrs. —— and ——, two young clergymen jaunting about

---

[9]Lord Falmouth's uncle, Hugh Boscawen, first Viscount Falmouth, had eight sons and ten daughters.
[1]Boswell was misinformed; the Clutterbucks were an old Gloucestershire family.
[2]The Parliamentary district controlled by Edgcumbe.
[3]The British trading establishment.

and who left us after dinner. We had good parson's fare and in addition a pineapple, and claret and burgundy from Lord Camelford's, where we were invited to tea and supper.

I shrunk a little from going to the great house of a nobleman so high in the world, who lived so much on the Continent on account of his *health* (or perhaps of *ennui*) and whose daughter was married to Lord Grenville, Secretary of State for the Foreign Department.[4] Thus do my *early* sheepish sensations occasionally recur. However, I was consoled by hearing that my Lord and my Lady were quite alone. So we walked about a quarter of a mile of dry road through a wood, preceded by a lanthorn, and were conducted by various servants up a grand staircase splendidly lighted, and then through a gallery sixty-three feet long into a drawing-room at one end of it, where we were courteously received by Lord and Lady Camelford. Nobody else there but a decent, agreeable old lady, Mrs. Holroyd, who had been governess to their daughter. Lord Camelford's figure and manner, joined with his being head of the family of Pitt and his distinguished abilities, united to impress me with respect.[5] My Lady was exceedingly affable and very much resembled the Countess of Crawford. I was really happy. We drank tea. Cards were proposed faintly and declined. We were much better amused by conversation, and by being shown an extraordinary fine cabinet of ebony and tortoise-shell adorned with compartments of silver embossed with figures very well executed,[6] old china, and pictures. We were conducted to the other end of the gallery into my Lord's library, well stored with books but commonly used as an eating-room. Here a *real* supper was elegantly served: a roast hare, roast chicken and partridge and various other dishes, with choice wines, particularly white hermitage, which I never before had tasted. I was *studiously* moderate. We talked naturally a great deal of the horrid scenes in France. Lord Camelford mentioned the prophecies of Nostradamus called his *Centenaires,* some of which had been pointedly fulfilled in the very years foretold. This his Lordship *admitted,* but maintained that it was only chance (because the greatest part had not happened) and proved that if you would throw upon paper a number of events as predictions, no

[4]Thomas Pitt, first Baron Camelford, had suffered from ill health since his student days. This was his last stay in England; he had arrived in June, left later in September, and died in Florence in January 1793. His daughter Anne had married the diplomat William Wyndham Grenville, 1st B. Grenville, two months earlier.

[5]A grandson of Robert Pitt, he represented the senior branch of the family; his first cousin William Pitt, the Prime Minister, belonged to the junior branch. Camelford had served in the House of Commons for many years before he was raised to the peerage in 1784.

[6]A well-known curiosity, decorated with figures of Ovid's *Metamorphoses.*

matter what, *some* of them would be fulfilled. This I did not like, supposing the predictions to be very *circumstantial,* so as to multiply very much the *chances* against hitting *a future fact.* I must see this curious collection of *second sight* and examine what has *happened* or been *proved* to correspond.[7] This was a visit which I shall always remember with satisfaction. In our way home we stopped at the stump of an oak-tree in which Charles I, who was twenty-seven days at Boconnoc, planted his standard when it was consecrated, and at which spot he received the Communion. The tree was cut over to found a place for the standard.[8] I beheld this with reverence, and next morning cut off some pieces of it and took them with me as *royal relics.*

SATURDAY 15 SEPTEMBER. At breakfast we had hot rolls and churned butter from Lord Camelford's. It seems his Lordship and Mr. Forster were companions at college, and Mr. Forster, a native of Essex, having accepted of the living here at Lord Camelford's request, his Lordship and family show him the kindest attention; and he on his part celebrates their praise and shows the domain to great advantage. Both of them were pleased with my saying that there was a good *alliance between Church and State* here. After breakfast Lord Camelford paid us a visit, politely apologizing for Lady Camelford's not waiting on us owing to a little indisposition. He talked with elegance and correctness, but, as Temple observed, in rather too formal and haranguing a manner. He said there was a word he wished to be struck out of our language—*liberty;* for that in truth the essence of civilized society consisted in a surrender of each man's liberty into a common stock for the advantage of individuals. He would substitute the word *protection,* by which person and property are secured. He wished also to abolish the political word *constitution.* His argument for this I do not accurately recollect. But I think he said that there was no definite political constitution of any country, as its *laws* were undoubtedly *alterable* at the will of the government. He scouted[9] the notion of *representation* in Parliament. Luckily I had lately read at Temple's for the first time his *Dialogue* on

---

[7]The predictions of the sixteenth-century astrologer Michel de Nostredame or Notredame (Nostradamus) were published as *Les Centuries.* Boswell had long been interested in clairvoyance and had discussed this phenomenon with Johnson on a number of occasions.

[8]Charles I had stayed at Boconnoc from 9 August to 4 September 1644 at a time in the Civil War when the Royalists seemed to be rallying. Although Boswell accepts the story that the oak was cut down to make room for Charles's standard, the destruction of the tree—only a nine-foot trunk remained in Boswell's day—was apparently caused by a strong wind in 1783.

[9]Treated as absurd.

that subject against the attempts of *reform,* and I showed I knew it pretty well, saying, "There is a pamphlet which your Lordship probably has *read*——" He smiled and said, "Yes, I *have* read it."[1]

Forster took us a pretty long walk and showed us considerable masses of this noble seat, the day being very fine. Temple laughed, knowing my want of relish of rural scenes, but allowed that I *acted* extremely well. Forster is a great friend of Mr. Mason, who once paid him a visit here. Yet he criticized some of his poetry as not intelligible. He thus put me out of conceit with two lines in *Elfrida* which I had been accustomed to admire:

> Hail to thy *living* light, *ambrosial* morn,
> All hail thy *roseate* ray![2]

He has something of an old maid in his habits and prattling. He has a number of favourite cats, two of which constantly sleep with him. No animal belonging to him is suffered to be killed. Yet he eats fish, flesh, and fowl which he buys.

I went in the chaise today, and Temple rode, twenty-one miles to Port Eliot, the seat of Lord Eliot, having stopped to change horses at Liskeard, one of his Lordship's boroughs.[3] I was struck with the appearance of Port Eliot, the house being part of the ancient Abbey of St. Germans, and the church, part of which is one of the first Christian buildings in Britain, standing so near to it that in some points of view the separation can scarcely be distinguished. The dining-room was the very space of the *refectory,* so that it has been eat and drunk in for more than nine hundred years.[4] We were received at the door by a servant out of livery and two or three footmen, and conducted through a hall and passages into a room seventy-five feet in length and twenty feet broad, a noble gallery indeed. In a little while his Lordship, whom I had informed of the time of our coming, made his appearance and

---

[1]*A Dialogue on the Actual State of Parliament* (1783) comments on the meaninglessness of the term *constitution* and the impracticability of fuller representation in Parliament. Camelford neither acknowledged nor denied authorship of this pamphlet, which Burke attributed to him in a speech in the Commons. The debate about the meaning of liberty and the unwritten English Constitution had recently been intensified by the publication of Burke's *Reflections on the Revolution in France* and Thomas Paine's attack on it in *The Rights of Man.*

[2]That is, Forster destroyed Boswell's good opinion of these lines, from Act I of William Mason's classical drama *Elfrida.*

[3]The Parliamentary seats of Liskeard were controlled by Lord Eliot.

[4]The Eliot mansion was built on the site of the original priory, founded in 429 by King Athelstan and dedicated to St. Germain, Bishop of Auxerre, France.

received us very courteously, nay, cordially, as did Lady Eliot soon afterwards.

There were now here Mrs. Yorke, widow of the late Charles Yorke,[5] and Mr. John Eliot and his lady, the daughter of Mrs. Yorke; and there appeared at dinner Miss Eliot, a maiden sister of a most unfortunate condition as to health, having had a kind of violent universal rheumatism a great many years ago, so as to be quite lame and almost blind and truly an object of disgustful sensation, being extremely fat and almost smothered in clothes, so that almost no part of her face is seen. Yet she talked some and eat and drank pretty well. Lady Eliot's humanity has made her stay in the country these last seven years to take care of this poor woman. Lord Eliot being much talked of for having no hospitality at all in London, I was curious to observe his establishment at his country-seat, and found it most excellent: good service, good dinner of two courses and dessert, madeira, hock, sherry twenty-seven years old, port, claret, and always after dinner a bottle of champagne and also canary.[6] Excellent cider and admirable beer—the wheat, the malt, and the brewing all *home*. His Lordship pleasantly and kindly said this was the first time a *Laird of Auchinleck* had been at Port Eliot, and he drank *Auchinleck* as a Cornish Baron drinking to a Scottish Baron. His conversation as usual was full of information and vivacity, so that Temple was highly pleased. I warmed myself well with wine, but was unreasonably displeased that neither my Lord nor his son were *jolly,* as the phrase is; that is, encouraged a brisk circulation of the bottle, which in many houses is required as a test of hospitable reception. Mrs. Yorke was a well-bred, agreeable woman, and Mrs. Eliot a pleasing young lady. It gave me a more than ordinary satisfaction to find Lady Eliot, with whom I was very little acquainted, to be remarkably affable and unaffectedly good. There was a good warm supper, and I composed myself with warm wine and water and sugar.

SUNDAY 16 SEPTEMBER. Still charming weather. An excellent breakfast, all decently at church in the morning. Then we went, my Lord on horseback and the rest of us partly walking, partly on a most social machine, an Irish car, running upon two low, broad wheels, covered by a spacious platform rendered comfortable by carpeting fixed over it, and on the three sides not next the horse, boards to support the feet on. Six or seven people can be moved about on it very easily, and it is drawn by a single stout horse, led by a man like a common

[5]Yorke, a prominent M.P. who had also served as Solicitor-General and Attorney-General, had died in 1770 only three days after having been appointed Lord Chancellor.

[6]A light, sweet wine from the Spanish Canary Islands.

carter. We surveyed different parts of the park, particularly a rising ground above a wood, on which is erected a summer-house from whence is an extensive prospect both of land and sea. Also a slate-quarry mixed with rock and rendered romantic by trees and bushes. It is in a circular form; the rocky compartments are singularly various and have a striking effect. Sir Joshua Reynolds admired it much. One passage into it is deeply excavated from the rock. Also a road for a considerable way along the River St. Germans, which flows up more than two miles above Port Eliot, and which his Lordship has embanked and gained considerably in addition to the beauty of the Place. He has also planted a great deal. His penetration found out soon that I had little and Temple much relish of rural scenes. We saw also about the middle of this road or walk a handsome artificial alcove in the form of a tent, but composed of wood with glazed windows. Miss Eliot appeared again at breakfast. But we saw her no more, of which I was very glad, for I could not help feeling uneasy at such a sight. Another hearty dinner, etc. And though I drank variety of wines, etc., in the time of dinner and a complete bottle of claret afterwards (Lord Eliot and Temple drinking madeira, and Mr. John Eliot, Mr. Penwarne the clergyman, and Mr. ———, one of the clerks of the Treasury, port), I was quite dissatisfied that there was no *spirit of drinking* displayed, and was so heated that in the evening I, in Temple's hearing, rated Lord Eliot eagerly, though with good humour, on the strange mode of Cornwall, where I could say I had never been *asked* to drink a little more. This was foolish, and Temple after....

[EDITORIAL NOTE. The journal of the Cornish jaunt ends here, at a time when Boswell's stay in Cornwall was coming to a close. "I have had a wonderful tour in Cornwall," he wrote to Malone from Port Eliot on 16 September, but then he continued: "When I say *wonderful,* I am not boasting of *happiness.* Would to GOD I were safe in London, which I hope to be on Saturday, the 29th."

Boswell returned to London in time to take the coach to Chelmsford on 1 October. The assizes of the Home Circuit brought him little business, however, and his fees of £1. 11*s.* 6*d.* did not cover his expenses of £3. 5*s.* 6*d.* While at Chelmsford, he was struck by a fit of hypochondria, the beginning of a black mood that remained with him for months.

Once back in London, Boswell was further depressed by the news that the Rev. John Dun, his old teacher and the parish minister at Auchinleck for almost forty years, had died after a long illness. As Laird of Auchinleck, Boswell had the deciding voice in the appointment of a new minister, and he took this responsibility seriously. For the next few months he was inundated with letters suggesting possible

candidates and engaged in lengthy correspondence about their qualifications.

Compliments on the *Life of Johnson* and suggestions for the second
edition continued to come in. James Abercrombie of Philadelphia, an
admirer of Johnson's who had written appreciatively earlier in the year,
sent news of Johnson material in America. By mid-October Baldwin
had already printed part of the third volume of the new edition. Yet
Boswell was not cheered. Soon after 29 October, his birthday, he resumed his journal in a despondent mood.]

MONDAY 29 OCTOBER. (Writing 31.) A severe fit of hypochondria, which had distressed me grievously for some time, still continued. This being the anniversary of my birthday, when I entered on
my fifty-third year, I prayed to GOD that I might employ the remaining part of my life better than the former. Yet in fact I did nothing all
day but write a letter or two and play at draughts with my children,
particularly my son James, who was confined by a cold and feverish
disorder.

TUESDAY 30 OCTOBER. (Writing 31.) I was much in the same
state, and passed my time much in the same way. I thought that if my
"weary soul" could be "soothed"[7] by any means not vicious, I was not
culpable. Yet I was vexed to waste life so. My daughters were out at
tea both these nights. My brother David paid me a short visit. I wondered at his rational, steady activity. Mr. Selfe, Mr. Baldwin's corrector, also was with me. I was quite despondent.

WEDNESDAY 31 OCTOBER. I awaked somewhat easier, and was
able to rise tolerably well, which for many days I could not do without
a miserable struggle. I vexed myself with fretful consideration of my
want of success in life, and of that constitutional melancholy which I
found still recurred. I had no hope of happiness in this world, yet
shrunk from the thought of death. Everything troubled me. I paid a
visit to Mr. Hamilton from the West Indies, nephew of my relation
Maj. Daniel Hamilton, as also to Lady Strange. I again played much at
draughts. My daughters had company at tea without first asking my
permission, which they had promised to do. I was hurt by this; did not
appear, and my mind cast about for plans of placing them somewhere,
as I found I was very unfit to have any charge of them. It appeared to
me that I should not have married, having no turn for the regularity

[7]Thomas Gray, *Ode on a Distant Prospect of Eton College*, l. 18: "My weary soul they seem
to soothe"—a reference to the breezes that come to the speaker from Eton, reminding
him of his happy youth.

of domestic life. But perhaps I judged too strictly and from too nice a sense of propriety. I thought of going to the Old Bailey sessions, which began today, but had not resolution. For two days I kept the house, and now for three I have tasted no fermented liquor.

THURSDAY 1 NOVEMBER. (Writing the 5th.) I continued in very bad spirits and much displeased with my daughters. My son James pleaded for them, and most sensibly said that I should not judge till my bad spirits were gone. I considered what a blessing it was to have such a boy, and the alarm of his illness made me reflect that I should not be disconsolate while he was preserved to me. I again played at draughts. In the evening I became reconciled with my daughters. I had such a nervous swimming in my head that I was exceedingly uneasy. I suppose the extreme change as to drinking had hurt me. Euphemia made me drink some warm port and water in bed, which did me good, I thought instantaneously. What a weak creature is man!

FRIDAY 2 NOVEMBER. (Writing the 5.) Was a little better in the morning, having had less disturbed sleep than for several nights. Breakfasted at the Chapter Coffee-house and read the file of the *Morning Post* since August, and found various squibs against me. Read also a file of Edinburgh[8] for the same period. The *names* and *ideas* strangely depressed me. I was brought back in imagination to an uncouth, low state, as I recollect Sir John Pringle in one of his last visits to Edinburgh telling me that he felt a kind of impression as if all his life since he left it had been a dream, and that he had not been President of the Royal Society.[9] The giddiness in my head was painful. Dilly was in the country; Hingeston not at home.[1] I dined cordially with Baldwin and drank a good bottle of old port. I then found Sir William Scott at home, and on his assuring me that he was quite at leisure, agreed to stay and eat oysters. I drank here some more port and had excellent Tory conversation, but could not help feeling very unpleasantly my having no employment, of which I complained to him, but did not perceive much sympathy. I walked home safely.

---

[8]Presumably the *Edinburgh Advertiser.*

[9]Pringle, an intimate friend of Lord Auchinleck's and later of Boswell's, had a brilliant career after leaving Edinburgh in the early 1740s. He served as Physician-General to the British forces in Flanders, introducing sanitary measures in military hospitals; he then developed a successful practice in London and was appointed Physician to the King; and he was President of the Royal Society from 1772 to 1778. But when he tried retirement in Edinburgh, he found it so depressing that he returned to London. Boswell saw him for the last time in Edinburgh in the summer of 1781, a few months before his death.

[1]John Hingeston was an apothecary.

SATURDAY 3 NOVEMBER. I was restless and fretful. I paid a visit to Courtenay, whom I had not seen since Tuesday sennight when he and I dined at Windham's. We got into too warm a dispute as to tolerating praise of the French Revolution as now become republican,[2] for I maintained that of necessary consequence this must attack our government. His feelings and notions were so different from mine upon that subject that I should not have argued it with him, for he is a friend to whom I have been much obliged. I wrote some letters, and then went to the Old Bailey and heard part of the proceedings before the Recorder, with whom I went up to dinner at half past five. I was grievously hypochondriac and had not the least relish of the scene which usually pleases me, except of the dinner and wine. Sir Watkin Lewes observed that I was not in spirits.[3] I however sat late with him and drank a great quantity of hock, so as to be much intoxicated. He set me down at Charing Cross.[4] I made a short call in Queen Street, where I must have made a strange figure. Happily I got home in safety. This is a wretched life for a man of talents, and a Christian. Let me record that this day my son James appeared for the first time *in print* in the *St. James's Chronicle*. A letter signed *Numa* attacking Mr. Burke for his *Reflections,* and also the subscription for the unfortunate refugee French priests, appeared in that paper on Tuesday. James happened to see it. His resentment kindled. He said I should answer it. I said I was unable; he had better do it. He in a very short time wrote a wonderfully good short answer signed *Hospitalis,* which I carried yesterday to Baldwin's, and it was inserted.[5]

SUNDAY 4 NOVEMBER. (Writing the 7.) As I well deserved, I awaked ill and vexed and lay very late. Worthy Dilly called. I rose and took a walk with him along the Paddington Road as far as to South-

---

[2] By its decrees of 21–25 September the newly elected National Convention had abolished the monarchy and proclaimed France a republic.

[3] Lewes was an alderman and former Lord Mayor of London.

[4] Boswell has inked out the following passage in the manuscript from "I made a short call" to "a Christian," apparently referring to an illicit visit.

[5] In answer to *Numa,* who blamed Burke's *Reflections on the Revolution in France* for needlessly involving the English in French politics and who opposed helping the priests recently expelled from France because their religion had been long rejected by the English, Jamie wrote: "What! would he have had them remain in a country where they were not only robbed by a licentious rabble of their property but where their lives were every day in danger? And if they had, by an abject submission to the will of the mob and by joining in the massacre of all their countrymen who were enemies to unbridled anarchy, kept a precarious fortune for a little while, would not their meanness and perfidy have met with their just reward, when the misleaders of the populace receive condign punishment?" Baldwin was the printer and publisher of the *St. James's Chronicle*.

ampton Row and then to Great Ormond Street. I called on Sir Francis Bourgeois, who told me that when M. Desenfans was *nervous*, Sir George Baker advised him to do nothing, but just to keep himself quiet.[6] My daughters had been at church in the morning. I went in the afternoon, but without any effect except being kept in apparent calmness for some time. When I came home, I found that Windham had called and asked me to dine with him. Though sadly low-spirited I went, and found with him Dr. Laurence of the Commons, Dr. Brocklesby, and Mr. Young, a young Quaker (his nephew), a youth of extraordinary information.[7] After dinner when we were in the drawing-room or library, Dr. Laurence maintained a very good argument for the existence of *mind* in man, which exercises *judgement* concerning various *impressions* or *perceptions*. I was firmly of opinion with him, but felt uneasiness at the reasonings of the Quaker and Windham on the opposite side, I suppose to carry on conversation. Windham, Laurence, and I remained some time by ourselves, and talked with earnestness of the seditious exertions in Britain, founded on a wild approbation of the proceedings in France.[8] We agreed in thinking that it was the duty of our Government to take speedy and vigorous measures to check such sedition and not suffer it to increase and strengthen, and Windham thought that men of this way of thinking should meet prudently and concert what ought to be done. Laurence and I agreed in this. I felt as if in the reign of Charles I.[9] But my wretched hypochondria depressed my spirit.

MONDAY 5 NOVEMBER. (Writing 7.) Though I had drunk moderately at Windham's, I was very much indisposed in the morning. My son James was now so well that I allowed him to go out, and he dined at a Mr. Babb's in Westminster, uncle to Mr. Whitfield the actor, with Mr. and Mrs. Whitfield, Mrs. Inchbald, and three Westminster boys

[6]Sir Peter Francis Bourgeois, a painter and an associate member (later full member) of the Royal Academy, lived with the art-dealer Noel Joseph Desenfans. The latter had reason to be nervous because he was buying paintings from aristocratic French *émigrés* for King Stanislaus II of Poland without proper reimbursement; indeed, when Stanislaus lost his throne in 1795, Desenfans was left with the works on his hands (after his death, they formed the nucleus of the Dulwich Gallery). Sir George Baker was President of the Royal College of Physicians.

[7]Although only nineteen, Thomas Young, who was Brocklesby's grandnephew, was already known as a classical scholar and student of exotic languages. He became a physician, made important discoveries about the functioning of the eye and the circulation of the blood, and was also the first to decipher the Rosetta Stone.

[8]A number of organizations in London and in the provinces were declaring their support of the French Revolution and demanding Parliamentary reform in England.

[9]When the Royalists resisted the rise of Cromwell and his Parliamentarians.

who with him were to act in English this winter.[1] I was very uneasy about him, not knowing where he was, and there being one of the thickest fogs that ever was known in London. However, he returned at night, safe though a good deal wet, and having one of his knees hurt by a fall. I had him put to bed and all care taken of him. I had walked out, but not far; and having met my brother David, he dined with me on cold victuals, and *porter*[2] *only*, a fancy of his. He also drank tea with me. Veronica dined at Mrs. Stevenson's.

I had no relish of life, and could do nothing. I am wrong in saying I did not walk far, for I was as far as Baldwin's; and I called at Bigg's in the Temple[3] and gave up my chambers against the expiration of the second year—in January next—having found them to be an ineffectual expense of about £40 a year. Counsellor Leach[4] had suggested to me that I could not expect to catch practice like a young man who is always waiting, but what business I could have must be from persons to whom I was known, who would come to me wherever I was. I felt an unwillingness to cease having chambers, but I consoled myself with speculating that I should be as much a lawyer as was consistent with my various other circumstances as a gentleman of estate and extensive acquaintance—and an author; that at any rate the chambers which I had were not suitable for me, and that if I should fortunately, either by practice or any other way, become richer, I might have them in due form. In the meantime the saving of about £40 a year was at present an object to me. I could thus reason very justly as to economy.

TUESDAY 6 NOVEMBER. (Writing the 7.) Instead of being refreshed with sleep, I in my present state am so disturbed while in bed that I dread lying down, though I feel it at night as a momentary ease. When I awaked this morning, I felt such a kind of general horror that I forcibly exclaimed, "GOD have mercy upon me!" I however rose and went to Westminster Hall, it being the first day of term. I shrunk from the brisk and hearty salutations of some of my brother barristers. I was fretted by observing the crowds of candidates for practice, and I was indignant at seeing briefs in the hands of many, while I had none,

---

[1] John and Mary Whitfield had been minor actors at Covent Garden, Drury Lane, and the Haymarket for the past eighteen years. Elizabeth Inchbald had begun as an actress but was now a prolific writer of sentimental dramas and had also recently published *A Simple Story*, a popular novel of passion. The boys were planning to act in English, not Latin, plays. Boswell did not approve of Jamie's acting and gave his permission only reluctantly.

[2] A dark beer.

[3] Joseph Bigg was the chief butler of the Inner Temple.

[4] Like Boswell, Thomas Leach belonged to the Inner Temple.

nor even a prospect of any. I was a little while both in the King's Bench and Common Pleas, and sat a considerable time in Chancery.[5] Dined at home and wasted all the afternoon and night at draughts and cards with my children. Was quite in despair as to doing any good in life.

WEDNESDAY 7 NOVEMBER. Still grievously ill. My son James accompanied me to Westminster, and after showing myself in Chancery and at the entrance of the King's Bench, he being with me, I walked with him to Baldwin's and showed him that his *Hospitalis* had excited a reply; for that in the Notes to Correspondents *Philo-Numa* was rejected.[6] We went to Westminster by water and I delivered him over to Mrs. Clough, his boarding-mistress, and Mr. Dodd the usher, his private tutor. I paid a visit to Mrs. Reynolds, Sir Joshua's sister,[7] but was quite languid, and without any hope of being better. Dined at home and suffered sadly the rest of this day, being only a little relieved by reading the life of Smart prefixed to his *Poems*,[8] and writing part of this journal, and two letters. I wondered if I could ever be at all in spirits again. I had an absolute indifference as to everything except *immediate* ease. Yet I was *conscious* this was wrong. Lucky are they who can maintain, or in whom is maintained, a constant earnestness about the *delusion* of this world; for a delusion it certainly is whenever reason calmly considers it and attempts to investigate its rationality.

THURSDAY 8 NOVEMBER. (Writing the 12.) Was too late for the Courts at Westminster, they being up before I reached the Hall. Dined at Metcalfe's with the Rev. Dr. Walker King and Dick Burke. Was quite hyp'd,[9] and disgusted by Metcalfe's boisterous puppyism. Drank too

---

[5]The three courts—King's Bench, the highest court of common law, for criminal and civil cases; Common Pleas, for civil cases between private persons; and Chancery, for cases involving trusts and property—all sat in Westminster Hall.

[6]This reply, apparently agreeing with Jamie's position, was not printed. Jamie's article was, however, mentioned in a later note signed Urbanitas, which acknowledged the virtue of Hospitalis's benevolent feelings towards the exiled French priests but voiced deep suspicions of the "prodigious number of *émigrés*" and their reasons for remaining in England (*St. James's Chronicle*, 20–22 November 1792).

[7]Frances Reynolds, Sir Joshua Reynolds's youngest sister, was a painter, chiefly of miniatures, and had been a favourite of Johnson's. Perhaps it was during this visit that Boswell saw Johnson's letters to her—letters which she would not allow him to publish.

[8]By Christopher Hunter, Christopher Smart's nephew. Published in 1791, this was the first collected edition of Smart's poems.

[9]Boswell's spelling of "hypped" or "hipped," the eighteenth-century term for experiencing hypochondria or depression.

liberally. Went at night to the *Mount* and added to my intoxication by taking porter and punch. Had some conversation with Bosville, Tierney, and Sir James Murray, in whose company I had never been before.[1] It was late before I got home. ——.[2]

FRIDAY 9 NOVEMBER. (Writing 12.) Awaked ill and vexed. As it was Lord Mayor's Day, did not go to Westminster Hall, but walked to the City to try what effect the Show and crowd would have on my spirits. But I was too *dull* to be at all agitated. I could get no farther than Baldwin's, whence I saw the procession move along Bridge Street, Blackfriars.[3] I met Malone in Fleet Street. He had returned last night.[4] Seeing him again animated me a little for a moment. I dined at Freemasons' Tavern with the Royal Academy Club,[5] our first meeting for the winter. I had some enjoyment from a good dinner, a cheerful but moderate glass of wine, and *the society of the artists,*[6] which I compared with a comfortable sense of superiority over any *Edinburgh society*. Yet I was not as I should be. Mr. Cosway set me down at the top of Bond Street.[7] I foolishly wandered about for some time, but got home safe and at a good hour.

SATURDAY 10 NOVEMBER. (Writing 12.) Paid a visit to Malone. Found him, as I always have done, engaged in literature, so as to have no weariness. Did not go to Westminster Hall. Dined quietly by appointment with my worthy bookseller Dilly, who consoled me as much as he could, for I was still woefully depressed. He accompanied me as far as Great Ormond Street, and then I proceeded to Malone's, who had asked me to dine; but I was engaged, and said I would call in the evening. I found Windham and Courtenay with him, drank two glasses of old

---

[1]Both George Tierney and Sir James Murray of Clermont, Bt., were M.P.s. Murray had also had a varied army career, having served in America and the West Indies from 1778 to 1783; he was currently a Major-General and aide-de-camp to the King.
[2]The dash may suggest a sexual encounter on the way home.
[3]Lord Mayor's Day was a public holiday celebrating the new Lord Mayor, who was elected each year on Michaelmas Day (29 September), was sworn in on 8 November, and on the following day took part in an elaborate procession, riding by special gilded coach from the Guildhall to Blackfriars Bridge, by state barge from there to Westminster Hall, and back in the same way. This procession and the accompanying pageants mounted by the livery companies were called the Lord Mayor's Show.
[4]Malone had been doing scholarly research at Oxford.
[5]This Club was restricted to the members of the Royal Academy. The Freemasons' Tavern adjoined Freemasons' Hall in Great Queen Street.
[6]Perhaps partly an allusion to the Society of Artists, which was the immediate precursor of the Royal Academy.
[7]Richard Cosway, a successful and fashionable painter, had been an acquaintance of Boswell's since 1785. Boswell had been more friendly with his wife, the Italian-born Maria Cosway, who was also an artist and had been an intimate friend of Paoli's.

mountain and coffee, and had some conversation, but without any true relish. Windham engaged us to dine with him on Monday. I was *conscious* of the good fortune of such society, though I did not *feel* it.

SUNDAY 11 NOVEMBER. (Writing 12.) Had been troubled with disagreeable dreams. Could not force myself out of bed till it was too late for morning service, and my children were in the same fault. I despised myself for having no order or proper authority in my house. I visited Malone and revised some additional Johnsoniana; also visited Mrs. Wood, not finding her husband at home. My son James and I then took a walk, and he and I and my two daughters went to church in the afternoon. Dined dully at home. Veronica drank tea at Mrs. Paradise's, and Euphemia, James, and I at my brother David's. Wherein does *this* London life excel a life at Edinburgh or any other town? But I have accustomed myself to expect too exquisite a relish of existence. I received a just check this evening in a sentence of the fifth sermon *Left for Publication* by Dr. Taylor, in which *Dr. Johnson* observes that disquietude of mind often proceeds from our overrating our own abilities and forming too high expectations.[8] I this day began to drink a decoction of woods against the scurvy, of which I had for some time had appearances, and imagined that my bad spirits might be partly occasioned by it.[9]

MONDAY 12 NOVEMBER. (Writing 15.) Was at Westminster Hall, partly in Chancery, partly at a sitting in the King's Bench before Lord Kenyon. Was quite dejected and fretful. Dined at Windham's with Malone and Courtenay. Felt myself sadly *under* them in conversation, and had no relish of it. Drank moderately there, but went to the Free and Easy at the Thatched House, and after winning a rubber at whist, supped and drank too freely and sat up late.[1] And most improperly *domesticated*, but not all night. It was, however, a temporary feverish relief from gloom.

TUESDAY 13 NOVEMBER. (Writing 15.) Awaked ill and upbraiding myself. To add to my distress, a note came from my son James that he was ill again and requesting to be sent for home. I instantly

[8]"A man that has a high opinion of his own merits, of the extent of his capacity, of the depth of his penetration, and the force of his eloquence, naturally forms schemes of employment, and promotion, adequate to those abilities he conceives himself possessed of; he exacts from others the same esteem which he pays to himself, and imagines his deserts disregarded, if they are not rewarded to the extent of his wishes" (*The Yale Edition of the Works of Samuel Johnson*, xiv. 57–58).

[9]The standard treatment for scurvy was drinking a liquid derived from boiling parts of certain medicinal trees such as sassafras, guaiacum, and aloes. Melancholy or hypochondria was thought to be a side effect of scurvy.

[1]Boswell has inked out the rest of this entry in the manuscript. By "domesticated" he seems to mean a sexual encounter, perhaps with a married woman.

complied. I lounged till it was too late for Westminster Hall, and went to Baldwin's to get a sheet corrected. Dined with him, in weary dejection. When I came home, found little James not at all well, but not so ill as I apprehended. Was tenderly affected.

WEDNESDAY 14 NOVEMBER. (Writing 15.) Was late in going to Westminster Hall, but made a point of being there. The King's Bench was up, but I was a little while both in Chancery and the Common Pleas. I was vexed to find myself quite idle. I walked a little while in the Court of Requests with Fielding,[2] who said that though ever so well occupied at home, he felt he had not done his duty if he did not attend in Westminster Hall. I met the Attorney-General in the Court of Requests, and asked him with some warmth why the fellows calling themselves the Society for Constitutional Information were not prosecuted for seditiously advertising for subscriptions to support the French in their efforts for *liberty*—in truth for overturning all order.[3] He answered, "Will you draw an Indictment against them?" He shuffled[4] pitifully. Windham gave much praise to Counsellor Adam's description of him: "He's a stay-maker."[5] I saw Mr. Nepean at the Secretary of State's office concerning the poor people who escaped from Botany Bay.[6] He said Government would not treat them with harshness, but at the same time would not do a kind thing to them, as that might give encouragement to others to escape. I hoped their time of transportation would be allowed to expire while they were in prison. I thought poorly of myself for being now so indifferent about them when I was so zealous in summer, but I was not *myself* now.

---

[2]The Court of Requests dealt with claims involving small debts. William Fielding, a barrister, was the son of the novelist Henry Fielding.

[3]Founded in 1780 and recently revived, the Society for Constitutional Information energetically advocated political reform, chiefly by circulating books and pamphlets. Since May, when a royal proclamation was issued, the Government had tried to control subversive publications and other activities by ensuring that offenders were prosecuted vigorously.

[4]Was evasive.

[5]As Attorney-General, Sir Archibald Macdonald was in charge of the case against Thomas Paine, who was accused of seditious libel in Part II of *The Rights of Man*, a pro-revolutionary work, more radical than his earlier writings, that had been published in February of this year. Summoned in May to trial in June, Paine had left for France to take part in the National Convention and never returned to England. William Adam's pun on "stay-maker" refers both to Paine's training as a maker of stays or corsets and to Macdonald's supposed reluctance to proceed with the trial because he did not approve of the prosecution—a rumour so widespread that Macdonald felt impelled to deny it publicly when Paine was finally tried *in absentia* in December.

[6]Evan Nepean was Under-Secretary of State for the Home Department, working under Dundas, and as such had jurisdiction over the prisoners.

On Monday when at Windham's, where I had dined thrice lately, my heart warmed, and though conscious of my embarrassed circumstances, I invited the company to dine with me today, which they did, as also my brother David. I was able to say little, and drank in moderation. I could not however relish, as I have often done, such society. Windham and Malone and my brother talked well against Courtenay's wild ravings in favour of the French. Malone sat some time after the rest. I felt a kindly[7] regret that I was not at Auchinleck amongst my good, honest tenants. But I dreaded the irritating task to *me* of receiving company. I was quite in the frame of

> Shall helpless man, with ignorance sedate,
> Roll darkling down the torrent of his fate?[8]

I did not "feel myself a man."[9] I was a weak, relaxed[1] creature. I slunk into bed with a pitiful, low-spirited sluggishness.

THURSDAY 15 NOVEMBER. (Writing 2 December from a note kept by my servant.) Was miserably dejected. An invitation to dine with Mr. Wilkes next day revived me somewhat. In the evening had Dr. Warren to visit my son James. He found him to be a little feverish and prescribed a draught for him, but said he would soon be well. Warren perceived me not to be in spirits. I envied his firmness and activity. I am not sure whether I went abroad today. I played a good deal at draughts with my son James.

FRIDAY 16 NOVEMBER. (Writing 2 December from notes, etc.) Was a little while at Westminster Hall. Dined at Mr. Wilkes's in Grosvenor Square. Company: he and Miss Wilkes, Mr. Swinburne the traveller,[2] Jack Devaynes, a gentleman from the City, and a French *aristocrate* refugee. There was an elegant dinner and a general gaiety, but nothing to record. It was however truly pleasant to me to see John Wilkes enjoying life as I have seen him do in Italy six-and-twenty years ago.[3]

SATURDAY 17 NOVEMBER. (Writing 4 December from notes, etc.) [No entry for this day.]

---

[7]Real or true.

[8]Johnson, *The Vanity of Human Wishes*, ll. 345–46. The first word in the original is "Must."

[9]Thomas Gray, "*Ode to Adversity*," ll. 45–48: "Teach me to love and to forgive, / Exact my own defects to scan, / What others are, to feel, and know myself a Man."

[1]Enervated.

[2]Henry Swinburne was a writer of travel books. Boswell had read his *Travels Through Spain* in 1780.

[3]During their meeting in Naples, Boswell had been struck by Wilkes's cheerfulness in spite of his exile and other political difficulties. "WILKES. 'I'm always happy. I thank God for good health, good spirits, and the love of books'" (Journal, 15 March 1765).

SUNDAY 18 NOVEMBER. (Writing 4 December from notes, etc.) My daughter Betsy came, went to church with us and dined, and I allowed her, *for the first time since last winter,* to stay all night. Veronica, Euphemia, and I drank tea at Mrs. Paradise's. I was quite low and could hardly speak.

MONDAY 19 NOVEMBER. (Writing 4 December from notes, etc.) Was at Westminster Hall a short while. Having been kindly entertained at the house of my relation Maj. Daniel Hamilton near Exeter, I wished to show attention to his nephew from the West Indies and niece, Miss Hamilton. So had them at dinner today with my brother and his wife, Mr. Robert Boswell's two daughters,[4] Major Green, Counsellor Leach, Mr. Dilly, Mr. Lumisden. Mr. and Miss Hamilton, the Miss Boswells, and Mr. Leach stayed the evening and supped. I got through this *operation* very well.

TUESDAY 20 NOVEMBER. (Writing 4 December from notes, etc.) Was very dull, and moping at home, when Mr. Richard Penn called on me, and I walked with him into the City and introduced him to Mr. Dilly, and sauntered about with him; and as he had come to town from Richmond, and was quite alone, agreed to dine with him at the Piazza Coffee-house, where I had not dined for some years. The scene of noise disgusted me, but he and I ate and drank cordially, but too much, for I was a good deal intoxicated. He carried me home in a coach.

WEDNESDAY 21 NOVEMBER. (Writing 4 December from notes, etc.) Was *justly* ill. Lay till late. Walked to Baldwin's. In my way met with the Bishop of Salisbury, who had come to town with his lady and family for two days. Kindly asked me to dine with them at the Royal Hotel, Pall Mall, which I did very comfortably, but had not much conversation. Went to the Essex Head Club and met Barrington, Brocklesby, Gregory, and Wyatt.

THURSDAY 22 NOVEMBER. (Writing 4 December from notes, etc.) A very bad day. Did not go to Westminster. My brother T.D. dined with me on a hare sent by Mr. Leach.

FRIDAY 23 NOVEMBER. (Writing as before.) Was at Westminster Hall, unprofitably as usual. Sir Francis Bourgeois, according to his obliging custom, carried me in his coach to the Royal Academy Club and brought me home from it. I relished the club as much as I could do anything in my hypochondria.

SATURDAY 24 NOVEMBER. (Writing as before.) This was the day fixed by Mr. Dilly for settling accounts with me and Mr. Baldwin as to the quarto edition of my *Life of Dr. Johnson,* etc. I was somewhat animated by the prospect, and walked pretty briskly to my worthy

---

[4]Presumably Jane and Sibella, the oldest of Robert Boswell's eight daughters.

bookseller's, where I had a hearty breakfast, after which he produced to me the clear produce of the sale, exclusive of presents, amounting to £1,555.18.2. This was very flattering to me as an author. We proceeded to Baldwin's, where I cleared off a bond for £400 (part of the price of Knockroon advanced to me by him and Mr. Dilly) and a note of hand for £100 lent to me by himself. There was great satisfaction in thus paying principal and interest to two worthy friends who had assisted me with their credit. I then returned to Mr. Dilly's, and after allowing for various sums which I owed him, there was a balance due to me of £608. I dined heartily at Baldwin's, and in the evening came Mr. and Mrs. Curtis[5] and Mr. Dilly, and we played whist and supped. I was however observed not to be in good spirits.

SUNDAY 25 NOVEMBER. (Writing 5 December from notes, etc.) At chapel with my children, morning service; then my two daughters and I paid a visit at the Adelphi Hotel to Mrs. McAdam and her daughter, Mrs. Forbes, who was ill of a consumptive disorder and going to Madeira.[6] We proceeded and paid a visit to Mrs. Baldwin, and invited her to dinner on Thursday; but she declined, saying she rarely went out to dinner. Mrs. McAdam drank tea with us. I was very dull. Little James returned to Westminster. I wondered at his spirit.

MONDAY 26 NOVEMBER. (Writing as before.) Dined with Malone tête-à-tête, having first tried an experiment on three (one new), but without any cheering effect.[7] Malone's conversation, however, always animates me in some degree.

TUESDAY 27 NOVEMBER. (Writing as before.) Was impatient and fretful. Walked into the City; met Hingeston in Holborn, who asked me to dine with him at four with some company; and though I had no wish to dine with him today, I would not refuse him, as his table at three is heartily open to me as often as I please. I tried an experiment on one new, but with no good influence on my spirits. The dinner today was plain, which I am ashamed to say disappointed me, as I thought *company* ensured something more. The company was well enough, but not remark-

---

[5]Thomas Curtis was a wholesale stationer with premises on Ludgate Hill. His wife was Baldwin's sister.

[6]In a letter to Mrs. McAdam written a few days later, Boswell apologized for his unfriendly behaviour during this visit, attributing it to her daughter Margaret Forbes's lack of attention to his wife during her long illness. In 1783, before her marriage, Margaret McAdam had been a frequent companion of both Margaret and James Boswell's in Edinburgh, and he had found her so charming that he had jokingly referred to her as a possible future wife.

[7]Presumably Boswell is using "experiment" in its eighteenth-century sense of "remedy" and is describing another self-treatment of sores, as on 4 July 1790. Perhaps these were scurvy sores.

able. We drank good port freely while our host exulted in his situation, "London being the first city in the world and the corner of King Street, Cheapside, the first spot in London."[8] We stayed, all or most of us, to tea and whist and a barrel of oysters and punch. I walked home safely.

WEDNESDAY 28 NOVEMBER. (Writing as before.) Punch always hurts me. I was very uneasy this morning and lay long. Dined with my brother T.D., and was somewhat soothed by his rational conversation. We went together to the Essex Head Club and met Brocklesby, Reed, Gregory, Calamy, and Sastres.[9]

THURSDAY 29 NOVEMBER. (Writing as before.) Was a little while at sittings in the King's Bench before Mr. Justice Buller. Felt myself quite languid, and wondered at the exertion all around me. As I walked homewards, I was vexed to compare my present *indifferent* sensations from London scenes with that warm glow with which they formerly affected me. A little momentary revival of spirits occurred by my meeting Dr. Langford, under-master of Eton School, and being asked in his frank, lively manner to dine with him next day at the Chaplain's Table, adding, "Dr. Fisher has desired me to take care of the Table in his absence.[1] I think it cannot be better taken care of than by you and me." To find myself regarded by the second man in that noble school, Eton (though he owed nothing at all to me, as my son was never in the under school), raised me pleasingly in my own opinion.

This day I gave a dinner, a kind of feast, two courses and a dessert, upon the success of my first edition of Dr. Johnson's *Life;* present, Mr. Malone, Mr. Deputy Nichols, his son-in-law the Rev. Mr. Pridden, Mr. Reed, Mr. Dilly, Mr. Baldwin, and his son Charles, printer with him, Squire Dilly, my brother T.D., my daughters Veronica and Euphemia, and son James. I got into a pretty good state of joviality, though still dreary at bottom. We drank "Church and King," "Health and long life to the *Life of Dr. Johnson,*" "the pious memory of Dr. Johnson," etc., etc. We did not drink to excess, but went to tea and coffee at a

---

[8]Hingeston's apothecary shop was located at this corner.

[9]Edmund Calamy was a barrister at Lincoln's Inn; Francesco Sastres, an Italian teacher and translator. A close friend of Johnson's, Sastres had provided Boswell with material in 1786, but two years later he gave several Johnson letters to Mrs. Thrale, knowing that she would include them in her *Letters to and from Johnson* long before Boswell could publish them in his work. Boswell scarcely mentions him in the *Life of Johnson* or in his journals although they continued to meet occasionally at the Essex Head Club, of which Sastres was an original member.

[1]William Langford, D.D., who was also a canon of Windsor, was Chaplain-in-Ordinary to the King in December. John Fisher, D.D., likewise a canon of Windsor, was a favourite chaplain of the King's; he had served as preceptor of Prince Edward Augustus, Duke of Kent, the father of Queen Victoria.

reasonable hour, and played whist, and part of the company stayed and partook of cold meat and a moderate glass.

FRIDAY 30 NOVEMBER. (Writing as before.) I found in the morning that there was yet no real *thaw* of the hypochondriac frost, for I was dejected and irritable. I do not recollect how I passed the morning, but at four I was at the Chaplain's Table, where Dr. Langford had with him old Mr. Southwell, whom I have met at an Old Bailey dinner, a gentleman of seventy-five and quite of the last age, two sons of the Rev. Mr. Wilson, canon of Windsor, who was private tutor to Pitt, and a son of Dr. Langford's, who had just taken a degree at Cambridge and was going for three years to *Tripoli* to reside with Mr. Lucas, the consul, and learn languages and commerce.[2] Dr. Langford whispered me to talk in favour of this plan, which I did as well as my *dead small-beer spirits*[3] would allow, calling it a pretty *trip* and expatiating on its advantages both in respect of curiosity and being fitted to rise in life. The Chaplain's Table has to me something very comfortable: a warm room, a solid English dinner of a few good things (as today soles boiled and broiled with a particularly good sauce of oysters and shrimps mixed, roast mutton, boiled fowls and tongue with plenty of vegetables, a damson tart and tartlets) and liquors enough, particularly a rich cider-cup. Today we had madeira (pretty well), hock (good), burgundy and claret (both rather poor), champagne and port (excellent). The glasses are uncommonly large. I was *gravely heated,*[4] and though the night was very cold, wandered in St. James's Park unwisely. Afterwards tried an experiment. Home early.

SATURDAY 1 DECEMBER. (Writing 6 from a note.) Breakfasted with Malone as usual on the first day of the month. Was asked to dine with him, but thought I was engaged to the Stationers' Company. On calling however at Baldwin's, found that Dilly, who was to have been in the concert,[5] had deserted. I therefore went to Malone's and was hospitably received, and had as good a day as my bad spirits would allow.

SUNDAY 2 DECEMBER. (Writing as before.) Sir William Scott, on whom I called yesterday, had engaged to get me a good seat in Lambeth

---

[2]The Rev. Edward Wilson, rector of Binfield, Berkshire, had tutored William Pitt, the Prime Minister, from the age of six. Langford's son, William Wass Langford, had studied at Peterhouse, Cambridge, since 1789 but received his B.A. only in 1793. His stay in Tripoli must have been a success, for he succeeded Simon Lucas as British consul there in 1803.

[3]Extremely low spirits—small beer being a thin, inferior beer.

[4]Boswell has inked out the following passage from "and though the night" to "experiment" in the manuscript. Presumably the "experiment" is the same as on 26 and 27 November.

[5]A participant in the plan to go to Stationers' Hall.

Chapel today to see the consecration of Dr. Buller as Bishop of Exeter,[6] a ceremony which I had never before seen. This made me get up more easily than usual. I took my son James with me, and (writing 13 from a note) we were well seated, and I had real satisfaction from the whole solemnity though inwardly melancholy. Mrs. McAdam dined and drank tea with us. I passed as dull a day as if I had been in Edinburgh. James however read to us Dr. Vincent's excellent *Discourse* on government.[7]

MONDAY 3 DECEMBER. (Writing as before.) It was so very cold that I got out of bed with the utmost difficulty and did not go to Westminster Hall. Dined at Baldwin's cordially, and then sat some time at Malone's with him and Courtenay, who was more reasonable than usual tonight as to French politics, waiving the subject and saying, "Why should men who love one another get into warm disputes about it?"

TUESDAY 4 DECEMBER. (Writing as before.) Malone and Courtenay dined with me, and Miss Monro, daughter of Dr. Donald Monro, was my daughters' guest. Courtenay in a slight instance or two showed the cloven foot. I was wretchedly destitute of intellectual relish.

WEDNESDAY 5 DECEMBER. (Writing as before.) Dined at home. Went and saw the King's Scholars at Westminster play the *Andria*.[8]

THURSDAY 6 DECEMBER. (Writing from note, 23 December.) Dined at home.

FRIDAY 7 DECEMBER. (As before.) Dined at the Royal Academy Club. For the first time *there* felt myself a good deal intoxicated. But luckily was as usual brought home by Sir Francis Bourgeois in his coach.

SATURDAY 8 DECEMBER.[9] Dined tête-à-tête with Malone. As he had been one of my encouragers to try my fortune at the English bar, I lamented to him my want of success. He said if I had confined myself to it, I possibly might have had practice. But I had chosen a wide and varied course of life. I had no reason to *complain*. This was *just* enough, but I could not help being *vexed*.

SUNDAY 9 DECEMBER. (As before.) Was at Portland Chapel part of the day as were my children. Mrs. Bosville dined and drank tea with us. My brother joined us in the evening. Little Betsy was with us.

MONDAY 10 DECEMBER. (As before.) I walked out to her boarding-school with Betsy, and was much pleased with her sense and vivacity and good English. I dined at Mr. Dilly's with the Rev. Mr. Collinson,

[6]William Buller, D.D. had been Dean of Exeter and Dean of Canterbury.

[7]*A Discourse Addressed to the People of Great Britain* argues against giving up the rights of the rich to help the poor. Only seventeen pages long, it was published in May of this year under the auspices of the Association for Preserving Liberty and Property against Republicans and Levellers.

[8]A comedy by Terence.

[9]This entry also must have been written on 23 December.

author of the *History of Somersetshire,* and his lady, and carried Dilly and his author to the Royal Academy, where Mr. West delivered his first discourse as President, a very good one;[1] but my wretched hypochondria still continued, I having never yet since 4 October at Chelmsford, when this fit began, had any fair remission.

TUESDAY 11 DECEMBER. (As before.) Having called at Baldwin's, he carried me to dine at the *Shakespeare* with the partners of the *London Packet,* where we had Dilly, little Davis (the son of Lockyer), Lowndes (bookseller), Crowder (printer), and Chalmers (their former editor) as a guest.[2] Two courses and a dessert. I was not in *author-like* humour and left them early to go with my daughters to a party at Dr. Monro's, which was crowded and hot, and to me disagreeable from hearing many Scotch tongues.[3] I however escaped into a kind of abstraction by playing at whist.

WEDNESDAY 12 DECEMBER. (Writing 25 from note.) Dined at home. Drank tea with T.D. and went with him to Essex Head Club.

THURSDAY 13 DECEMBER. (Writing as before.) T.D. and I dined with Mr. Ross Mackye, on whom I had called yesterday. Nobody there but the Hon. Dunbar Douglas, son of the Earl of Selkirk, who chattered indecently in favour of French Revolution wildness. I wondered to see an old gentleman past four score quite cheerful.[4] But I was tired hearing his Scotch stories.

---

[1] The Rev. John Collinson, vicar of Long Ashton, Somerset, was not Dilly's author at this time—a Bath publisher had brought out *The History and Antiquities of Somersetshire* in 1791—but perhaps Dilly was planning to publish a new work of Collinson's. Benjamin West, an American artist who had worked in England for more than thirty years and was admired for his history paintings, had been appointed President of the Royal Academy in March. Addressing the students at their annual prize-giving in a speech that mingled the inspirational with the platitudinous, he reviewed the development from classical to more recent art, emphasized the improvements in British art under Reynolds, exhorted the students to cultivate honour and virtue, and urged them not merely to follow the taste of their teachers but rather to develop their own bent or genius. Boswell has inked out the phrase "a very good one" in the manuscript, apparently having changed his mind about the quality of West's discourse.

[2] The Shakespeare Tavern and Coffee-house, also known as the Shakespeare's Head, was in the Piazza of Covent Garden. The *London Packet* was a newspaper that had appeared three times a week for more than twenty years. Baldwin and the booksellers Lockyer Davis and Thomas Lowndes had been among the original owners; the current partners, now that Davis and Lowndes were dead, appear to have included Dilly, Davis's son, and Thomas Lowndes's son William. John Crowder was the paper's printer and Alexander Chalmers its former editor.

[3] Donald Monro, M.D., a respected London physician now retired, was a native of Scotland.

[4] Boswell means Mackye. Douglas, who was only twenty-six years old, was a lieutenant in the navy at this time.

FRIDAY 14 DECEMBER. (As before.) Dined at Brompton Row with Mr. Humphry the painter, with Mr. Malone, Mr. West, Mr. Farington, Dr. Petrie of Lincoln, and his brother who paid £10,000 damages for *crim. con.*[5] He talked well, and with much information as to France in particular, though with too much leaning to the present horrible anarchy. Humphry gave us a good dinner.

SATURDAY 15 DECEMBER. (As before.) Dined at Mr. Baldwin's.[6]

SUNDAY 16 DECEMBER.[7] Was a short time at St. Andrew's Church, Holborn, my son James with me. Dined at Sir William Scott's with Lord Radnor, Mr. Burke and his son, Dr. Laurence, Mr. Malone, Mr. Metcalfe, Mr. Cholmondeley, Sir Charles Bunbury, and Mr. Windham, all *good men and true*[8] for our excellent Constitution. Mr. Burke proposed as a toast, "Old England against New France," and it having been proposed that we should be a club, Burke asked us for next Sunday; but Windham having insisted on its being at his house on that day, it was so settled. Even this company could not dissolve my atrabilious,[9] gloomy cloud. I drank to warmth, but not beyond that. Windham's chariot carried me home. I then went to the Mount and sat some time with Governor Penn, etc., and had a little negus.

MONDAY 17 DECEMBER. (As before.) Dined according to invitation, 30 November, at the Chaplain's Table with Dr. Langford. His guests were Sir Joseph Banks, Sir George Baker, a Mr. Peacock, the two Mr. Wilsons who were there last time, and Lord Brownlow; a very agreeable day which in some degree "soothed my weary soul."[1] Dr. Langford most kindly invited me to come there whenever it was convenient for me while he was in waiting, observing that room could always be made. "Yes," said I, "locus est et pluribus umbris." "I am sure, Sir," said he,

---

[5] Joseph Farington was a well-known landscape-painter and an influential member of the Royal Academy. Dr. Robert Petrie had been the physician in the Tower of London before practising in Lincoln; his brother had been found guilty of "criminal conversation" with a married woman (i.e., adultery).

[6] Presumably it was either on this day or on the following Wednesday that Boswell added his signature to the Declaration of Loyalty issued by the Stationers' Company on 12 December. Similar statements were published by a number of municipalities, parishes, and guilds following the Royal Proclamation of 1 December, which called upon the militia to quell what the Government regarded as increased seditious activities. The Stationers had set aside a six-day period, starting on Friday, to allow those who approved of their Declaration to sign it; Boswell may well have been encouraged to do so by Baldwin, who was this year's Master of the Company.

[7] This entry, too, was no doubt written on 25 December.

[8] An allusion to the "twelve good men and true" who make up a jury, a quintessentially English institution.

[9] Hypochondriac or melancholy.

[1] See above, 30 October 1792.

"you are not an *umbra*."[2] We sat later than usual. I went to the Thatched House and played whist, but for the first time did not stay supper.

TUESDAY 18 DECEMBER. (Writing as before.) As my daughters had with my consent invited some time before the meeting of Parliament was known a number of company to a *party* this evening, I abstained from the first meeting of the Literary Club for this season in order to keep myself cool and be ready to receive the ladies and gentlemen from the beginning of the rout,[3] which I had never done before. I set myself *doggedly* to it, and, though in sickly spirits, did very well. I at last sat down to whist and played eagerly, but lost.

WEDNESDAY 19 DECEMBER. (As before.) Dined at Baldwin's. Then called on Dilly and took him as my guest to the Essex Head Club.

THURSDAY 20 DECEMBER. (As before.) Went spontaneously to the Chaplain's Table, and had a hearty welcome from Dr. Langford. There were only other three guests: the Rev. Dr. Baker, Dr. Langford's eldest son, and Mr. Shadwell, a solicitor. In the evening I went to the Lyceum in the Strand and saw a part of *The Fair Penitent* and the whole of *Love à la Mode* performed by Westminster boys. From some association which I cannot trace, theatrical entertainments of every sort still produce a kind of irritation of my feelings. My son James acted Sir Archie MacSarcasm exceedingly well.[4] He came home last night for the Christmas holidays.

FRIDAY 21 DECEMBER. (As before.) I had been during all this fit of hypochondria miserably restless. I had some gratification, but a poor one, and that mixed with upbraidings, by lying long in the mornings in a kind of half sleepy stupefaction. When I came downstairs I was listless and fretful. I breakfasted without appetite, having as it were a bitter taste which communicated itself to everything. *Sincerum est nisi vas*, etc.[5] I often called on Malone, and found him fully occupied in

---

[2]Horace, *Epistles*, I. v. 28, trans. H. R. Fairclough, Loeb ed.: "There is room, too, for several shades." Horace, inviting a friend to a simple dinner, uses *umbris*, the dative of "shades," to refer to uninvited guests; Langford implies that Boswell is always a welcome guest and also that he never casts a shadow or gloom on the company.

[3]A large evening party or reception.

[4]Nicholas Rowe's bourgeois tragedy and Charles Macklin's farce were the English plays performed by Jamie and his classmates (see above, 5 November); Jamie had the famous part of the comic Scottish suitor in the farce. The Lyceum, used originally for the exhibitions and concerts of the Society of Artists, had been converted into a theatre in 1790.

[5]Horace, *Epistles*, I. ii. 54, trans. H. R. Fairclough, Loeb ed.: "Sincerum est nisi vas, quodcumque infundis acesit: Unless the vessel is clean, whatever you pour in turns sour."

historical and biographical researches,[6] on which he was intent while I had absolutely no pursuit whatever. The delusive hope of *perhaps* getting into some practice at the bar was *now* dead, or at least torpid. The printing of my second edition of Dr. Johnson's *Life* was the only thing I had to do. That was little, and was now nearly ended. I hurried into the streets and walked rapidly, shunning to meet people as much as I could, my perceptions being liable to such soreness from even looks and manner that I suffered acute pain on being accosted, and this was augmented by an unhappy imagination that it must appear how inefficient and troubled I was. Indeed Devaynes, my apothecary, said to me, "You are not ill enough to stay at home, and yet you should not be going about." I had scorbutic eruptions on different parts of my body, which fretted in the night, and I supposed that the *humour* which they indicated to be in my blood[7] was one cause of my present indisposition.

I called on an old acquaintance near Maiden Lane, and had a momentary change of ideas; but no vivid sensation of existence.[8] Dined at the Royal Academy Club, which always does me good, as I am there amidst *Englishmen* and those, men of talents and celebrity. I today sat next to Sir William Chambers, who said, "I have made great collections for a history of the Royal Academy. I intended to have done it myself, but I shall give them to Mr. Boswell." I said I was much obliged to him. Some of our brethren joined in the conversation and approved much, and it was proposed that there should be a biographical sketch and a head[9] of each deceased member. West and Cosway both spoke of it, and how agreeable it would be to the royal founder, and mentioned that the records of the Academy would be open to me, and many individuals could furnish anecdotes. Sir William mentioned that Miss Moser had some papers that would be of use.[1] This scheme gave me a little *fillip*. I drank too freely today. West and Cosway accompanied me to the Lyceum and saw the farce. I was, it seems, not a little intoxicated, as I was sorry to hear from my son James, with whom I went in a coach with Mrs. and Miss Keir to the bottom of Bond Street, and from thence in another by ourselves.

SATURDAY 22 DECEMBER. (As before.) Lord Henry Petty, son of the Marquess of Lansdowne, who was with us at breakfast a morning or

---

[6]Malone was working on a study of John Aubrey, the seventeenth-century biographer, as well as continuing his Shakespeare researches.

[7]That is, the sores that Boswell attributed to scurvy chafed him, and he believed that these sores were a sign of diseased fluid (humour) in his blood.

[8]Boswell has inked out the preceding sentence in the manuscript.

[9]An engraved portrait.

[1]Chambers was the Treasurer of the Royal Academy. He was a founding member, as was Mary Moser, a painter of flower-pieces. Nothing ever came of this scheme.

two ago, dined with us today, as did Sir Francis Bourgeois, both to go to the Lyceum in the evening. Sir Joshua Reynolds and I were last year much struck with Lord Henry, as having extraordinary talents, and I sent him a present of my *Life of Johnson.* Being but a year younger than my son James and in the same remove[2] with him at Westminster, I was desirous that James should cultivate his acquaintance, and spoke to him of it; but with Westminster independence he would not while he had no fancy for him. Luckily however they by degrees became better acquainted, and were now intimate, and James had his promise that when he should be Prime Minister, James should be Lord Chancellor. It will be curious if this should come to pass.[3] I attended the whole of the play as well as the farce and made up by my decorum for last night's impropriety. I was however vexed that my London sensations were not as they should be.

SUNDAY 23 DECEMBER. (Writing 9 January 1793 from note.) Was part of the day at Portland Chapel with my children and then dined at Windham's with the two Burkes, father and son, Dr. Laurence, Mr. Cholmondeley, Mr. Metcalfe, Sir William Scott, Mr. Malone, and young Jephson, who had arrived from Ireland the night before. We drank *Old England against New France,* but I was still not *up* in spirits. I recollect no part of the conversation except Mr. Burke's observing that Milton in prose was like Milton in verse, for in both he produced some very fine passages and some of a very different nature.

MONDAY 24 DECEMBER. (As before.) Had been afflicted in the night with that strange complaint called the nightmare. Stayed uneasily at home all day. Went to Malone's in the evening and was somewhat relieved.

TUESDAY 25 DECEMBER. (As before.) It vexed me that even on the festival of Christmas I was melancholy. I went with my son James to St. George's, Hanover Square, and had some elevation of heart in that hallowed dome. Saw Miss Upton at a distance, and admired her as formerly. Sir Michael Le Fleming, who was in town for a short time, paid me a visit. My brother David dined with me on our family turkey on this good day.

WEDNESDAY 26 DECEMBER. (Writing 26 January 1793 from note.) Dined at Chaplain's Table by invitation to eat true old English plum-porridge, of which a portion had been reserved from yesterday's

---

[2]Intermediate class.
[3]Boswell had inscribed the copy of the *Life of Johnson* to Lord Henry Petty as follows: "When his Lordship shall hold a high station in public life, let it be remembered how early I foresaw it." Petty, who succeeded his half-brother as third Marquess of Lansdowne and later took the name of Petty-Fitzmaurice, served as Chancellor of the Exchequer and held other high Government offices but, unlike his father, Lord Shelburne, never became Prime Minister.

feast. It was served up in a silver tureen as soup, but did not well to *precede* fish and other dishes. It was good of itself, however. It seemed to be just rich plum-cake boiled down in wine with spices. Hon. Daines Barrington and Mr. Brereton were there as antiquarians. We had also Mr. Reeves, chairman of the Association at the Crown and Anchor, and Mr. Topham, their secretary, and some more company.[4]

THURSDAY 27 DECEMBER. (Writing as before.) Home all day playing draughts with my son James. Was quite relaxed.

FRIDAY 28 DECEMBER. (As before.) No better; dined home.

SATURDAY 29 DECEMBER. (As before.) Ditto. Ditto.

SUNDAY 30 DECEMBER. (As before.) With difficulty for some time past did I get out of bed. I was not at church today. It being Dr. Langford's last day this year at the Chaplain's Table, I went on his general invitation, as I had never been there on a Sunday, when soup is served. I was afraid there might be a crowd, but we were only five, and he made me heartily welcome, saying as a plain Englishman, "he believed me to be *a very good man.*"[5] The other guests were a Mr. Peacock, father of the gentleman whom I met here some dinners ago, and two young gentlemen. We had not only soup and other good things but a haunch of venison. Three days dining frugally at home and not tasting wine made the entertainment here relish highly. But the various liquors I found affected me rather too much after I got into the street. Yet I arrived safely at home and went early to bed.

MONDAY 31 DECEMBER. (As before.) Dined at Baldwin's, where I generally *warm* myself with wine; but today, though we cordially ended the year, I was more moderate than usual, as I was to go to a card-party at Miss Campbell's in Suffolk Street, Cavendish Square. I hoped to have met Miss Upton there, but her mother and she had colds, so I was disappointed. Strange that I have never yet been in her company. I liked this party. It was really small.

---

[4]Owen Salusbury Brereton was not only an antiquarian but also a barrister of Lincoln's Inn, Recorder of Liverpool, and a former M.P. John Reeves had just become the head of the Association for Preserving Liberty and Property against Republicans and Levellers, which met at the Crown and Anchor Tavern and which tried to counteract the supposedly seditious activities of the supporters of the French Revolution, chiefly by issuing cheap publications that defended the British monarchy and Constitution. Reeves had returned to England in the autumn of this year after serving as a judge in Newfoundland. John Topham, a respected barrister of Gray's Inn and editor of state papers including the Parliamentary Rolls, was the Association's Treasurer. Boswell was proud to be "one of the earliest of the Associators at the Crown and Anchor" (Boswell to Andrew Erskine, 6 March 1793).

[5]Perhaps Boswell is recalling a conversation in which he boasted of being a "*very* good man" and Lord Graham, later third Duke of Montrose, rejoined, "You only know what a good man is" (Journal, 13 May 1781).

1793

TUESDAY 1 JANUARY. (As before.) Breakfasted with Malone according to custom and looked at new monthly publications. Went with him to the LITERARY CLUB, where were the Bishop of Dromore, Dr. Burney, Sir Joseph Banks, Messrs. Burke, Senior and Junior, Sir William Scott, Mr. Windham. I have lost my faculty of recording. I recollect only that the Bishop of Dromore said "he was *sure* Cleland did not write the *Woman of Pleasure*, though the *wretch* owned it." His Lordship added that he had occasion to make particular inquiries as to the fact, and he was satisfied that it was written by Sir Charles Hanbury Williams. This I could not help thinking was erroneous. I knew Cleland pretty well. He had very good talents. He told me, or rather acquiesced as an *undoubted* fact, of his having written that extraordinary book; and, what is very strange, he said he had kept it nine years before he published it.[6] I had little relish even of THE CLUB. I enjoyed chiefly the wine.

WEDNESDAY 2 JANUARY. (Writing 8 February.) Dined at Hingeston's. Evening, Essex Head Club.

THURSDAY 3 JANUARY. (As before.) Called on Mr. Wilkes and paid him £100 which he in the handsomest manner put into my hands without a note some years ago. I drank chocolade and had

---

[6]John Cleland's notorious novel, published in 1748–49, is better known as *Fanny Hill*. In his journal of 13 April 1779 Boswell mentions Cleland's remark that he had kept the first part and half of the second for twenty-five years before publishing the novel. But Cleland was an unreliable informant: he had tried to gain his release from imprisonment for pornography by blaming the work on Hanbury Williams, a diplomat who also wrote erotic verse, thus contributing to the rumour that Williams was the author, but then he claimed that he had rewritten a text given to him by a well-connected young man eighteen years earlier.

some pleasant conversation. He was clear for my publishing my travels.[7] I was seized today with a pretty severe cold. (I cannot read the note where I dined.) In the evening drank a little mountain with Malone.

FRIDAY 4 JANUARY. (As before.) Dined at Royal Academy Club. Sir Francis Bourgeois accompanied me to a party which my daughters had, and a little music. Salomon only stayed to an egg, etc.[8]

SATURDAY 5 JANUARY. (As before.) To cure my cold, lay in bed all day and eat plentifully of leek soup. Enjoyed a pretty good share of tranquillity.

SUNDAY 6 JANUARY. (As before.) Still more tranquil than for some time past. Called on Mr. Leach, Barnard's Inn.[9] Had Jamie with me. Was at chapel in the afternoon. Dined at Metcalfe's with Malone, Sir William Scott, Burke and son, Windham. Drank rather too much. Metcalfe observed it petulantly.

MONDAY 7 JANUARY. (As before.) Home all day. The three young Cookes drank tea with us, and we had a Twelfth Day cake.[1] Evening, Thatched House Club.

TUESDAY 8 JANUARY. (As before.) Took Jamie with me to Hicks's Hall, where he heard a little business. He then went with me to Dilly's, where we dined with Leach, Phineas Bond,[2] Counsellor Burrough, Counsellor Allan, etc. I was too intemperate, lost at whist, stayed supper, but got home in safety.

WEDNESDAY 9 JANUARY. Not well, but knew why. At home all day, doing nothing but sorting some papers.

[EDITORIAL NOTE. At this point the journal again lapses, this time for nearly seven months. In mid-January Boswell went to Chelmsford for the Essex Epiphany Sessions, with the same disappointing results as at the earlier assizes: £3. 3s. in fees but £3. 6s. in expenses. He was

---

[7] Boswell was beginning to consider the publication of the journals he had written during his tour of Germany, Switzerland, and Italy in the 1760s.

[8] Salomon was a violinist and composer as well as an impresario.

[9] Perhaps separate visits. Leach was a member of the Temple; Barnard's Inn, which provided living quarters for students of chancery law, belonged to Gray's Inn.

[1] A special frosted spice-cake, elaborately decorated, was served on the twelfth day after Christmas (6 January) to mark the end of the Christmas festivities and the festival of Epiphany. By tradition the cake contained a bean to designate the king of the feast and a pea to designate the queen.

[2] A native of Philadelphia but a loyalist, Bond had practised law in England during the American Revolution; he was now British consul to the Middle States of America. Boswell included a note of Johnson's to Bond—sent by James Abercrombie from America—in the second edition of the *Life of Johnson*.

still not feeling well. In fact, illness prevented him from attending the Royal Academy dinner on 18 January.

But at the end of the month the momentous political events in France roused him to new exertions. Louis XVI, who had been on trial since 11 December 1792, was guillotined on 21 January; he was buried unceremoniously in the Madeleine cemetery, and quicklime was poured on his body to destroy it as soon as possible. The news reached England three days later. In burning indignation Boswell conceived the extraordinary scheme of planning a monument for the French monarch in Westminster Abbey and wrote the advertisement for the subscription.]

[Draft, dated 31 January 1793]

MONUMENT IN HONOUR OF LOUIS XVI, KING OF FRANCE

The anarchy, assassination, and sacrilege by which the Kingdom of France has been disgraced, desolated, and polluted for some years past cannot but have excited the strongest emotions of horror in every virtuous Briton. But within these days our hearts have been pierced by the recital of proceedings in that country more brutal than any recorded in the annals of the world. Not contented with murdering their sovereign with every circumstance of rude and barbarous insult, previous to and during the execrable act the ruffians who have now usurped the power of France not only inhumanly refused to allow his remains to be reposited in the sepulchre of his fathers but with unexampled malignity have taken measures to prevent that honour being paid to him at any future time. To express therefore to surrounding nations and to posterity the generous indignation and abhorrence felt by the humane, free, and happy subjects of this realm at such savage atrocity, it is proposed that a subscription be opened for a monument to be erected in Westminster Abbey, the venerable repository of our own monarchs, to the memory of Louis XVI, King of France, whose patience, piety, dignified deportment, and fortitude in his last moments entitle him to the admiration of mankind.

T.D. Boswell produced a French translation, adding a sympathetic allusion to the French *émigrés*. Before publishing the appeal, Boswell did however take the precaution of writing to Dundas so as to get at least unofficial approval from the Government. Dundas, after checking with Pitt, quickly discouraged the scheme in a brief letter of 5 February: "He [Pitt] thinks that the public mind is sufficiently alive on the subject of the death of the King of France, and that any immediate expression of it in the manner you suggest would not be attended with any real beneficial effect and might raise discussions unnecessary to be agitated."

In a lighter vein Boswell seems to have indulged in one or two romantic fancies. For instance, he clipped a lock of hair belonging to Miss Harriet Cotton—a lady not mentioned elsewhere in his writings—and kept it among his papers with the note "cut by me, 5 February 1793." He was, moreover, corresponding with Temple about Maria Lemon, who had flattered him during his visit to Cornwall. Temple in his letter of 6 February held out some hopes of a possible union: "The lovely Maria! the idea is transporting! Such a connection would be like beginning life anew." But he felt obliged to add a warning: "We frequently mistake our strength and deceive ourselves, and when we fondly hope to gather only roses, fill our hands with thorns and prickles."

At the end of February Boswell set out for Scotland, primarily in order to appoint a new minister for Auchinleck parish. He knew what sort of clergyman he wanted—someone who would be both an intelligent companion to his family and a helpful minister to the humblest in the parish—and he decided to hear the views of his parishioners at first hand. To Temple, who repeatedly urged him not to undertake the strenuous journey, he played up his role as Laird of Auchinleck with a touch of self-irony: "Only think, Temple," he wrote on 26 February, "how serious a duty I am about to discharge, *I, James Boswell, Esq.* You know what variety that name includes. I have promised to come down on purpose, and *his Honour*'s goodness is gratefully acknowledged." After his favourite candidate preferred a ministry among the Glasgow poor, Boswell chose John Lindsay, the candidate of the elders of Auchinleck Church.

On 20 March Boswell sent Malone the revised ending of the *Life of Johnson* for the second edition. He had added some anecdotes about Johnson's last days and a final paragraph in praise of Johnson. Although he invited corrections, he was obviously pleased with his effort. He also reported: "I have been wonderfully active, and in health and spirits almost incredible, and never once drunk." Boswell's spirits must have been dampened, however, on receiving a grief-stricken letter from Temple with the news that Mrs. Temple had suddenly died after a three-week illness.

On his departure from Auchinleck Boswell spent a day and a night in Glasgow. There he briefly renewed his acquaintance with Wilhelmina Alexander, the sister of his neighbour Claud Alexander of Ballochmyle, who had caught his fancy nine years earlier. Boswell had, in fact, kept a running account of the flirtation and now added the concluding entries.

[Record of Miss Wilhelmina Alexander, Autumn 1784 to March 1793]

1st time. Autumn 1784 in chaise—something genteel and gay. I have seen her, etc.

2nd. Winter after dancing at Dunn's.[3] Was not near her. Did not strike me much—but still uncommonly genteel.

3rd. Autumn 1785 at Ballochmyle in a forenoon—her eyes delightful—her vivacity enchanting.

4th. At Auchinleck dinner and dance. Sensible, lively, beautiful. Though one in London,[4] floated in fancy, was captivated.

5th. Autumn 1786 talked to her for two minutes as she stopped in a chaise. Was actually afraid—dreaded the fire—and prudently did not see her more.

6th. At Auchinleck forenoon—told her I had seen nobody like her—put me in mind of Solomon.[5]

7th. Autumn 1787. Dined at Ballochmyle—sat next her—danced with her. *Liked* her still better and was not *burned*.

8th. At Ballochmyle breakfasted—she did not please me so much on horseback.

9th. At Auchinleck dinner and dance—elegantly dressed—most charming. Told her how much I admired—danced with her. She told me confidentially of F. and W.[6] I applauded her. I told her confidentially of a romantic illicit connection and how I had owned it to wife[7]— she informed me that it had been told—and others—which were not true. At supper she happened to touch my hand—my sensibility was such that I suddenly drew back. She said: "That was a proper *reproof to me.*" I was quite elevated with gay spirits.

10th. Having the night before rode several miles round on purpose to see her at Ballochmyle and heart having strangely failed so as not to go in, breakfasted. Saw her to be most pleasing. She showed a love of genealogy and knowledge of it which won my heart.

11th. Moment at Auchinleck to take my daughter with her—most engaging.

12th. Evening at Ballochmyle. The fondness was gone too deep. It

---

[3]In February 1785 Boswell had attended two of the subscription assemblies held at least once a week at Dunn's Hotel in Edinburgh.

[4]Presumably Boswell means Mrs. Margaret Rudd, the celebrated adventuress with whom he had carried on an affair from November 1785 to April 1786.

[5]I Kings 3: 12: "Lo, I have given thee a wise and an understanding heart; so that there was none like thee before thee, neither after thee shall any arise like unto thee." Boswell is referring to Wilhelmina Alexander's special qualities.

[6]Not identified.

[7]Boswell had confessed his transgressions with Mrs. Rudd in the summer of 1788.

was painful, it was serious—I spoke earnestly. She said: "You make me laugh"—I was hurt by this. When I talked slightly[8] of a licentious connection of Lady ——, she said with much feeling and dignity of virtue in her eye, "I am sure *you* think justly." I was really sick and resolved to keep aloof.

13th. A forenoon call at Ballochmyle. She came and talked with me while I sat on horseback, and gave me her hand at parting.

14th. At Ballochmyle in the forenoon—was more indifferent. She dined at Auchinleck—quite accommodating and pleasant. Sorry to part from her. Saluted twice.[9] Had been thinking at night, none fair as she, etc.

15th. Night between 21 and 22 October. In a dream—very fond. She allowed fifty kisses and said: "Now this only kindness."

16th. At Ballochmyle, autumn 1791, after almost three years not seeing her. Before dinner thought I saw a *little* change—a little fading. But when I saw her dressed, could not perceive a difference. Lively and pleasant, but not quite so frank as when I was a married man. Evening, when asked to play whist, said "I *think* I can employ my time better," looking at her. She acquiesced and we sat chatting together all the time.

17th. Next morning, had dreamed twice that I saw her. Looked very well. Pressed her to come and dine at my house with her brother, but could not prevail. Felt a *little* of the passion.

18th. On Tuesday, 11 October, returning from Fairlie and drank tea at Ballochmyle. She had a pleasing and engaging appearance, but I was not captivated. The *connections* did not suit my taste, and I recalled my *English* fondnesses.

19th. At Glasgow in a forenoon, March 1793, cheerful and agreeable. At night at play. A Mrs. Clarke made room in box. Admired her at a public place.

20th. Had been asked to sup night before but was engaged to a client at my inn. Breakfasted gaily and liked—without fever. Joked and said jointure lands were not vacant yet[1] as my parish had been, to which I had just presented a minister.

The record of Boswell's flirtation with Wilhelmina Alexander ends here, and so, presumably, did his infatuation. Soon he was in any case busy with other matters. On his return to London, for instance, he once more turned his attention to the Botany Bay prisoners and, quite pos-

---

[8]Slightingly.

[9]Kissed in a gesture of farewell.

[1]Jointure lands were landed property that were part of a marriage settlement. Boswell is suggesting jokingly that Lady Auchinleck's continued possession of several rent-producing farms when she became Lord Auchinleck's second wife in 1769 makes them unavailable to him as a marriage settlement if he were to remarry.

sibly as a result of his urging, Dundas set in motion the granting of a royal pardon to Mary Bryant, who was released in early May. But the four men remained in Newgate, and Boswell tried to help them by writing an appeal to Evan Nepean, Under-Secretary of State for the Home Department, arguing that if they were set free they would find work and the support of friendly relations.

[Draft of a Petition for the Botany Bay Prisoners—14 May 1793]

Case of the Convicts who Escaped from Botany Bay
General Observations

Not one of these poor men has been either a highwayman or a housebreaker.[2] Their offences, though justly punishable, have been of a slighter degree of malignity. For this they have atoned: by an imprisonment before trial—by confinement on board the hulks[3] at Portmouth—by a severe passage to New South Wales—by servitude and almost starvation there—by a series of most distressful sufferings in the course of making their escape—by imprisonment since, in the gaol of Newgate. They did certainly in the impatience of misery subscribe a petition praying to have their wretched captivity exchanged for a situation on board His Majesty's fleet. But it is humbly submitted to Government whether, all things considered, they should not have a second chance to be good members of society and be permitted to do the best they can for themselves and their families. It should seem to be of the genius of our Constitution to act with mildness and compassion where there is no obvious call for severity.

Particulars

William Allen, born at Kingston-upon-Hull, in his fifty-sixth year, served both the last wars in His Majesty's fleet under Captain Moutray in the *Ramillies* and after he was broke Captain Marotter and Admiral Graves. Was in her when she was cast away.[4] "Water I must follow" are his words, but would rather go where he can get most by it; viz., in

---

[2]At the top right-hand margin Boswell later added in parentheses: "This I afterwards found not to be true as to Lilley. See certificate of his conviction."

[3]Prison ships.

[4]In July 1780 John Moutray, the widely experienced captain of the *Ramillies,* lost the convoy of merchant ships for which he served as escort by sailing into the midst of the combined French and Spanish fleets near Gibraltar. He was subsequently tried by court-martial and stripped of his command. Allen served under him not only in the 1780 engagement but also presumably before that in the North American war. The *Ramillies* was wrecked in a violent storm in September 1782. Vice-Adm. Thomas Graves was on board at the time of the shipwreck but escaped to a nearby ship.

a merchantman: "I have the world to begin again." Has a wife at Beccles in Suffolk, from whom he has heard since he came home.

John Butcher, born in the parish of Kidderminster, Worcestershire, in his forty-ninth year, was always a husbandman, unmarried. Has heard from Mr. Woodward, who keeps the Lion at Kidderminster. Would be kindly received and get his bread in his own country.

Nathaniel Lilley, born at Sudbury in Suffolk, in his thirtieth year, by trade a weaver and fish-net-maker. Has a wife and four children (one since his return home). Has an uncle, Richard Wardel, who married his aunt, who is a cabinet-maker and joiner in Gatney Street, Pimlico, no. 4, and a brother Robert Angus, a waiter at —— in Old Russell Street, corner of New Hummums,[5] who married his sister who keeps a laundry. By these he would be supported and put in a way of getting a livelihood by his own trade. In the meantime he has worked night and day in gaol as a net-maker to support his family, being employed by Mr. Mason, Fleet Street.

James Martin, born at Balymenoch,[6] county of Antrim, Ireland, in his thirty-sixth year, by trade a bricklayer and mason. Had worked in England seven years before the misfortune happened to him. Has a wife at Exeter, from whom he has heard several times, also one child, a son. Could get a guinea a week, being a very good workman as he proved when at Botany Bay, where he worked a great deal for the settlement. Is willing either to return to his own country, where his mother, brother, and sister are—and he has heard from them—or he will get work in London.

All of them would go to sea in any manner that Government thinks fit rather than remain in prison. But it is hoped that in consideration of their extraordinary sufferings, they will be allowed to do the best they can for themselves, in an honest way.

Conclusion

It is therefore earnestly requested that in this extraordinary case the clemency of the Crown may be benignantly exercised.

At the same time that he was writing this petition Boswell tried to interest Lady Jean Dundas in the plight of the four prisoners, but she,

[5]Perhaps Tom's Coffee-house at the corner of Russell Street and Covent Garden. The New Hummums was a hotel at the location of an older hotel called The Hummums and before that of Turkish baths (the name was derived from the Arabic "hammum," a warm bath).
[6]Ballymena.

having only recently become Dundas's second wife, declined to interfere with her husband's professional duties.

Meanwhile the printing of the second edition of the *Life of Johnson* was being completed. Boswell had collected new material and had added lengthy explanatory footnotes throughout. But important new material arrived after the first two volumes were printed. Unable to include the additional letters and anecdotes in their proper chronological place, Boswell put them where he could. For instance, he inserted thirteen letters from Johnson to Bennet Langton at the end of the second volume, followed by two important letters from Johnson to the Prime Minister, Lord Bute, on the subject of his pension. Additional Johnson anecdotes, which the Rev. Dr. William Maxwell sent from Ireland in May, were tucked away in the first volume, immediately after the Table of Contents, with the heading "Additions to Dr. Johnson's Life Recollected and Received after the Second Edition Was Printed." Altogether, the second edition was a somewhat disorganized affair.

Unabashed, Boswell provided a new Advertisement that did not stint self-praise. After expressing his aim of making the second edition even better than the first, regretting the death of Reynolds, and extolling Johnson's character and principles as antidotes to the subversive ideas coming from France, Boswell could not resist dwelling on the praise he had reaped from many eminent persons. In particular, he quoted a friend who said, "You have made them all talk Johnson," and continued with obvious satisfaction: "Yes, I may add, I have *Johnsonized* the land, and I trust they will not only *talk,* but *think,* Johnson." In a further passage Boswell expressed his pleasure at being praised by the King himself. "It is impossible for me, an enthusiastic *Tory,* not to tell the world what I feel and shall express with that reverential fondness which characterizes a true royalist. Soon after the death of my illustrious friend, HIS MAJESTY one day at the levee, after observing that he believed Dr. Johnson was as good a man as ever lived, was graciously pleased to say to me, 'There will be many lives of Dr. Johnson: do you give the best.' I flatter myself that I have obeyed my SOVEREIGN's commands."

Because of these remarks Boswell suddenly had to deal with a protest from an unexpected quarter. In an angry note dated 13 May, Malone accused Boswell of having written a "wild rodomontade" and demanded that if Boswell persisted in his self-praise, he was to delete all references to Malone in the Advertisement for the first edition so as not to harm his reputation. He signed himself, "Yours always very sincerely in *private* but by no means wishing to be *pilloried* with you in *public.*" As Malone explained to Sir William Forbes some years later, he had encouraged Boswell to rewrite the Advertisement for the second edition and to end with the comments on Johnson. When Malone saw the supposedly revised version at the press, he found that Boswell had, instead, added several paragraphs of self-congratulation, including the quotation from the King that was especially objectionable because the monarch's remarks, when made in private, were by convention not to be published. Boswell endorsed Malone's note "a strange letter," consulted Courtenay, and then wrote a conciliatory reply, offering to submit the Advertisement to their mutual friend John Douglas, Bishop of Salisbury, for his decision. Presumably it was at the latter's suggestion that Boswell dropped the paragraph that implied a royal imprimatur,[7] but he retained the four paragraphs of self-praise that now appear at the end of the Advertisement.

At about this time Boswell also took steps to counteract an irritating rumour that he had visited Lady Salisbury, the leading Tory hostess, at Hatfield House without her invitation after the preceding summer's Hertford Assizes. Writing to her on 16 May, he not only asked her to deny this rumour but also reminded her of her promise to dance with him at the next assizes, asserting with characteristic pride: "Believe me, Madam, if I were not conscious of having such blood in my veins as entitles me in one respect to that distinction, such is my aristocratic enthusiasm that I should not only not aspire to it, but should not accept it if offered. But I have been the partner, at a ball, of many princesses, and even of the sister of my sovereign, the present reigning Duchess of Brunswick when she was Hereditary Princess."[8] He even offered to postpone a tour of the Continent that he was planning in order to claim the promised dance. And he took the opportunity to enclose some of his verses that he knew would please her, entitled "On hearing Lady Salisbury say at the Orleans Gallery, 26 April 1793, 'I do love Charles the First,'" which expressed his own monarchical sentiments and "loyal Tory soul." Lady Salisbury replied immediately, confirming that she had indeed invited him the preceding summer and had promised him a dance, but declaring that she was unable to dance with anyone at the present time.

As his letter to Lady Salisbury reveals, travels on the Continent were now much on Boswell's mind. France had declared war on England and Holland in February, and Boswell was planning a visit to Flanders to observe the Combined Armies—the British, Dutch, Hanoverian, and Hessian troops who were fighting against the French. In addition, he

[7]A proof-page with this paragraph has survived and is now in the Yale collection.
[8]In August 1764 Boswell had danced a minuet with the Duchess Augusta of Brunswick-Lüneburg, the sister of George III, as well as with the Princesses Elizabeth and Auguste-Dorothea, two of the daughters of the reigning Duke.

was giving more thought to revising and publishing the journals of his earlier Continental tour. To Sir William Forbes, who was travelling in Italy, he described this projected book—it would include conversations, anecdotes, and letters from Voltaire, Rousseau, and other famous people he had met—and suggested that it would be ready for publication the following winter. Boswell was already visualizing several small duodecimo or octavo volumes that travellers might conveniently take with them, projected a large edition in English, and asked Forbes to approach foreign booksellers who might publish translations.

But these plans had to be suspended when a serious accident befell Boswell on the night of 5 June, as he was coming home intoxicated.

[From the *London Chronicle*, 8–11 June 1793]

Last Wednesday night, as James Boswell, Esq., was returning home from the City, he was attacked in Titchfield Street, knocked down, robbed, and left lying in the street quite stunned, so that the villain got clear off. A gentleman happening to pass that way, with the assistance of the watchman and patrol conducted him safe to his house in Great Portland Street, when it was found he had received a severe cut on the back of his head and a contusion on both his arms; he has ever since been almost constantly confined to his bed with a considerable degree of pain and fever.

Boswell was so badly hurt that even two weeks later he had to dictate his letters to his servant rather than write them himself. He took his mishap as a solemn warning and promised—once again—to reform.

[To Temple, 21 June 1793]

The robbery was only of a few shillings. But the cut on my head and bruises on my arms were sad things, and confined me to bed in pain and fever and helplessness as a child many days. By means of Surgeon Earle and Apothecary Devaynes I am now, thank GOD, pretty well. This, however, shall be a *crisis* in my life. I trust I shall henceforth be a sober, regular man. Indeed, my indulgence in wine has, of late years especially, been excessive....Your suggestion as to my being carried off in a state of intoxication is awful....It impressed me much, I assure you.

By early July the *Public Advertiser* could report that Boswell had almost recovered; it had the grace to add that "Mr. Boswell's death would have caused a vacancy in the mirth as well as the instruction of the nation."

In spite of his mishap, Boswell still planned to visit the armies on the Continent. But first, in mid-July, he went to Chelmsford on the circuit and from there to Warley Camp, where he could gain a taste of military life in a more peaceful setting. Bennet Langton, who was serving as Major in the Royal North Lincolnshire Militia, welcomed him warmly and placed a tent at his disposal for the night of 17 July. But the experience proved disappointing; Boswell was unable to sleep and caught cold. Cutting short his stay, he returned to London. From there, on 24 July, he wrote apologetically to Langton: "I was sorry to leave you sooner than you kindly wished. But it was really necessary for me to be in town, and, as I candidly owned to you, I had enough of a camp. In my convalescent state, another disturbed night would have hurt me much." He was also having doubts about his Continental trip. "I hesitate as to Valenciennes, though I should only *survey* a camp there," he confided to Langton, referring to the town just inside the French border that the British and Austrians were besieging. "Yet my curiosity is ardent."

On 17 July, while Boswell was away from London, the second edition of the *Life of Johnson,* "corrected and considerably enlarged by additional letters and interesting anecdotes," was finally published. Boswell sent two copies to Langton with his letter of 24 July, no doubt because Langton had provided so much new material, and could inform him that four hundred copies had already been sold.

But he was still ailing. To Sir Michael Le Fleming he complained on 31 July: "I am not yet free from the consequences of the *villainous accident* which *befell* me, being feeble and not in my right spirits." He resumed his journal on the following day.]

THURSDAY 1 AUGUST. Was very low-spirited. I think I dined at Baldwin's.

FRIDAY 2 AUGUST. Seward dined with me, and we got time off tolerably well till between nine and ten when he left me and I went to bed.

SATURDAY 3 AUGUST. Seward carried me with him to Sir William Chambers's at Whitton,[1] where I had once dined with the Knight and enjoyed it much. Nobody there today but his lady and daughter, Mrs. Harward, with her husband, a lieutenant in the Guards, who left us after dinner. I was vexed that I had not a true relish of the beauties of this spot. But the hospitality and good living pleased me. We were to stay till Monday.

[1]Chambers's country-house in Twickenham, near Hounslow.

SUNDAY 4 AUGUST. Experienced in the morning, as I have often done, that when I am in a state of uneasiness from that inexplicable disorder which vexes a great part of my life, the most beautiful prospects and all other circumstances of enjoyment when a man is well in body and mind, avail nothing. Seward's animated conversation did me some good, as did Sir William's tranquil, rational, and entertaining talk. After breakfast they went with me in Sir William's chariot to Twickenham and set me down at the church, where I saw a genteel congregation, had some relief by pious exercise, and heard Dr. Du Val preach.[2] When service was over, I found them waiting for me, and they carried me back to Whitton. It is no small comfort to me that in all situations my religion still continues. It was strange that my two friends should instead of going to church today drive about airing. Mosnier the painter and his wife (whose French language and manners were offensive to me) and Captain d'Auvergne of the navy (said to be heir of the Duke of Bouillon) dined with us.[3] I had "the load of life"[4] heavy upon me. I was better in the evening when the *company* was gone, and liked some calcavella[5] which we had after supper. In this journal I am not to *expatiate* on the comfort and elegance of Sir William Chambers's living. But it dwells on my mind.

MONDAY 5 AUGUST. After breakfast Seward and I sauntered a good while with Sir William, who then went out in his chariot with his lady; and Seward carried me over to Castlebar near Ealing to the seat of Mr. Smith, where my daughters had been some weeks this summer. The Place is beautiful, or rather the view from it is delightful.[6] Our host came from London, to which he goes every day to manage his business as a stockbroker, and returns. The wife and family of Mr.

---

[2]Philip Du Val, D.D., F.R.S., was the vicar of Twickenham, a canon of Windsor, and chaplain to the Duke of Gloucester.

[3]The portrait-painter Jean Laurent Mosnier, formerly a member of the Académie Royale, had left France at the outbreak of the French Revolution and was now exhibiting his work at the Royal Academy. Philippe d'Auvergne had been adopted by Godefroid-Charles-Henri, Duke of Bouillon, and was to succeed the Duke's feeble-minded, childless son in the Duchy of Bouillon, a small territory adjoining France to the north-east. D'Auvergne's nomination to the Duchy had been officially recognized by George III in February 1792, but later wars and lawsuits prevented D'Auvergne from ever gaining control of Bouillon.

[4]Johnson, Prologue to Goldsmith's *Good-Natured Man*, ll. 1–2:
>Pressed by the load of life, the weary mind
>Surveys the general toil of human kind.

[5]A sweet white wine from Lisbon.

[6]The highest elevation of Ealing, called Castle Bear by Boswell.

Parke, the famous hautboy-player,[7] were here. In the evening Seward returned to Whitton. I stayed, and we had music and dancing; but I wearied.

TUESDAY 6 AUGUST. Felt the same listlessness and fretfulness as at any house in the country in Scotland. Was glad to be carried to *town* by Mr. Smith. After seeing my daughters, walked into the City and dined at Baldwin's. The printing of the *Additions* to my first edition of my *Life of Dr. Johnson* was my only *business* at present.[8]

WEDNESDAY 7 AUGUST. Only sad idleness to record. Dined at home.

THURSDAY 8 AUGUST. My brother Thomas David dined with me. I had called on Windham, returned from the Combined Armies, and heard part of his story.[9]

FRIDAY 9 AUGUST. Breakfasted with Windham and heard him out. Dined with Dilly by chance at three. Then having called at Baldwin's to see a sheet of my *Additions*, was told that Mr. Noorthouck, author of a *History of London*,[1] was there, I had never seen him, so went in and drank a glass of wine with Baldwin and him, whom I found to be a good-talking, knowing man. He had now retired to live at Peterborough.

SATURDAY 10 AUGUST. I reflected how sadly London was changed to me of late: no General Paoli—no Sir Joshua Reynolds—no Sir John Pringle—no Squire Godfrey Bosville—no General Oglethorpe.[2]

SUNDAY 11 AUGUST. Was at Portland Chapel in the morning, by myself. Then sauntered to St. James's Park and as far as Dilly's. Was

[7]First oboist at Drury Lane, John Parke also played in the Queen's band, at the Concerts of Ancient Music, and at the Haydn concerts of 1791–92 and 1794–95.

[8]A quarto pamphlet entitled *The Principal Corrections and Additions to the First Edition of Mr. Boswell's Life of Dr. Johnson* was to provide the owners of the first edition with what Boswell regarded as the most important new material included in the second edition.

[9]Windham had spent three weeks on the Continent, two of them at Valenciennes. Strongly opposed to the French Revolution, he had wished to see for himself how the war was progressing.

[1]In his *New History of London* (1773) John Noorthouck provided not only a history of London in various periods but also a survey of buildings existing at this time. He was an index-maker and corrector of the press by profession.

[2]Paoli was in Corsica; the others had died within the last few years. Gen. James Edward Oglethorpe, founder of the colony of Georgia, had been a friend since 1768, when he called on Boswell because he admired the *Account of Corsica*. After this entry Boswell originally started a new paragraph with the statement, "I have neglected to keep any memorandum of my useless life until Sunday 18 August" and began the entry for 18 August with: "This morning a Mr. Kestle, a glazier at." He must then have remembered his activities from 11 to 17 August, for he inked out these statements and continued his daily entries.

feeble and fatigued. Mr. Cooke's son and daughters dined with us and drank tea. I had been alarmed by my daughter Euphemia's having a cough and other symptoms which might tend to that dismal disease, a consumption, but she was now better. In the evening I got Veronica and her to say *short* divine lessons. I was uneasy at their having very little attention to religious duties. They had however been at Portland Chapel this afternoon.

MONDAY 12 AUGUST. My brother Thomas David dined with us, and Miss Watsons, Mrs. and Miss Keir drank tea. I walked out in the evening, and was somewhat amused with the illuminations by some club-houses and tradesmen in honour of the Prince of Wales's birthday, and then I went to the Free and Easy at the Thatched House, where I had not been for more than two months. We were only five; played cards and supped. It was half past one when I got home. I thought of giving up this club, which was expensive and of no service to me, and the amusement overbalanced by the late hours.

TUESDAY 13 AUGUST. Dined at Baldwin's. I always drink tea there when I dine. It is truly comfortable to me to have such a hospitable table at my printer's, where there is good cheer and hearty welcome, and my coming in as a guest makes no difference. Mr. Graham of St. Paul's Churchyard, the great upholsterer, Mrs. Baldwin's brother, called, and Baldwin and he and I walked nearly to the obelisk in St. George's Fields.[3] I then went quietly home, carrying with me a haddock and five whitings which I bought for eighteen pence, and had a little fish supper for myself and my daughters.

WEDNESDAY 14 AUGUST. Sauntered out *wearily*. Visited Cosway. Dined at home. Then—for a wonder!—went to the play, to try to *dissipate* my mind. It was at the Haymarket Theatre. I was somewhat entertained by *The Mountaineers*, a new piece by young Colman; that is to say, I liked the scenery and one or two of the songs and some parts of the dialogue. But the mixture of tragedy was much too deep; and indeed the distress even to insanity of a lover who imagined he had forever lost his mistress was to me disgustingly extravagant, and Kemble in acting it "outdid his usual outdoings."[4] There was a silly after-piece called *Carnarvon Castle, or, The Birth of the Prince of Wales*.[5] Upon the whole I was tired and found my theatrical taste gone.

-

[3] A cabinet-maker and upholsterer, Joseph Graham was a member of the Court of Assistants (the governing body) of the upholsterers' livery company. The obelisk had been erected about twenty years earlier in honour of the then Lord Mayor, Brass Crosby.
[4] Pope, *The Art of Sinking in Poetry:* "They continue to outdo even their own outdoings." George Colman the Younger's play, with music by Dr. Samuel Arnold, had opened on 3 August and was a great success, with twenty-six performances in its first season.
[5] By John Rose, with music by Thomas Attwood.

THURSDAY 15 AUGUST. Courtenay, who had come to town, called on me, and he and I dined at Windham's. Only Mr. Lukin of the navy, Windham's nephew, there.[6]

FRIDAY 16 AUGUST. [No entry for this day.]

SATURDAY 17 AUGUST. Windham and Courtenay, who had now his family in town, and my brother David dined with me.

SUNDAY 18 AUGUST. This morning there called on me Mr. Kestle, at no. 12 Cross Street, Carnaby Market, a glazier, who told me that he was a native of Fowey[7] and knew all the relations of Mary Broad very well, and had received a letter from one of them directing him to me; that he wished to see her and inform them about her, and also to introduce her sister Dolly to her, who was in service in London. He mentioned that a large sum of money had been left to Mary Broad's father and three or four more—no less than three hundred thousand pounds. I had a suspicion that he might be an impostor. However, I carried him to see her, and from his conversation it appeared that he really knew her relations. She did not recollect him, but he had seen her in her younger days. I was pleased with her good sense in being shy to him and not being elated by the sound of the great fortune. He said he would bring her sister Dolly to her in the evening. I walked away with him nearly to Oxford Street, and then returned to Mary and cautioned her not to put any trust in anything he said till he had brought her sister. I sauntered restlessly. Went to afternoon service in Whitehall Chapel, but the minister drawled so, that I did not stay sermon, but went and walked more. Dined at Mr. Nealson's, Great George Street, with Mr. Maurice Morgann, Counsellor Cooke, and Mr. Webster, attorney. Was languid and low-spirited, but conversed tolerably. Called on Mary in my way home, and found that Kestle had actually brought her sister Dolly to her, a fine girl of twenty, who had been in great concern about her, and showed the most tender affection.

MONDAY 19 AUGUST. Visited an old acquaintance in Queen Street; excellent. Dined at Baldwin's. Then went to Newgate to see the four men who had escaped from Botany Bay and assure them personally that I was doing all in my power for them. I first called on Mr. Kirby, the keeper,[8] who kindly invited me to drink tea, which I did with his wife and niece and several other *ladies*. It was a curious thought that I was in *Newgate;* for the room was handsome and everything in good

---

[6]William Lukin was presumably a midshipman; he became a lieutenant in October of this year. A favourite of Windham's, he eventually became his heir.

[7]A seaport in Cornwall.

[8]John Kirby had become the keeper of Newgate after the death of Richard Akerman in November 1792.

order as in the drawing-room of any good middle-rank family in any part of London. Mr. Kirby did not partake with us, saying he did not drink tea above once in a month. He obligingly attended me into the gaol by the door from his house, which Akerman had built up for fear of the prisoners' breaking in, but he had opened. He invited me to eat beef with him on the 3 of September, the eve of St. Bartholomew's Day, when the famous fair which goes by his name is proclaimed by the Lord Mayor,[9] and he wrote a truly respectful note which he gave me to keep me in mind of it. I had frequently been in Newgate before, and had felt the crowding of the prisoners and their importunity for money very uneasy. But now when the commander-in-chief was with me, there was a wonderful difference. They were all uncovered,[1] fell back on each side, and did not utter a word. It was so far pleasing that there was at present here nobody under sentence of death. After having comforted the Botany Bay men, we were returning, when we were accosted by Lord William Murray, to whom Mr. Kirby had introduced me in our way going to the men. I was struck with his family likeness both to the late and present Duke of Atholl.[2] He asked me to walk up to his apartment. Mr. Kirby also went; and there I saw Lady William, a genteel young woman, sitting on a bed without curtains, in a room with bare stone walls. Both Lord William and she talked very easily. I felt strangely. I then called on Mr. George Dance, the City architect, in Gower Street, and found him just returned from the country, sitting with his son, a young student of Cambridge, and another young gentleman to whom he was guardian. We had bread and cheese and bottled porter, and ended the evening with pleasantry. I refused to join them in a glass of wine.

TUESDAY 20 AUGUST. Dined at Mr. Hingeston, the apothecary's, in Cheapside, with Mr. Salte, a clergyman, and Mr. N———, a dry-salter; stayed the evening and played sixpenny whist. Walked home, which I should not have done at night from the City.[3] *Domest.;* almost discovered. Never again.

WEDNESDAY 21 AUGUST. Uneasy and still in sad spirits. Courtenay insisted that Windham and I should dine with him and eat a trout

---

[9]See below, 3 September 1793.

[1]That is, they had removed their hats as a sign of respect.

[2]Murray, who had been in the King's Bench prison for debt, had been transferred to Newgate in 1792 for supposedly taking part in an attempt to blow up the prison walls. Boswell had known both his father, John Murray, the third Duke of Atholl, and his brother, John Murray, the fourth Duke.

[3]Boswell has inked out the rest of this entry. *Domest.* is no doubt an abbreviation for *domesticated* and suggests a repetition of the experience on 12 November 1792.

which he had bought *cheap* in the City. We complied. His family was now in town and dined with us.

THURSDAY 22 AUGUST. At breakfast I read in the newspaper that there had been an action in Flanders, in which Colonel Bosville was killed. This agitated me much, and I hastened to his friend Colonel Morrison of the Coldstream, who I was pretty sure would have certain information. As I was going along Upper Seymour Street, in which he lives, I met a sergeant of the Coldstream, to whom I spoke, and was informed by him that the sad report was real. I found Colonel Morrison with tears in his eyes; he put into my hand a letter which he had just received from Captain Hewgill, adjutant to the Coldstream and secretary to the Duke of York, communicating the melancholy event.[4] I was deeply affected—running back in my mind on the many scenes in which I had seen the Colonel since I first saw him a little boy at his father's in London. I called on Windham, who regretted him much; and he accompanied me first to the orderly room of the First Regiment of Guards, which I happened to know, and then to the office of Mr. King, Under-Secretary of State, at both of which places we got more particulars. We afterwards walked to different places, and I parted with him in Long Acre and went to my brother at Somerset House,[5] who joined me in condolence, saying that the Colonel was *an emblem of life*. It was indeed difficult for some time to bring our *imaginations* to *believe* that he was dead. We went together and left our cards at the lodgings of his brother, and then dined at my house. I was in a kind of distraction of mind from time to time. My *military ardour* was quite extinguished. I resolved not to go to the Continent this year.

FRIDAY 23 AUGUST. I could not rest. I walked into the City, though I felt much pain from feebleness. I dined at home.

SATURDAY 24 AUGUST. I called on Mr. Bosville and was let in. He seemed wonderfully calm. He showed me a letter from Colonel Grinfield announcing to him with much feeling the great loss.[6] He gave me several letters from the Colonel to read, which showed perfect firmness of mind but at the same time showed that he had no favourable opinion of the prospect of success in the present war, supposing the French to unite. The Rev. Dr. Palmer at Grantham, who has often entertained

[4]Thomas Bosville, a Lt.-Colonel in the Coldstream Guards, was killed on 18 August at Lincelles, where the British and Dutch forces routed the French. Six feet four inches tall, he was struck by a bullet that passed over the head of another officer. Frederick Augustus, Duke of York, was the commanding officer of the regiment.
[5]The location of the Navy Pay Office in which T.D. Boswell was employed.
[6]Col. William Grinfield was Major in the 3rd Regiment of Foot, another of the three regiments fighting in Flanders.

me hospitably there,[7] Mr. Hingeston, who is with Mr. Devaynes and attended me when ill, and my brother T. D. dined with me. Mr. Hingeston went away before tea.

SUNDAY 25 AUGUST. I and my two eldest daughters were at Portland Chapel forenoon and afternoon, and I dined at home with them. In the evening I went to Mary Broad's to meet her sister Dolly, who was very desirous to see me and thank me for my kindness to Mary. I found her to be a very fine, sensible young woman, and of such tenderness of heart that she yet cried and held her sister's hand. She expressed herself very gratefully to me, and said if she got money as was said, she would give me a thousand pounds. Poor girl, her behaviour pleased me much. She gave me, on my inquiring, her whole history since she came to London, from which it appeared that she had most meritoriously supported herself by good service. She was now cook at Mr. Morgan's in Charlotte Street, Bedford Square; but the work was much too hard for her, a young and slender girl. I resolved to exert myself to get her a place more fit for her. It was now fixed that Mary should go by the first vessel to Fowey to visit her relations, her sister there having written to me that she would be kindly received. She had said to me as soon as she heard of the fortune that if she got a share, she would reward me for all my trouble. This scene was a relief from the thoughts of Colonel Bosville.

MONDAY 26 AUGUST. Dined at home.

TUESDAY 27 AUGUST. Dined at Baldwin's. Drank more mountain than was proper for me, but grasped at immediate temporary relief.

WEDNESDAY 28 AUGUST. Still bad. Walked to Camberwell, called on Thomas Stothart, the smith, and was glad to see our old smith's son in a prosperous state, with men under him, an English wife, etc. Dined with Dr. Lettsom, the company almost all medical men; played at bowls. Came to town in the Doctor's chariot.

THURSDAY 29 AUGUST. [No entry for this day.]

FRIDAY 30 AUGUST. Had been twice called early in the morning to take a place in one of the coaches that pass through Farnham, in order to visit my daughter Betsy at Mr. Williams's at Badshot Place, but had not resolution to get up; so I determined that today I would go in one of the afternoon coaches. After tedious waiting, got a place in the Gosport coach, and was set down about midnight at Farnham, at the Bush Inn, a very good one.

---

[7]Richard Palmer, D.D., rector of Scot Willoughby in Lincolnshire and a prebendary of Canterbury, had been an acquaintance of Boswell's for more than twenty years. Boswell had last visited him at Grantham in March 1786.

SATURDAY 31 AUGUST. Rose in good time to go and view the Castle of Farnham, the residence of the Bishop of Winchester,[8] and fine park belonging to it, and to walk a mile and a half to Badshot Place, where I was well received by the family, and found Mrs. Yeldham and Colonel Teesdale visitors. Betsy was highly pleased at seeing me. I had a little saunter in his fields with Mr. Williams. I accompanied him, his lady, and visitors to Sir Nelson Rycroft's, who rented a Place close to Farnham, as they were engaged there. Mr. and Mrs. Bradburn, neighbours of Mr. Williams, dined there. I found myself quite in English society, and relished it as much as my vile hypochondria would allow. We stayed the evening and had whist and supper.

SUNDAY 1 SEPTEMBER. It rained hard. Mrs. Williams had prayers and sermon with the ladies, and I in my own room. I felt the same weariness as at a house in the country in Scotland. Dinner was a relief. I drank rather too much. We had also supper.

MONDAY 2 SEPTEMBER. Mr. Williams and the Colonel went out a-shooting early. I breakfasted with the ladies, walked to Farnham, and got a place in the long coach from Southampton. It was a fine day. I got to London between five and six; dined on bread and milk. Called on my brother and sat awhile with him. Went early to bed.

TUESDAY 3 SEPTEMBER. According to Mr. Kirby's invitation on the 19 of August, I repaired to Newgate to his house and saw the ceremony of the Lord Mayor, sheriffs, etc., calling on the keeper of Newgate and drinking cold tankard out of a large silver cup which he presents to them at his door, and then the proclamation of Bartholomew Fair.[9] I then called on Dilly, and then dined most substantially with the keeper of Newgate, who had the ordinary, the water-bailiff of the City,[1] and three other gentlemen and myself as his guests. We had table beer and porter and Yorkshire ale and sherry and port, and drank liberally. We had also a repetition of the cold tankard. Our

---

[8]With its deep moats, thick walls, and well-placed towers, Farnham Castle was imposing but at this time somewhat dilapidated. It was only the summer residence of Brownlow North, Bishop of Winchester.

[9]Originally a cloth fair but long a carnival with booths, shows, and raucous entertainments, Bartholomew Fair was held in Smithfield for several days starting on 3 September. It was officially proclaimed open by one of the Lord Mayor's attorneys in the presence of the Lord Mayor, sheriffs, and aldermen. Their stopping at Newgate for a cool drink from a special tankard was a traditional part of the ceremonial procession to and from Smithfield.

[1]The Rev. John Villette was the ordinary (chaplain) of Newgate. H. Smith was the water-bailiff, in charge of regulating shipping; he also served as deputy to the Lord Mayor.

conversation was chiefly of London, and particularly of convicts. I got home about nine and went to bed.

WEDNESDAY 4 SEPTEMBER. As I was walking in the street in sad spirits, I was hailed by Lord Inchiquin in his chariot, who asked me to dine with him at four. He and his lady were in town for a day or two, as they occasionally are, not keeping house regularly; but I was invited as a friend; only themselves and I. My spirits were very bad, but the Earl and I drank a bottle of claret each, besides glasses enough in the time of dinner. I felt painfully the loss of Sir Joshua.[2] They went to the play, and when I found myself in the street, just warmed with wine and having nobody on whom I could call, I thought the best thing I could do was to steal into bed, which I did a quarter before seven. Strange kind of life.

THURSDAY 5 SEPTEMBER. Lay as usual till past nine, so had been fourteen hours in bed. Was still no better. Dined at Dilly's with Mr. Baldwin, Mr. Pote, bookseller of Eton, Mr. Bell, bookseller of Edinburgh, Mr. Isaac Reed, Mr. Watt, formerly captain of a ship, and Dr. Gillies, who to my no small satisfaction went away early. So did Bell and Watt. Dilly, Baldwin, Reed, and I played whist, Pote sitting by, helping us with wine and betting. I was very unlucky tonight and lost every rubber—£3.8. Was vexed more than I should be.

FRIDAY 6 SEPTEMBER. Malone had come to town the day before and sent me a note, which I found on my return from Dilly's. I this morning found him busily engaged in arranging old papers which he had found at Stratford-upon-Avon, in hopes of illustrating Shakspeare's history more or less. I envied him the eagerness with which he examined them. My son James came this morning, having travelled in the coach from Glasgow without going to bed.[3] He was in good health and spirits, and I was truly comforted by seeing him again. My friend Temple's eldest son, Francis, a midshipman returned from a voyage to Guinea, was now in town. He and my brother and his wife and daughter Maria and old Mrs. Green dined with me. A number of other people having come to tea, I shrunk from the motley crowd and drank tea at Malone's.

SATURDAY 7 SEPTEMBER. Dined at Malone's with Courtenay. Felt a tolerable oblivion of unhappiness.

SUNDAY 8 SEPTEMBER. Was not at all in spirits. Went to Marylebone Church, but not finding a seat, came home and (I think) made

[2]The meeting with the Countess of Inchiquin, the former Mary Palmer, and their conversation reminded Boswell of Reynolds.

[3]Having spent the summer at Auchinleck, Jamie was coming back for the new term at Westminster School.

Veronica read one of Dr. Johnson's sermons to me. Jack Devaynes called and asked me to dine with him at the *Bush,* his fine little villa at the one-mile stone from Hyde Park Corner, and bring my son James with me. We went and met a Dr. Budd and his son, Rev. Mr. Peter,[4] a Mr. Norris, and Mr. Hingeston. Had a tolerable day of it. But my son James with uncommon propriety spoke to me against dining out on Sundays.

MONDAY 9 SEPTEMBER. [No entry for this day.]

TUESDAY 10 SEPTEMBER. [No entry for this day.]

WEDNESDAY 11 SEPTEMBER. Dined at Malone's with Courtenay, and was somewhat relieved.

THURSDAY 12 SEPTEMBER. Malone and Courtenay were engaged to dine with me, but Courtenay was taken ill; so I had Malone only, whose conversation did me good, though I felt a grievous inferiority from my low spirits.

FRIDAY 13 SEPTEMBER. Dined at the three o'clock dinner at the Old Bailey with the Lord Mayor, the Recorder, Mr. Sheriff Brander, and Judge Heath, to whom I sat next and was pleased with his conversation.[5] Drank a dish of tea with the ordinary in the parlour. Heard one trial only of two pick-pockets, the court was so hot. Had tea comfortably at Malone's in the evening. Found a letter at my house informing me that my friend Temple was coming to town to exert himself to get his son Francis made a lieutenant in the navy.

SATURDAY 14 SEPTEMBER. Expected Temple this morning by the mail-coach. He accordingly came before I was up, accompanied by his son John James, whom he was going to place at Eton School. It was settled that my friend should lodge at my house and John James at my brother's. To see Temple again "soothed my weary soul";[6] and partly sauntering a little way in the street and partly conversing, time passed well enough till dinner, when my brother T.D. joined us. The evening was easier to me than usual of late.

SUNDAY 15 SEPTEMBER. My friend was with me at Portland Chapel in the morning. Sir Christopher Hawkins sat with us awhile afterwards. We stayed at home conversing calmly in the afternoon.

---

[4]Possibly Dr. Richard Budd, a distinguished physician attached to St. Bartholomew's Hospital, his son, and perhaps the Rev. Edward Peter of Great Wigborough, Essex.

[5]The company included Sir James Sanderson, the Lord Mayor; Alexander Brander, one of the two London Sheriffs; and John Heath, Judge of Common Pleas, who had shown his independence by refusing the knighthood customarily bestowed on the holder of this position.

[6]The third time within the year that Boswell uses this quotation from Gray's *Eton College* ode.

Frank Temple had returned last night. This evening I was in a very irritable frame and broke out into too violent a passion against my daughters, who, however, had provoked me by contradiction. I was conscious that I was to blame for not keeping an uniform authority over them.

MONDAY 16 SEPTEMBER. My uneasiness of mind continued. Temple saw how unhappy I was, both from increased irritability and from finding myself disappointed in all my high views of rising in life and having no occupation, nor even any reasonable prospect of obtaining promotion. I read to him part of my correspondence with Dundas, from which we both thought that Dundas would never do anything for me if he could avoid it. Here I was deserting the seat of my ancestors and wasting my life in absolute idleness. Yet my friend, upon considering my unhappy constitution and long habits, thought that I must continue on, living with economy and hoping that something good might happen to me. I sat a little while with Malone. My friend Temple dined with my daughters and excused my dining (first time) at Mr. Desenfans', where were Mrs. Desenfans, sister of the famous Mr. Robert Morris;[7] and Miss Mackworth, only daughter of the late Sir Herbert,[8] a charming young woman, whose figure and looks and manner and voice and conversation charmed me, and amidst my gloom made me imagine for the first time for many months that I could really be made happy by a female companion, M. l'Abbé de Calonne,[9] M. Bukaty the Polish Minister,[1] Mr. Agar, Mr. Cosway, a Captain Purcel, Sir William Chambers, Mr. Northcote,[2] and Sir Francis Bourgeois, who lives in family with M. Desenfans. We had much conversation about pictures and other topics. The dinner, dessert, and wines were exquisite. The *tout*

[7]Robert Morris, a barrister, had defended Frederick, Lord Baltimore in a trial for rape in 1768; after his client's death, he had eloped with Baltimore's daughter, and had then let her divorce him two years later.

[8]Eliza Anne Mackworth's father, who had died two years earlier, had been an M.P. for twenty-four years and was known for his independent views.

[9]Jacques-Ladislas-Joseph de Calonne, a prominent French abbé, had come to London in 1789 to join his more famous brother, Charles-Alexandre de Calonne, the former French Minister of Finance who had been accused of fiscal mismanagement and had left his country in disgrace a year earlier. From 1790 to 1792 the Abbé had been repeatedly on the Continent to raise money for a counter-revolution planned by the Bourbon princes. The Abbé de Calonne was now editor of the *Courier de Londres,* a bi-weekly French-language newspaper published in London.

[1]Franciszek Bukaty was the Polish Ambassador Extraordinary and Envoy Plenipotentiary. He had been a diplomat in London for over twenty years.

[2]James Northcote, a portrait-painter and member of the Royal Academy, had worked as assistant to Reynolds in the 1770s and later wrote an important memoir of him.

ensemble operated upon me and revived my spirits so much that as I was walking home, I said to myself, "A Lord of Session? I would not be the Lord President." So much did I at the moment look down on a narrow, provincial situation. But surely in *solid reason* I was wrong. I found my brother T. D. sitting at my house. The difference in my humour tonight was very visible.

TUESDAY 17 SEPTEMBER.[3] I was called half past six in order to accompany my friend Temple to Eton, where he was to place his son John James. We did not however set out till eight, breakfasted at Cranford Bridge, went to Windsor and viewed St. George's Chapel and the Castle and the noble prospect (none of which made any impression upon me, my spirits were so bad), and then came to Eton to the Christopher Inn, where we dined, and by sending notes were visited by Mr. Briggs, who was to be Temple's son's tutor, and by Mr. Goodall, with whom we talked as to placing him. They went away, and we supped by ourselves.

WEDNESDAY 18 SEPTEMBER. I was little better, and shrunk from the animated system of the discipline of a great school. Could hardly believe my own son had been three years here. After breakfast Mr. Briggs came and went with us to Dr. Heath's and to Mrs. Griffinhoofe's, the boy's dame, and all was soon arranged. I introduced Temple to Dr. Davies, the Provost,[4] whose vivacity pleased him much. Both he and Dr. Heath invited us to dinner, but we were resolved to return to London. We paid visits to Mr. Goodall and Mr. Briggs, and I was going to ring at Dr. Langford's door when he hailed me from his horse and was heartily affable as ever. I took Temple and his son to see the library, both the schools, and the dormitory;[5] and then (leaving the boy somewhat disconsolate) we drove to town. Upon the road I observed to my friend how much depended on the state of our minds. The time was when being at Eton College, etc., as described by Gray, and that too in company with *him,* would have been a luxurious treat to me;[6] and now not only was it altogether insipid, but I was sadly vexed at its being so. We had no dinner today, but only tea.

THURSDAY 19 SEPTEMBER. Today I gave a dinner to a pretty large company: Sir Christopher Hawkins, Principal Gordon of the Scots

[3]Boswell inadvertently dated this entry 16 September and continued the mistake in the next three entries.
[4]Jonathan Davies had become Provost two years earlier, at which time George Heath had become Headmaster.
[5]The library is in the inner quadrangle, the Upper and Lower schools and dormitory in the outer quadrangle, known as the School Yard.
[6] By "*him*" Boswell means Temple.

College, Paris,[7] Mr. Lumisden, my brother David, Mr. F. Temple, Mr. Dodd, my son James's tutor at Westminster, and James with him. Also Sir Francis Bourgeois. I exerted myself as well as I could, though I had no enjoyment. They drank tea and coffee.

FRIDAY 20 SEPTEMBER. The day passed on heavily. Mrs. and Miss Keir drank tea. Temple and his son Francis and I breakfasted at my brother David's.

SATURDAY 21 SEPTEMBER. I went with Temple and saw the statuary of Mr. Bacon and Mr. Nollekens,[8] Sir Joseph Banks's library, and the pictures of Sir Francis Bourgeois and Mr. Desenfans. I was still destitute of all relish. My brother David dined with us.

SUNDAY 22 SEPTEMBER. My friend Temple waited on Mr. Dundas by appointment concerning his son Francis. I went with my brother David to the seat of Mr. Dolan, the great Irish brazier, in the Bavarian Chapel and heard High Mass, also a very good sermon by a Mr. Gregg. I looked back to my first being present at the Roman Catholic service in this chapel.[9] Temple returned with good hopes from Dundas,[1] but disgusted at having found his language and manners as Scotch and coarse as ever, and provoked at his excessive advancement. I went to evening service at Portland Chapel. At night I was miserably weary and irritable.

MONDAY 23 SEPTEMBER. Temple dined at Lady Strange's and I at Malone's, tête-à-tête. My spirits still bad.

TUESDAY 24, WEDNESDAY 25, and THURSDAY 26 SEPTEMBER. I group these three days together because they were not distinguished from the general insipidity and gloom of my existence at this time, except that on Thursday I showed Temple Westminster School—where I had a dim perception of its celebrity as impressed on my early imagination—and brought my son James home to dinner. Temple was to leave me on Friday, being to go with Sir Christopher

---

[7]Alexander Gordon had fled to England in 1792 after his college, which educated Scottish Catholics for the priesthood, was closed by decree of the National Assembly in its move against foreign property-owners. He and Lumisden were friends and fellow Jacobites. Boswell had visited Gordon in Paris in 1766.

[8]John Bacon and Joseph Nollekens were both successful sculptors and members of the Royal Academy. Bacon was working on the Johnson monument at this time; Nollekens was known for his busts of Garrick, Sterne, Pitt, and Paoli, among others.

[9]The Bavarian Chapel in Warwick Street, supposedly intended for the use of the Bavarian envoy, was one of the mission churches where Mass was said for the public. Boswell had heard his first Mass there during his stay in London in 1760, when he had contemplated becoming a Catholic. The Irishman whose seat he took was presumably the ironmonger Dennis Dolan.

[1]Frank Temple in fact received his lieutenancy in this year.

Hawkins in his carriage to Cornwall. It vexed me exceedingly that both the last time when my old friend was with me, and now, my spirits were miserably bad, worse indeed now than then; and he observed to me that my temper was sadly changed for the worse, especially when I was at home with my daughters, at whom I was almost perpetually fretting. He saw that they did not treat me with the respect due to a parent. But he imputed this to the unsteadiness of my behaviour, as I sometimes was too free with them, and then attempted to keep them in too much restraint. I agreed with him in this, and also that they had good sense and good dispositions; but I maintained, and he admitted, that they ought not to go abroad so often, or to have company at my house in an evening without previously informing me and obtaining my approbation. He was so good as to speak to them; and it was settled that they should not go abroad in an evening or have company more than three days in each week, and never on Sunday, it being however understood that their being at their uncle's should not be counted. It hurt me a good deal that they were at no pains to acquire the English pronunciation and tone, and were fond of associating with Scotch people who could do them no credit. I was indeed sensible that from the narrowness of my circumstances I could not maintain them in such a style as, according to the ways of the age, they could be much in fashionable life.

I was now not only disappointed in any views of ambition in the wide sphere of London, but from my having addicted myself almost entirely to English society, and my aversion to Scotch manners and contempt of provincial consequence being known, I had too much reason to apprehend that should I apply for the office of Lord of Session, I should not be able to obtain it. I was in truth in a woeful state of depression in every respect. The animating delusion that I might get practice in Westminster Hall had vanished; for I saw plainly that all my habits and appearances in public were, as Malone well observed, against me as a lawyer; and I was conscious that I had never applied seriously to English law, and could not bear the confinement and formal course of life which practice at the bar required. I yet shrunk from the thought of retiring to my seat in the country, and considered that as my profession was *Jurisconsultus*,[2] it would be a sad thing to abandon it. Temple kindly said that he found me more wretched than he could have imagined; that he thought if I retired to Scotland, there was danger that I would sink into deep melancholy, or take to hard drinking. He was therefore for my just hanging on here, living with prudent econ-

[2] A consultant in Civil Law.

omy, so as not to embarrass my circumstances more, and hoping that something favourable might happen, but that I should every year spend some time at Auchinleck. Thus my worthy friend and I speculated, while I considered that years were rolling on and age approaching. He however allowed that when my spirits were good, I was as youthful as he had ever known me, and thought that I might marry an agreeable woman of fortune who might soothe my mind and be of essential benefit to my family; but that he apprehended she would be very unhappy with a man of such a disposition and mode of life as I was. It was a valuable consolation to me to find that my friend and I were as much attached to one another as ever, and that whenever I was alone with him in free conversation, I experienced a calm relief from my "vexing thoughts."[3] I find it almost impossible to *take off an exact impression*[4] of the state of my mind at this time.

FRIDAY 27 SEPTEMBER. I went and saw my friend Temple set out for Cornwall with Sir Christopher Hawkins and Principal Gordon of the Scots College at Paris. I dined at Malone's.

SATURDAY 28 SEPTEMBER. According to my invitation I repaired to Guildhall to Mr. Kirby; and after seeing part of the ceremony of the election of a Lord Mayor, attended the keeper of Newgate at the Paul's Head Tavern in Cateaton Street, where I had never been before. I was peculiarly pleased with this well-known City tavern, quite in an ancient style in all respects. The room was spacious, the finishing solid, and the furniture plain and substantial. Mr. Kirby had twelve friends to dine with him. The ordinary of Newgate supported him on one hand and I on the other. There were two deputies of wards, etc., etc. The dinner was abundant, the dessert and wines excellent. The keeper of each of the four gaols within the jurisdiction of the sheriffs, viz., Newgate, New Compter, Poultry Compter, and Ludgate, entertains his friends at dinner on this day, when the prisoners are *turned over*, as it is called, i.e., put under custody of the new sheriffs, according to a schedule;[5] and in the evening there is at the joint expense of

---

[3]An unidentified quotation.

[4]To make a copy, as in engraving or in clay or wax modelling.

[5]A definite time-table was apparently followed when the new sheriffs ceremoniously took responsibility for the prisoners under their jurisdiction: debtors and felons in Newgate, debtors only in the three other prisons ("compter" being the term for a city prison for debtors). The new sheriffs—chosen like the Lord Mayor and the aldermen from members of the City livery companies—were Peter Perchard and Charles Hamerton. In this year the election of the Lord Mayor, the swearing in of the previously selected sheriffs, and the celebrations to mark these events were taking place one day before the customary date, no doubt because Michaelmas fell on a Sunday.

the whole an entertainment in the largest room of the Paul's Head, a very old custom, when the company who are invited crack walnuts and drink *sack,* as the *mountain* furnished nowadays is called,[6] and there are also other wines and ale, as also cold meat on a side-table. The sheriffs, several aldermen, the Recorder, Common Serjeant,[7] and a great many other respectable persons were there. Mr. Kirby, who now made his *turnover* for the first time as keeper of Newgate, according to usage presented the new sheriffs with hammers to crack their walnuts, and paid the same compliment to a number (about fifty) of his friends, of whom I was one. I know not whether the hammers given to the sheriffs were different from the rest, which were little, neat, polished, iron heads with wooden handles. They had been made at Birmingham. I felt curiously to be thus one of a true City of London company. I did not drink too much and got home well. I should have mentioned that I was this morning surprised by the arrival of my nephew James Cuninghame from the East Indies, who had been obliged to come home on account of bad health.[8] I insisted on his lodging at my house.

SUNDAY 29 SEPTEMBER. This being Michaelmas Day I had my brother David and his wife and Mr. Malone to share my goose,[9] to which I added a brace of moorfowl, which had come quite fresh from my eldest son, the first I had received for three years. I relished my dinner tolerably (though still troubled with the strange smell and taste with which I have been affected for about three months, owing either to my having catched cold by sleeping in Warley Camp, or by the nerves of the nostrils or what is called Sleider's membrane[1] being impregnated with a very strong vapour of tobacco smoke at an inn at Brentwood the evening after), but my spirits were still very bad.

MONDAY 30 SEPTEMBER. Two days ago I had a visit from Mr. John Johnston, nephew and heir of my old friend Grange. I was pleased to find him a very sensible, genteel young man, a surgeon's mate in

[6]As a general name for Spanish white wines, *sack* had been in use since the early sixteenth century, but it was now apparently replacing *mountain,* the name of the wine from Malaga made of mountain-grown grapes.

[7]The second highest legal officer of the Corporation of London, who served as judge in the Lord Mayor's court and the central criminal court—a post held since 1790 by John Silvester, Boswell's acquaintance from the Home Circuit.

[8]A liver complaint had dogged Cuninghame since at least 1785 and had forced him to return from his service in the East India Company three times, this last time permanently.

[9]The traditional Michaelmas fare, thought to ensure prosperity in the following year.

[1]Boswell means the mucous membrane of the nose, called *membrana Schneideri* after the seventeenth-century scientist Konrad Victor Schneider, who studied it.

the army. He dined with me today, and I entertained him as well as my bad spirits would allow.

TUESDAY 1 OCTOBER. I dined at Gen. Sir William Medows's with his lady, Mr. and Mrs. Pierrepont, and Col. James Stuart from India, whom I had not seen for thirty years.[2] Sir William had called on me and politely written a note of invitation in my parlour. Attention thus shown to me by a gentleman so eminent was flattering, and the elegant dinner and pleasant conversation animated me somewhat, though in the present state of my nerves I inwardly shuddered at the thoughts of the fatigues and dangers of war.

WEDNESDAY 2 OCTOBER. Dined at Malone's with Courtenay and Colonel Loftus of the Guards. Felt myself pretty well for a time.

THURSDAY 3 OCTOBER. Dined at Baldwin's, who kindly gave an entertainment on occasion of the second edition of my *Life of Dr. Johnson;* present, Alderman Clark,[3] Mr. Malone, Mr. Deputy Nichols, Mr. Dilly, Mr. Chalmers, editor of the *Public Ledger,* and my brother David, also Counsellor Tomlins. It was an excellent City dinner at which I did my part as well as I could, but my gloom was heavy. In the evening played whist and lost. Took a coach home with Malone.

FRIDAY 4 OCTOBER. Dined at Dilly's; only his brother the Squire with him. I was still dismal. Mr. Sharp came to us after dinner. I won at whist. Stayed and supped, and took a coach from Cheapside to Oxford Street; so shunned St. Giles's[4] and other bad scenes.

SATURDAY 5 OCTOBER. Was so relaxed and dismal that I could with difficulty get up. Thought I would try what abstinence would do for me. But Courtenay called and insisted so kindly on my dining with him that I could not refuse. I first accompanied him in a long walk, which was of some use to me, and then dined with him and his family at a little neat house which he had for two guineas a week in Portland Road, two doors from the corner of Great Portland Street. I grew better.

[2]Maj.-Gen. Sir William Medows had recently returned from India, where he had served as Commander-in-Chief of the British troops of Madras in the campaign against Tipu, Sultan of Mysore. Charles Pierrepont (formerly Medows) was his brother. James Stuart had assumed increasingly commanding positions in various Indian campaigns from 1782 to 1792; in 1790 he had served under Medows in the war against Tipu.

[3]Richard Clark, alderman for the past seventeen years and former Lord Mayor, was also the president of Christ's Hospital. Highly regarded by Dr. Johnson, who had invited him to join the Essex Head Club, he had later provided Boswell with several Johnson letters.

[4]Perhaps Boswell means that he avoided the temptations of Queen Street (see above, 19 August 1793), which was located in the parish of St. Giles-in-the-Fields.

SUNDAY 6 OCTOBER. Was at Portland Chapel both morning and evening. I this morning dreamed for the first time since his death that I saw my friend Grange.[5]

MONDAY 7 OCTOBER. Courtenay called and pressed me to dine with him again today and meet Malone. I complied, and had "the load of life"[6] somewhat alleviated.

TUESDAY 8 OCTOBER. Worthy Langton, having come to town, called on me. Though I had walked as far as Lambeth, I went out again with him and accompanied him as far as Parliament Street, where he was to dine with Mr. George Stubbs, an eminent solicitor and great manager of his canal business.[7] He asked me earnestly to go with him. But my spirits were not as usual, and I refused. I walked to the other side of Westminster Bridge, intending to take a bit of dinner at an hotel there which I had heard much commended. But looking in at the windows, my fastidiousness did not like it. So I bought sixpenceworth of plum-cake and carried it to the hotel on this side of Westminster Bridge and eat it, and drank a glass of punch. As I was walking up Parliament Street, I was descried from Mr. Stubbs's parlour window, and worthy Langton came running after me with a pressing invitation from Mr. Stubbs to drink a glass of wine. I complied and found him to be a steady, sensible, and hearty man. There were there only his lady and a Miss Hutton, his ward, whom I liked very well, Lord Portmore,[8] and Mr. Langton. It was, after I had a little wine, a good place as I could wish. We had also tea and coffee. I was asked to dine there next day, but was engaged. Langton left us and went to the play. I came home.

WEDNESDAY 9 OCTOBER. Dined by appointment at Newgate with Mr. Kirby in a plain family way; only his niece and nephew and Mr. Wood, his wife's son, with us. I would drink only ale, and a little brandy to finish. In the evening Langton came to me by appointment, and he and Paradise supped.

[5]Boswell had been deeply disturbed by the death in July 1786 of John Johnston of Grange, whom he considered his oldest intimate friend. On this day Joseph Farington noted in his diary: "Met Boswell, who, I think, is much altered for the worse in appearance."

[6]The second time in about two months that Boswell quotes this phrase from Johnson's Prologue to Goldsmith's *Good-Natured Man* (see above, 4 August 1793).

[7]Langton had inherited a half-interest in the company that owned the Wey River Navigation, a waterway near Weybridge in Surrey, and that also received income from all ships coming through from the Basingstoke Canal. Stubbs was keeper of the records of the Court of Common Pleas.

[8]William Charles Colyear, third Earl of Portmore, was co-owner with Langton of the Wey River Navigation.

THURSDAY 10 OCTOBER. By invitation of Mr. Richard Sharp, one of the Court of Assistants of the Fishmongers' Company, I dined with them at their Hall, which is truly a grand building.[9] We had three courses and a dessert, madeira, sherry, hock, port, and claret. I did not drink too much. After tea and coffee Sharp and I, Dr. Dale,[1] a physician, and Mr. ———, one of the wardens, went to a room above stairs and played whist. I won, and regaled myself with cold roast beef and rummers[2] of punch. Took a coach home.

FRIDAY 11 OCTOBER. Awaked easier today than I had been for many weeks. Mr. Johnston of Grange and my brother David dined with me.

SATURDAY 12 OCTOBER. Still somewhat easier. I had fixed that Mary Broad should sail for Fowey in the *Ann and Elizabeth,* Job Moyse, Master, and it was necessary she should be on board this night, as the vessel was to be afloat early next morning. Having all along taken a very attentive charge of her, I had engaged to see her on board, and in order to do it, I this day refused invitations to dinner [from] both Mr. Ross Mackye and Mr. Malone. I went to her in the forenoon and wrote two sheets of paper of her curious account of the escape from Botany Bay.[3] I dined at home, and then went in a hackney-coach to her room in Little Titchfield Street, and took her and her box. My son James accompanied me and was to wait at Mr. Dilly's till I returned from Beal's Wharf, Southwark, where she was to embark. I sat with her almost two hours, first in the kitchen and then in the bar of the public house at the wharf, and had a bowl of punch, the landlord and the captain of the vessel having taken a glass with us at last. She said her spirits were low; she was sorry to leave me; she was sure her relations would not treat her well. I consoled her by observing that it was her duty to go and see her aged father and other relations; and it *might* be her interest, in case it should be true that money to a considerable extent had been left to her father; that she might make her mind easy, for I assured her of ten pounds yearly as long as she behaved well, being resolved to make it up to her myself in so far as subscriptions

---

[9]Although a hat-maker by profession, Sharp had been admitted to the Fishmongers Company ten years earlier "by redemption" (i.e., by payment of a fee) and had been elected to the Court of Assistants, the guild's governing body, in 1790. By this time the livery companies were no longer exclusively guilds for specific trades but had also become social organizations. The Fishmongers had an imposing building at the corner of London Bridge.

[1]A well-established physician who was also a linguist and classical scholar.

[2]Large drinking glasses.

[3]This account has not survived.

should fail;[4] and that being therefore independent, she might quit her relations whenever she pleased. Unluckily she could not write. I made her leave me a signature, "M. B.," similar to one which she carried with her, and this was to be a test of the authenticity of her letters to me which she was to employ other hands to write. I saw her fairly[5] into the cabin and bid adieu to her with sincere good will. James had tired at Dilly's, waiting so long, and was gone home. I followed him. I paid her passage and entertainment on the voyage, and gave her an allowance till 1 November and £5 as the first half year's allowance per advance, the days of payment to be 1 November and 1 May.[6]

SUNDAY 13 OCTOBER. Before I got up I had a letter from Mr. Pughe, the young Templar who had kindly taken care of me when I was knocked down in the street, dated no. 2 White Lion Street, Islington, and requesting a little pecuniary assistance, as he was in great distress.[7] After breakfast I went and found him and left a guinea with him, intending to make after[8] inquiries. I was pretty well today, though affected with a kind of stupor, mixed with regret, from having seen in the newspapers a morning or two ago that my old friend and correspondent and confidant in hypochondria, the Hon. Andrew Erskine, was dead.[9] I revolved a thousand scenes. I paid a short visit to an old acquaintance in Queen Street, whom I had not seen since Monday 19 August. My children had been at Portland Chapel in the morning. I was there at evening service; dined at home and my children said divine lessons. I allowed my daughters to drink tea quietly at Mrs. Cooke's,

---

[4]Boswell tried to raise this subscription but eventually paid for most of this annuity himself, sending it to Mary regularly through the Rev. John Baron of Lostwithiel.
[5]Directly, right up to.
[6]The last sentence is a later addition.
[7]Signing himself only as J. Pughe and claiming to be a member of one of the Inns of Court, Boswell's good Samaritan had just sent a desperate plea for help. His father, disapproving of his marriage, had stopped his allowance, his wife had just been delivered of a child, and he was destitute. Boswell, in calling him "Templar," assumes that Pughe belonged to the Middle or Inner Temple, but no record of him has been found.
[8]Later.
[9]Boswell and Erskine, who had been close friends in Edinburgh at the age of twenty but who had then drifted apart, had recently begun to correspond again and had exchanged confidences about their melancholy. Erskine, the youngest son of the fifth Earl of Kellie, had been an army officer in his youth and also a mildly talented writer. He and Boswell had published their earliest poems in the same miscellany—*A Collection of Original Poems by the Rev. Mr. Blacklock and Other Scotch Gentlemen* (1760)—and their exuberant correspondence under the title *Letters between the Honourable Andrew Erskine and James Boswell, Esq.*, two years later. But after leaving the army in 1770 Erskine had found no satisfying occupation; indolent, impecunious, and often in debt, he had been living discontentedly with his sisters in Edinburgh.

for I had refused to dine with Malone (who had been in the country since Monday) both yesterday and today; and thinking from poor Erskine's death of the uncertainty of life, I felt an uneasiness at twice disappointing so good a friend as Malone. So I went to him and passed the evening tête-à-tête over wine and tea and cold meat.

MONDAY 14 OCTOBER. Intended to have dined at home, but Mr. Turing and Mr. Saunders called, and being East Indians,[1] I presented wine, a glass of which set my spirits afloat. So I walked into the City and dined with Mr. Hingeston; a small company with him. We had one *game* at whist, as he was obliged to go out. I found that I had taken wine enough to affect me rather too much.

TUESDAY 15 OCTOBER. Walked out in the sun and felt a benignant sensation. Thought that my continuing a member of the Free and Easy at the Thatched House occasioned late hours and expense and did me no real good. I wrote to Mr. Maule, the King's Aurist,[2] as follows:

"Mr. Boswell presents his compliments to Mr. Maule. Understanding that he is now treasurer to the Free and Easy at the Thatched House, and that tomorrow is the day on which it is the rule to signify continuance or not for the ensuing year, he begs leave to acquaint Mr. Maule that finding a late hour of being abroad is not now convenient for him, he is unwilling to stand in the way of a better member, and therefore resigns his place in that society, wishing it all happiness. Great Portland Street, 15 October 1793."

WEDNESDAY 16 and THURSDAY 17 OCTOBER.[3] On both these days, as well as the day before, I dined quietly but dully at home. On Thursday evening I drank one glass of wine and coffee with Malone, who had with him *dreary Downes* (as I called him), an old Irish schoolfellow, son of a Bishop, but a poor, commonplace, mean-looking, sordid creature, though rich, with a living in Essex besides.[4]

FRIDAY 18 OCTOBER.[5] It is unnecessary to repeat my listless,

[1]Very likely John Turing and Edward Saunders, respected residents of Madras for more than thirty years, whom General Medows had appointed to the Madras Council on his arrival in 1790. Turing had also been mayor of Madras and became Provisional President of the Council while Medows was on his campaign against Tipu.
[2]William Maule, an ear specialist.
[3]Boswell inadvertently dated this Wednesday and Thursday as 14 and 15 October.
[4]Presumably Andrew Downes, the son of Robert Downes, Bishop of Raphoe in County Donegal, Ireland.
[5]Compounding the mistake in his dating, Boswell recorded this day as 15 October and the next two days as 16 and 17 October. He corrected the dating only for Monday 21, Tuesday 22, and Wednesday 23 October.

fretful, and desponding feelings, which, when I do not mention some-thing different, must be understood to continue. I walked out about nine or somewhat later this morning and called on my brother David, whom I accompanied to Somerset House, and then called on Baldwin, and on Mr. Kirby at Newgate, and missed breakfast. On my return Courtenay and I happened to meet at Malone's door, and called on him together and were asked to dine with him, which we did. Mr. Kenneth Courtenay[6] was there. I had as usual a temporary relief, but not the high enjoyment which I have had in the company of these two friends.

SATURDAY 19 OCTOBER. Fasting so long the day before and eating and drinking too heartily at *dinner,* if a meal at *six* should have that name, had combined to put my stomach and bowels in disorder, so that I had been ill in the night and in the morning had violent evac-uations. I was so ill that I kept my bed very long; then grew better, dined at home, and kept my intention of going to see *The Beggar's Op-era* at Covent Garden. Incledon played Macheath really very well, and pleased me peculiarly by his having a look of Counsellor Fielding to my eye. Miss Poole in Polly for the second time sung charmingly, but dis-gusted me by her bad acting.[7] The music and indeed the dialogue of the piece had not lost their power of animating me. I sat next to old Mack-lin, who had placed himself very near to the orchestra, and appeared to be wonderfully well. He said he had played in *The Beggar's Opera* when it first came out. He might possibly be in a mistake after the lapse of such a number of years.[8] I came home in somewhat better spirits.

SUNDAY 20 OCTOBER. Lay so long that I was too late for morn-ing service. My daughter Betsy came home from her boarding-school, and looked exceedingly well. Euphemia was at church in the morning. The other three and Mr. Cuninghame accompanied me to it in the afternoon. My brother David and his wife dined and drank tea with us. My bowel complaint was still uneasy, and alarmed me somewhat.

MONDAY 21, TUESDAY 22, WEDNESDAY 23 OCTOBER. Dur-ing these three days I kept the house and lived on rice-milk only. My bowel complaint was thus cured, but my dejection of mind was very distressing. Seward called on [me] this evening and did me some good.

---

[6]Courtenay's son, about twenty-four years old.

[7]The tenor Charles Incledon had been performing at Vauxhall Gardens for the past seven years and at Covent Garden since 1790. His Macheath, in the 1793 revival of *The Beggar's Opera,* confirmed his popularity. Maria Poole, later Mrs. Dickons, had just made her debut at Covent Garden in this month and had sung Polly for the first time on 12 October.

[8]Macklin was confusing two events. He did not act in the first production of *The Beg-gar's Opera* (1728)—he began his famous role of Peachum nine years later—but he at-tended the first performance.

THURSDAY 24 OCTOBER. I continued much in the same way. Malone, who had asked me to dine yesterday and had an answer from me mentioning how much I had been indisposed, called on me. The horrible murder of the Queen of France, an intimation from Sir William Forbes that my old friend——had killed himself,[9] which I had received when in bed late on Monday morning, and my present state of body and mind all conspired to affect me so much that I wondered at his active vivacity. I eat half a roast chicken today, but without relish, and drank some port and water. I forced myself to go in the evening to a party at Mr. Turing's. Veronica was somehow not ready in time. Euphemia and Mr. James Cuninghame and I went. We had music and a numerous company, and I was dissipated into a little ease. I played at whist. I eat a crayfish[1] and drank a little both of port and madeira. After confinement, the streets of London seemed very brilliant.

FRIDAY 25 OCTOBER. What an insignificant life is this which I am now leading! I played a long time today at draughts with my son James, who had a holiday, and played for money, which was wrong. I should rather have heard him read some Greek or Latin. But my mind was very sickly. I called for a few minutes on Malone. He and Courtenay and his son Kenny dined with me. I was flat, and unable to talk much. I eat some mutton broth and boiled mutton and some potatoes, and drank a little port wine. My total want of relish for literature was wretched. I was incessantly thinking on myself. I have for a long time now read nothing except Johnson's *Grammar of the English Language,* the first volume of Harington's *Nugae Antiquae,* and Orton's *Letters to a Young Clergyman* (the Rev. Mr. Stedman, vicar of St. Chad's, Shrewsbury, who sent me them in a present).[2] One comfort I had, which was in reading the

[9]The news that Marie Antoinette had been guillotined on 16 October reached London six days later and was reported in the 22–24 October issue of the *London Chronicle.* The blank in the manuscript stands for Andrew Erskine, whose name Boswell apparently could not bring himself to write; although he had recorded Erskine's death on 13 October, he had not known of the suicide. From Sir William Forbes Boswell learned in successive letters that Erskine, in ill-health and severely depressed for several months, had filled his pockets with stones and had walked into the sea near his home.

[1]A spiny lobster, also known as *langouste.*

[2]"The Grammar of the English Tongue" was a thirteen-page prefatory essay in Johnson's *Dictionary.* In *Nugae Antiquae* ("Trifles from Olden Days") Henry Harington, D.D., compiled the verses, letters, and other prose pieces written by his forebear, Sir John Harington, the Elizabethan courtier, poet, translator, and wit. *Letters to a Young Clergyman* (1791) consisted of letters written by the evangelical Presbyterian minister Job Orton to the Rev. Thomas Stedman, who edited them and saw to their publication after Orton's death; he had recently presented this and another book to Boswell in return for the pleasure he had received from the second edition of the *Life of Johnson.*

Holy Scriptures. I was now going regularly through the Epistles. But the melancholy now oppressing me prevented my having the *felicity* of piety.

SATURDAY 26 OCTOBER. Dined at home. Mr. Young from India, son of Sir George of the navy,[3] passed the evening with us.

SUNDAY 27 OCTOBER. Seward asked me to take a seat in his hack-chaise to visit Sir William Chambers at Whitton. I was drearily ill, but after morning service at Portland Chapel, went. Sir Francis Bourgeois also went with us. We found a good family dinner and hearty welcome. Conversation did me some service; and as there was nobody else there, we were quite comfortable, which favoured our plying the bottle too freely both at dinner and supper.

MONDAY 28 OCTOBER. I had been very much intoxicated and was so ill that I did not get up till half past three, just in time to take a brisk walk and sit down to dinner. Sir Francis was gone. We had another comfortable day and drank liberally, though not so hard as yesterday.

TUESDAY 29 OCTOBER. The wine of yesterday had affected me so that I was by no means easy. However, I rose between ten and eleven. My spirits were wretched, so that I had not the just relish of a very entertaining copy-book of letters between our host and several great and eminent men, a good many of which Seward read aloud. From the sickly wish of change of place, I set out on foot in order to return to London. Seward accompanied me to Hounslow, and I walked as far as Turnham Green[4] and then took a seat in a return post-chaise. Dined quietly with my daughters. Though it was my birthday, I had nothing particular at table. Neither was my mind animated as it should be on such an anniversary. I found a note from Malone to dine with him next day.

WEDNESDAY 30 OCTOBER. Called on Malone. Called also on Sir William Scott, who was to have dined with us but sent an excuse. I was dejected by contrasting my idle, dejected state with his occupation and prosperity. Only Courtenay and I dined at Malone's. My faculties were dull.

THURSDAY 31 OCTOBER. Attended on the bench of the Old Bailey for a short time, and dined at the three-o'clock table; Sir William

---

[3]Samuel Young was a civil servant in Madras. His father had been a naval captain for fifteen years and would soon be promoted to Rear Admiral; his plans for establishing a colony in New South Wales paved the way for the establishment of a penal settlement at Botany Bay.

[4]A distance of four or five miles from Hounslow.

Plomer in the chair, Baron Hotham and Judge Heath, Alderman Combe,[5] Sheriff Hamerton, etc., there.

FRIDAY 1 NOVEMBER. Dined at Mr. George Dance's with Mr. Hodges and Mr. Edwards, painters, Mr. Cockerell and Mr. Brettingham, architects,[6] and though still clouded by hypochondria, had some immediate enjoyment. An excellent dinner, good wine not to excess, and rational and pleasant conversation, of which our host can always furnish a happy share, and some pleasing music, he playing on the pianoforte and singing and Edwards playing on the violin, altogether had a benignant effect on me. I recollected with a curious feeling my intimacy in early life with Mr. Love, the player, Mr. George Dance's brother.

SATURDAY 2 NOVEMBER. Went to Mr. Pollock, first Clerk in the Secretary of State's Office for the Home Department, and as I had often done before, applied to him for the men who had escaped from Botany Bay. The time of only one of them, James Martin, was expired; so I left the certificate of his conviction which Mr. Follett, Clerk of Assize on the Western Circuit,[7] though I was not personally known to him, had on my calling on him at his chambers in the Temple humanely furnished without any fee. A pardon was to be made out for this man. On my coming home to dinner I found to my surprise that all four men had been set at liberty and had been at my door. I dined at home. James Cuninghame dined with me. I found that he was intending to pass the winter in London; and though I willingly meant to make him live with me in case of his making a short stay, I felt it by no means convenient that he should be a whole winter's guest, as I found that

---

[5]Plomer, a member of the Tiler and Bricklayer's Livery Company, had been an alderman for the past twenty years; he had served as both Lord Mayor and sheriff and was knighted in 1782. Beaumont Hotham, a member of the Middle Temple and former M.P., had long been a Baron of Exchequer and, as such, served as judge in matters of revenue and taxation; Boswell had met him in 1778 when he officiated as judge at the Carlisle Assizes. Harvey Christian Combe, alderman since 1790 and sheriff the following year, had the rare distinction of belonging to two Livery Companies: the Brewers and the Fishmongers.

[6]William Hodges, R.A., was known for his paintings and drawings of the South Seas (he had accompanied Captain Cook on his second voyage, 1772 to 1775, around the world) and for his later landscapes of India and Russia. Edward Edwards was Professor of Perspective at the Royal Academy. Samuel Pepys Cockerell built or renovated important residences and had recently designed a guard-house at St. James's Palace. Robert Furze Brettingham was a respected architect of private mansions and more recently also of prisons.

[7]Martin had been convicted at Exeter, on the Western Circuit; presumably the certificate was needed to prove that he had now served out his sentence. Apparently Boswell did not realize that the other three men had also, in fact, completed their original sentences.

the expense of my housekeeping was considerably increased by him. He insisted on taking a lodging, which I opposed. He said he then would certainly insist on furnishing wine. I kept the matter in a kind of wavering state.

SUNDAY 3 NOVEMBER. Went to Newgate to inquire concerning the Botany Bay men; found they had been discharged by proclamation, which Mr. Kirby imagined to be a complete acquittal. (But upon afterwards conversing with several barristers and Mr. Shelton, Clerk of Arraigns at the Old Bailey, I was satisfied was a mistake.)[8] I saw Lilley and Broome,[9] who on being sent for came freely into Newgate. The other two had gone to take a walk. Time passed on till it was too late for me to go to church. I and my daughters and son James drank tea at my brother David's.

MONDAY 4 NOVEMBER. At home.

TUESDAY 5 NOVEMBER. At home. Mr. Dilly called in the evening and eat bread and cheese.

WEDNESDAY 6 NOVEMBER. This being the first day of term, I went to Westminster Hall; but my servant having neglected to take down my wig and gown, I only shook hands with some of my brethren and walked into the City. Having had a note concerning my *Life of Dr. Johnson* from Mr.———, under-librarian of Sion College,[1] I called on him and showed him I was right. The supposed mistake was quoting two numbers of *The Idler* wrong. But the true history was, Johnson left out a paper against war, which changed the numbers after the first edition. The under-librarian's was the Irish one, from the first.[2] He introduced me to Mr. Clements, the librarian, a

[8]The men were discharged by a special procedure whereby the clerk of the court—in this case, Thomas Shelton—issued a proclamation asking anyone who wished to prosecute the defendants to do so now. Since neither the Government nor anyone else came forward, the prisoners could be released even though they were not granted a complete acquittal, which would have included a pardon for their escape from Botany Bay. No doubt they were helped by a letter sent to Nepean on behalf of Lord Grenville, Secretary of State for Foreign Affairs, that stated: "When they were committed to Newgate Lord Granville [sic] had little disposition to prosecute them, and as their sentence is expired the prosecution may not be necessary. So shall they be discharged?" (From Joseph White to Evan Nepean, 1 Nov. 1793.)

[9]Presumably an *alias* of John Butcher's.

[1]The Rev. Robert Watts, at this time assistant librarian and later for thirty-three years the librarian of Sion College. Located at the London Wall in the City, Sion had been a centre for London clergymen since the sixteenth century—it was headed by the Bishop of London—and was renowned for its library; at this time it received, by royal order, all books recorded in the Stationers' Register.

[2]The discrepancy in the numbering was due to the inclusion in the Dublin edition (1762) of an extra *Idler*, no. 22, that changed the numbers of the subsequent papers.

venerable man between eighty and ninety, who expressed himself much pleased with my *Life of Dr. Johnson,* with whom he had frequently been in company. He in a frank, old-fashioned way asked me to dine with him, saying he dined early. I told him I was engaged to dine with Dr. Lettsom, the Quaker physician. "Sir," said he, "you will have no grace.[3] I once dined with a Quaker in the Strand. As I was a clergyman, he would not directly ask me to say grace, but addressed me thus: 'Friend, if thou hast anything to say before sitting down to thy meat, now is thy time.' So I said grace." I thanked the worthy man for his courtesy, and said I would pay my respects to him at another time. I liked to view the large, grave-looking library of the *London clergy.* At Dr. Lettsom's was a numerous company, several of those whom I had seen at his house at Camberwell. We sat late and drank a great deal of wine. Sir John Peter, late consul at Ostend,[4] carried me in a coach with his lady to their lodgings in Leicester Square, and made me go up and take a glass of liqueur; and then was so kind as to proceed with me in the coach to my own door and see me safely at home, I being a good deal intoxicated.

THURSDAY 7 NOVEMBER. Venner, who had come down on a special retainer to the Essex Sessions, very handsomely invited all the counsel to dine with him today at his house in Essex Street. We were all there but Gascoyne, who was engaged, and Webb, who was ill. He gave us an admirable dinner and excellent wine, and we were "roaring boys." I came off "mellow," and left some of them sitting, who I heard *kept it up* till pretty late.

FRIDAY 8 NOVEMBER. The Royal Academy Club at Freemasons' Tavern began today for the winter. I relished it as much as the present state of my spirits would allow. I sat between Farington and Humphry.

SATURDAY 9 NOVEMBER. The counsel of the Essex Sessions are peculiarly lucky as *bons vivants.* At Chelmsford each new Justice presents them with a dozen of claret, so that they have a liberal supply of that generous wine. Venner entertained us on Thursday; and today Mr. Henniker-Major, one of the chairmen of the Sessions, gave us a dinner and wine in a very good style at his house in Portman Square.[5]

The essay was originally published in 1758 in the weekly *Universal Chronicle* but was not reprinted in the first two editions of *The Idler* in 1761.

[3] With their emphasis on great simplicity of worship, the Quakers dispensed with the saying of grace at meals.

[4] Peter had just completed his service of almost twenty years as consul for the Circle of the Lower Rhine (Flanders).

[5] John Henniker-Major—he had adopted the second name a year earlier—was a barrister of Lincoln's Inn and an antiquarian. His family came from Stratford in Essex.

Webb, who was yet ill, and Lemaistre for some other reason were not there. He had also Stanley, Baker, and Heath, who had formerly been of our number, Mr. Johnstone, the surveyor of the county, and Mr. Dacre, an Essex attorney. I had almost resolved to quit the Sessions. But so many pleasant circumstances made me think of continuing at them some time, just as an amusing variation of life.

SUNDAY 10 NOVEMBER. Went in the morning to High Mass at the Spanish Ambassador's Chapel, and heard a curious sermon by Father Robertson on the duty of praying for the souls in Purgatory. For the first time for many months I was struck with the face, person, dress, and manner of a lady, who seemed to be a foreigner, perhaps a milliner or a singer or dancer at the opera. But she inspired once more those sensations and irradiations of fancy which have innumerable times in my life been experienced by me. When she came down from the front of one of the galleries where she sat and walked out of the chapel, accompanied by a decent elderly woman, I followed her at a becoming distance. She walked a great way through Cavendish Square, Charlotte Street, Rathbone Place, the crowd coming out of the Methodist chapel in Tottenham Court Road, and in short to Thornhaugh Street, no. 5, where I saw her and her duenna fairly housed. I resolved to inquire afterwards in the neighbourhood who she was. I dined at home after having attended evening service at Portland Chapel. I and my children drank tea at my brother David's.

MONDAY 11 NOVEMBER. Called on Seward, whom I now visit often, as he has lodgings within seven doors of me. He showed me a striking account by Lord Clarendon of a gentleman miserable from idleness.[6] He and I dined with Parsons at his lodgings, he being confined by indisposition.

TUESDAY 12 NOVEMBER. Dined with Malone, by ourselves. During this term I do not particularly specify *when* I was at Westminster Hall. I went a few times only. I could not get a seat in the crowded King's Bench. I was disgusted by the dulness of Chancery, and hated to see Wedderburn sitting in the highest seat of the law.[7] Yet I made a pretence of being seen in my barrister's dress.

[6]Seward lived at no. 40 Great Portland Street, Boswell at no. 47. The account by Edward Hyde, first Earl of Clarendon, has not been identified, but a general statement of Clarendon's abhorrence of idleness appears in his essay "Of Industry" (*Miscellaneous Works*, 1751, 2nd ed., p. 145).

[7]Alexander Wedderburn, Baron Loughborough, was appointed Lord Chancellor in January of this year. Boswell had experienced similar pangs of envy earlier, telling Malone, "I was tortured to see Lord Thurlow, Lord Loughborough, Lord Amherst, and all who had risen to high situation while I was nothing" (Journal, 26 April 1788).

WEDNESDAY 13 NOVEMBER. Dined at Mr. Smith's, attorney in Basinghall Street, Solicitor to the Ordnance, whom I had seen at Dr. Lettsom's last week. Two of the physicians who had been of that company were here. We had a very good dinner and wine enough without excess, and joined the ladies at tea and coffee. I then went to the Essex Head Club, a pretty numerous meeting.

THURSDAY 14 NOVEMBER. [No entry for this day.]

FRIDAY 15 NOVEMBER. Was at Mr. Gunning's, Surgeon General to the army, with Johnston of Grange, in the view of getting him promoted.[8] Laid a foundation for it by and by.

SATURDAY 16 NOVEMBER. Johnston of Grange and my brother David dined with me. I do not mark when Mr. Cuninghame dined. He was often out at dinner.

SUNDAY 17 NOVEMBER. Was at Portland Chapel, I think both services. Dined at Mr. Paradise's with Sir Charles Blagden, just returned from his travels, Dr. Bancroft,[9] Mr. Planta, and several more. I was somewhat entertained.

MONDAY 18 NOVEMBER. [No entry for this day.]

TUESDAY 19 NOVEMBER. Was restless. Wandered into the City. Called on Captain Preston, whom I had not seen for a long time, and was asked to dine with him (this being commonly his day of dining in town). I accepted, and found Mrs. Preston, Sir Richard Pearson,[1] Captains Cotton and Sealy, and Mr. Martin, his clerk. The scene was hearty and did me some good. Captain Cotton set me down in Bedford Square, and I then walked home safely.

[8]Boswell was trying to help the nephew of his old friend, John Johnston of Grange, to obtain the post of regimental surgeon so that he would not have to go to Jamaica, where he had been offered a position at the government hospital. On this day, either before or after this call, John Gunning wrote to Boswell that although he would consider Boswell's recommendation in the future, he could not find a place for Johnston at the present time. Johnston thereupon decided to take the Jamaica post and embarked in late November. On the voyage he served as surgeon's mate during the capture of Martinique and Guadeloupe, contracted the prevalent tropical fever, and died in April or May 1795, soon after reaching Jamaica.

[9]Edward Bancroft, M.D., Paradise's friend and financial advisor. Many years after his death he was discovered to have been a double agent, spying not only for the Americans but also for the British during and after the American Revolution.

[1]Pearson may well have known the other guests from his younger days in the East India Company. But he spent most of his life in the navy, fighting in both the Seven Years' War and the American Revolution. He lost a ship in an engagement with John Paul Jones in September 1779 but was exonerated by a court-martial and created Baronet for his efforts (Jones is reported to have said that the next time they met, he would make him a lord). Pearson was now retired and lived at Greenwich Hospital, which he later headed.

WEDNESDAY 20 NOVEMBER. Was more restless than yesterday. Wandered over London Bridge all the way to Thrale's brewhouse and paid a visit to Mr. Perkins, one of his successors,[2] thinking I might dine with him, but I found that he was as yet at his country-house. Neither Dilly's nor Hingeston's (the last of whom was not at home) suited me today. I felt myself in a kind of desolate state. However, I found the hospitable Malone at home by himself a quarter past five and dined with him comfortably. What a wretched thing is it that I have such an aversion to dining quietly at home!

THURSDAY 21 NOVEMBER. Found Hingeston at home and dined with him, and then went to Dilly's and had a rubber at whist with him and Millington and Sharp. Was set down by Millington in Berners Street[3] and got well home.

FRIDAY 22 NOVEMBER. Dined at the Royal Academy Club. Sat between Sir William Chambers and Mr. Humphry, who observed to me how valuable a Society it was, and always improving by age. It was a question among us today whether we should not have a commemoration of this our twenty-fifth year since the foundation of the Royal Academy; and several of us signed a request to the President to call a meeting of all the members of the Academy to consider of it.

SATURDAY 23 NOVEMBER. Dined at Mr. Ross Mackye's with my brother David, Hon. Col. Cosmo Gordon,[4] a French emigrant, and a clergyman who had travelled with Lord Mountstuart. It was wonderful to find a man of *eighty-five* as social as any of us, with little diminution of memory,[5] yet he said a man was a fool who wished to live to a great age. His claret was excellent, and I indulged too much in it. But it produced a temporary relief from melancholy. This evening Mr. James Cuninghame went to lodgings very near my house. This was a relief to us, for an inmate is a considerable expense and trouble, and our seeing him often occasionally[6] must be much more agreeable.

---

[2]John Perkins, formerly the superintendent of the brewery and now one of its owners, lived in the former Thrale house in Southwark. Boswell had recently sent him a copy of the second edition of the *Life of Johnson* in return for some Johnson letters he had provided.

[3]Langford Millington, a respected merchant, spent most of his life in Barbados and now lived in this street.

[4]Cosmo Gordon, Baron of the Scottish Court of Exchequer and Boswell's acquaintance for almost twenty years.

[5]This is the third time that Boswell comments on Ross Mackye's age (see above, 22 July 1790, 13 December 1792).

[6]That is, only on particular occasions

SUNDAY 24 NOVEMBER. Was at Portland Chapel both services. Dined at home. My son James and I drank tea at my brother David's.

MONDAY 25 NOVEMBER. My daughter Betsy not being very well, I had her brought home, that we might take better care of her than was done at the boarding-school. I had been disturbed in the night by a strange dream of a statue stepping down from its pedestal,[7] and my running from it in fear. Dined at home. Went afterwards to Mr. Malone's and drank some wine and coffee.

TUESDAY 26 NOVEMBER. Signor Masseria, who had come (as he said) from General Paoli to try to negotiate with our Ministry for assistance to the Corsicans against the French,[8] had been some days in London, and I called on him on Saturday. Mr. Robert Boswell was also unexpectedly in town. Both of them and Mr. Cuninghame and my brother David and his wife dined with us today, as did my son James.

WEDNESDAY 27 NOVEMBER. Dined at home. Went in the evening with my brother to the Essex Head Club, a small meeting.

THURSDAY 28 NOVEMBER. Dined at Malone's with Courtenay. Was too eager in drinking.

FRIDAY 29 NOVEMBER. Dined at home. My daughters had *literally* a small party[9] to tea and cards and a little music and dancing. I was in a tolerable frame of mind and played whist and won a trifle. Betsy was now pretty well.

[7]Mozart's *Don Giovanni* was not performed in London until March of the following year, but Boswell may have been familiar with Molière's *Don Juan* (1665) or its adaptations. The Don Juan story was performed as ballet and pantomime, and the final scene as opera, in 1785 while Boswell was in London.

[8]Paoli had written to Boswell about these negotiations in a letter dated 12 October 1793, in which he defended his decision to take up arms in necessary self-defence against the French, whom he now called "the anarchists of the Convention." Since the deposition of Louis XVI he had become increasingly disenchanted with the revolutionaries, whom he could no longer regard as the guardians of liberty who had invited him back to Corsica in 1790. Although he was in control of the island, his authority was undermined in Paris by Corsican deputies, more radically republican than he, who questioned his loyalty to France. He was blamed for the failure in early 1793 of the French invasion of Sardinia (part of the Kingdom of Piedmont), in which he had participated only half-heartedly, and he was increasingly suspected of having developed pro-British sentiments during his many years in England. After the National Convention ordered him arrested for treason in July 1793, he led the Corsicans in openly opposing the French. But fearing that Corsica could not remain independent for long, he secretly sent Filippo Masseria, who had been his trusted aide during his English exile, back to London in October to secure the protection of the British government. Boswell had met Masseria in 1783 while staying in Paoli's house in London.

[9]Not merely unpretentious but also small in the number of guests.

SATURDAY 30 NOVEMBER. After a long interval I took a share of Mr. Baldwin's family dinner cordially, and drank in moderation. At tea were Mr. Richard Baldwin's widow and daughter, whom I had not seen for a great many years.[1]

SUNDAY 1 DECEMBER. It was a damp day. My daughters kept the house, but James and I were at Portland Chapel both services. In the evening I made Veronica read aloud one of Johnson's sermons.

MONDAY 2 DECEMBER. Breakfasted with Malone as on the first *lawful* day of the month, when the magazines and reviews come out.[2] I was pleased with my own letter in the *Gentleman's Magazine* in refutation of an attack by Miss Seward of Lichfield.

[EDITORIAL NOTE. Anna Seward, the prolific poet known as "The Swan of Lichfield," with whom Boswell had carried on a mild flirtation in 1784–85, had provided him with several anecdotes about Johnson's early days in his native Lichfield. In the October issue of the *Gentleman's Magazine* she protested that on the very first page of his *Principal Corrections and Additions* to the first edition of the *Life of Dr. Johnson* Boswell had impolitely rejected her account of Johnson's writing his "Verses on Receiving a Sprig of Myrtle from a Lady" for Lucy Porter, the daughter of the future Mrs. Johnson. (Instead of this romantic story, which he had used in his first edition, Boswell now accepted the report published by Mrs. Piozzi in her *Anecdotes* that the verses had been written at the request of Johnson's boyhood friend Edmund Hector.) Miss Seward suggested that Johnson might have written the verses first for Lucy Porter and later used them again for Hector. Johnson's telling Mrs. Piozzi that he had written the verses for Hector could be regarded as just a small untruth, Miss Seward argued, and much less significant than the many other "false assertions" Johnson had uttered, notably the statement that the poet George Buchanan was the only genius Scotland had ever produced.

Boswell's long and forceful reply, written on 16 November but not published until this day, revealed his concern both for protecting Johnson's reputation and for accepting only trustworthy evidence in his biography. After remarking on Miss Seward's "poetically luxuriant" prose and her apparent prejudice against Johnson, he proceeded to comment on several of the anecdotes she had sent him in March 1785. He was irritated to find that in her October letter to the *Gentleman's Magazine*

---

[1] Boswell had met the bookseller Richard Baldwin, the uncle of Henry Baldwin, together with his wife Elizabeth and his daughter at the Stratford Shakespeare Jubilee of 1769.

[2] Since 1 December fell on a Sunday, the journals that Boswell and Malone read together at the beginning of each month could not be published until Monday.

she still accepted as factual the story, denied by Johnson himself, that he had at the age of three written an epitaph on a duck he had accidentally killed. Nor could Boswell accept Miss Seward's 1785 account of a conversation Johnson had supposedly had with his mother in which she refused her consent to his marriage to the much older and impecunious Mrs. Porter. Boswell, having failed to get confirmation of this story from another Lichfield lady, had, in fact, said the opposite in the first edition—that, being a fond parent, Mrs. Johnson had consented to the marriage—and now declared: "As my book was to be a *real history* and not a *novel*, it was necessary to suppress all erroneous particulars, however entertaining."

As for the sprig of myrtle verses, Boswell found it "an awkward tale" that they had supposedly been addressed to the young woman whose mother Johnson later married. Having in the mean time received a letter from Hector explaining that he had requested the verses, Boswell declared: "*Conjecture* must at once yield where *fact* appears, and *that* we have from Mr. Hector." Then, indulging in some conjecture of his own, he argued for the reverse of Miss Seward's hypothesis—that perhaps Johnson wrote the poem first for Hector and only later gave it to Lucy Porter. In any case, he insisted: "That they were written for Mr. Hector…is all that is necessary to be proved; and it has been proved."

Boswell was particularly eloquent in contradicting Miss Seward's aspersions on Johnson's truthfulness: "From the veneration and affection which I entertain for the character of my illustrious friend, I cannot be satisfied without expressing my indignation at the malevolence with which she has presumed to attack that great and good man. In the present letter she seriously accuses HIM of '*conscious falsehood*' in an '*assertion*' that 'Buchanan was the only man of genius which his country had ever produced.' From the frequency of what she calls '*similar false assertions*' she concludes that 'his veracity was of that species which, straining at *gnats*, swallows CAMELS.' Miss Seward does not perceive that such sallies as those which are recorded to show Dr. Johnson's wonderful dexterity in retort, are not assertions in the sense which concerns truth or falsehood; they are evidently *ardentia verba* (*glowing words*—I ask her pardon for quoting a Latin phrase) uttered in witty contest. They are not even expressive of his *opinion*; but, if they could be supposed to convey his real opinion, still they would have no concern with his *veracity*." Indeed, Boswell insisted, "Dr. Johnson's strict, nice, and scrupulous regard to *truth* was one of the most remarkable circumstances in his character."

Boswell could not resist ending with some further remarks sure to irritate Miss Seward: "I have, in my *Life of Dr. Johnson,* spoken of her in as handsome terms as I could; I have quoted a compliment paid by him

[Johnson] to one of her poetical pieces;[3] and I have withheld his opinion of herself, thinking that she might not like it." He suggested that her hearing of Johnson's true opinion of her from other sources might have inspired her recent attempts "to undermine the noble pedestal on which the public opinion has placed Dr. Johnson," and as a parting shot he hinted that she belonged to "a cabal of minor poets and poetesses" whom Johnson, were he still alive, would surely have despised.

We now resume with the remainder of the journal entry for 2 December.]

I was in a very restless state, and quite unwilling to dine at home. I sauntered down Bond Street and St. James's Street, hoping to meet somebody who would ask me. But all in vain. I stood dejected in the court of St. James's Palace, and heard half past four strike. I could no longer expect an invitation. The evening was dusky and dull. As I was walking up St. James's Street, I heard a voice saying, "I cannot let an old friend pass without speaking to him." It was Lord Eardley[4] who had observed me. After shaking hands, and being *politely* told that he had been looking in a wrong street for my house in order to call on me, we joined in lamenting the loss of Colonel Bosville, and his Lordship said, "A great friend of his dines with me today, Colonel Morrison. I wish you would come. Let us press you into the service." "Shall I be in time?" "Oh yes, we'll wait for you. There are only men. Go and change your coat, and take a hackney-coach." I agreed quietly. When hurrying home, I felt a wonderful elation. After a dreary despair, here was not only a dinner, but a capital dinner. "There is no place but London," I exclaimed, "where this could have happened!" My spirits rose. I carried my daughters a stately bunch of grapes, was soon dressed as much as was necessary, and got to Lord Eardley's in good time. Our company was a French *aristocrate* who was going to join Lord Moira,[5] a clergyman, Colonel Morrison, whom I had a cordial satisfaction in meeting, Lord Eardley's eldest son, and Mr. Culling Smith, his son-in-law, and three young gentlemen, their companions. We were entertained in his Lordship's magnificent dining-room, lately built and

[3]Boswell had recorded Johnson's remark to Anna Seward that nothing in *The Colombiade*, an epic poem about the New World written by Anne-Marie du Boccage, equalled Miss Seward's description of the sea in her poem on the death of Captain Cook.

[4]Formerly Sir Sampson Gideon, he had officially changed his name to Eardley (a name in his wife's family) in July 1789 and had been created Baron Eardley of Spalding two months later. A long-time M.P., he was the only son and heir of the great financier Sampson Gideon, through whose influence he was created Baronet at the age of thirteen after becoming a convert from Judaism.

[5]Francis Rawdon-Hastings, second Earl of Moira, was the commander of an expeditionary force that was leaving for Brittany to support a royalist insurrection.

which I had never seen (as in truth I was not asked to his house all last winter),[6] and the dinner was truly admirable, the wines excellent. I considered calmly the irresistible effect of such an entertainment, while I experienced it. I drank liberally, but not to excess. Colonel Morrison set me down at the top of Bond Street, and I got well home.

TUESDAY 3 DECEMBER. Betsy returned to Blacklands. As the meeting of *the members of the Royal Academy* to consider of a commemoration of their institution in its 25 year was to be held tonight, I dined at home, but was unreasonably dull and even drowsy. It is a sad thing to have so *un*domestic a disposition. Before eight I was taken up, I know not in whose coach, by Sir Francis Bourgeois, Mr. Cosway, etc., and we took up Mr. West, our President. There was a pretty full meeting and many speakers. I was really animated in delivering my sentiments, and met with so much applause that it vexed me to think I could not have an opportunity of being heard in the courts in Westminster Hall.[7] We came to no conclusion, though we (at least a part of us) remained together till more than half past eleven. But I understood that a foundation was laid for our President's sounding the royal inclination before Tuesday the 10th, on which day there was to be a regular general meeting of the *Academicians*. George Dance, Farington, Hamilton, Hoppner, and I eat Welsh rabbits and drank two pots of porter and a bottle of port at Holyland's Coffee-house,[8] and were pleasant, and agreed to meet at Freemasons' Tavern on the evening of the tenth, the very anniversary of the institution, and commemorate it over a glass with such other good men and true of our number as might be selected. We took a joint hackney-coach in the London fashion, and I got home a better man than I came out.

WEDNESDAY 4 DECEMBER. Resolved to dine with the Lord Mayor at the Old Bailey, but did not get there in time; so heard some of

---

[6]Eardley lived in Arlington Street, Piccadilly, which was known for its elegant residences. Boswell had last been at his house after meeting him and his youngest daughter Selina at Court; on that occasion he had written close to thirty lines of verse, "On seeing the Honourable Selina Eardley appear at Court 5 July 1792 in a gown trimmed with furze," the gist of which was that she wore the prickly flowers to discourage presumptuous advances—possibly including his own. Culling Smith had married Eardley's second daughter, Charlotte Elizabeth, in September 1792.

[7]Farington, who recorded some of the discussion, also noted: "As to the mode of commemoration, Mr. Boswell made a very good speech on the necessity of doing it in a becoming manner.... His speech was very well received" (*The Farington Diary*, ed. James Greig, 3 December 1793, i. 22).

[8]William Hamilton specialized in portraits and, more recently, in paintings of literary, historical, and Biblical subjects; John Hoppner, a prolific and admired painter of portraits, was court-painter to the Prince of Wales. Holylands Coffee-house in the Strand was an expensive establishment with an international reputation.

the proceedings,[9] and dined after five with the Recorder, Common Serjeant, Sheriff Hamerton, and a small company. Was not in full spirits, but had some enjoyment. Did not drink too hard. Nine struck as I reached Malone's door. Found him and Mr. Humphry, the painter, who had dined with him, I suppose. Sat awhile and went home quietly.

THURSDAY 5 DECEMBER. Dined at home with my daughter Euphemia only, Veronica being at Mrs. Stevenson's. Drank tea at my brother David's, where was the Countess Dowager of Dundonald, whom I was almost ashamed to meet, as she had been in London many months and I and Veronica had only called on her once, and I had once invited her to dinner, when she excused herself by indisposition, so that she had not seen either me or my daughters, though she had called twice. However, I should have been sorry not to see her tonight. My daughters unluckily were engaged at Mrs. Cooke's. Lady Dundonald, as my brother observed, was almost the only person now remaining of those whom in our younger years we used to *look up* to.[1] I found her quite courteous and ready to keep up an intercourse of visiting. Her son John[2] was of the party tonight. I felt curiously.

FRIDAY 6 DECEMBER. My daughters went to the country-house of *Citizen Smith*[3] at Castlebar. I was not very fond of this. But as they were very desirous to go, did not restrain them. I dined at the Royal Academy Club, and sat between Sir Francis Bourgeois and Yenn.[4] I enjoyed the good living and conversation, but drank really too much, so that after I came home, I sallied out foolishly into the street, and running fast on the foot pavement slippery with mire, fell and hurt my left elbow a good deal. I then perceived that I had not £50 in banknotes, which I had inadvertently taken to the tavern in my pocket. I returned home and mentioned my loss, but was so confused by intoxication as not to think of making a search, or I fancy was not able to do it. In much agitation I hurried away to the tavern in a hackney-coach, and being shown into the room where we had dined, looked in vain, and could get no account of my notes. I came home vexed, and went to bed.

[9]This day marked the beginning of the new sessions at the Old Bailey, the court at which the Lord Mayor—this year, Paul Le Mesurier—officiated as judge. As reported in the *St. James's Chronicle*, six prisoners were convicted of felonies, six were acquitted.
[1]Boswell had last seen Jean Cochrane, Dowager Countess of Dundonald, the widow of his maternal granduncle, the eighth Earl of Dundonald, in Edinburgh in January 1786. Always a commanding figure, she was now seventy-one years old.
[2]The Hon. John Cochrane was deputy commissary to the forces in North Britain.
[3]The appellation "Citizen" suggests that Smith sympathized with the French republicans, who used this egalitarian form of address.
[4]John Yenn, R.A., was an architect and Clerk of the Works at the Queen's House (now Buckingham Palace).

SATURDAY 7 DECEMBER. I was very uneasy at having lost such a sum so unknowingly. I could not conceive how it could have happened, for I had put the notes into my fob.[5] My housekeeper told me that the first time when I came home last night, I had opened my cabinet. Upon opening it this morning I found the notes, which was no small relief. Strange that I was utterly unconscious of having put them there last night. But one in liquor is sometimes wonderfully cautious and cunning. I dined at Dilly's upon a long previous invitation to meet Mr. Butler, the Roman Catholic lawyer who undertook to finish the edition of *Coke upon Littleton* begun by Mr. Hargrave.[6] It seems he wished to be acquainted with me. I was somewhat afraid of so well-informed and shrewd a man, but was glad to find him more communicative than inquisitive. He discovered great variety of literary knowledge, particularly of the poets, and he was a true admirer of Dr. Johnson, whose character of Milton as a poet[7] he thought the most eloquent piece of prose in the English language. In this gentleman I saw a living instance of one who is truly a hard student, for I think he told us he took only five hours sleep. I observed that he ate and drank heartily, and he said he had consulted Dr. Warren as to abstemiousness, but was advised by him to the use of port wine as salutary in our climate. The rest of the company were Mr. Isaac Reed, Counsellor Thomson, Mr. Rogers, author of *The Pleasures of Memory* and other poems, Mr. Tuffin, the great brandy-merchant, Mr. Sharp, and Mr. Pinkerton, *alias* Robert Heron,[8] who behaved himself very well and moreover went away early. The rest of us remained together in good talk and without excess till

[5] A small pocket in the waistband of breeches that was designed to hold money or a watch.
[6] Sir Edward Coke's *First Part of the Institutes of the Laws of England* (1628), a commentary on Sir Thomas Littleton's treatise on landlord-tenant relations entitled *Tenures* (c. 1481), was the most respected authority on real property law. In 1785 Charles Butler took over from Francis Hargrave the work on the thirteenth edition (1788) and supplied invaluable notes, making it the basis for all further editions. For many years his Catholicism prevented Butler from practising as a barrister, but he became a successful conveyancer (a specialist in estate law), and when the Catholic Relief Act of 1791, which eased the restrictions on Catholics, exempted barristers from taking the usual religious oaths, he became the first Catholic since 1688 to be admitted to the bar.
[7] In the last part of his "Life of Milton," included in the *Lives of the Poets*.
[8] Samuel Rogers, at this time a junior partner in a bank, had aspirations as a writer and later headed a literary circle; his *Pleasures of Memory* (1792), a long reflective poem on scenes conjured up by memory, was already in its fifth edition. John Furnell Tuffin, a successful vintner, was also a collector of fine books and paintings as well as a lively conversationalist. John Pinkerton had published his *Letters of Literature* (1785) under the pseudonym Robert Heron; he was an argumentative eccentric, notorious for insisting, in other works and in conversation, that the Celts (whether Scottish, Irish, Welsh, or Spanish Biscayan) were the only survivors of the original Europeans but, still savage, had produced no great men whatsoever.

past twelve. I walked as far as Red Lion Square to Mr. Butler's door with him, steady Reed also being with us. Mr. Butler engaged us both to dine with him next Thursday.

SUNDAY 8 DECEMBER. My son James and I passed the day by ourselves very well. We were both morning and evening at Portland Chapel, and he read and explained to me a chapter in the Greek New Testament. I began today to read what it is strange I should not have read before, Law's *Serious Call to a Devout and Holy Life,* the book which I have mentioned as having made Dr. Johnson first think earnestly of religion after his childhood. I wondered at his approbation of it; for though there is not a little vivacity in it, and many characters very well imagined, the scope of it is to make a religious life inconsistent with all the feelings and views which animate this state of being, and in short to make us ascetics upon the monastic plan.[9] It had a dreary influence on my mind, at present disposed to be gloomy. My son James, to whom I read some of it, very sensibly observed, "Such books do a great deal of harm." I resolved however to read it through.

MONDAY 9 DECEMBER. I was in wretched spirits. Yet I had benevolence at my heart. A considerable time ago Courtenay and I found in our street a lad of about fourteen sitting on the steps of a house and crying bitterly. We inquired of him what was the matter. He said he had lost a silk handkerchief worth six shillings belonging to his master, and he durst not go home for his master would beat him unmercifully, for he used him very cruelly. We bid him be quiet, and we would go along with him and satisfy his master. The boy's name was John Constantin and his master was Mr. Horton, a tailor in Mount Street, Grosvenor Square. The master was not at home, but we saw a foreigner, manservant to Madame de Coigny, a lodger in the house,[1] and Horton's maid, both of whom assured us of the cruel usage of the boy. We left word that the handkerchief should be paid, and I gave the boy my card to take to his mother, who might call upon me. She accordingly did so, and appeared to be a genteel woman. Her husband was an old Frenchman, cook to

[9]William Law's work, published in 1729, is a powerful exhortation to devote oneself to a life of piety and prayer, cultivating the Christian virtues of humility and charity while rejecting all worldly concerns. To dramatize his teachings Law used character-types with allegorical or classical names. In the *Life of Johnson* Boswell had described the book's impact on the twenty-year-old Johnson following a period of religious indifference. Boswell's own copy, inscribed with his name and the date December 1792, is preserved at Yale.

[1]Presumably Horton's lodger was the manservant, not his mistress, Louise-Marthe de Conflans, Marquise de Coigny, a French émigrée with republican sympathies who had become an accepted member of London society.

Earl Thanet,[2] at whose country-house he now was. She paid for the handkerchief, and was willing that a farther trial should be made of Horton's behaviour. It seems he continued as harsh as ever; so after a considerable time I went with Mrs. Constantin and the boy to the office of Westminster Justices in Great Marlborough Street, and upon complaint made, had Horton summoned to appear next day, when Mr. Scott, one of the Justices, took the oaths of the foreign servant, the maid whom I had seen, and another maid who had been in Horton's service, and by them very bad usage was proved.[3] He on the other hand brought several of his men, who swore that Horton used the boy very well, though he was perverse, gave bad language, stayed long out when sent errands, and pilfered little sums out of the change. The maid now with Horton said that the boy had lately threatened to stab her with a knife. Thus was the case perplexed. The apprentice fee being above £10, the affair could not be decided but at the Quarter Sessions. I suggested that the master and boy should certainly be separated; and luckily Horton said he was willing to give up the indentures, and leave it to one of the Justices, or two persons mutually chosen, to settle how much of the twenty guineas which had been paid should be returned.[4] I thought that the boy's father should be consulted. He accordingly came to town, was of the same mind with his wife, and signed a letter to me authorizing me to act for him. After various delays, when I had taken the trouble to go to Horton's house and could not find him, I wrote to him today insisting that the business should be brought to a conclusion.

I dined alone on cold beef and a glass of water. Horton called, and fixed half past five. I attended, and Mrs. Constantin brought as her referee Mr. Enoch, an old Quaker, master tailor in Oxford Street. Mr.

[2]Boswell first wrote "Stanhope," then changed it to a name beginning with Th but stopped after making a large ink blot, leaving "Thnhope" in the manuscript. Sackville Tufton, ninth Earl of Thanet, was the only British or Irish earl at this time whose title begins with Th.

[3]By a statute of 1562, still in force, Justices of the Peace had the authority to regulate the working conditions of apprentices, and a single Justice could serve as mediator in a dispute between an apprentice and his master. John Scott was a permanent judge at the Great Marlborough Street Office, one of seven police offices established in 1792 to replace the rotation offices with their changing magistrates (see above, p. 33 n.2).

[4]Normally an apprentice was obligated to serve for seven years without salary, and an agreed-upon premium for his training was paid on his behalf, usually by his parents, while a master was obligated to teach his craft and to provide food, clothes, and housing. But the indentures, the contract between an apprentice and his master that specified the conditions of employment, could be voided—that is, the apprenticeship could be ended—by the consent of both the master and the apprentice, who could then arrange for the division of the premium according to a mutually agreeable plan.

Horton had Mr. Bishop, also a master tailor. After a great deal of altercation, I proposed that the two referees should retire and consider by themselves how much should be allowed for the boy's board and lodging, deducting at the rate of sixpence a day for what advantage was gained by his going on errands; and that the overplus should be restored. They withdrew; and after (I reckon) an hour, Mr. Horton and I were asked to come upstairs, when we found that they could not agree. Mr. Enoch insisted on ten guineas being restored; Mr. Bishop would allow only five. The boy had been nine months maintained by Horton, and could not in that time be considered as of any service in the business. I gave it as my opinion that as there were mutual charges of misbehaviour, which were not now to be discussed, and as both parties must suffer loss by the apprenticeship being dissolved, it seemed fair that there should be an equal division of the money advanced; that if Mr. Horton would not himself determine between the differing arbitrators, a third must be called in. That as acting for the father, I could not agree to five guineas when one of the arbitrators thought ten should be restored. But I would agree to a medium of seven guineas. Horton then observed that he had furnished the boy clothes to the value of a guinea, and he would pay six, which would make up the sum. Thus it was settled. The indentures were both put into the fire;[5] Mrs. Constantin pocketed the gold. The late apprentice was allowed to go home with his mother, and his young brother carried upon his head a small box which contained his few clothes. The fond mother was overjoyed, and pressed me to accept four of the guineas, which I absolutely refused, telling her that my reward was the satisfaction of having done a humane action. "O Sir," says she, "you have saved a soul from death." The boy was now to be taken under his father's care and be made a cook.[6] I charged the mother to look sharp after him and prevent his having bad habits, which I was convinced he was in danger of, and not to indulge him too much; and I desired that she would let me know how he went on. She had a very good house, no. 5 Edward Street, Portman Square, and let lodgings. Her husband and she had six children.

TUESDAY 10 DECEMBER. I walked into the City and called on Dilly and Captain Preston. Dined at home with my daughter Euphemia,

---

[5]There were two documents because, by law, the indenture deed had to be torn into two pieces at the beginning of the apprenticeship, the master and the apprentice each keeping his part. The term "indenture" is, in fact, derived from the jagged indentations in the torn document; matching the parts was a means of authenticating the deed. When an apprenticeship was dissolved by mutual consent, the indentures had to be actually cancelled, whether by a written statement or, as in this case, by the destruction of both parts.
[6]A father was permitted to prepare his son for his own trade without formal apprenticeship.

who returned this morning.[7] About nine I repaired to the Royal Academy to get certain intelligence as to the meeting concerted last Tuesday to be held on this the anniversary of our institution. I had Mr. Farington called out, who to my surprise told me that I had disappointed them very much, for that they met at *dinner* at the *Bedford Coffeehouse.* It seems this had been settled, and I had been informed of it on Friday at our Club, but had been so much inebriated that I had totally forgotten it. He however told me that they were to sup, and desired me to go and wait with some associates till the Academy broke up. The company at the Bedford were dispersed, but I waited in the coffee-room till some of them returned. The Academicians sat so late that we did not begin to our cold supper till a quarter before twelve, and it was about one when we were all collected; namely, George Dance, Tyler, Zoffany, Smirke, Rooker, Hamilton, Farington, Lawrence, Westall,[8] and myself. Paul Sandby[9] had dined, and Opie joined them after dinner. We were very joyous, and kept it up till past four. Farington walked a good part of the way with me, and I reached home in safety.

WEDNESDAY 11 DECEMBER. Was somewhat disturbed *hesterno Iaccho.*[1] John James, the son of my friend Temple, came from Eton for the holidays to lodge at my brother's and eat with me. My brother dined with me, as did Mr. Richard Cooke. I drank tea at Malone's by a note of invitation.

THURSDAY 12 DECEMBER. Dined at Mr. Butler's. His lady was a genteel woman. Only she and a governess and Mr. Serjeant Marshall with us at table. Steady Reed was ill and could not come out. I felt curiously when I looked back and now found myself comfortably dining with a great Roman Catholic lawyer in Red Lion Square.[2] We had *good talk,*

---

[7]Euphemia had been visiting Mr. and Mrs. Smith at Castlebar.

[8]The company included William Tyler, a sculptor and architect; John or Johann Zoffany, a German-born portrait-painter who had settled in England in 1758 and won fame by painting Garrick and other actors in their roles; Robert Smirke, a painter of Biblical and literary scenes; Michael Angelo Rooker, an engraver, painter of water-colour landscapes, and principal scene-painter of the Haymarket Theatre; Thomas Lawrence, Reynolds's successor as portrait-painter to the King, who would eventually succeed West as President of the Academy; and Richard Westall, a history painter and water-colourist. Most were full members of the Academy, but Rooker remained an associate all his life while Westall and Lawrence were associates who became full members in 1794.

[9]Sandby, a water-colourist, engraver, and caricaturist, was a founding member of the Academy.

[1]"With yesterday's wine"—alluding to the description of the sleeping Silenus in Virgil's *Eclogues* (vi. 15, trans. H. R. Fairclough, Loeb ed.): "inflatum hesterno venas, ut semper, Iaccho: his veins swollen, as ever, with the wine of yesterday."

[2]Possibly Boswell is recalling his visits to a perfumer in Red Lion Square in 1769 to purchase a special medicine, the Lisbon Diet Drink, which was thought to cure gonorrhoea.

as Johnson used to say;[3] an excellent dinner and wine enough. The emigrant Bishop of Périgord, a lively little Frenchman,[4] came in after dinner. Mrs. Butler made coffee and went out to a party. The governess made tea, at which a little Miss Butler assisted. Butler kept me for the evening, and he and I, his lady and the governess had a bit of supper.

FRIDAY 13 DECEMBER. Dined tête-à-tête with Parsons.

SATURDAY 14 DECEMBER. Dined at Malone's with Humphry, the painter. Rather *dry*. But I was too eager for wine.

SUNDAY 15 DECEMBER. At Portland Chapel in the morning, and was disgusted by a charity sermon preached by the Rev. David Gilson, curate of St. Saviour's, Southwark, and of St. Magnus, London Bridge. He had an abominable Scotch (at least northern) pronunciation, and affected such oratory as the Presbyterian preachers use.[5] Having received a note from Betsy that she was invited for the holidays to Mrs. Williams's, and asking my permission to go, though she had before declined it on account of Miss Williams's bad treatment of her, I thought it best to see her; so I walked out to Blacklands, and discovered that Mrs. Hockley had made her write the note, and that in reality she did not wish to go. I therefore made her happy by telling her she should be allowed to pass the holidays at home, and told Mrs. Hockley and Miss Williams that I had settled she should be at home. After dining quietly at my own house, I went with Euphemia, Jamie, and Master Temple and drank tea at my brother David's, who always entertains me with rational conversation.

[3]Perhaps an allusion to the witty verbal cut and thrust that Johnson enjoyed: "'Well' (said he), 'we had a good talk.' BOSWELL. 'Yes, Sir; you tossed and gored several persons'" (*Life of Johnson*, summer 1769). For Johnson's distinction between "talk" and "conversation," see above, p. 131 n.2.

[4]Charles-Maurice de Talleyrand-Périgord had been Bishop of Autun, but perhaps Boswell associated him with the Périgord because he belonged to a noble family of that region. Worldly and cynical, he had joined the revolutionaries, had approved of their anti-clerical measures (whereupon he was excommunicated in 1791), and came to England as unofficial representative of the French government in January 1791 and again in May 1792. But he favoured a constitutional monarchy and was shocked by the execution of Louis XVI. Suspected of royalist sympathies, he barely escaped the September 1793 massacres of aristocrats and clerics by fleeing with a special passport issued by Georges-Jacques Danton, then Minister of Justice. The British government viewed him with suspicion as a possible spy and soon invoked the newly passed Alien Act to force him to leave the country. After some years in America he returned to France and gained fame as the statesman who served Napoleon, helped to bring about the restoration of the Bourbons, and became a key figure at the Congress of Vienna.

[5]Boswell either did not properly remember or miswrote his name, which was David Gibson. He may have indulged in the highly emotional rhetoric or the special whining delivery used by Presbyterian ministers of the older school.

MONDAY 16 DECEMBER. Was restless and unwilling to dine at home. The streets were so dirty, I could not go into the City; and no other good opportunity of finding a dinner abroad presented itself to my mind. At last I thought that perhaps Dr. Langford was now come to preside at the Chaplain's Table, St. James's; so I resolved to take that one chance. I found that he entered on attendance this very day; so after sauntering about St. James's Street and the Palace, and hearing four strike, I repaired to the hospitable room. Mr. Lewis, who superintends that table as butler and waiter and knows me well, received me courteously. Dr. Langford was not yet come, but when he arrived he welcomed me heartily. We had Governor Devaynes, a Mr. Bourchier who had been eight-and-thirty years in the East Indies,[6] Dr. Robert Willis, physician, Mr. Peacock, whom I had met there several times, and two of his sons. The dinner was as usual substantial and well dressed. The war with France having obstructed the importation of champagne, that exquisite wine was cut off. But we had madeira, sherry, hock, port, and claret, and good malt liquor; and I took enough to warm me rather too much. Dr. Langford asked me to dinner the next Sunday. The early breaking up of this table is an objection. I wandered about foolishly for some time. Cw.[7]

TUESDAY 17 DECEMBER. Cw.[7] I was in a dilemma how to act, for there was to be another meeting of the members of the Royal Academy to consider of the commemoration, at eight in the evening; and Mr. Dodd, the usher, had obligingly given me two tickets for all the three nights of *Ignoramus*,[8] played by the King's Scholars of Westminster. The first night had escaped my memory. On the second (last Wednesday) I had sent Richard Cooke and John James Temple. Tonight I had furnished one to Hatter Sharp, and if I did not go myself I thought Mr. Dodd might justly take it amiss, and my son James be vexed. I dined quietly at home, and at last resolved that I would *first* attend the Academy and *afterwards* hurry down and take a part of the play, which I had no wish to see wholly. I managed so as to be at the Academy till the question was carried (a very few only dissenting) that we should have our commemoration. The *mode* was then to be considered, subject to His Majesty's approbation or negative. I then posted to Westminster, heard a very little of the play, and was so pleased with

[6]William Devaynes, M.P., a London banker and Director of the East India Company, the brother of Boswell's apothecary Jack Devaynes; and perhaps Charles Bourchier, member of the Council of Bombay.

[7]A private symbol that looks like a C with a wavy tail.

[8]This comedy in Latin by George Ruggle, satirizing an ignorant lawyer, was first performed in 1615, was popular in its own time, but had not been produced in the licensed London theatres in more than fifty years.

the good speaking of the boys that I regretted I had not heard more. I got so far within one of the doors as to *see* also when the Epilogue was spoken. I then called at Mrs. Clough's; but by some negligence of the servant my son was not informed of my being there, though Mr. Dodd sat some time with me, and I got off decently as to the play by mentioning that the Academy had made me late. Mr. Dodd invited me to supper, but I pleaded the business of the Academy still going on; so back I went and found that by reason of tedious speaking they were still sitting. Mr. West, the President, had brought forward a proposition for an exhibition of all the choicest pieces of painting, sculpture, and architecture during the first twenty-five years of our Academy, with an ode by the Laureate,[9] music vocal and instrumental, a discourse by the President as a kind of *summing up* of what had been done in the arts during that period; and to this the royal family should be respectfully invited the first day, and the second, patrons and patronesses of the arts, dignitaries of church and state, etc. This proposition (which he had read to me yesterday when I called on him[1]) was indeed splendid in theory, but I found that the artists thought it might be very dangerous for them, as invidious comparisons would be made of the works of the dead with those of the living. I said to Farington that if there should be such an exhibition, it should be only of the works of the dead: a kind of exhibition *omnium animarum,*[2] an *All Souls* Exhibition. Mr. West was so much set on his own plan that he said to myself and some others privately that if it was rejected, we who had signed the request of calling a meeting to consider of a commemoration should withdraw our request, and let the matter go off.[3] But I could not go into this. Mr. Farington had this morning communicated to me his plan, which was 1st, that we should dine together in our own apartments at the expense of the fund; 2nd, that a loyal Address should be presented to His Majesty signed by all the members present; 3rd, that a medal should be struck on the commemoration; 4th, that four impressions should be in gold and presented to the King, the Queen, the Prince of Wales, the Princess Royal;[4] 5th,[5] that silver impressions should be given to all

[9]Henry James Pye, who had become Poet Laureate following Thomas Warton's death in 1790.

[1]Boswell had forgotten to record this meeting with West and his subsequent visit to Farington in his journal entry for 16 December.

[2]The Catholic Church's commemoration of the faithful dead, now in purgatory.

[3]That is, drop the idea of the commemoration.

[4]Charlotte Augusta Mathilda, the Princess Royal, was George III's oldest daughter. In his diary Farington noted that the idea of presenting medals to the royal family had come from Seward by way of Boswell.

[5]Boswell inadvertently repeated "4th" for this point and designated the next as "5."

the members of the Royal Academy; 6th, that a committee of six Academicians should be named to obtain the royal pleasure on these propositions, and if approved, to carry them into execution. This plan was adopted unanimously; and by plurality of strokes annexed to their names in the printed list, the following six were chosen the committee: West, Richards, Farington, Tyler, Copley,[6] Hodges. Mr. West, Sir Francis Bourgeois, and I walked to Covent Garden and took a hackney-coach home. Veronica returned this morning.[7]

WEDNESDAY 18 DECEMBER. Paid Malone a short visit in the morning. Dined at home. Went with my brother to the Essex Head Club, where we met Barrington, Brocklesby, Reed, and Rose. This day Jamie came home for the holidays.

THURSDAY 19 DECEMBER. Betsy came home for the holidays. I dined at Seward's with Malone and Courtenay. I drank too much.

FRIDAY 20 DECEMBER. Dined at the Royal Academy Club. Sat between Farington and Bonomi.[8] After dinner Mr. West announced to us that His Majesty had graciously approved of our plan for celebrating the twenty-fifth year of our institution. This put us into high spirits, and we were unusually lively. I however did not drink to excess. It should not be forgotten that I had good reason to think that if the King had put his negative on our plan, there would have been violent discontents in the Academy; and that there were some democratic[9] members who wished for a negative, to afford them an opportunity for discontent and disturbance. They were now obliged to dissemble and go along with the tide. Mr. Nollekens set me down in my own street at the corner of Mortimer Street, and I came well home.

SATURDAY 21 DECEMBER. Sat awhile with Seward, as I often do in a morning; also with Parsons. Dined at home.

SUNDAY 22 DECEMBER. Was at Portland Chapel in the morning with Betsy and Jamie. My two eldest daughters went in the afternoon. I dined according to invitation at the Chaplain's Table with Dr. Langford, his son, Mr. Peacock and his son, and the Rev. Mr. Gibbons

---

[6]John Inigo Richards, a landscape-painter and principal scene-painter of Covent Garden Theatre, who was the Academy's Secretary, and John Singleton Copley, the American painter who had worked in London since 1775.
[7]From her visit to the Smiths at Castlebar.
[8]Guiseppe Bonomi, an Italian architect who practised in England from 1767, had been Reynolds's candidate for the Royal Academy Professorship of Perspective and the cause of Reynolds's temporary resignation from the Royal Academy in 1790 when other academicians preferred Fuseli (see above, p. 43). Bonomi, who was an associate of the Academy (he never became a full member), had recently designed the new Spanish Embassy Chapel.
[9]The term, associated with the French republicans, suggested a radical outlook.

of St. Paul's and his son. I relished the good dinner, and was too forward in drinking, which I fear was observed. Was somewhat intoxicated. Found Mr. and Mrs. Paradise by themselves, eat a bit of cold veal and drank some mountain.

MONDAY 23 DECEMBER. Was in a sad listless state, and made my son James play at draughts with me the whole day, by which I was quite stupefied.

TUESDAY 24 DECEMBER. John James Temple went to pass part of the holidays at Mr. Claxton's at Shirley near Croydon. I stayed at home all day. In the evening resumed reading of the papers given in to the Court of Session in a cause, Stewart against Newnham, Everett, and Company, and began to draw a case for Stewart, respondent in an Appeal to the House of Lords.[1] Imagined myself ill-qualified for such kind of labour, yet did it well enough.

And here let me try to recall what passed between Lord Thurlow and me of late. I had some time ago written to him expressing an earnest desire to wait on him, "as I was very unhappy." My application was totally neglected. In the Appeal, Gillespie and Reid against Bogle, which was heard at the bar of the House of Lords in March last, though he was no longer Chancellor, he gave great attention to it, and I was lucky enough to make a very good speech.[2] When I had done, he came down to the bar, shook me by the hand, and very courteously asked me how I did. This capricious change to the better pleased me to a certain degree. But I had presence of mind sufficient to make him perceive that I was sensible of his strange conduct before; for I asked his Lordship if he had not received a letter from me. He was somewhat embarrassed, and said something importing that in the multiplicity of business he must have overlooked it, adding, "For I should always be

---

[1]Boswell's client, David Stewart, represented a group of creditors who had sued the London bank of Newnham, Everett, and Co. for seeking to collect the total value of a bond, thereby preventing the other creditors from collecting their share of the funds. The decision of the Court of Session in favour of Stewart was now being appealed by the bank.

[2]William Gillespie and Matthew Reid *v.* Adeliza Hussey or Bogle and Husband was a complicated case involving creditors and land rights. In 1724 Reid, one of the appellants whom Boswell was representing, had taken possession of some land in payment of a debt. But when he sold it in 1787 to Gillespie, Boswell's second client, other creditors of the original owner claimed that now that Reid had been repaid through the sale of the property, they had a right to it and also to many years of back rent. The Court of Session had decided against Reid and Gillespie. In their Appeal to the House of Lords, Boswell argued that his clients had a right to the property because they had held it far longer than the ten years required by statute, and that they had no obligations towards the other creditors. The case was heard in the House of Lords in April, not in March as Boswell thought, and was decided on 3 May 1793. In spite of Boswell's efforts, his clients lost their Appeal.

very glad to *wait* upon you," meaning to *receive* me or *wait upon me* at his own house, which I thought had been a Devonshire phrase, as I first heard it in that sense there.[3] "So then," said I, "My Lord, I may have the honour to see your Lordship?" He assented.

I was not in a great hurry to make the trial; but some time, I think in May, I one morning called at his house in King Street, St. James's, looking into the Square. The servant said he was ill and could not see anybody. So I left my card. The servant having carried it to his master without delay, I was soon followed by him and told that my Lord would see me. So I was introduced into his library, or study, where he was sitting, confined with the gout and reading a Bill to be brought into Parliament, or some such sized paper. After a polite reception, he resumed the reading of this paper. I made myself quite easy by rising and looking at the backs of the books on some of his shelves, and then took my seat again on the sofa opposite to that on which he sat. When he had done with his reading, he began to talk in a frank manner, and asked me what news there was. I said I heard of none except the accounts which we had from the Allied Army. Battles being mentioned, he said he had read the history of *many*, but never could understand *one*. He had been lately reading the account of the battle of Minden, and it appeared to him that Prince Ferdinand must have been drunk, and that Lord George Sackville was the only man who knew anything about the matter.[4] *Being now out of Administration,*[5] he seemed to be adverse to the war against the French; yet when I asked him if he thought the old government of France oppressive, as now so loudly asserted,

---

[3]Thurlow was using an old-fashioned turn of phrase, obsolete at this time except in dialect.

[4]An iconoclastic remark, since Prince Ferdinand of Brunswick was, and still is, generally regarded as the hero of Minden, a battle fought by Hanoverian, British, and Hessian troops against the French in August 1759, whereas Sackville, Ferdinand's second-in-command, was disgraced. He was blamed for disobeying orders, tacitly accused of cowardice for delaying the advance of the cavalry he commanded, and declared unfit for all further military service at the end of the court-martial he had requested to clear his name. As Sackville argued at his court-martial, he had not sent in the cavalry as quickly as Ferdinand expected because he felt obliged to verify conflicting orders. There is no evidence that Ferdinand was drunk during the battle, but his orders, unclear from the start, became still more confusing when transmitted by two rival aides-de-camp, and personal hostility made him publicly shame Sackville after the battle without further inquiry. Although Sackville subsequently won the favour of the new King, George III, and became Secretary of State during the American Revolution, he never escaped the shadow of Minden. As late as 1782, when he retired from his Ministerial position and took his seat in the House of Lords for the first time as Viscount Sackville, some of his fellow peers protested that he was unworthy of the seat. On that occasion, he was eloquently defended by Thurlow.

[5]Thurlow had ceased to be Lord Chancellor in June 1792.

he exclaimed in his *swearing manner,*[6] "Damn their bloods; there was not as much oppression under the old government as would justify shedding the blood of a single chimney-sweep." He said the best thing which he had seen upon the subject of the wonderful changes in France was a pamphlet entitled *Causes et principes de la Révolution Française.*[7] This I think was the title. He said he could not find another copy. Lord Hawkesbury[8] had his.

He asked me what I would have for breakfast: tea or coffee or what, and what I would eat. I mentioned coffee and buttered toast. He ordered accordingly, and by and by we were told breakfast was ready, and then we went into a parlour. He drank tea, and I took my pot of coffee in all comfort. He asked me if the toast was as I liked it. I said, since his Lordship had asked me, I should tell him freely, no. I liked it better done, as they do it in inns. He rung his bell and ordered it in my very words. Such a minute particular of a man who has been considered as so formidably sulky is curious. He was in a talking humour, and I listened to him with high satisfaction. I introduced the Appeal of Gillespie, in which I had appeared. He said he was clear that after the long lapse of time and the circumstances in evidence, there was a sufficient *presumptive proof* that the other creditors were satisfied, and therefore Reid's Adjudication now held by Gillespie was good.[9] "Why then," said I, "did not your Lordship reverse the Decree?" His answer was, "If it had been the judgement of an English court, in which I know or, which is the same thing, *think* I know all that could be said on the subject, I certainly should have reversed the Decree. But as the point had not been argued in the Court of Session, and that court is as a foreign court to me, I thought it decent that the judges should have an opportunity to consider it." *This* was encouragement enough for a second Appeal, should the Court of Session again give the cause against my client. He said there was no

---

[6]Thurlow's profanity was legendary.

[7]*Des principes et des causes de la Révolution en France* (1791), written after the fall of the Bastille and published anonymously in St. Petersburg, was pro-monarchist in tenor but attributed the Revolution to mismanagement under Louis XVI—frequent changes in administration, undermining of authority at Court and in the army, and financial irregularities. It also pointed to fatal misjudgements by Jacques Necker, the Swiss banker who became Minister of Finance in 1788 and recommended calling the States-General in 1789, thereby unleashing republican ideas about the power of the people's representatives.

[8]Charles Jenkinson, Baron Hawkesbury, later Earl of Liverpool, President of the Board of Trade and Chancellor of the Duchy of Lancaster, had been Secretary at War during the American Revolution.

[9]Thurlow therefore agreed with Boswell's position that his clients had the rights to the property after holding it for so many years, and added the further argument that during this time the other creditors were presumably compensated to their satisfaction.

system of judicial forms more excellent than that of the Court of Session in *theory,* or more detestable in *practice.* He went over the whole train of it in the most luminous manner, and showed how sadly the practice deviated from the rules. He reprobated[1] the voluminous idle proofs, idle in a great measure, taken by ignorant commissioners; and also copying and recopying all the arguments and quotations into the record.

I asked him to give something to Mary Broad. He exclaimed, "Damn her blood, let her go to day's work." But when I had described her hardships and heroism, he owned I was a good advocate for her, and said he would give something if I desired it. He expressed a wonder at my activity, enumerating several scenes which I had mentioned, and adding, "I should not be able to do all this in a month," or, "It would take me a month." I told him in direct terms how desirous I had been of his acquaintance, and that I had formed several schemes for meeting him, one of which was to lie in wait for him at Buxton.[2] I said I hoped his Lordship would do me the honour to come and eat roast beef with me, and if he liked music *(which I knew he did),* my daughter would play. He said he would be glad to wait on me, or words to that effect, adding, "Why should not you come and eat with me, and bring Miss Boswell? Miss Kitty would be happy to see her." *Here* was a *rub.* I knew his wish to bring his *natural daughters* into good company. But I have always disapproved of putting them on a level with those lawfully born; and besides, whatever ladies of great weight and consequence might do,[3] I could not think of my daughters forming such an acquaintance. I flattered myself I should shift this embarrassment.

My being knocked down in the street and consequent illness so sunk my spirits that I had no heart to renew my visit. But some time in the autumn I met him suddenly one forenoon in the narrow walk on the right of Storey's Gate,[4] when he shook hands with me and hoped I was well. I mentioned the accident by which I had been hurt, but that

---

[1]Condemned.

[2]A spa in Derbyshire, where Thurlow sought relief for his gout.

[3]Catherine ("Miss Kitty") was the second of Thurlow's three illegitimate daughters by Polly Humphreys, whose mother owned Nando's Coffee-house. Thurlow remained averse to marriage throughout his life but was a devoted father. He had been gravely disappointed by the recent elopement of his oldest daughter, but he saw to it that Catherine and her younger sister were received in society—among others by Lady Kenyon and the Marchioness of Donegal. Eventually, after Thurlow's death, Catherine married Alexander George, seventeenth Lord Saltoun.

[4]A gate on Birdcage Walk, St. James's Park, named for Edward Storey, keeper of Charles II's aviary, whose house had been on this spot.

I was now recovered, having pretty good *stamina*. "And excellent spirits" (or "always good spirits"), said he. I answered, "Alas, no, my Lord. I have sometimes very bad spirits." "How then do you do to dissemble?" said he. I know not whether he or I introduced the state of Europe, as to which I expressed uneasiness. "That," said he, "is of more consequence to younger people than we are. I am satisfied with what is." When we parted, he said, "GOD bless you." I wonder if any advantage will ever come to me from this acquaintance.

WEDNESDAY 25 DECEMBER. Christmas Day is always more or less a *hallowed time*[5] to me. Having heard that Dr. Horsley, now Bishop of Rochester and Dean of Westminster,[6] was to preach in the Abbey today, my son James and I went thither, and though late, heard a part of the service. But observing another clergyman mount the pulpit, we came away; first looked into Whitehall Chapel, which not hitting my fancy at the moment, proceeded to St. Martin's,[7] where we heard sermon. My brother David and his wife dined with us. I was in tolerable spirits. But had no real enjoyment of life.

THURSDAY 26 DECEMBER. Was listless and dined at home.

FRIDAY 27 DECEMBER. Walked into the City; called at Dilly's and had a pretty good account of the sale of my second edition of Johnson's *Life*.[8] Took Baldwin's family dinner cordially, and *went under the rose* with him, as the phrase is, for being at his evening club at St. Paul's Coffee-house.[1] Did not get home till between one and two in the morning.

SATURDAY 28 DECEMBER. Dined with Captain Calland at the mess of the Life Guards; Turing and Saunders and others there, particularly the Hon. Capt. James Stuart of the Guards, son of my old friend, now Earl of Bute. He paid me handsome compliments on my writings, and I lamented the difference between his father and me,[2]

[5]Perhaps an allusion to Shakespeare's reference to Christmas: "So hallowed, and so gracious, is that time" (*Hamlet*, I. i. 164).
[6]Samuel Horsley, D.D., had just become Bishop of Rochester and Dean of Westminster in November. A powerful speaker—he had preached a memorable sermon of warning against the new revolutionary spirit earlier in the year in Westminster Abbey—he also had scientific interests and had edited the works of Newton.
[7]Presumably St. Martin's-in-the-Fields, north of Whitehall.
[8]The record of sales kept by Boswell reveals that by the end of December 712 copies were sold. At 17*s.* a copy, Dilly had taken in more than £550.
[1]Apparently Boswell went to an evening club in St. Paul's Coffee-house as Baldwin's personal guest. "Under the rose" (*sub rosa*) suggests that this was a private club.
[2]The Hon. Evelyn James Stuart, a captain in the 1st Regiment of Foot Guards, was the son of Lord Mountstuart, who had succeeded his father as fourth Earl of Bute in 1792. For the cause of the coolness between Mountstuart and Boswell, see above, p. 140 n.9.

saying I would go to the end of the world to serve him. Turing and Saunders and I and one or two more stayed whist and supper. I lost, which did not please me.

SUNDAY 29 DECEMBER. Lay the greatest part of the forenoon. Was at Portland Chapel in the afternoon. Mrs. Cooke and her children drank tea with us.

MONDAY 30 DECEMBER. Dined at home today, as I did yesterday, *dieting* myself, as I said, for the Academy celebration.

TUESDAY 31 DECEMBER. This was the day of celebration of the twenty-fifth year of the Royal Academy from its institution. The members repaired to their apartments in Somerset Place; first went into the Secretary's parlour and signed a loyal Address to His Majesty on the occasion; then assembled in the library till dinner was upon the table; and then proceeded to the council-room, where we had a most excellent dinner of two courses and a dessert, madeira, sherry, port, and claret, and a glass of champagne. We were in the best convivial frame and should have enjoyed ourselves to the utmost, had not Mr. West, with good meaning but injudiciously, engaged Cramer, Borghi, Shield— in short a number of musicians both vocal and instrumental, whose performances interrupted the flow of our festivity and irritated many members.[3] There was tea and coffee. And afterwards we resumed the bottle. "When the light troops were gone, and only grenadiers remained," as was observed by Farington, between whom and Wyatt I sat. Supper was served, it being now the new year. Then after some more wine we parted. I was not the worse.

[3]The chief entertainers were a chamber-music group: Wilhelm Cramer, chamber-musician to the King and a highly regarded violinist; Luigi Borghi, manager of the Italian opera company at the Pantheon and second violinist in some of Cramer's concerts; and William Shield, known chiefly as a composer but also until recently first viola at the King's Theatre, Haymarket. According to Farington, the musicians disrupted the celebration by having a harpsichord brought in and set between the tables, displacing several members from their seats. "From this time it became rather a concert with intervals, than a meeting where conversation could have any share. Boswell and others disliked it much" (*The Farington Diary,* ed. James Greig, 31 December 1793, i. 32).

1794

WEDNESDAY 1 JANUARY. Lay long. Dined at home. Sat awhile in the evening with my brother David.

THURSDAY 2 JANUARY. I and my three daughters and son James dined at my brother David's. Masseria was of the party. At tea were Mr. and Mrs. Paradise.

FRIDAY 3 JANUARY. Found Malone, who had returned last night from a visit to Mr. and Mrs. Crewe[4] in Cheshire, on which he had been absent about ten days. Dined at home. I and my children drank tea and spent the evening at my next-door neighbour Mr. Watson's, whose history I do not know save that I have heard he was a stockbroker, and I found out from himself tonight that he was a Cumberland man from Wigton and has an estate in that country which he visits once in seven years. Our opposite neighbours, Mr. and Mrs. Poole and *his* three children, were there. We had a supper of a great variety of dishes and a cheerful glass. I had played whist and lost a trifle. Upon the whole, I forgot my "vexing thoughts"[5] pretty well.

SATURDAY 4 JANUARY. Courtenay called on me, and I fixed with him to meet him at Malone's at dinner. The Commentator,[6] at whose door I left word that I was to come, received me very cordially. Courtenay joined us when we had half done. I had rather a *goodish* day.

[4]John Crewe, a long-time M.P., and Frances Anne Crewe, a great hostess and much-admired beauty, whom Reynolds painted three times and to whom Richard Brinsley Sheridan dedicated his *School for Scandal*.
[5]Quoted earlier by Boswell on 26 Sept. 1793, but not identified.
[6]A favourite appellation of Boswell's for Malone. He was now working on an ambitious new edition of Shakespeare, which was to appear in fifteen volumes. Still unfinished at his death in 1812, it was completed by James Boswell, Jr., finally appeared in twenty volumes in 1821, and came to be known as the third variorum edition.

SUNDAY 5 JANUARY. My daughters were at chapel in the morning; I with my son James in the afternoon. I dined at home, and in the evening my children said divine lessons.

MONDAY 6 JANUARY. Last week Veronica had called on Colonel Bosville's widow, who returned her visit, and invited us all to her house on Twelfth-Day, which this was, to tea and spend the evening. Understanding that she was by no means in deep affliction, I had also called on her, and found her wonderfully composed, in a small house in Half Moon Street, and a Miss Prior living with her. My two eldest daughters and I, after dining at home, went to her this afternoon. She had a Mr. and Mrs. Bisset, a Miss Evans, a foreigner who passed by the name of a Count, Lord Macdonald's five sons,[7] and a brother, brisk and noisy, and a little sister. We had tea, and I played whist and won; and then we had supper and a Twelfth-cake.[8] There was much laughing and singing. But I could not share in the merriment, for I thought of the loss of my gallant kinsman, and felt with wonder and some disapprobation the seeming indifference of his widow, to whom however I resolved to pay attention.

TUESDAY 7 JANUARY. Idled away my time and that of my son James at draughts, at which he now beat me numbers of games. Dined at home. There had been for some time a hard frost. The little Miss Cookes drank tea with Betsy and Jamie and me.

WEDNESDAY 8 JANUARY. Nothing to record but dining at home, and there being in the evening a party with my daughters, Mr. Richard Johnson and his wife, and Courtenay's two eldest sons, Mr. and Mrs. Smith and Miss Dennison, a Miss Waghorn and Miss Damen, a Dutch singer,[9] and Mr. Masseria.

THURSDAY 9 JANUARY. Courtenay had insisted on Malone and me dining with him today. I thought it wrong in his situation to entertain at all.[1] But I could not refuse. Mr. Blair of Portland Place was there. The day went off well enough.

---

[7] Alexander Macdonald, first Baron Macdonald of Sleat, had seven sons, the eldest aged twenty. Their mother, the sister of the late Thomas Bosville, was the former Elizabeth Diana Bosville, who had been one of Boswell's matrimonial candidates many years earlier. Boswell had been engaged in a fierce public quarrel with Macdonald after criticizing him anonymously but recognizably in the *Tour to the Hebrides*.

[8] See above, 7 January 1793 and n. 1.

[9] Richard Johnson, M.P., the son of a former client of Boswell's, had married one of Courtenay's daughters. The singer was perhaps a member of the Dutch musical family Dahmen or Damen; Wilhelm Dahmen and Johan Arnold Dahmen are known to have been in England at about this time, but we have found no record of the women of the family.

[1] Courtenay was, as usual, in great financial difficulties.

FRIDAY 10 JANUARY. Called on Malone, who asked me to dine with him, to which I agreed; and Windham having come to town yesterday, called on him and acted as ambassador to invite him to be of the party. But he was engaged. Malone and I did very well tête-à-tête.

SATURDAY 11 JANUARY. It was a dark, misty, moist, cold day. Yet I resolutely walked to Dilly's and heard that the sale of my book was going on as might be expected. He had dined early, so I went to Baldwin's and shared his good family dinner. Walking home in the cold, damp air at night, I found myself faint and apprehensive of falling down in the street. I bought some Shrewsbury cakes at Mr. Paul's in —— Street, Covent Garden,[2] eating some of which supported me somewhat. But still I was feeble. I betook myself to Atkinson's Coffeehouse in Dean Street, Soho, where a glass of warm brandy and water, with some of my Shrewsbury cakes, and the warmth, and several newspapers, and variety of faces set me quite to rights, and I got well home and went to bed directly, I believe about nine, and instantly fell asleep.

SUNDAY 12 JANUARY. Awaked relaxed[3] and with some degree of headache. Lay and indulged, had rice-milk in bed, and Betsy and Jamie read to me the first and last chapter of the Bible. I got up between one and two and called on Malone, with whom I found Courtenay. My two eldest daughters were at chapel in the morning. I and Jamie and Betsy went there in the afternoon. My brother David dined with us. I sat quietly at home with my children in the evening.

MONDAY 13 JANUARY. Took an early dinner with Dilly, and went in the Norwich coach to Chelmsford, to the Epiphany Sessions. Supped with the counsel.

TUESDAY 14 JANUARY. Breakfasted with the counsel. Visited my worthy friend Major Langton, now commanding the Royal North Lincolnshire Militia here. Was pleased to see them do some part of their exercise. Attended Sessions in the morning. Almost no business. Only two causes. Dined at the counsel mess. Sat the afternoon drinking claret with Fanshaw,[4] Gascoyne, and some others. Drank tea and a dram with Miss Lakin, one of the landladies of the Saracen's Head,[5]

---

[2]Shrewsbury cakes were small, flat, round, crisp biscuits (American: cookies). Peter Paul owned a confectioner's shop at no. 2 Bridges Street, Covent Garden.
[3]Weak and enervated.
[4]Either Counsellor John Gascoyne Fanshaw or Counsellor Charles Fanshaw.
[5]Lakin was one of three owners of the Black Boy, which Boswell seems to have confused with the Saracen's Head. Both were good inns at Chelmsford.

along with Gascoyne, whom I took with me to supper at Langton's, where I was engaged. Lady Rothes[6] was ill and did not appear. Some of the Miss Langtons and Captain Gardiner, the adjutant, were at table. I was too visibly intoxicated.

WEDNESDAY 15 JANUARY. Breakfasted with the counsel. Attended the court in the morning. Went by polite invitation from Sir John and Lady Dalling to dinner at Danbury Place,[7] in Langton's coach with him and some of his young family. Hearty welcome. A great dinner and wines in abundance. Various company, particularly Dr. and Mrs. Kirkland of Chelmsford. Did not get home till near twelve; saw Lady Rothes.

THURSDAY 16 JANUARY. I did not get a single fee of any sort these Sessions, and therefore resolved to take them only occasionally, if at all. At nine got into the Chelmsford coach for London, reached Dilly's a little before three, left my baggage and repaired to the Old Bailey. Alderman Curtis carried me up to dinner, where were the Lord Mayor, Lord Chief Baron, Judge Grose (all of whom did me the honour to drink a glass of wine with me), Judge Rooke,[8] Sheriff Hamerton, etc. Went into court again and heard Lord Chief Baron try a prisoner very well. At night found George Dance, looked at a number of his drawings, and had some cold meat and port. Liked to be in my own bed again.

FRIDAY 17 JANUARY. I was now in better spirits, less unhappy, but without any vivid relish of life. I went to the Old Bailey between three and four and heard some trials by the Recorder. Alderman Hopkins[9] and he invited me to the second dinner, where I was hearty enough but not too much so, and got home safe.

SATURDAY 18 JANUARY. Went to Malone's at five and waited till he came home, and was made welcome to a share of his dinner. He pressed a second bottle, the greatest part of which I could not resist drinking. However, we had good talk. I did not join the Royal Academicians to

[6]Bennet Langton's wife. She was the widow of the Earl of Rothes and continued to use her style of Countess of Rothes after her second marriage. Boswell had known her for many years.

[7]Boswell had taken an immediate liking to Sir John Dalling at their earlier meeting at the Mount Coffee-house in April 1783. Dalling is not listed as the owner of Danbury Place, a handsome house four-and-a-half miles south-east of Chelmsford; perhaps he was renting it.

[8]The group included Sir Archibald Macdonald, the former Solicitor-General, who had become Lord Chief Baron of the Court of Exchequer in February 1793; Sir Nash Grose, a highly respected judge of the King's Bench; and Sir Giles Rooke, who had been promoted from serjeant-at-law to King's Serjeant in 1793 and who later that year had been named Puisne Judge, with the usual attendant knighthood.

[9]Sir John Hopkins had been Lord Mayor in 1792 and was knighted in that year.

celebrate the Queen's birthday,[1] as some improper guests find their way.

SUNDAY 19 JANUARY. I had a little of a headache. My children and John James Temple, who had returned a few days ago, went to Portland Chapel in the morning. I sat at home and read a part of the Bible, and *Opinions of Sarah, Duchess of Marlborough,* published by Lord Hailes from a manuscript.[2] I thought them so trifling as not to be worth publishing. I was at chapel in the afternoon, dined at home, and with my children and J. J. Temple drank tea at my brother David's and partook of Edinburgh bun. Lord Townshend having left a card for me the day before, I called on him today and saw him for a few minutes. Then sat awhile with my Lady,[3] etc.

MONDAY 20 JANUARY. Having called on Seward, who was asked to a family dinner at Mr. Cator's in the Adelphi, I accompanied him, and was cordially welcomed. Only a Mrs. Scott and a niece of Cator's and her husband there. A good dinner, and I managed so that Seward and I had wine enough. We had whist in the evening and I won.

[EDITORIAL NOTE. On this day Boswell wrote again to the *Gentleman's Magazine* in reply to a second letter of Anna Seward's that had meanwhile appeared in the December issue. She had renewed her complaints about his impoliteness to her, repeated her assertions about the Johnson anecdotes she had provided—concerning the duck and the sprig of myrtle verses, Johnson's conversation with his mother about his impending marriage, and the rest—and intensified her criticism of Johnson. Moreover, she had concluded with a well-chosen battle image, declaring with considerable dignity that "Into paper-war with a man, who, after professing himself my friend, becomes causelessly my foe, I will no farther enter."

Boswell took up the battle image with gusto. "Why should I be my fair antagonist's *foe?* She never did me any harm, nor do I apprehend

---

[1]This day was a public holiday to celebrate the Queen's birthday. The royal family did not attend the festivities at the Royal Academy.

[2]Published anonymously in 1788, this small volume consisted of about forty brief excerpts from a diary written by Sarah Churchill, Duchess of Marlborough, between 1736 and 1741. Sir David Dalrymple, Lord Hailes, had been one of Boswell's early models; an advocate who had become a Lord of Session, he had also cultivated literary and antiquarian interests.

[3]George Townshend, first Marquess Townshend, had had a distinguished military career and had now attained the rank of General. Boswell had been his guest in 1769 while he was serving as Lord Lieutenant of Ireland and had dined with him repeatedly since then. The Marchioness was his second wife.

that she ever can. She protests against entering farther into a *paper war* with me. If there be such *war*, it is all on one side, for it is not in my thoughts." He then reviewed the causes of contention all over again, revealing new evidence to support his interpretations. On the subject of Johnson's conversation with his mother, for instance, he pointed out that the Lichfield lady whom Miss Seward had cited as her source was the very lady who had denied the story when he wrote to her for verification. He could also point out a number of inaccuracies in Miss Seward's criticisms of Johnson.

The sprig of myrtle controversy was more awkward for Boswell, for he had just received a second letter from Edmund Hector revealing that he was not the suitor for whom the verses had been written, as Boswell had assumed, but that he had requested them for a friend. Still, Hector's explanation was proof that the verses had not been written for Lucy Porter, and Boswell took the opportunity to quote Hector's letter in full, including his harsh comment about Miss Seward: "If you intend to convince this obstinate woman and to exhibit to the public the truth of your narrative, you are at liberty to make what use you please of this statement" (Hector to Boswell, 9 January 1794).

Not having spared Miss Seward's feelings in the course of his long letter, Boswell ended on a conciliatory note: "Let the *duck* be changed into a *swan*, and the *myrtle* into an *olive*. Instead of railing, let us have the song. Instead of war, let us have peace." To this letter, which appeared in the January issue of the *Gentleman's Magazine* (published on the first day of February), Miss Seward did not bother to reply. Although the February issue still printed letters by supporters of both combatants, the editor expressed the wish to receive no further comments on the subject and declared an end to the controversy that had been played out in the pages of his journal.]

TUESDAY 21 JANUARY. This day the Parliament met, and the Literary Club for the first time this winter; I in the chair. Having been afraid we should have a very thin meeting on account of the Parliament,[4] I had written to Dr. Warren to request his attendance. He accordingly came. Dr. Warton and Malone were the others. We had pretty good conversation, but I was too much bent on drinking, and certainly took greatly more wine than I should have done. Walking up

---

[4] Boswell's concern was justified. Courtenay, Windham, and Fox were present in the House of Commons and presumably earlier in the House of Lords for the official opening of Parliament, when the King gave his Address on the progress of the war to the combined Houses.

Bond Street I met an old acquaintance whom I was very happy to see and whom I was induced to pass a little time with.

WEDNESDAY 22 JANUARY. Being in fermentation[5] from last night, which had not been the case with me since December 17, I walked into the City, and having called at a house in the Old Bailey, found

A *new* repast and (*to me*) untasted spring.[6]

Called a second time—better. Dined quietly with Dilly, drank sufficiently both of frontignac and port, and after coffee got well home, having first drunk a glass of negus at the Mount.

THURSDAY 23 JANUARY. Dined at home with my three daughters, having found Malone engaged out. Betsy and I drank tea in a family quiet style with Mr. and Mrs. Cooke and their children. I did not go to Westminster Hall today, though the term began, being too late and having truly little motive.

FRIDAY 24 JANUARY. Dined at Mr. John Devaynes's with Baron Dimsdale, Mr. Birch, a surgeon,[7] and Mr. Jones, a clergyman. A pretty hearty day. But how insignificant is my present life!

SATURDAY 25 JANUARY. Dined at home.

SUNDAY 26 JANUARY. At Portland Chapel in the afternoon. Dined at home. In the evening sacred lessons with my children.

MONDAY 27 JANUARY. When I awaked, there was a heavy snow. I lay till past one. Dined at home. For these three days I have drunk only water.

TUESDAY 28 JANUARY. Had not yet been in Westminster Hall this term. Sat awhile with Malone, who walked with me into the City, as Captain Preston had requested I would call on him that we might fix a day for dining with Mr. Bleaden, master of the London Tavern, who above two years ago had asked me to come and view his *world below,* as he justly called his cellars, etc., and afterwards to do the landlord the honour to *eat a beefsteak* with him. And lately he had reminded

[5]Emotional excitement.
[6]Joseph Addison, *Cato,* I. iv. 70: "A new repast, or an untasted spring." Boswell has inserted "to me" in parentheses above the line and has introduced a sexual innuendo not found in the original line, which describes the simple pleasures of native Africans who live by hunting. The place of his rendezvous was the narrow street between Ludgate Hill and Newgate Street, best known as the location of the Old Bailey court-house.
[7]Thomas Dimsdale, M.D., an authority on inoculation against smallpox, who was granted the hereditary title of Baron by the Empress Catherine of Russia in gratitude for inoculating her and members of her family; and either John or Nicholas Birch. The more prominent, John Birch, surgeon extraordinary to the Prince of Wales, was, like Dimsdale, an advocate of inoculation.

me of it and told me that Captain Preston and Mr. Cameron[8] would be of the party. He had desired me to bring half a dozen friends, but I invited only Gov. Richard Penn, who I was sure would relish it highly; and having reminded him of it at the Mount last Wednesday, he chuckled and said, "I shall lie upon my arms."[9] Tuesday 4 February was fixed by Preston today. I found with him to my great surprise his brother Sir Charles and his niece Miss Preston. His lady and Captain Sealy and Dick Grindall and his two clerks were our party. We had plenty of wine. In the evening came his brother-in-law, Brown. We had whist and I won; and after a bit of supper had a coach and got well home.

WEDNESDAY 29 JANUARY. Called on Malone, who engaged me to dine with him. He had asked me yesterday. I walked boldly through the snow to the London Tavern and settled the dinner day with mine host. Sat awhile at Dilly's, and found that the sale of my *Life of Dr. Johnson* had stagnated for some time,[1] which discouraged me. There was a great thaw and a drizzling rain; the cold was penetrating, and I felt it take effect on me. I was very comfortable at Malone's. Little Betsy went back to Blacklands today. I had called at the Old Bailey. ᴍ .[2]

THURSDAY 30 JANUARY. It was a very cold day. I read the service appointed for it[3] to my son James. I had a note from Mr. Spottiswoode, the solicitor, desiring to have draft of case, Stewart against Newnham and Company, to put to press. Luckily I had not much remaining to do of it. So I finished it and sent it in the evening. This gave me some rational satisfaction. I dined at home. Veronica had a headache. Euphemia and I went to a party at Mrs. Poole's. I played whist and won.

FRIDAY 31 JANUARY. Dined at the Royal Academy Club. I know not how it happened, but I drank too much, so that I scarcely remembered being brought home in his coach by good Sir Francis Bourgeois. I sat between Sir William Chambers and Catton,[4] two of the old original members. West told me, as he and I went together in a hackney-

---

[8]Almost certainly Donald Cameron, a partner in the banking-house of Harley, Cameron, and Son, and former sheriff of Essex, whose father, Dr. Archibald Cameron, was executed in 1753 for having supported the Jacobite cause in 1745. Boswell had toasted Donald Cameron at one of the Chelmsford Assizes as "not only a *High* Sheriff but a *High*land High Sheriff" (unidentified newspaper, probably 6–9 Aug. 1791, in Boswell's collection of newspaper clippings).

[9]That is, be ready for battle; in other words, well prepared and waiting eagerly.

[1]Only twelve copies had been sold during the month of January.

[2]A private symbol.

[3]Commemorating the execution of Charles I.

[4]Charles Catton, a landscape- and animal-painter, who was coach-painter to George III.

coach to our club, that the King had looked with great attention at the Address from the members of the Royal Academy, and had particularly observed my signature, and said, "Boswell writes a good hand; a very good hand" (laughing) "for a Scotchman."[5]

SATURDAY 1 FEBRUARY. Breakfasted with Malone according to custom on the first day of the month. Visited Seward a little while. When I had been a few minutes at home, Windham called on me, and he and I went to Malone's, Windham having asked us to dine with him next day, and having recollected a prior engagement which made him put it off. I walked with Windham to Upper Grosvenor Street and we left our cards at Mr. Ranby's,[6] where I was asked to dine on Sunday 9th. I parted with Windham at his own door, feeling my inferiority when I thought of him as an active statesman.[7] I dined at home. My cold troubled me a good deal. Veronica, Euphemia, Jamie, and I drank tea at Mrs. Cooke's. At night I bathed my feet in warm water, and drank warm negus, and laid myself quiet for repose. I had a good deal of comfort from this nursing of myself.

SUNDAY 2 FEBRUARY. Awaked in a fine perspiration and breakfasted in bed. Rose about one and went by engagement to visit Mrs. Fitzgerald, who was now at the hotel in Cleveland Row, corner of St. James's Street. She had a charming apartment on the second floor; a bow-window which fronted Pall Mall and commanded on one side St. James's Palace, on the other, St. James's Street. The view quite animated me. I sat awhile with this lady very agreeably. Then Jamie and I went to Portland Chapel. Euphemia had been there in the morning. Veronica had a cold and kept the house. With much difficulty I allowed Euphemia to go to Mrs. Smith's in the evening, she having promised that she would not again ask to go abroad on a Sunday. I dined at home, and was quiet all the evening.

MONDAY 3 FEBRUARY. Having had a cold for a day or two, I kept the house today and was pretty tranquil.

TUESDAY 4 FEBRUARY. This was the great day of dining with Mr. Bleaden, mine host of THE LONDON. I sat quietly at home till Gov. Richard Penn called on me a little after three in his coach, and we proceeded to the jovial spot. Bleaden received us most courteously

---

[5]Although the Academicians had signed the Address on 31 December 1793, its presentation to the King had been delayed until the medals were ready.

[6]John Ranby, a writer on political subjects, shared Boswell's views on the slave trade. In the *Life of Johnson* Boswell praised Ranby's *Doubts on the Abolition of the Slave Trade* (1791) with the witticism (not his own): "HIS *Doubts*...are better than most people's *Certainties*" (23 September 1777).

[7]Now one of the leaders of the Opposition, Windham was being urged to join the Government; he reluctantly accepted the position of Secretary at War in July of this year.

and went himself with us through his cellars, which we found to be of wonderful extent and replenishment. He told us he sold wine *out of the house* to the value of £5,000 yearly. He then conducted us to that elegant Apollo, his dining-room,[8] and by and by we sat down to dinner, in number twelve: himself and we two, Mr. Cameron and his son, Mr. Preston and his brother Sir Charles, Mr. Newte, a Mr. Dent, Captain Fraser in the East India naval service, Mr. Lewin (I think), who had been one of their captains, and a Mr. Wigram. There was a course of two soups, two dishes of fish, stewed beef, boiled lamb and spinach, roast mutton, fricandeau of veal, *petit pâté*[9]—in short, substantial and choice. Our host then said, "Gentlemen, there's a beefsteak coming." "Ay," said I, "that's what you promised." We had exquisite beefsteaks, hot and hot,[1] *after which* was a second course of game, omelette, pastry, etc.—in short, what the season could afford. Madeira, sherry, port, old hock circulated, and we had a glass both of burgundy and champagne. And lastly came an elegant dessert and *Scotch pints*[2] of very capital claret. I admired the manner in which Bleaden conducted himself. He made no speeches of any sort, but sat at the head of his own table with the ease of a plain, sensible English gentleman. I alone pleasantly remarked on our dinner, "Mr. Bleaden, I observe your beefsteak appears in a variety of forms. It seems to be woodcocks before you, and here it looks like partridges." Even then he assumed nothing on his grand feast. I sat next to Governor Penn, who enjoyed the scene hugely and whispered me, "It is the best thing we shall have this month." We were admirably served by at least seven waiters, who had now a motive to diligence and ambition when they beheld their master in such a situation, who, as he once told me himself, had been a waiter at White's.[3] The generous bottle circulated so as to produce in me a total oblivion till I found myself safe in my own bed next morning. Governor Penn, who according to agreement carried me safe home, afterwards informed me that Bleaden became very gay, sang several good songs, insisted that this meeting

[8]An allusion to the Apollo, the room in the Devil's Tavern in which the playwright and poet Ben Jonson held forth in his later years to his tribe of enthusiastic disciples. The dining-room of the London Tavern, decorated with Corinthian columns, was known as the Pillar Room.

[9]Veal fricassee and small patty shells filled with chopped meat or fish (considered a great delicacy).

[1]Served as soon as cooked and hence very hot.

[2]About three times as large as English pints.

[3]White's Chocolate House, which was opened in 1693, was a popular establishment in the early eighteenth century (it was the fictional setting of many papers in the *Tatler*, 1709–10), then became known for gambling, and came to an end in 1755, when it changed its name and location. John Bleaden, now in his fiftieth year, must have worked there as a mere boy.

should be an anniversary, and made all of us who could speak promise that we should attend; that one half of the company dropped off, and the rest gathered round our host and continued to drink till there was a full stop from inability, and then he brought me off. *I since find that his recollection was not perfect, for several of the company sat long after us.*

WEDNESDAY 5 FEBRUARY. Awoke with a violent headache and had recourse to *a drop of brandy*, which I have found to be a certain remedy. Walked into the City, being restless, and took a quiet dinner with Dilly.

THURSDAY 6 FEBRUARY. M. Esnard, one of the emigrant French priests, whom I had accosted in the street and given him my card, had called on me sometimes, and offered to read French with Veronica. He was a well-behaved man, and told me he had taught theology five years at Nancy in Lorraine. I invited him to dinner today, and had also the two lay emigrants with whom I had made an acquaintance at Salomon's concert: Vicomte D'Alzon and Chevalier Fieulieux,[4] and my brother David to assist me to entertain them. The day went off wonderfully well. Only I thought it lasted too long.

FRIDAY 7 FEBRUARY. Went to Westminster Hall for the first time this term. The Master of the Rolls sat in Chancery,[5] which I attended a short time with no satisfaction. I relished more a peep into the King's Bench, which is somehow congenial with my feelings. I then walked to Dilly's, where I was engaged to dine and play whist. The company were Seward, Syms, Sharp, and the Rev. Thomas Belsham, who left us after dinner; and then the remaining five (one being out in his turn) played games at whist till about eleven. We did not drink wine to excess; and some warm punch, which went about in tumblers, was very agreeable. I lost. But I had now been less irritable, and, from what cause I know not, more easy for some time. Seward carried me home in *his own hackney-coach,* according to Goldsmith's phrase.[6]

SATURDAY 8 FEBRUARY. My son James, it being a holiday, came home early in the forenoon with his eyes and cheeks so discoloured and swelled that I absolutely should not have known him. He had boxed with an Irish boy of the name of May so long ago as Tuesday. This custom in the great schools still prevails, and the masters wink at it. Mr. Dodd, the usher, on whom I called, told me that they never inquired much into such quarrels, but left them to be settled by the boys. He said

[4]Perhaps the twenty-year-old André-Henri Daudé, Vicomte d'Alzon, and a Chevalier Fieulieux or Feulieux (the spelling of whose name caused Boswell great difficulty).
[5]Sir Richard Pepper Arden, M.P.
[6]Notoriously short of funds and in no position to keep a carriage of his own, Goldsmith had presumably relished the paradox of this phrase, a hackney-coach being not privately owned but only hired for an occasion.

he understood my son had shown great spirit, for though he found his antagonist too powerful for him, he would not *give up* (or *give out*, I know not which is the phrase), and was fighting on till the boys separated them. I was uneasy to see him and from apprehending that he might perhaps receive some permanent injury. But I did not say much.

Before I was out of bed this morning I received an earnest letter from M. Fieulieux informing me that he was under arrest for debt at a sheriff's officer's, and entreating my coming to advise him what to do. After consulting with Seward and Malone, who asked me to dine with him, but which I could not by reason of the time which this disagreeable business would take, I repaired to the *lock-up house*,[7] Ship and Anchor Court, Temple Bar, where I found not only M. Fieulieux but M. D'Alzon, one for £10, the other for £11.6, which last, however, was on a bill at a twelvemonth's date, a few days only being expired since its date. The creditor of both was a Mr. Price, their tailor. I went to his brother and attorney in Northumberland Street and conversed with him, and agreed to meet him at Nando's Coffee-house between six and eight. I took a hasty dinner at home and a glass or two of wine with Malone, and then went to my brother David and got him to go along with me. We first called on our acquaintance Mr. Bicknell, attorney in Norfolk Street, to whom Seward had recommended to me to apply. He was very distinct and obliging in giving information how to act, said he should be at home all the evening, and from humanity would be ready to do anything in his power if called upon. My brother and I went to Nando's and met the tailor and his brother, and after many proposals and conversations both with them and the French gentlemen, it was agreed thus: the sum owing by both, including £3.3, said to be *half* the charges of the arrest, being £24.10, the 10/- was thrown out. M. D'Alzon paid down £12, and he and his friend granted their joint bill at a year's date for £12. The former bill was delivered up, and a receipt granted by the tailor for the new one, which, when paid, should be in full for clothes furnished to both, declaring that one or both might leave the kingdom and return without being troubled till after the year was elapsed. On these conditions they should be set at liberty. All this was accordingly done, and my brother and I saw the gentlemen fairly home to their lodgings. I however told them that in justice, and for the honour of the laws of this country, an action should be brought by M. D'Alzon for false imprisonment, as by special agreement credit was granted for a year for the contents of his bill. I came home much satisfied with my benevolent exertions.

SUNDAY 9 FEBRUARY. I went to St. George's, Hanover Square,

---

[7]A house used for the temporary detention of offenders.

and attended part of the morning service, standing in the passage where I could see Miss Upton, who looked as elegant as ever and suggested pleasing imaginations, which, however, reflection told me could hardly be realized. In truth I had a consciousness that not only from my uncertain spirits and temper, but from my strong affectionate attachment to my dear departed wife and my tender regard for my children, I could not reasonably expect to have comfort in a second marriage, except with a very excellent woman indeed who should also bring a considerable fortune; and how vain would it be for me to think of obtaining such a match! I next went and heard part of a sermon by Dr. Parker at St. James's Church.[8] Then found Lord Kellie and walked with him on Lord Fife's terrace, and got a most particular account of my late old friend, his brother Andrew.[9] I came home and heard my son James say divine lessons, his *face* preventing him from appearing at church, to which I think my two daughters went. I dined at Mr. Ranby's, with Sir William and Lady Scott, Mr. Palmer of Somerset Street, Mr. Crosbie, my old acquaintance at the Duke of Montrose's,[1] and a gentleman whose name I do not recollect; a good day enough. Came home quietly.

MONDAY 10 FEBRUARY. The day was passed *nihil agendo;*[2] at least no trace remains.

TUESDAY 11 FEBRUARY. Both yesterday and today I dined at home and drank only water. In the evening was at a party at Mrs. Cooke's, played whist and lost.

WEDNESDAY 12 FEBRUARY. Dined at Mr. Farington the painter's with Mr. George Dance, Mr. Tyler, Mr. Garvey, Mr. Richards, all R.A.s, Mr. Howard the surgeon, and Mr. Farington's brother, captain of an East Indiaman,[3] and his lady. Mrs. Farington, the mistress of the house, made up *ten.* I was struck with wonder and a kind of feeling of the inferiority of my situation when I saw a house and furniture and table belonging to this painter, all so much better than mine. But I enjoyed all and passed a truly joyous social day. In the evening played whist and lost a little.

THURSDAY 13 FEBRUARY. Called on Farington and looked at the book of the Royal Academy Club from its foundation in 1788, containing an exact state of the members present at each meeting, the

---

[8]William Parker, D.D., who had officiated at St. James's, Westminster, for more than thirty years and was much admired for his sermons.
[9]See above, p. 245.
[1]Boswell and Crosbie had met at the house of William Graham, second Duke of Montrose, in 1781 and had taken to each other immediately.
[2]With nothing accomplished.
[3]The party included Edmund Garvey, a landscape-painter, and either Richard Farington or William Farington (both East India captains).

money received, the bills and complete expenditure. I dined tête-à-tête with Malone very cordially. He talked like a practical philosopher against my being discontented with my lot in life; and when I showed him an exact view of my affairs, my income, deductions, and calculation of expense under different articles, from which it appeared that my fund for living was truly narrow, he did not think I had reason to complain, and observed that I was educating my children in the most laudable manner, and that ten dinners in a year to my friends would not make a difference of more than thirty pounds. At the same time he allowed that a few hundreds a year of addition would be most desirable for me. My constant cause of repining is having indulged hopes of attaining both to consequence and wealth, so as to raise my family to higher consideration; and finding no prospect of attaining my ambitious objects, I tried to soothe myself with the consideration of my fame as a writer, and that by the good management of my estate, and saving, I might in time pay my debts, in which case I should, besides raising at least one third the rent of what I inherited, add Dalblair £115, Willockshill £50, and Foardmouth £5—£170 yearly to the family estate—Dalblair too being princely in extent,[4] and should also give my second son the pretty little property of Knockroon. And supposing me to achieve only one half of these additions, I should be no unworthy *Laird*.

FRIDAY 14 FEBRUARY. I dined at Mr. Nealson's, stockbroker in Great George Street, Westminster. This was one of the days of the meeting of the Royal Academy Club, which I never missed when in town, and was exceedingly unwilling to miss on any consideration whatever. But Nealson, who is remarkable for giving capital dinners, had sent me a card of invitation for this day a fortnight before, which I concluded must be on account of some extraordinary *feast*, and having some time ago refused an invitation from him, I resolved to go. But I upbraided myself for deserting my Academical brethren, for though we had, as *mos est*,[5] a table excellently covered, there was no particular luxury; and the company were only Falstaff Morgann[6] and his niece, Miss Kingston, a large, smiling, and pleasant woman, Counsellor Cooke, Mr. Webster the attor-

---

[4] All three properties were in the vicinity of Auchinleck. Boswell was especially proud of Dalblair, a large moorland farm which he bought at auction in 1767, thereby becoming a laird in his own right. He acquired Foardmouth, a small farm, in 1783 and Willockshill in 1785.

[5] According to custom—a common Latin tag.

[6] Maurice Morgann was known for his *Essay on the Dramatic Character of Sir John Falstaff* (1777), a detailed character analysis attempting to refute the commonly held view that Falstaff is a coward. Boswell found the essay "very ingenious," but Johnson was not convinced, declaring: "as he has proved Falstaff to be no coward, he may prove Iago to be a very good character" (*Life of Johnson*, iv. 192 and n.1).

ney, his wife, son, and daughter (in short, the ordinary guests at this board), with the addition of Mr. Parsons and Mr. Coutts Trotter. However, I was invited to dinner also next day to meet Mrs. Abington[7] and Mr. Morgann, which I liked much, and we lived well, and the Websters and I stayed the evening and played whist, and then we had a pretty supper of roast chickens, etc. Time passed so that when I got home I thought it had been only between twelve and one, when in truth it was after three.

SATURDAY 15 FEBRUARY. I had been for three days in a good deal of concern on account of something interesting to another person as well as to myself, and therefore I kept it *secret,* and endeavoured to act with as much prudence and gentleness as I could from my own mind only, without any advice. I dined again at Nealson's. Mrs. Abington, Mr. Morgann, and Mr. Webster were there. Mrs. Abington's fame and elegance and vivacity pleased me much, notwithstanding that she was now past fifty and grown very fat. The dinner was admirable, and ingeniously varied from that of yesterday. We talked of Pope, who Mrs. Abington said got into the best company and had the good sense to keep himself in it. Morgann observed that he was always received as a gentleman, and never treated merely as a poet. We talked of Sir Richard Steele, and Morgann quoted (as the test of high fashion, I think—I know not from whom. I must ask):

To wear red stockings and to dine with Steele,[8]

and Swift's ill-natured lines

jails
Wales.[9]

[7]The popular comic actress Frances Abington, now temporarily in retirement, was a great friend of Nealson's and inherited £100 from him a few years later. Boswell had first met her in 1785.
[8]Pope, *Macer,* l. 4—a satirical line describing the ambition of a social-climbing poet newly arrived in town.
[9]Swift, *A Libel on Doctor Delany:*

> Thus, *Steele,* who owned what others writ,
> And flourished by imputed wit,
> From perils of a hundred jails,
> Withdrew to starve, and die, in *Wales.*

This exaggerated account of Steele's life reflects the rumours that he took credit for some of Addison's essays in the *Tatler* (1709–11) and did not acknowledge Colley Cibber's contributions to his last play, *The Conscious Lovers* (1722). Swift's reference to prisons recalls the numerous judgements against Steele for debt, and the last line alludes to his final retirement to Carmarthen in Wales. In actual fact, Steele was incarcerated only twice (both times briefly), and he withdrew to Wales by arrangement with his creditors, spending his last three years comfortably on a small property near the relations of his late second wife.

Mr. Morgann said he could give me some particulars of him after he retired to Wales; for I had observed that his works had never been collected, and that they should be; and Mrs. Abington having politely said (*looking to me*) that an honourable friend would do it very well, I had owned that I intended to do it and write his life.[1] Mr. Morgann went early. The rest of us had beefsteaks and stewed oysters for supper.

SUNDAY 16 FEBRUARY. Was at Portland Chapel morning and evening service. At night M. D'Alzon paid me a visit.

MONDAY 17 FEBRUARY. Dined at home; drank only water.

TUESDAY 18 FEBRUARY. Ditto. Ditto. Stayed from the LITERARY CLUB this day as I did last meeting, merely to save expense, being sadly vexed by my straitened circumstances.[2]

WEDNESDAY 19 FEBRUARY. Dined at the Old Bailey between five and six with the Recorder, Sheriff Hamerton, etc., a very small party, having first heard some trials. Then was at the Essex Head Club with Barrington, Brocklesby, Farmer, Weston, Calamy.

THURSDAY 20 FEBRUARY. Seward carried me to dine at the Thatched House Tavern with the subscribers to the Westminster Library.[3] He was one of the stewards, and I was one of his guests. I never saw a coarser collection of beings, a few excepted. I was quite disgusted and came off early. Fortunately I found Malone, and Courtenay with him, and had some hours of good conversation and some good wine. Blessed change!

FRIDAY 21 FEBRUARY. Dined at Baldwin's. Was in a drinking frame, and wildly took between two and three bottles of mountain. Was much intoxicated, and guessed afterwards, from a dim recollection, that I had talked with impropriety, which gave me uneasiness; but I thought it was best to let it pass away as if I had been utterly unconscious, which in truth I was. I had the judgement to take coach home.

SATURDAY 22 FEBRUARY. Mr. Robert Boswell had some days ago surprised me by his unexpectedly returning to London, along with Mr. Kerr, King's Printer for Scotland, to solicit an abatement of the new duty on paper. They dined with me today. Seeing a *bailie of Edinburgh* and a *Writer to the Signet* and hearing contracted topics low-

---

[1] Being of an old Welsh family, Morgann knew of Steele's experiences in Wales. Nowhere else does Boswell mention his plan to collect Steele's works (which have still not been published in a complete edition) or to write a biography of Steele.
[2] A number of tenants had not paid their half-yearly rents, which were due in January.
[3] Founded in 1789, this was one of two subscription libraries in London, used chiefly by middle-class and professional people.

ered my spirits and made me shrink from returning to my native city.[4]

SUNDAY 23 FEBRUARY. At Portland Chapel in the morning. My daughter Betsy came home. I (as an exception from my general rule as to Sunday) dined at Mr. Nealson's with Mrs. Abington, Counsellor Cooke, Mr. Webster, Citizen Smith, and Mr. Wood the painter.[5] An excellent dinner. Mrs. Abington and I, and I do not remember how many more, stayed supper.

MONDAY 24 and TUESDAY 25[6] FEBRUARY. Dined at home both these days. Nothing particular to mark.

WEDNESDAY 26 FEBRUARY. My daughter Betsy returned to school. I dined quietly at Mr. Dilly's.

THURSDAY 27 FEBRUARY. Dined at Mr. Cator's with Mr. Collinson (late of the house of Brown and Collinson), Mrs. Cator's cousin, and Lawyer Lysons.[7]

FRIDAY 28 FEBRUARY. This being the Fast ordered by His Majesty on account of the war, I was at Portland Chapel both morning and evening; and having thus done my duty, accepted of an invitation from Kemble to dine with him; and there I met Mr. and Mrs. Siddons and two daughters, his other sister Mrs. Twiss and her husband[8] and son, and Mr. Malone. We were quiet and sober, and went in good time to tea and coffee and whist, and stayed supper.

SATURDAY 1 MARCH. On account of the Fast, our Royal Academy Club was held today instead of yesterday; a pretty numerous company. I was present in the morning at a curious scene at Kemble's: a manager trying a young candidate for the stage. This was Mr. Pughe,

---

[4]Robert Boswell was a Writer to the Signet (a senior solicitor who prepared papers for hearings before the Court of Session); Charles Kerr was a bailie (a municipal magistrate). By "contracted topics" Boswell means narrow, provincial ones.

[5]The landscape-painter and water-colourist John George Wood.

[6]Boswell inadvertently wrote 26 in the manuscript.

[7]Thomas Collinson had been a partner in the London banking-house of Brown, Collinson, and Tritton, which apparently ceased to function in the early 1780s; he was a cousin of Cator's wife, the former Mary Collinson. Samuel Lysons was at this time a special pleader (a specialist in the technicalities of pleadings in civil and criminal suits) but not yet a barrister. A few years earlier he had helped Mrs. Piozzi by trying to gather material for her *Anecdotes of the Late Samuel Johnson, LL.D.* and seeing it through the press, then by collaborating with her in editing the *Letters to and from Johnson.* Also a talented engraver, he provided etchings for his brother Daniel Lysons's *Environs of London* (1792–96) and would soon collaborate with him on the famous topographical survey entitled *Magna Britannia* (1806).

[8]Frances Twiss, Kemble's younger sister, and her husband Francis Twiss. On her marriage in 1786 she had given up a moderately successful acting career; Twiss was a scholarly man who later published a Shakespeare concordance.

who had kindly assisted me home last summer when I was knocked down. He repeated a part of *George Barnwell;*[9] but Kemble perceived no strong talent in him, but only imitation. He advised him to try first to be employed in the Bath or York or Norwich theatre. My son James was with me at this ceremony.

SUNDAY 2 MARCH. Was, I think, at Portland Chapel in the morning. Walked out to Kensington Gore and dined with Mr. Wilkes, with two ladies besides Mrs. Arnold and his young daughter,[1] Jack Devaynes, and a captain whose name I forget; a cheerful day. Devaynes brought me to town in his chariot.

MONDAY 3 MARCH. Dined at Lord Inchiquin's with Malone, Sir Charles Blagden, Mr. Edward Gwatkin, and Mr. Charles Dundas;[2] a hearty day.

TUESDAY 4 MARCH. Dined at the LITERARY CLUB with the Duke of Leeds, Lord Spencer, Lord Lucan, Dr. Burney, and Windham. It was not as in the days of Johnson. I drank liberally.

WEDNESDAY 5 MARCH. Dined at home and prepared myself for an Appeal, Newnham and Company against Stewart, in which I was counsel.[3]

THURSDAY 6 MARCH. The Appeal came on in the House of Lords. Grant and Macdonald were heard for the appellants, and it was adjourned till Monday. I dined at Gov. Richard Penn's with Mr. Pinckney, the American Minister,[4] and his lady, and a pretty numerous company, chiefly Americans. A capital dinner and good wine; enough yet not to excess.

FRIDAY 7 MARCH. Dined quietly at Mr. Dilly's.

SATURDAY 8 MARCH. Dined at Mr. Nealson's with Mrs. Abington, Mr. Morgann, Mr. Webster, and Mr. Parsons. We were invited to a beefsteak dinner. But the steaks were ushered in by mock-turtle soup and a turbot, and followed by a very good second course and dessert.

---

[9]*The London Merchant, or The History of George Barnwell* (1731), George Lillo's bourgeois tragedy about an apprentice who is seduced by a wicked woman, robs his master, kills his uncle, and ends repentant on the gallows.

[1]Amelia Arnold, Wilkes's mistress since 1777, and his natural daughter Harriet, aged fifteen. He had installed them in a small house in Kensington Gore, in the south-west of London, and visited them frequently.

[2]The counsellor Charles Dundas, whom Boswell had met in Edinburgh in December 1780 and in London in May 1781; a former M.P., he was returned again this year.

[3]See above, 24 December 1793, p. 268 and n. 1.

[4]Thomas Pinckney had been at his diplomatic post in England since 1792. A native of Charleston who had served as Governor of South Carolina, he was popular in English society, in part because he was educated at Westminster School and Christ Church, Oxford.

I stayed the evening, played whist and won, and partook of a comfortable bit of supper.

SUNDAY 9 MARCH. From having drunk too much yesterday I lay long today, then walked as far as Peele's Coffee-house[5] and had some tea and a muffin, and did not get home till it was too late for afternoon service. Found the Bishop of Salisbury's lady and daughter, who had come to invite me to dine with his Lordship in an easy way. I went with them in the coach to Hill Street, Berkeley Square, no. 13.[6] Nobody else at dinner but his son and the Provost of Eton. A pleasant day. But I drank too freely. Well home, however, in the evening.

MONDAY 10 MARCH. I spoke in the House of Lords for Stewart against Newnham and Company. Want of use made me feel awkward and not clear. But I got on sufficiently well. Adam, who was with me, was quite easy. The Decree was affirmed.[7] I dined at Dilly's with Cumberland, Sharp, Rogers, Dr. Towers,[8] my brother David, and Mr. ——from Manchester, a friend of Sharp's. A great deal of conversation.

TUESDAY 11 MARCH. Dined at Malone's with Windham.

WEDNESDAY 12 MARCH. A quiet dinner with Mr. Dilly on good fragments of Monday. He and I then went to Braithwaite's and took an additional cheerful glass with him and Seward and Sewell, bookseller, Cornhill. After which I was at the Essex Head Club. I recollect not who were present.

THURSDAY 13 MARCH. Dined at home, my brother David with me.

FRIDAY 14 MARCH. Dined at the Royal Academy Club; a small party, only eleven. I sat between Farington and Rooker at Mr. Tyler's end of the table. Drank moderately.

SATURDAY 15 MARCH. Took a beefsteak dinner with Mr. Hingeston. Was somewhat heated with wine. ㅿㅿ.

SUNDAY 16 MARCH. Not at chapel in morning. ㅿㅿ. ㅿㅿ. But was there in the afternoon.

MONDAY 17 MARCH. It occurred to me that as Corsica was by the assistance of British force ere this time free from the French power, some person might be employed to go thither on the part of this country as Minister or Commissioner, or under some denomination, to ne-

---

[5]In Fleet Street. It stocked English, Irish, and Scottish newspapers.

[6]While in town the Bishop and his family were staying in a rented house at this address (information kindly supplied by Mr. Francis Sheppard).

[7]That is, the House of Lords upheld the decision of the Court of Session, the Appeal of the Newnham-Everett bankers was denied, and Boswell's client won the suit.

[8]Joseph Towers, LL.D., author of a biography of Johnson published in 1786 that respectfully but firmly criticized his political ideas.

gotiate with the inhabitants, who would probably form a connection with us,[9] and I thought I had a good claim to that appointment. I consulted with Sir John Dick, who said, "Time and chance happen to all men. I really think this will succeed." I therefore wrote a letter to Mr. Dundas, of which Sir John approved, dined at home quietly, and sent it in the evening.

[Boswell to Henry Dundas]

Great Portland Street, 17 March 1794

DEAR SIR,—Eleven years are now elapsed since I received from you a letter expressing in very cordial terms your inclination to befriend me in my views of obtaining some promotion; and during all that period in which I have seen numbers successful, and found myself entirely neglected, I trust I have given you as little trouble as any person who was flattered with reasonable hopes of your kind assistance. It is four years since I last had a conversation with you by appointment at Somerset Place;[1] and painful as its fruitlessness has been, I have made every allowance for the multiplicity both of your occupations and of those who press upon you from various quarters.

An occasion, however, so peculiar now offers for my applying to you, that I should upbraid myself if I omitted it. The success of His Majesty's forces by sea and land against the French and their adherents in Corsica leaves no doubt that by this time that island is totally free from any subjection to the horrible power to which I am at a loss to give a name. Of course the brave inhabitants will wish to form a connection with Great Britain, which certainly may be of considerable advantage to us. Whatever shall be the nature of that connection, some person must necessarily be appointed there as Minister or Commissioner or under some denomination on the part of this country. Permit me, then, to offer my services, and to request that I may be recommended to His Majesty to be employed in that capacity. My knowledge of Corsica, and my having been the first man by whose means authen-

---

[9]Starting in January 1794, British land and sea forces helped the Corsicans to drive out the French garrisons, and negotiations were now under way to determine the status of the island. In a letter to the Rev. Andrew Burnaby and Tiberius Cavallo, dated 22 February 1794, with a postscript to Boswell, Paoli expressed the hope of seeing Corsica "free under the protection of or in union with Great Britain"; that is, he welcomed the annexation of Corsica by the British as long as the Corsicans retained their internal self-government. The British, in turn, were interested in acquiring Corsica as a military base in the Mediterranean.

[1]Dundas's encouraging letter has not survived, nor does the journal record a meeting with Dundas in 1789 or 1790 when, as Treasurer of the Navy, he occupied an office in Somerset Place.

tic information of its importance was obtained,[2] my long and continued intimacy with General Paoli, and the consideration how agreeable it would be to him and to the people in general, that I should be sent thither, seems, I cannot help thinking, to have such weight as almost to preclude competition, and should I be so fortunate as to be honoured with a trust which would of all be to me the most pleasing, you may be assured of my utmost attention and zeal to fulfil its duties.

Should I be supposed too confident upon this subject, give me leave to refer you to Sir John Dick, whom you will unquestionably look upon to be a most competent judge, from his long residence as British consul at Leghorn and from his long acquaintance both with General Paoli and myself. I am, dear Sir, your faithful and most obedient servant,

JAMES BOSWELL

TUESDAY 18 MARCH. Dined at Mr. Wilkes's in Grosvenor Square; Mr. Trevanion, Member for Dover, a Bristol merchant, and a jolly, conversable man who Mr. Wilkes said was the keeper of the wild beasts in the Tower,[3] and Miss Wilkes made the company; there was pleasantry united with jollity. I drank too liberally and ended the evening at the MOUNT in an intoxicated state with Dick Penn, Sir Charles Farnaby, etc., and made an appointment for a dinner the following Friday at Freemasons' Tavern.

WEDNESDAY 19 MARCH. Called at Dilly's and had by chance an agreeable dinner with him and Cumberland, though it was somewhat clouded by Millington being there. We played whist and I lost, as I generally happen to do at Dilly's. Then went to the Essex Head Club.

THURSDAY 20 MARCH. Dined at the Bishop of London's, where I met my friend Langton, who had called on me the day before, and for the first time the Rev. Mr. Cracherode, the celebrated scholar and collector of books, whom I was surprised to find a very pleasant man; also Mr. Jacob Bryant.[4] We had the best day that I ever had at my Lord

---

[2]Boswell was not overstating his case. It was he who after his tour of Corsica in 1765 had given the British public a vivid impression of the state of the island in newspaper articles and his *Account of Corsica,* and who had tried to persuade the Government, which was following a policy of strict non-intervention, to help Paoli and his followers in their struggle for independence.

[3]Apparently three different guests: John Trevanion, M.P.; a Bristol merchant; and the keeper of the popular menagerie in the Tower.

[4]The Rev. Clayton Mordaunt Cracherode was a recluse who devoted himself to buying rare early editions, prints, coins, and gems; on his death in 1799 he bequeathed his huge collection of rare books to the British Museum. Bryant, the former librarian of Blenheim Palace and fellow of King's College, Cambridge, had written much-discussed treatises on ancient history, mythology, and the Old Testament.

of London's. Langton and I having been both asked to dine at Windham's, went thither in the evening and found him and Malone, who had dined tête-à-tête, and had a cold collation and wine and good talk.

FRIDAY 21 MARCH. Was for a rarity one of a tavern party, as fixed at the Mount. We met, eight: Dick Penn, Sir Charles Farnaby, Sir John Honywood, Colonel Wasey, late of the Horse Guards, Charles Dering, late of the Foot Guards, brother to Sir Edward,[5] Parson Newman, Mr. Thornhill, a Berkshire Squire, and myself. Our dinner was excellent, our wines abundant and good, our conversation that of hearty *bons vivants*. We drank copiously. But Sir John Honywood and I had a cordial bottle of claret after all the rest of the company were gone.

SATURDAY 22 MARCH. Was much heated and somewhat giddy. But walked a good deal and recovered. Dined at Mr. Hastings's, a small company: only he and his lady, Miss Payne who lived with them, Miss Bristow, born in India and about to go there again—*a beautiful export*, as I called her—Major Scott, and the Rev. Mr. Burn, formerly chaplain at Calcutta. The same elegance of entertainment.[6] Mrs. Hastings mentioned her having shot a tiger, and signified an inclination to do the same to *a man in this country from his resemblance to a tiger* (very naturally resenting Burke's persecution of her husband). Major Scott told us that Gibbon had said, "I have heard of eternity of punishment, but never of eternity of trial." I stayed the evening and played whist and lost a little. But what is very strange, I do not recollect whether Mr. Hastings played.

SUNDAY 23 MARCH. Was at Portland Chapel, I think both morning and afternoon. Dined at Malone's with Langton, Windham, Courtenay. I have lost the faculty of recording conversations. Or perhaps I have seen and heard so much now that no conversation impresses me much.

MONDAY 24 MARCH. I had a curious and pleasing party. Mr. Rham, a German who had been at Utrecht when I was there in 1763 and 4, and whom I had not seen for thirty years all but three months, was now in London. I had him, the Rev. M. de la Guiffardière, Reader to the Queen, and the Rev. Mr. Rose, who had all been with me there

[5]Farnaby, Honywood, and Sir Edward Dering were M.P.s for various Kent constituencies. Charles Dering was Farnaby's brother-in-law.
[6]By Miss Bristow Boswell presumably means Marian Brisco, the daughter of Hastings's aide-de-camp, who was born in the Hastingses' house in Calcutta and lived with them in England for several years before returning to India in 1794. Major John Scott had been another of Hastings's aides-de-camp and a major in the East India Company's armed forces; from 1781 he served as Hastings's representative in England, where his excessive zeal on behalf of Hastings was thought to have goaded Burke into starting the impeachment proceedings.

at the same time and were members with me of a *société littéraire,* to dine with me today.[7] It was luckily to be a holiday at Westminster next day, so that my son James came home in time to see us *four worthies*[8] enjoying ourselves; and he engaged that we should all dine with him on that day thirty years. I felt some uneasiness that I was so far advanced in years without having any employment in the state. Mr. Masseria and my brother T.D. and his wife were also with us.

TUESDAY 25 MARCH. Dined at Marquess Townshend's with Langton, Mr. Greenwood the agent, Mr. John Beresford (son of the Honourable John, quite a Teague), Miss Shaw (an elderly, fat, vulgar Scotchwoman), the widow of Menzies of Culdares who had married Miss Shaw's brother, Miss Menzies, her daughter by Culdares,[9] Lady Townshend, two daughters, and son, Lord Frederick. A weary day, and little wine. Early to tea. Colonel Barré was added then to the company.[1] But I had got into bad humour, sat at a distance with Lord Frederick, and stole home soon. I am become too fastidious.

WEDNESDAY 26 MARCH. Dined at home. Drank only water. Some days before, I had received a cold Ministerial letter from Dundas, informing me that my services in Corsica could not be accepted.[2]

[7] Rose, a fellow Scotsman, tutored Boswell in Greek and became his frequent companion in Utrecht; he had taken holy orders in the mean time. The Rev. Charles de Guiffardière, already a clergyman in Utrecht, surprised Boswell by his worldly views on love and manners; he was now established in London as French Reader to the Queen, teacher of French to the princesses, and preacher in the Protestant French chapel in St. James's Palace. The literary society, of which Boswell was a founding member, consisted of students who met once a week to speak French and listen to each others' speeches. Johann Christoph Wilhelm von Rham spoke on the passions on 30 March 1764.

[8] Exemplary figures—an allusion to the Nine Worthies, historical and legendary figures from ancient and medieval times.

[9] John Claudius Beresford was the son of Boswell's acquaintance John Beresford, the influential M.P. in the Irish House of Commons; Teague, the Anglicized version of the Irish name Tadhg, suggests the stereotyped Irishman. In March 1795 young Beresford married Elizabeth Mackenzie Menzies, the only daughter of Boswell's Edinburgh acquaintance Archibald Menzies of Culdares and his widow, now Mrs. Shaw.

[1] Isaac Barré, whose name reflects his Huguenot descent, had served as lt.-colonel in various North American campaigns (the American city Wilkes-Barre is named after him together with John Wilkes). As an M.P. from 1761 to 1790, he was known for his fiery invective in the House. He was now blind.

[2] "I regret that it is not in my power to avail myself of your services in this instance, but I think it right to apprise you that should our endeavours in Corsica be crowned with ultimate success, the powers already vested in Sir Gilbert Elliot fully embrace all objects relative to that island which in such case may be brought under consideration" (Dundas to Boswell, 23 March 1794). Elliot, who had arrived in Corsica in December 1793 as representative of the British government and was carrying on the negotiations with Paoli, did not yet have an official title. He was named provisional Viceroy in June.

Courtenay was clear from it that Dundas had no inclination to do anything for me, but the contrary. I was not very sorry that this particular application had failed, for I had begun to shrink from the thoughts of quitting London and going among foreigners, etc., etc. But it hurt me to think that Dundas, after his apparently cordial professions, was minded to neglect me totally. However, I thought of pressing him resolutely.

THURSDAY 27 MARCH. Again dined at home and drank only water. Felt myself really the better for this regimen. Having said to Cumberland that I would go and see his new comedy, *The Box-Lobby Challenge*, went tonight to the Haymarket Theatre and saw it and *The Children in the Wood*.[3] Was pleased to find that I yet could relish theatrical entertainments pretty well.

FRIDAY 28 MARCH. Dined at Royal Academy Club, a small party. Relished wine. We had tonight after tea and coffee a couple of bottles of madeira *extra*, paid by those who remained, individually.

SATURDAY 29 MARCH. Dined at the Bishop of Salisbury's with Hon. Daines Barrington, Mr. Malone, Sir Grey Cooper, and Master Graves,[4] whom I never had met before. We had a good rational day, yet wine enough.

SUNDAY 30 MARCH. Was, I think, at Portland Chapel in the morning. Dined at Mr. Ross Mackye's with Dr. Stuart, Bishop of St. David's (who had asked that I might be of the party), and Lord Glasgow. It was quiet and agreeable. After the Bishop was gone, I asked and had another bottle, which was rather too much. Mackilston's brother[5] was engaged to dine with me. My children took care of him.

MONDAY 31 MARCH. Dined at home, having Langton, Courtenay, Malone, Windham, and Mr. Humphry the painter with me. A good day.

TUESDAY 1 APRIL. Dined at the LITERARY CLUB; Sir Charles Blagden there for the first time.[6] I sat between the Bishop of Salisbury and Sir Joseph Banks. In the morning Windham, Langton, and I and my son James had been at Blackwall and seen a detachment from sev-

[3]*The Box-Lobby Challenge* dealt with a challenge to a duel in the lobby outside the boxes of a theatre. *The Children in the Wood* was a popular opera with libretto by Thomas Morton and music by Samuel Arnold.
[4]Cooper was a former M.P. and had also held posts in the Treasury. William Graves was a master of Chancery and a bencher of the Middle Temple.
[5]The brother of John Shaw Alexander of Mackilston, a former client of Boswell's who had lent him £500 some years earlier.
[6]Sir Charles Blagden—he was knighted two years earlier—had been elected to The Club on 18 March.

eral regiments of cavalry embark for Ostend; part of George Campbell's corps and himself.[7] The fatigue had made me more susceptible of the effects of wine. I talked too much and too confidently of insisting on the object of our war with France being *defined*. The Duke of Leeds and Langton and I sat a long time after the rest were gone.

WEDNESDAY 2 APRIL. Was restless. Walked into City. ᗰ . Dined at Hingeston's. As he went out soon, was loose.[8] Sat a long time at the Chapter Coffee-house. Then went to Essex Head Club. Had an apprehension that I was not in good health.

THURSDAY 3 APRIL. Mackilston's brother dined with me. He was going out surgeon's mate in an East India ship. In the evening at Mrs. Poole's and played whist.

FRIDAY 4 APRIL. Dined at Mr. Cator's with Mr. Jeffreys, town clerk of Bath, a great crony of Lord Camden's,[9] a sly, talking old fellow with an affectation of heartiness, and withal such a knowledge of legal forms and their history as made me ashamed of my ignorance. Miss Dennison came to stay some nights with my daughters.

SATURDAY 5 APRIL. My apprehension of illness had now vanished. Dined at Mr. Syms's, wine-merchant, with Mr. Dilly and some more company. Played whist and won.

SUNDAY 6 APRIL. Was at Portland Chapel, evening service, and dined at home.

MONDAY 7 APRIL. Dined at Mr. Malone's, only he and I.

TUESDAY 8 APRIL. Had at dinner Mr. Dilly and his sister, who had come to see him, Counsellors Leach and Const, Seward, Mr. James Cuninghame. Whist in the evening.

WEDNESDAY 9 APRIL. Sauntered about a great deal and had no dinner. Excess yesterday had heated me.

THURSDAY 10 APRIL. Miss Dennison left us. My daughters and I dined at Mr. Dilly's with his sister and Mrs. Dickenson, his opposite neighbour, a genteel woman, Deputy Nichols, and Counsellor Leach; an extraordinary good dinner even for Dilly. Played whist in the evening.

FRIDAY 11 APRIL. Dined at the Royal Academy Club, a pretty numerous meeting, but was obliged to leave it earlier than usual, as

---

[7]Blackwall, which owes its name to the blackish embankment of the Thames, was an important dock area in the East End. George James Campbell, the orphaned son of James Campbell of Treesbank and of Margaret Boswell's sister Mary, was Boswell's ward; he had been a cornet in the 7th Regiment of Dragoons since 1786.

[8]That is, at loose ends.

[9]Charles Pratt, first Earl Camden, formerly Lord Chancellor and now Lord President of the Privy Council, had been Recorder of Bath since 1759.

my daughters called on me by appointment to go to a party at Mrs. Cator's, where I played whist and had some conversation with Dr. Vincent, master of Westminster School.

SATURDAY 12 APRIL. Walked into the City, and being kindly asked by Dilly, dined with him and his sister. Nobody could be found to play whist with us. In the evening I was lucky enough to find Mr. George Dance at home, and ended it pleasantly with him.

[EDITORIAL NOTE. This entry marks the end of Boswell's full journal. Only a few more notes, all of them fragmentary, have survived. Fortunately, however, Boswell's extensive correspondence together with the reports of his friends and acquaintances makes it possible to trace his manifold activities during the remaining thirteen months of his life.

In April Boswell involved himself even more energetically in the affairs of the Royal Academy. At issue was the Professorship of Ancient History, which had been made vacant by the death of Edward Gibbon on 16 January. Boswell began a determined campaign to secure the appointment of William Mitford, of whose conservative *History of Greece* he approved, and to prevent the appointment of John Gillies, whom he suspected of "democratical" principles. In a letter dated 28 April 1794 and addressed to the members of the Academy, Boswell drew attention not only to Mitford's distinction as a historian but also to "his respectable character as a gentleman, a Member of Parliament, and a colonel of militia." So strong were Boswell's feelings that as late as 29 December he wrote to Farington threatening to resign as Secretary for Foreign Correspondence if Gillies were elected. Because of the violent disagreements among the Academicians, the King refused to fill the vacancy at this time; when the appointment was finally made nearly a quarter of a century later, it went to Boswell's candidate, Mitford.

Boswell had planned to be at Auchinleck early in June but delayed his departure. Perhaps he did so to hear Burke's long summation of the prosecution's case against Hastings, which began on 28 May. Farington noted in his diary that Boswell accompanied him to the trial on 14 June and that "Burke was very dull and tedious." When Burke completed his statement two days later, Boswell sent a note to Hastings congratulating him on no longer having to submit to public abuse in the House of Commons. Not that this was the end of Hastings's trial; only in April 1795 did the House of Lords finally acquit him of wrongdoing in his management of Indian affairs.

Before leaving London, Boswell tried to get a grip on his finances. He could count on some income from the sale of the second edition of the *Life of Johnson*—108 sets since the beginning of the year. But as his jottings of 24 June reveal, he had to make various payments, including the sum of £37 to Mrs. Hockley, whose school Betsy was about to leave. Moreover, taking the two older girls with him to Auchinleck threatened to be costly. As early as 10 May Boswell complained to Sandy: "I really cannot afford the expense of carrying them down and back again, and their making a suitable appearance in Scotland." On the other hand, he realized that the girls needed marital opportunities and that "to give them a chance of being *properly established,* they should be in their own country."

Taking the two girls with him, Boswell left London on 26 June and arrived at Auchinleck on 1 July. Sandy, who had spent the winter studying in Edinburgh, had been in Ayrshire since the end of May. Betsy and Jamie stayed behind in London, the former starting at Mrs. Stevenson's boarding-school in Soho Square, the latter attending the summer term at Westminster School. To keep in touch, Boswell wrote long weekly letters to Jamie, and these give as vivid an impression of his concerns and shifting moods as did his journals of earlier days. The first of the following excerpts was written at Carlisle; the subsequent ones at Auchinleck.]

[Boswell to James Boswell, Jr., 30 June 1794]

Your sisters were so weary...that I resolved to stay quietly here, where we have been very well....Your sisters have upon the whole behaved better than I expected, though they have sometimes irritated me by talking wild nonsense about London. You know their topics. I trust that they will grow insensibly more rational. As for myself, I am in wonderfully good spirits, and looking forward with glee to being tomorrow at the seat of our ancestors.

[Boswell to James Boswell, Jr., 7 July 1794]

Soon were we in the parish of Auchinleck, which warmed my heart. Your sisters were not at all pleased and talked a deal of nonsense, such as that...the country appeared naked and wild. When we arrived at the Place, your brother was somewhere between [it] and the Old House. But Andrew Gibb having seen him at a distance and made him a signal, he came running with great speed and joyfully met us severally on the green behind the house. We had comfortable tea as usual at Auchinleck, a little walk out, and a good supper. Your sisters continued to talk strangely, but finding themselves not minded, they very sensibly begin to reconcile themselves to their situation, as well they may, for it is both agreeable and respectable. The weather is very fine. I have walked about with much satisfaction....

I am not as yet able to write a long letter, being relaxed by the heat and out of the habit of writing. My spirits, however, are wonderfully good, and I have never once since I came here been in that state of irritation in which you have so often seen me.

[Boswell to James Boswell, Jr., 14 July 1794]

MY DEAR JAMES,—Your letter of the 5th instant gave me no small pleasure. It suggests solid, wise counsel concerning your sisters. The distinction between what *ought* to be, and what as affairs now stand *can* be done, is exceedingly just; and you will be glad to know that I act in conformity to it in a degree far beyond what I expected I could do. I now and then have broke forth a little, but I assure you not often and by no means with that violence which you have observed in London. I have not drunk half a bottle of wine any day since I came here, some days not more than two glasses, some none at all. This moderation I am convinced has produced a calmness in my blood and spirits very different from the effects of too free living in the metropolis....

Your brother I found very desirous of going to Leith races[1] which are this week, so he left us on Friday. I heard him read some of Horace only one morning. When he returns, I shall hear him read both Greek and Latin every day, and shall be also at pains gently to correct a loud familiarity of manner and a very broad pronunciation which he has acquired by being so long in Scotland and so much of late among his inferiors.

[Boswell to James Boswell, Jr., 21 July 1794]

It gave me great concern to find that you had found no letter on Saturday sennight, which with reason made you uneasy, and you would have had just cause to complain, had I failed to write, which was not the case. I do not forget what you mention, that holding a kind of conversation with us every Saturday is a comfort which you should have during our absence. You are certainly well entitled to it, considering your manly behaviour in not only not complaining of your being left in London without us but even steadily advising me to carry your sisters down, as it might probably be of great advantage to them. And I

---

[1] Horse races on the sands of Leith, a seaport near Edinburgh, that were carried on in a carnival atmosphere.

really flatter myself that it will. They seem to be fully as well entertained as in London, and that in a manner which does not dissipate their minds and fret me, so that there is scarcely any degree of that feverish altercation which was so painful to me and which you saw with so much concern. They both of them improve in riding. The little piebald pony is perfectly quiet and carries them well. They have had strawberries and raspberries preserved and black-currant jelly made....To tell you the truth, I like this quiet life much better than if I had much company to entertain.

[Boswell to James Boswell, Jr., 30 July 1794]

I have very little inclination to visit, and to tell you the truth, am heartily weary. My only satisfaction is in showing kindness to the people.[2] I am reading Clarendon's *History*,[3] but have as yet gone on slowly. It is shocking to observe the abominable conduct of the rebellious rascals in the beginning of Charles the First's reign. I shall see it grow worse and worse as I proceed.

[Boswell to James Boswell, Jr., 11 August 1794]

My old friends the Corsicans are (between ourselves) a strange people. They were enthusiastically fond, or professed to be so, of the *Republic of France,* a part of which they agreed to be. Now they are or profess to be equally so of the *British Monarchy*, of which they have agreed to be subjects. I own I do not much relish their throwing themselves under a foreign power,[4] and I do not think it was necessary because I think an *alliance* might have been made, which would have been more honourable for them. Perhaps, however, this could not be adjusted, and if our King's authority be only *nominal*, and the essential interests and independency of Corsica be maintained, that brave little nation may after struggling for ages be at last in a flourishing and happy state. I cannot on this occasion but feel somewhat indignant, both because the administration of this country was formerly deaf to all my represen-

---

[2]The tenants on the estate.

[3]The monumental *History of the Rebellion and Civil Wars in England.*

[4]Boswell's misgivings were justified. Corsica had become a British protectorate, but the arrangement proved to be short-lived. Mutual irritation developed between Paoli and Sir Gilbert Elliot, who was formally appointed Viceroy in the autumn of 1794. In October 1795 Paoli was eased out and returned to England, where he spent the remaining twelve years of his life in comfortable retirement; and the Corsicans soon rose up against the British, forcing them to evacuate the island in September 1796. Thereupon the French returned and once more made Corsica their province.

tations in favour of our protecting the Corsicans…and because I am totally neglected in a business which I have certainly the best claim to be employed in.…

My spirits are very bad at present, so that I cannot write to you so much or so well as I could wish. Today we are putting in hay, which makes no small stir. Tomorrow the shooting-season begins, and Sandy is all impatience to begin.

[Boswell to James Boswell, Jr., 22 August 1794]

MY DEAR JAMES,—Believe me I have been and am at this moment (half past eleven at night) not a little uneasy to think that tomorrow you will not receive a letter from me as usual upon Saturday. The reason is, that upon due consideration it appeared that it would have given great offence should your sisters have gone to Edinburgh the very week previous to the administration of the Holy Sacrament in our parish church, as it would have been obvious that they intended to shun it and the days of public worship which you know are by the custom of this country appropriated to that occasion.[5] They therefore agreed to return on Saturday night from Mrs. Montgomerie's, and the week after they remained here, and I had the satisfaction to have them attending the Sacrament with all the days appointed on account of it. Veronica made at first some scruple to be a communicant here, as she had taken the Sacrament in the Church of England, which she maintained made her of that church, so that it would be wrong in her to communicate in another. But I satisfied her, I trust, that the difference is only in form, and that both churches are fellow Christians who commemorate the death of our Saviour in obedience to his sacred dying commands. Euphemia objected for some time that she was not fit. But when the day came, both of them communicated decently. I was sorry that I could not persuade your brother to join. After having been confirmed, in which ordinance[6] he took the vows of a Christian upon himself, he needed not have had any difficulty to partake of the Lord's Supper, as I am convinced that both his faith and practice are such as are not unsuitable to a Christian. He however attended church regularly unless[7] on Saturday, when he was indisposed. I hope he shall ere

[5]The taking of Communion on Sacrament Day—preceded by a week of intense preaching—was an important annual event in Ayrshire. The stern sermonizing of the Presbyterian clergymen and the more worldly concerns of their congregation are satirized in Robert Burns's *Holy Fair* (1786).
[6]Religious ceremony.
[7]Except.

long come to think it both his privilege and his duty to be a communicant.

[Boswell to James Boswell, Jr., 6 September 1794]

I am ashamed to say that I have been so idle as not yet to have finished the first volume of Clarendon's *History,* though it be but a small one.... The explanation is that since I came to this place, and indeed for a considerable time before, I have had an indolence of mind and a kind of deadness as to all intellectual pursuits. But I will try to rouse my spirit and do better.

For all my hopes of writing enough, I must now (Monday 8 September) finish this as I am setting out for the Circuit at Ayr. But I shall write more next post.

[Boswell to James Boswell, Jr., 12 September 1794]

MY DEAR JAMES,—So I did go to the Circuit at Ayr on Monday, and dined with Lord Abercrombie, the judge,[8] who had with him about thirty at table. But alas, your sagacious counsel to think of the *Lord of Sessionship* was counteracted, for I felt that a very moderate situation in London is to *me* far preferable to one of the most respectable in Scotland. I am afraid there is no help for this long-continued and rooted way of thinking. I must be as long at Auchinleck as I can, and do the estate and the people as much good as may be in my power. But truly the manners of England and the infinite variety of acquaintance and of important objects in the metropolis give me such a gratification that I may at least say that "the load of life," as Johnson calls it in his Prologue to *The Good-Natured Man,* is three-fourths lighter to me. And I still indulge a visionary, pleasing hope that I may obtain some preferment of consequence. You may depend on my resolutely remaining at Auchinleck this year till after Christmas. But I cannot hold out longer than January or at farthest February.

[Boswell to James Boswell, Jr., 24 September 1794]

I am glad to find that there are no more disturbances in London. The war, I am afraid, is pretty generally unpopular. It is astonishing how these abandoned wretches the French hold together and act with so

---

[8]Boswell had known Alexander Abercrombie in Edinburgh for at least twenty years. He had been a Writer to the Signet, was elevated to the bench of the Court of Session as Lord Abercrombie in 1792, and was now on circuit at Ayr.

much resolution. Lord Eglinton named me one of his deputies as Lord Lieutenant of Ayrshire. But I did not choose to accept of any commission under a man of whom I have a sorry opinion,[9] and besides, he named so many, and some of these such persons that it was no credit to be of the number. I however do what I can, as a landholder and a Justice of the Peace, to inculcate good principles of loyalty and due subordination.

[Boswell to James Boswell, Jr., 6 October 1794]

I have finished one volume of Clarendon's *History* and am a good way in the second. But I read heavily. I never was in a more stupid state of mind than at present. To have no prospect of promotion in London quite vexes me. I must contrive to live there as economically as possible, and indulge the hope that something good may yet happen, for indeed I cannot settle in Scotland, though I am very willing to be a part of the year at Auchinleck. I long much to see you, and the time till Christmas seems very, very long.

[In answer to Boswell's complaining letters, Jamie wrote consoling comments that are remarkable for their maturity. Soon they were engaged in a lively exchange concerning Boswell's depression and expectations.]

[James Boswell, Jr. to Boswell, 18 October 1794]

Am sorry to find you writing about "your dull and depressed spirits." Pray, Sir, do not suffer yourself to be melancholy. Think not on your having missed preferment in London or any of these kind of things, the unreasonableness of which you yourself upon reflection must be sensible of if you consider that your manner of living has never been that of a man of business and that, in short, you have been entirely different in every respect from those who have been (in that line) more successful—they who have obtained places and pensions etc. have not the fame of having been the biographer of Johnson or the conscious exultation of a man of genius. They have not enjoyed your happy and convivial hours. They have not been known to Johnson, Voltaire, Rousseau, and Garrick, Goldsmith, etc., etc. They have not visited the patriots of Corsica. In short, would you rather than have enjoyed so many advantages have been a rich, though dull, plodding lawyer? You cannot expect to be both at the same time. Every situation in life has

[9]See above, 8 April 1791.

its advantages and disadvantages....Let me then have in your next letter a declaration that you are now in excellent spirits.

[Boswell to James Boswell, Jr., 27 October 1794]

MY DEAR JAMES,—Last night I had the pleasure to receive a most sensible and animating letter from you concerning my depression of spirits and complaining of want of success in life; and truly, I must acknowledge that "thou reasonest well."[1] For I am at all times satisfied that the circumstances in my lot which you enumerate are to me more valuable than any place or pension which I could have had without them. But unluckily I have all my life indulged fond hopes of raising myself, and of consequence my family, by obtaining some preferment which would be both honourable and profitable. In the common estimation of mankind a Lord of Session's place would have realized that hope. In mine, however, whose views were enlarged by being so much in England, any provincial appointment has long appeared beneath me. The manners of Edinburgh, too, disgusted me and, in short, LONDON has for these thirty years and upwards been the object of my wish as my scene of exertion. Much enjoyment have I had there, but as yet every ambitious aim has been disappointed. My constitutional melancholy is ever lurking about me, and perhaps I should impute to this the chief part of my unhappiness. The country does not at all suit me. I have no relish of its amusements or occupations. My temper is gloomy and irritable, and I am continually fretted by hearing of trespasses upon my woods and lands, and tenants falling behind in their rents. Add to this that my circumstances are so straitened that I am in a wretched state of uneasiness how to get my family supported, and at the same time pay the annuities and interest of debts which must be annually cleared. The expense of living here is much greater to me than in London. The wine and corn and hay consumed cost me half as much every week or more than all that is laid out in town; and then there must here be every day a dinner sufficient for a company, as we cannot be sure of being alone. I do not think I have had two comfortable days, putting together all the hours which should be reckoned so, since the 1st of July when I arrived here. Entertaining company is a weary labour to me, and when I pay visits I seem to myself to be fighting battles, yet I dread returning to London with your sisters, who distressed me so much there.

[1]Addison, *Cato*, V. i. 1—Cato's praise of Plato for having recognized the human longing for immortality.

[James Boswell, Jr., to Boswell, 10 November 1794]

I have now two letters of yours to answer....In that of the 27th of October you say, "I am at all times satisfied that the circumstances in my lot which you enumerate are to me more valuable than any place or pension I could have had *without them.*" By which you seem to mean that you wished for preferment with them. Look round the world; observe them who are rising at the bar, in the state or any occupation. Do they live in that manner? Very differently indeed! Hard at work, surrounded with papers, poring over Coke upon Littleton, etc., without one moment to themselves, hardly. When you see Warren rising from the middle of his dinner to go (perhaps out of town) to a patient, Mansfield (as his son informs me he very frequently was obliged to do) going to bed with his papers by his bedside, do you envy him his money? I dare to say you do not. Such is the life that must be led by those who acquire money.

You complain of your constitutional melancholy. That, to be sure, together with other vexatious circumstances, sometimes harasses you. But who so merry and gay as you in company, though at times gloomy at home? Why may it not be so their happiness may be as much put on as yours is? I have since your absence been pretty frequently at my uncle's and I know that he (for one) is very far from being happy. ...With such a share of felicity as you have now, and have had, I see no reason why you should be discontented. Read Clarendon, or if you find that he is tedious lay him down and take up some other book....Or rather, what I would advise you to do is something in the way of an author—any little pamphlet or anything to keep you going. Write a play. What's become of *The Pawnbroker* and *The Improver,*[2] etc., etc. Don't give way to your melancholy but drive it off; there are a thousand ways.

[Boswell to James Boswell, Jr., 21 November 1794]

MY DEAR JAMES,—Before me lies your admirable letter of the 10th, in which you write *de consolatione*[3] like a true philosopher, who has observed human life and made just reflections. I will try to avoid repining. Yet at the same time I cannot be contented merely with literary fame and social enjoyments. I must still hope for some creditable employment, and perhaps I may yet attain it.

---

[2]These projects are not mentioned in Boswell's journal or other writings.
[3]An allusion to the medieval Roman philosopher Boethius's *De consolatione philosophiae,* which teaches that there is no security in worldly goods or honours but only in virtue.

[Boswell's depression seems to have been intensified by the many guests who, according to the Auchinleck Book of Company, came for dinner or overnight in increasing numbers after the summer. A few of the young women invited by Veronica and Euphemia stayed for two weeks or a month apiece. But Boswell also encouraged guests. In mid-November he invited three officers of the 4th Dragoons to a fête for which twenty-two persons spent the night at Auchinleck and dancing went on until four in the morning. So successful was this party that the girls invited the officers and an equally large company to similar festivities in December.

For the most part, however, Boswell remained gloomy and full of misgivings about his future. To Malone he wrote on 18 November: "I have little more business to transact here. But why go to London? What have I to do there? I can see no prospect in life but a thick fog. Could I but recover those pleasing delusions which braced my nerves when I first entered Westminster Hall! In short, could I have any object!" And in his fragmentary "Pathetic Song" begun at Mauchline on 11 December, Boswell expressed a more general disenchantment:

> 'Tis o'er, 'tis o'er, the dream is o'er,
> And Life's delusion is no more.

After these two lines, the only ones he set down, he summarized the rest: "The subject must be the gay hopes indulged in youth, and the apathy which years and disappointment produce."

Still, Boswell derived some satisfaction from taking care of estate affairs—meeting his tenants, getting roads built, riding out to inspect his farms. He also enjoyed a brief exercise of his legal talents in solving a local mystery. In the spring of 1793 a young man named Mungo Miller had been found dead in a Mauchline street. Although foul play was suspected, the evidence at the time was considered insufficient to bring anyone to trial. But rumours persisted, and Boswell, together with three judges, held renewed hearings in September and December 1794. When they eventually concluded that Miller had indeed been murdered, Boswell wrote the report to the Lord Advocate, showing his skill in marshalling the evidence.]

[Boswell to Robert Dundas, Lord
Advocate, 27 December 1794]

It now clearly appears that Mungo Miller's death was not occasioned by a fall where his body was discovered, as was industriously reported by the persons liable to suspicion, because the witness by whom he was first found lying on the street (and who never was examined till he appeared before us) describes him to be lying in such a situation as is totally inconsistent with that supposition, and the surgeon of Mauchline, an intelligent man, gives his reasons for thinking it impossible that he could have received the cause of his death on the spot where his corpse was found. Therefore, the natural conclusion is that there must have been either murder or manslaughter. The last place where he was ever seen alive was in the house of John Thomson, innkeeper in Mauchline, where he was drinking the night before, and certain persons were there with him, one of whom is proved to have been owing him money on the Saturday before his decease. It is positively denied by John Thomson and his family, as also by those persons, that he was drinking there or passed any time there; it is only admitted that he called at the door and promised to return in a quarter of an hour to pay two notes but never did. The supposition of his having died a violent death in that house is strongly confirmed by tracing drops of blood from John Thomson's backyard towards the place where his corpse was found, and the strong presumptive evidence that his watch was the very night of his death seen in the hands of Janet Thomson, the innkeeper's daughter, one of the persons who was drinking with him, who gave a false account of it, and imposed upon the sheriff another watch which she had borrowed at Cumnock for the purpose, and sold a watch at Dumfries, which we can have no doubt was Mungo Miller's.

[Describing the Miller case to Jamie on 15 December, Boswell declared: "I have a real satisfaction in taking so much pains and trouble for the sake of justice and quieting the minds of the relations of the deceased." He also mentioned that his spirits had suddenly improved. Clearly, he was enjoying the peace and quiet of Auchinleck after Sandy returned to the university and while Veronica and Euphemia were visiting Lady Auchinleck in Edinburgh before their return to London. On 27 December he expressed his newly found sense of well-being to Jamie: "On Christmas Day I sat down by myself in my own dining-room to excellent leek soup, a roast turkey and a minced pie, with all which, having regaled myself sufficiently, I drank a bottle of rich *gold wine*.[4] In the evening I had coffee and Edinburgh seed-cake. But I read devoutly the service for the day, morning and evening." To celebrate New Year's Day he went to Rozelle, the Countess of Crawford's estate. He was pleased that his tenants paid their rents—more than £50—ten days earlier than usual, at his request, and that he could therefore pay

---

[4]Perhaps madeira, a heavy amber-coloured wine. At this time Boswell had several dozen bottles of 1777 madeira at Auchinleck.

off a bond that included part of the price of Knockroon. In the second week of January he left Auchinleck and by the nineteenth he was back in London.

Boswell threw himself into town life with relish. To Sandy he wrote on 23 February: "The *intellectual* luxury of London, after so long an absence from it, has no doubt *occupied* me much—or *dissipated* me so much, I believe I should rather say—that I have not been able to settle either to read or write with composure. But *wine* has had its share in the *effect*." He was, in fact, drinking heavily once more but was quite unconcerned about possible damage to his health.

His lifelong interest in Shakespeare led him in February to inspect the manuscripts and relics supposedly discovered but actually forged by William Henry Ireland, an enterprising eighteen-year-old lawyer's clerk, who sought to profit from the prevailing Shakespeare mania. According to Ireland, Boswell carefully examined both the appearance and the style of Ireland's Shakespeare papers, quenched his thirst with a brandy, and then, kneeling down, exclaimed: "I now kiss the invaluable relics of our bard: and thanks to God that I have lived to see them!" (*The Confessions of William Henry Ireland*, 1805, p. 96.) Malone, on the other hand, was not deceived and later published a pamphlet attacking the authenticity of Ireland's material.

Boswell's good mood persisted. Clearly feeling benevolent, he fulfilled an extraordinary promise he had made more than twenty years earlier to reward the infant Veronica for showing affection to Dr. Johnson during his visit to Edinburgh, when other members of the family had not shared Boswell's enthusiasm for Johnson.[5] At the 3 March meeting of The Club Boswell had several members witness a document granting Veronica a special gift of £500 to be paid after his death. Unhappily, Veronica had no opportunity to enjoy this gift, for she survived her father by only a few months.

On 4 March Boswell gave a carefully arranged dinner party at which he brought together a group of friends, including Malone and Farington, with Capt. George Wynyard, who had achieved a certain notoriety for his part in an extraordinary incident of second sight. While dining with another officer in Nova Scotia ten years earlier, Wynyard had seen an apparition of his brother John, who was then in England, and both Wynyard and his companion had discussed this strange happening with their fellow officers. Several months later news came from England that John Wynyard had died at precisely the time when he appeared to his brother in Nova Scotia. Boswell, who was always fas-

---

[5]"Her fondness for him endeared her still more to me, and I declared she should have five hundred pounds of additional fortune" (*Tour to the Hebrides*, 15 August 1773).

cinated by such stories, had readily accepted the truth of Wynyard's story when he heard it from Temple in 1789, but Reynolds and Malone had been highly sceptical. No doubt Boswell now took pleasure in letting Malone and other scoffers hear about the experience from Wynyard himself.

The next day, 5 March, Boswell asked George Dance, who had missed the Wynyard dinner, to a more intimate gathering. At the bottom of his copy of the invitation Boswell later described the evening: "He came, and he and I and Bourgeois and Seward and my brother and my two eldest daughters and my son James were most exceedingly pleasant and merry, talking all manner of lively nonsense mixed with sense, singing, dancing, acting *The Beggar's Opera,* in short, everything but drinking. We kept it up till about one in the morning, gay and uninflamed." Boswell was planning to write an essay on his favourite play.

He was, moreover, becoming involved with a real Newgate figure. Maj. James George Semple, alias Semple-Lisle or Lisle, was a notorious adventurer, a confidence man who had served in several armies on the Continent but who had also been repeatedly imprisoned for cheating people out of goods and money. Boswell heard of this colourful swindler by chance in a stage-coach from the wife of a stablekeeper, and his last known journal entry includes her account of how Semple tricked her.]

MONDAY 9 MARCH. Coffee and egg and marmalade. Wrote *éloge* for Sir Joshua's sale of pictures, and note to Sir Francis Bourgeois from Lady Inchiquin.[6] Too late at Golden Cross. Gravesend coach just gone out of the yard. Ran to overtake it. Jumped into the Woolwich *long.*[7] A fine, lively miss eat biscuit; asked a bit and got it. Pitt was abused by several male passengers and one, a sea-captain, said he wished he had him on board.[8] Mrs. ———, wife of a stablekeeper in Mark Lane, told us how she had been swindled by Major Semple, who drove into their

---

[6]Reynolds's collection of old masters was sold by the auctioneer James Christie on Friday, 13 March, and the three following weekdays. Prefixed to the sale catalogue is a tribute to Reynolds that may be Boswell's *éloge.* Presumably using part of the £200 legacy Reynolds had left him, Boswell bought three paintings at the sale.

[7]The stage-coach to Woolwich, a long coach that could seat about sixteen passengers. The Golden Cross Inn, Charing Cross, was a departure point for many coaches. Why Boswell was travelling in the direction of Woolwich and Gravesend, south-east of London, is unclear.

[8]Perhaps Pitt was being blamed for continuing the war against France—a war that had become increasingly unpopular. The Combined Armies had suffered crushing defeats on several fronts, and the remains of the British forces were being shipped back to England during this month.

yard in a hackney-coach, came out and talked with ——, ostler, saying he was Colonel Hale, brother of General (Bernard) Hale,[9] and just come from the Continent, that he had bought nine horses and wished them to stand in ——stables, and that ——would assist him to buy some more which he wanted. He then asked the ostler if he could change him a banknote, as he had not silver to pay his coach. He then pulled out a bunch of them seemingly and said he had not one under fifty. The ostler said he could not change it but he would run to some of the neighbours and try to get it changed. He did so but returned and said he could not. The ostler then said he might speak to his mistress. He accordingly conducted him to her; said....

[The fragment breaks off abruptly near the beginning of a line. But Boswell's connection with Semple did not end at this point. A few days later he received a note from Semple asking him to come to the prison where Semple was being held for the theft of a shirt. He was living comfortably enough in special lodgings, cheered by the visits of a woman friend, but his funds for such privileges were running out and he hoped for Boswell's help. After several visits, Boswell supported Semple's pleas to various officials to be allowed to leave the country permanently—to go to America, to undertake any military service, however dangerous—in short, to do almost anything to avoid being transported to Botany Bay. Boswell's letters on Semple's behalf were of no avail, however, nor were Burke's a few months later. In spite of a suicide attempt, Semple was transported and lived to experience further hair-raising adventures.

All this while Boswell was seeing old friends and making new ones. On 18 March he wrote to Sandy: "In truth I am wonderfully happy at present. What a varied life do I lead! Yesterday dined with Lord Delaval[1] at his princely house in Portman Square, where I am this winter for the first time *at home;* today at Newgate; tomorrow with the officer of the Guards at the Tower; Friday with a great clothier in Aldermanbury,[2] married to the niece of my rich friend Cator, the £30,000-at-least-man. The Earl of Inchiquin has given me dinner after dinner with admirable parties at his house."

[9]Gen. Bernard Hale, Lt.-Governor of Chelsea Hospital, in fact had a younger brother, John Hale, who was also in the army; he was, however, a general who had been promoted at the same time as Bernard Hale.
[1]John Hussey Delaval, 1st B. Delaval, now a widower in his late sixties, was known for his ostentatious living as early as the 1750s. He had been an M.P. from 1765 to 1786, when he was created Baron Delaval of Seaton Delaval and moved to the House of Lords.
[2]In the City, near the Guildhall.

But Boswell's drinking was becoming the talk of the town. When Charlotte Ann Francis, Fanny Burney's younger sister,[3] invited him and his daughters to a dinner-party, she was teasingly told by friends that he would not leave her house while he was still sober and might stay a week. At her dinner, he was highly entertaining but increasingly intoxicated. Mrs. Francis's description of the ensuing scene is the last glimpse we have of Boswell in society.]

[From the Journal of Charlotte Ann Francis, 11 March 1795]

We left the gentlemen a quarter before eight and they were so merry and jovial that we could not get them up till past ten....[They] at last came up, all very *lively,* but Boswell indisputably drunk. He hauled Veronica out of her seat that he might sit and have a quarter of an hour by Mrs. Francis, he said. He began by attempting to make love to me, but I was so grave that happily the love-fit wore off.

Before dinner I had put a dozen of wine on the chimney-piece in the back parlour with instructions to Charles to get out what was wanted. Somehow they discovered this *pile,*[4] as Boswell called it, and made merry with it accordingly.

I am sorry they were any of them tipsy, but as I have had so many merry visits at their houses, I am very glad they enjoyed themselves and were merry....I heard since they gave toasts from Shakespeare— when they were filling their glasses "measure for measure" was one.

[When a problem arose in relation to Johnson, however, Boswell showed that he could still be both firm and diplomatic. The Rev. Samuel Parr, LL.D., a classical scholar of note, had been asked by Reynolds and Seward to write the Latin epitaph to be inscribed on the Johnson monument. Parr had been working on it since 1791 and insisted that the members of The Club approve it sight unseen. Boswell knew Parr to be exceedingly touchy; in 1791 he had objected sharply to Boswell's suggesting in the *Life of Johnson* that several men of genius were competing to write the epitaph, and Boswell had soothed him by declaring that he had meant to suggest only that men of genius would or should compete with each other in undertaking this task. Now he was less willing to soothe Parr, and quite prepared to state plainly why a review of the epitaph was

---

[3]She was the widow of Dr. Clement Francis, a medical officer with the East India Company and Warren Hastings's surgeon, who had died in 1792. She later married Ralph Broome.

[4]Treasure. Charles was Mrs. Francis's brother, Charles Burney, Jr.

necessary. He expressed his views in a highly formal letter addressed to Malone, who may well have requested it in order to show it to Parr.]

[Boswell to Malone]

Great Portland Street, 13 April 1795

DEAR SIR,—Whatever respect you and I and all who take a concern in erecting a monument to Dr. Johnson may have for the learning and abilities of Dr. Parr, I am clear that we could not be justified in adopting implicitly without so much as having seen it, the inscription which that gentleman has written. We are answerable to the memory of our illustrious friend, to the present age, and to posterity. Let me add: we are answerable to another tribunal, without whose approbation of the epitaph the monument cannot be admitted into St. Paul's Church: I mean the Dean and Chapter of that Cathedral.

When Sir Joshua Reynolds asked Dr. Parr to furnish an epitaph, I cannot suppose that he meant to preclude even himself from all consideration, and all power of objection; far less that he could entertain a notion that the other gentlemen with whom he had not conferred on the subject, would be so tied up. He certainly understood that this epitaph, as in all similar cases, was to be subject to revision. He had before him the example of Dr. Johnson himself, who was requested to write Dr. Goldsmith's epitaph; and how did that great man conduct himself? You will find in my octavo edition of his *Life*, volume 2, page 448, a letter from him to Sir Joshua in which he says, "I send you the poor dear Doctor's epitaph. Read it first yourself; and if you then think it right, show it to The Club. I am, you know, willing to be corrected."

I trust that when Dr. Parr reconsiders his unusual proposition, he will be satisfied that, without any offence to him, it must receive a negative. I am with much regard, dear Sir, your faithful, humble servant,

JAMES BOSWELL

[It seems fitting that this letter, the last complete one written by Boswell, shows him not only trying to protect the memorial to Johnson but also invoking Reynolds, Goldsmith, and The Club.

On the following day, 14 April 1795, Boswell suddenly fell ill. At a meeting of The Club he was overcome with fever and chills, headache, and nausea, and had to be taken home and put to bed. He remained in great pain for three weeks, suffering from progressive kidney failure and uraemia, perhaps as a result of his recurring bouts of gonorrhoea. On 4 May T.D. Boswell wrote to Temple: "I am sorry to say my poor brother is in the most imminent danger; a swelling in his bladder has mortified, but he is yet alive, and God Almighty may restore him to us." On 8 May Jamie reported to Temple that his father felt better, and Boswell tried to write as well since he had heard that Temple and his daughter had been injured in a riding accident. After scrawling a few words, he let Jamie continue, although he signed the letter himself—the last time he was able to do so.]

[Boswell to Temple]

8 May 1795

MY DEAR TEMPLE,—I would fain write to you with my own hand but really cannot.

Alas! my friend, what a state is this. My son James is to write for me what remains of this letter and I am to dictate. The pain, which continued for so many weeks, was very severe indeed, and when it went off, I thought myself quite well, but I soon felt a conviction that I was by no means as I should be, being so excessively weak as my miserable attempt to write to you afforded a full proof. All, then, that can be said is that I must wait with patience.

But O my friend, how strange is it that at this very time of my illness you and Miss Temple should have been in such a dangerous state! Much reason for thankfulness is there that it has not been worse with you. Pray write or make somebody write frequently. I feel myself a good deal stronger today notwithstanding the scrawl.

God bless you, my dear Temple! I ever am your old and most affectionate [friend], here and I trust hereafter,

JAMES BOSWELL

[James Boswell, Jr., to Temple, enclosed with the preceding letter]

REVEREND SIR,—You will find by the foregoing, the whole of which was dictated to me by my father, that he is ignorant of the dangerous situation in which he was, and I am sorry to say still continues to be. Yesterday and today he has been somewhat better, and we trust that the nourishment which he is now able to take, and his strong constitution, will support him through. I remain with respect,

JAMES BOSWELL, JR.

[James Boswell, Jr., to Temple, 16 May 1795]

My father received your letter yesterday, which I read to him as he was unable to do it himself. He continues much in the same state as he was when I wrote last: he is very weak but it is to be hoped that by taking a sufficient quantity of nourishment he will recover strength and health.

[James Boswell, Jr., to Temple, 18 May 1795]

I am sorry to inform you that since I wrote last my father is con-siderably worse; he is weaker, and almost all the nourishment he takes comes off his stomach again. He had expressed a very earnest desire to be lifted out of bed, and Mr. Earle, the surgeon, thought it might be done with safety. But his strength was not equal to it and he fainted away. Since that he has been in a very bad way indeed and there are now, I fear, little or no hopes of his recovery.

[T.D. Boswell to Temple, 19 May 1795]

I have now the painful task of informing you that my dear brother expired this morning at two o'clock; we have both lost a kind, affec-tionate friend, and I shall never have such another. He has suffered a great deal during his illness, which has lasted five weeks, but not much in his last moments; may God Almighty have mercy upon his soul and receive him into His heavenly kingdom. He is to be buried at Auchinleck, for which place his sons will set out in two or three days; they and his two eldest daughters have behaved in the most affection-ate, exemplary manner during his confinement.

On 8 June 1795 Boswell was interred in the family vault at Auchinleck. At the funeral, Sandy and Jamie were joined by Sir William Forbes,[5] who later described his sentiments to Veronica in a letter of 13 June: "I went on Sunday to Auchinleck House and on Monday as-sisted at paying the last mournful tribute to the memory of a friend with whom I had lived in the strictest intimacy for thirty-six years, and to whose steady and unalterable regard and attachment I shall ever look back with gratitude and affection."

Boswell's other friends expressed their feelings more simply—par-ticularly Malone, who wrote to Windham on 21 May: "I suppose you know poor Boswell died on Tuesday morning, without any pain. I don't think he at any time of his illness knew his danger. I shall miss him more and more every day. He was in the constant habit of calling upon me almost daily, and I used to grumble sometimes at his turbulence, but now miss and regret his noise and his hilarity and his perpetual good humour, which had no bounds. Poor fellow, he has somehow sto-len away from us, without any notice, and without my being at all pre-

[5]Forbes was the sole executor of Boswell's will. He was also the literary executor, to-gether with Temple and Malone.

pared for it." And Sir William Scott wrote to Malone in late May or June 1795: "I regret with you most heartily that we have lost a companion in poor Bozzy whose place is never to be supplied. Poor fellow! I lament our loss of him beyond measure." Some years later Richard Cumberland remembered Boswell with special affection: "I loved the man; he had great convivial powers and an inexhaustible fund of good humour in society; nobody could detail the spirit of a conversation in the true style and character of the parties more happily than my friend James Boswell, especially when his vivacity was excited and his heart exhilarated by the circulation of the glass and the grateful odour of a well-broiled lobster" (*Memoirs*, 1806, p. 476).

But Boswell left much more than the warm feelings and affectionate memories of his friends. His enduring legacy is not only his *magnum opus*, which had already established him as "the great biographer" in his lifetime, as he had hoped, but also his astonishingly detailed and intimate journals. Covering more than thirty years of exertion and indolence, ambition and disappointment, high spirits and low, they provide an autobiographical record unparalleled in its scope and variety.

Unless otherwise stated, the documents listed here are owned by Yale University and stored in the Beinecke Rare Book and Manuscript Library. In our description of these documents we have drawn on Dr. Marion S. Pottle's exhaustive Catalogue of the Yale Boswell Collection, which is available in galley proof and typescript in the Yale Boswell Office.

A.   The text of the present volume is mainly furnished by the twelve sections of Boswell's journal and notes for journal listed below. For the periods when Boswell did not keep his journal we have included other documents such as his notes on special occasions, legal reports, verses, letters, contributions to newspapers and periodicals, and occasionally the report of another author. Documents printed for the first time, in whole or in part, are signalized at A1, 5, 9, 11, 13, 16, 17, 18, 22.

1.   Dreams, between 13 and 14 August 1789. Written on both sides of a small wrapper, slightly torn. Printed for the first time.

2.   Notes for journal and journal in London, 12 November to 31 December 1789. 3 quarto and 8 octavo leaves, unpaged, 21 sides written on, loose. Notes from 12 to 19 November; fully written journal from 20 November to 31 December.

3.   Journal in London, 1 to 19 January 1790. Quarto notebook with marbled paper covers, 8 unpaged leaves, 15 sides written on. Fully written journal.

4.   Notes for journal in London, 19, 23 January, 2 to 7, 15 February, 1 to 21 April, 1 to 10 May 1790. 10 unpaged leaves, of different shapes and sizes, 16 sides written on, loose. The notes for 1 to 21 April, 1 to 3, 9 to 10 May are in Veronica Boswell's hand. The notes for 18 to 21 April are written in the blank spaces of a letter from Charles Dilly. We quote selectively from 20 to 22 January and omit the notes from 24 January to 1 February.

5.   Note on the visit of Warren Hastings, 1 March 1790. Written on the reverse of a letter to Hastings, 28 February 1790, confirming the date and time of the visit. Printed for the first time.

6.   "Journal from the time that my old friend Temple arrived on a visit to London and me in 1790," 14 May to 16 June 1790. Written in the same notebook as the journal in London, 1 to 19 January 1790

(A3), starting from the other end. 16 unpaged leaves, 32 sides written on. Fully written journal.

7.   Journal at Carlisle, 17 June to 15 July 1790. 18 unpaged quarto leaves, 36 sides written on, loose. Fully written journal.

8.   Journal in London, 27 July to 10 September 1790. In the same notebook as that recording Temple's visit; begins immediately below the entry for 16 June 1790 and continues on 13 unpaged leaves, 26 sides written on. Fully written journal.

9.   Notes for journal in London, 11 September to 2 October 1790. Notes for 11 to 25 September on 2 leaves, in the Hyde Collection, now printed for the first time. Notes for 26 September to 2 October on 1 quarto leaf, folded into 3 sections (6 sides), unpaged, 2 sides written on, loose.

10.   "William Pitt, the Grocer of London" from the *Public Advertiser,* 11 November 1790.

11.   "Love at Church," lyric in the archives of the Earl of Crawford and Balcarres. Printed for the first time.

12.   Journal in London, 1 February to 10 April 1791. In a quarto notebook, full bound in vellum. 18 unpaged leaves, 35 sides written on. Fully written journal.

13.   "Lewes Home Circuit, 1791," 12 to 14 August 1791. 2 folio sheets, three sides written on. Addressed: "Alexr. Boswell, Younger of Auchinleck, Esquire, Machlin, Glasgow." Printed for the first time.

14.   Journal of a Jaunt to Cornwall, 17 August to 16 September 1792. Quarto notebook with marbled paper covers, 29 unpaged leaves, 58 sides written on. Fully written journal.

15.   Journal in London, 29 October 1792 to 9 January 1793. Quarto notebook, full bound in vellum, 21 unpaged leaves, 42 sides written on. Fully written journal.

16.   "Monument in Honour of Louis XVI, King of France," 31 January 1793. Single folio leaf. Printed for the first time.

17.   "Record of Miss Wilhelmina Alexander," autumn 1784 to March 1793. 2 leaves, loose, 4 sides written on. Printed for the first time.

18.   "Case of the Convicts Who Escaped from Botany Bay," 14 May 1793. 2 folio leaves, 3 sides written on. Printed for the first time.

19.   Journal in London, 1 August 1793 to 12 April 1794. 65 unpaged leaves, 128 sides written on. In the same notebook as the journal in London, 29 October 1792 to 9 January 1793, beginning after one blank leaf. Fully written journal.

20.   Journal in London, 9 March 1795. 1 quarto leaf, both sides written on. Fully written journal.

21.   Extract from the diary of Fanny Burney, October 1790, in *Diary and Letters of Madame d'Arblay,* ed. Charlotte Barrett and Austin Dobson, 1905, iv. 431–33.

22.   Extract from the diary of Charlotte Ann Burney Francis, later Broome, 11 March 1795, manuscript in the Henry W. and Albert A. Berg Collection of the New York Public Library (Astor, Lenox and Tilden Foundations). Printed for the first time.

23.   Forty-two letters printed in their entirety or in substantial extracts: 2 letters from Boswell to Lord Lonsdale, 8 June 1789, 15 June 1790. 1 letter from Lord Lonsdale to Boswell, 20 July 1789. 1 letter from Alexander Boswell to Boswell, October 1789. 1 letter from Veronica Boswell to Alexander Boswell, 21 November 1789. 6 letters from Boswell to W. J. Temple, 23 August 1789, 30 November 1789, 13 February 1790, 21 June 1790, 2 and 6 April 1791, 8 May 1795 (all Pierpont Morgan Library). 1 letter from W. J. Temple to Boswell, 4 July 1791. 1 letter from Boswell to Richard Penn, 26 June 1790. 2 letters from Boswell to Edmond Malone, 30 June 1790 (Yale), 13 April 1795 (British Library, Add. MS. 22549 f. 12). 1 letter from Boswell to Sir William Forbes, 2 July 1790 (National Library of Scotland, Fettercairn Papers, Acc. 4790). 1 letter from Boswell to Veronica Boswell, 9 July 1790. 1 letter from Boswell to Andrew Gibb, 6 November 1790. 1 letter from Boswell to Andrew Kippis, 11 July 1792. 1 letter from Charles Burney to Boswell, 16 July 1791. 1 letter from Nancy Temple to Padgy Peters, 8 September 1792 (Rear-Adm. P. F. Powlett). 1 letter from Boswell to Henry Dundas, 17 March 1794. 13 letters from Boswell to James Boswell, Jr., 30 June, 7, 14, 21, 30 July, 11, 22 August, 6, 12, 24 September, 6, 27 October, 21 November 1794. 2 letters from James Boswell, Jr. to Boswell, 18 October, 10 November 1794. 1 letter from Boswell to Robert Dundas, 27 December 1794. 3 letters from James Boswell, Jr., to W. J. Temple, 8, 16, 18 May 1795 (all Pierpont Morgan Library). 1 letter from T. D. Boswell to W. J. Temple, 19 May 1795 (Pierpont Morgan Library).

B.   Many other documents are quoted or referred to in the editorial notes and in the annotation. They include Boswell's Register of Letters, his Book of Company, legal papers, financial papers, journal memoranda, verses, newspaper paragraphs, the *Journal of a Tour to the Hebrides,* the *Account of Corsica,* the *Life of Johnson,* and upwards of sixty personal letters quoted in brief. One of these, a letter of 25 August 1790 to William Forbes of Callendar, is on loan to the Scottish Record Office (ref. GD.171/400/4). Other letters not located at Yale are in the Houghton Library of Harvard University, the National Library of

Scotland, the Pierpont Morgan Library, and the Hyde Collection, Somerville, New Jersey.

Non-Boswell material includes twenty-five letters quoted in brief, extracts from contemporary periodicals, poems, and other printed matter, as well as later sources.

C.   A selected bibliography. Boswell's journal was edited by Geoffrey Scott and F. A. Pottle and published without annotation in the eighteen volumes of *Private Papers of James Boswell from Malahide Castle in the Collection of Lt.-Colonel Ralph Heyward Isham* (1928–34), an expensive, privately printed edition limited to 570 sets. The Yale-McGraw-Hill edition initiated in 1950 is the first to make this material available to the general reader. The twelve volumes of journal published so far are listed on p. [i]. Much of the journal printed in *Boswell: The Great Biographer*, the final volume of the Yale-McGraw-Hill trade edition, appeared in the eighteenth volume of Isham's *Private Papers*.

The only general collection of Boswell's letters printed thus far is *Letters of James Boswell*, ed. C. B. Tinker (2 vols., 1924), but four volumes have been published in the Yale research edition of Boswell's correspondence: *The Correspondence of James Boswell and John Johnston of Grange*, ed. R. S. Walker (1966); *The Correspondence and Other Papers of James Boswell Relating to the Making of the "Life of Johnson,"* ed. Marshall Waingrow (1969); *The Correspondence of James Boswell with Certain Members of the Club*, ed. C. N. Fifer (1976), and *The Correspondence of James Boswell with David Garrick, Edmund Burke, and Edmond Malone*, ed. P. S. Baker, T. W. Copeland, G. M. Kahrl, Rachel McClellan, and J. M. Osborn (1986).

The authoritative edition of Boswell's *Life of Johnson* is that edited by G. B. Hill, revised by L. F. Powell (6 vols., 1934–64); the fifth volume of this edition contains Boswell's *Journal of a Tour to the Hebrides*, as published in 1785. Boswell's original journal of this tour appears as a volume in the Yale-McGraw-Hill trade series. A one-volume edition of the *Life of Johnson*, edited by R. W. Chapman, is available in a revised edition, with an introduction by Pat Rogers (1980). The edition of the manuscript of the *Life of Johnson* is now being prepared by Marshall Waingrow.

F. A. Pottle's *Pride and Negligence: The History of the Boswell Papers* (1981) was planned originally to accompany and introduce Marion S. Pottle's Catalogue of the Yale Boswell Collection, which will eventually appear in three volumes. Two catalogues of papers now mainly in the Yale Collection were printed more than fifty years ago: F. A. Pottle and M. S. Pottle's *Private Papers from Malahide Castle* (1931), and C. C. Abbott's *Catalogue of Papers Relating to Boswell...Found at Fettercairn House* (1936). The standard bibliography is F. A. Pottle's *Literary Career of James Boswell, Esq.* (1929); it is supplemented by Professor Pottle's article on Boswell in *The New Cambridge Bibliography of English Literature* (1971) and A. E. Brown's useful *Boswellian Studies* (2nd ed., 1972). F. A. Pottle's *James Boswell: The Earlier Years, 1740–1769* (1966) and Frank Brady's *James Boswell: The Later Years, 1769–1795* (1984) constitute the standard biography.

INDEX

This is in general an index of proper names with an analysis of actions, opinions, and personal relationships under the important names. Buildings, streets, and other locations in Carlisle, Edinburgh, and London are listed under those headings. Observations or opinions on a person are always listed under the name of that person and usually under the name of the person who is quoted or cited. Details of Boswell's personal and social relationships are indexed under the names of people concerned. That is, Boswell's relationship with his friend, John Wilkes, is indexed under Wilkes, not under Boswell. Part II of the article on Samuel Johnson is an analysis of Boswell's relationship with Johnson. Sovereigns appear under their Christian names; noblemen and Lords of Session under their surnames, with cross-references from their titles. The titles given in the index are those proper to May 1795. Maiden names of married women are given in parentheses. Titles of books are listed under the name of the author. Abbreviations used are D. (Duke), M. (Marquess), E. (Earl), V. (Viscount), B. (Baron), Bt. (Baronet), Kt. (Knight), W.S. (Writer to the Signet), JB (James Boswell), SJ (Samuel Johnson), MM (Margaret Montgomerie Boswell).

Index